KILLING ONE ANOTHER

GWYNN NETTLER

Professor Emeritus of Sociology
University of Alberta
Edmonton, Canada

CRIMINAL CAREERS VOLUME TWO

Anderson Publishing Co. / Cincinnati, Ohio

Rick Adams, Publisher's Staff Editor

CRIMINAL CAREERS VOLUME TWO: KILLING ONE ANOTHER

Library of Congress Cataloging in Publication Data
Nettler, Gwynn.
    Killing one another.

    (Criminal careers; v. 2)
    Bibliography: p.
    Includes indexes.
    1. Homicide. I. Title. II. Series: Nettler, Gwynn.
Criminal careers; v. 2.
HV6505.N47   364.1'523   81–70993
ISBN 0–87084–601–9   AACR2

Designed by William A. Burden

Criminal Justice Studies
Anderson Publishing Co./Cincinnati, Ohio

John L. Mason, President   Jean C. Martin, Executive Editor

KILLING ONE ANOTHER

CRIMINAL CAREERS

Volume One
EXPLAINING CRIMINALS

Volume Two
KILLING ONE ANOTHER

Volume Three
LYING, CHEATING, STEALING

Volume Four
RESPONDING TO CRIME

CONTENTS OF CRIMINAL CAREERS

DETAILED ANALYSIS OF VOLUME TWO

PREFACE

One way to study social behavior is to think about the courses of lives. All thoughtful people engage in this work, formally or informally. Journalists, novelists, and social scientists are vocationally dedicated to this task, but others who do not chart careers for a living also have opinions about what produces kinds of careers. Such opinions affect the guidance of one's own life and influence choices among public policies.

Professional students of social life have attended to segments of people's careers. These segments include childhoods, educational paths, marriages in happiness and misery, occupational shifts and continuities, and health and longevity.

The present work is in the tradition of such studies, but it attends to certain crimes as major nodes or characteristics of careers. However, the principles that inform our study have general applicability. These principles, tentatively formulated, can be applied to the interpretation of any style of life—criminal or lawful, successful, failed, or in-between. These themes provide, then, an introduction to the study of social behavior. An introduction is not a completion, of course, and our study is justified if it describes the difficulties of observing human action and of explaining it.

The text is divided into four volumes. The first part of Volume One (*Explaining Criminals*) describes interpretive themes. These are prescriptions for thinking about careers, criminal or lawful. These themes constitute assumptions that run like a thread through the substantive chapters on kinds of crime (Volumes Two, *Killing One Another* and Three, *Lying, Cheating, Stealing*) and on modes of responding to crime (Volume Four, *Responding to Crime*).

The second half of Volume One develops these themes by outlining major causes of conduct. These chapters show that human action is not spun out of a simple string of causes, as it is popular to assume. On the contrary, careers are produced in a dense web of influences. A conclusion that follows is that we can know something about what the causes of conduct *can be* without knowing what they *will be* for particular individuals and particular acts.

Volume Two describes homicidal occasions. Attention is addressed to description on both aggregate and individual levels. It is emphasized that description is part of scientific explanation, but that it is not the whole of such explanation, and that there is but little science in the study of conduct.

Volume Three applies our interpretive themes in description of varieties of dishonesty, and Volume Four discusses modes of responding to crime and their justifications.

This work is intended for students of criminology, deviance, and criminal justice. It also has relevance to studies of the relations between information, knowledge, and private and public policy.

Instructors in departments of psychology and sociology, and in schools of law, criminal justice, and social work may use one volume, or all, and in any order. However, this is a book that tells a story. It reads best from beginning to end.

A booklet of discussion and test questions for each volume is available as a teaching aid. In addition, each chapter begins with an abstract that provides a study and lecture outline.

ACKNOWLEDGEMENTS

William R. Avison, Rollin C. Dudley, and Robert A. Silverman read portions of this manuscript and I thank them, and anonymous reviewers, for their suggestions. None of these readers is to blame, of course, for any of my continuing errors.

Jennefer Fraser worked with me for two years as a "detective of data." I am particularly grateful to her for her diligence and enthusiasm. I wish also to thank the editor of these volumes, Rick Adams, for his attention, imagination, and editorial advice.

Gwynn Nettler

1 HOMICIDE: DEFINITIONS AND JUSTIFICATIONS

Abstract • Our attitude toward homicide is ambivalent. • Western criminal codes classify homicide as culpable and non-culpable. The classification rests on, and changes with, moral assumptions. Therefore, there is no universal concept of wrongful homicide. • A science requires a taxonomy of the objects and events of interest. There is no reliable taxonomy of homicide, in part because of moral quarrels about justifications of killing. • Moral quarrels are illustrated with a sample of homicidal recommendations and justifications.

ETHICAL STUDIES COMMONLY NOTE that our morals only prohibit what we are inclined to do. The inclination may be infrequently expressed, but moral commandments would be vacant if they were directed against impossibilities rather than proclivities.

It is because we fear death and yet are likely to kill one another that we prohibit some forms of homicide. However, our attitude toward deadly quarrels does not consistently condemn them. Our evaluation of homicide is accurately described as "ambivalent." Ambivalence is a term invented by the Swiss psychiatrist Paul Eugen Bleuler (1857–1939) to indicate that a person can have a split soul and be simultaneously attracted to and repelled by taboo persons, objects, and acts. And so it seems with us and homicide. We are both delighted and appalled by violence, and while we condemn brutality, we buy it in great quantities through markets in contact sports, the daily news, and mass entertainment.

It is not necessary to accept psychoanalytic doctrine in order to agree with one of the founders of this mode of thought, Sigmund Freud (1856–1939), who believed that "The basis of taboo is a forbidden action for which there exists a strong inclination in the unconscious" (1938, p. 832). Whether or not the inclination is "in the unconscious," murder is often in our hearts and it is against this temptation that morals and laws inveigh.

The prohibition of homicide expresses disapproval of the killing of our species, but it is a prohibition that varies with circumstance. Historically, homicide has been of secondary importance to the crimes of heresy and treason. The anthropologist Seagle (1932, p. 450) tells us that "horror of homicide is a modern phenomenon."

The fact that condemnation varies with circumstance is but another way of noting our ambivalence toward intentional homicide. For example, the Deputy Chief of Counsel for the United States in the Nuremberg "War Crimes" Trials has recently justified those proceedings as "fair and necessary" in punishment of "crimes against humanity" as defined by the two thousand year old "Commandment, 'Thou shalt not kill'." (Kempner 1978, p. 92). The victorious Allies indicted 22 Nazis as "war criminals." Of these, 19 were found guilty and 12 were sentenced to death. One of the condemned men, Hermann Göring, escaped his sentence by committing suicide (Jackson 1947, Smith 1977). The remaining 11 were killed for their crimes, and killed in a ritual manner—by being hung.

Noting our inconsistent application of commandments against homicide says nothing about the *justice* of any side in a deadly quarrel. Justice is quite another matter (Nettler 1979), and some people's sense of justice requires some kinds of homicide while it condemns others (Berns 1979). Thus, although all bands of people who regard themselves as "we" prohibit some kinds of killing of their "own kind," few, if any, nations condemn killing their foreign enemies and many allow the killing of domestic threats. In short, war and execution are legal; murder and manslaughter are criminal.

The names given to the different occasions for homicide indicate whether the killing is justified or not. The cynical journalist Ambrose Bierce (1842–1914?) put it this way in his *Devil's Dictionary* (1958, p. 57):

> *Homicide,* n. The slaying of one human being by another. There are four kinds of homicide: felonious, excusable, justifiable, and praiseworthy, but it makes no great difference to the person slain whether he fell by one kind or another—the classification is for advantage of the lawyers.

The classification is largely legal business, as Bierce contends, but the classification derives originally, as does the criminal law, from moral concerns and from moral definitions of the variety of homicide. Therefore, "there has never been a universal concept of wrongful homicide" (Seagle 1932, p. 450).

DEFINITIONS

Homicide is the general term for the killing of a human being, "directly or indirectly" and "by any means" (Martin & Cartwright 1974, Sec. 205). In the criminal codes of Western countries, homicide is divided into that considered to be "culpable" (blameworthy) and that which is considered to be non-culpable. By definition, non-culpable homicide is not a crime.

Homicide is considered non-culpable when it is "justifiable" or "excusable." Justifiable homicide is that committed in the service of a legal duty as in police killing of persons who resist arrest while committing an indictable crime (a felony) or in state execution of offenders. Justifiable homicide also includes that committed "in necessary self-defense, or in defense of habitation, person, or property against one who manifests, intends, or endeavors, by violence or surprise, to commit a known felony" (*Harris* v. *State,* 34 Ark. 469,477). Obviously, such justifications vary in time and place, yet all Western jurisdictions recognize some homicide as justifiable.

"Excusable homicide" overlaps that termed "justifiable" in some jurisdictions where homicide in self-defense is called "excusable" (*United States* v. *King,* 34 F. 302,306). However, a more common definition refers "excusable homicide" to that committed "by accident or misfortune in doing any lawful act by lawful means with usual and ordinary caution, and without unlawful intent" (*State* v. *Reynolds,* 22 P. 410,411; 42 Kan. 320; *People* v. *Fitzsimmons,* 23 N.Y.S. 1102,1105).

Not all accidental killing is excusable, of course, and the deaths accidentally induced through "negligence" or in the commission of other crimes are considered culpable. "Culpable negligence" that results in the death of another person "in cases where such killing is not justifiable or excusable homicide nor murder" is deemed "manslaughter" (*Rivers* v. *State,* 78 So. 343,344; 75 Fla. 401). Manslaughter, in turn, may be considered to be "voluntary" or "involuntary." It is considered "voluntary" when the killing is intentional but done "without premeditation in heat of passion or while unreasonably resisting an unlawful attack or threatened attack" (*Wingfield* v. *State,* 160 P. 945).

"Murder" is a term usually reserved for "the felonious killing of one human being by another with malice aforethought" (*State* v. *Donovan,* Del. 8, 876, 879). In some jurisdictions, "murder" may be charged even though no particular person was the intended victim of the lethal attack. Thus in Georgia, "If a person . . . recklessly discharges a gun into a crowd, although at no particular person, and death results to some one, such a killing is 'murder'." (*Hackney* v. *State,* 55 S.E. 2d 704, 706; 206 Ga. 64).

All these distinctions among the circumstances in which people kill one another are *legal* definitions, as Bierce observed. They vary, therefore, with jurisdiction. For example, the homicide called "infanticide" is given a different definition in the United States from that which it receives in England and Canada. In the United States, "infanticide" is so defined as to constitute "murder." In England and Canada, the definition is narrower and the penalties reduced more in line with those for "manslaughter" (Wootton 1978, p. 149). The American law says:

> " 'Infanticide' is the felonious taking of the life of a newborn child and constitutes murder" (*Gilpin* v. *Gilpin,* 94 NYS 2d. 706,708). "To constitute 'infanticide,' the child must have been totally expelled alive from its mother's body, must have lived an independent existence after such expulsion, and its death must have been caused by violence inflicted upon it by some other person after the commencement of its independent existence" (*Cordes* v. *State,* 112 S.W., 943, 945; 54 Tex. Cr. R. 204).

However, in England and Canada "infanticide" is so defined that only mothers can be guilty of it. The Canadian law reads:

> A female person commits infanticide when by a wilful act or omission she causes the death of her newly-born child, if at the time of the act or omission she is not fully recovered from the effects of giving birth to the child and by reason thereof or of the effect of lactation consequent on the birth of the child her mind is disturbed (Martin & Cartwright 1974, Sec. 216).

The maximum penalty in Canada for "infanticide" is five years imprisonment, a considerable reduction from the life sentence imposed for "murder."

Accomplices

In addition to the variety of morally tinctured legal definitions of homicide, Western law also holds guilty to some degree those persons who, while not actually doing the killing (or any other crime), are accomplices to the deed. Accomplices, in turn, are given several legal definitions and may be held culpable as "abettors," "accessories" before and after the fact, "counsellors," or "conspirators" (Smith & Hogan 1973). The fine legal distinctions among classes of accomplice need not detain us other than to note that culpability can extend beyond pulling the trigger or plunging in the knife.

CLASSIFICATIONS

To define an object or an event is to draw a boundary around it so that one can tell—publicly and reliably—which thing or which happening is which kind of object or act. Definitions classify. They group objects or events into "classes" of things or acts that share some property not similarly distributed among other "classes."

Every science starts with classification of the materials of interest. When a set of agreed-upon rules for classification has developed, it is recognized as a taxonomy. While there is more than one way to construct taxonomies (Sokal 1966), a taxonomy is the foundation of that kind of knowing called scientific.

If we cannot neatly define classes of acts, we cannot count them reliably; and if we cannot reliably count the events of interest, there is no ground on which to build scientific explanation (see Volume One, Chapter 4).

Unfortunately for studies of social relations, there are as yet no taxonomies of human acts that are sufficiently clear, consensual, and reliable as to provide the basis of a science of social action. This is not to say that social studies cannot improve upon common sense, but that the quality of the science in "social science" lacks the exactitude associated with that honorific label in studies of physical events (Mazur 1968).

There are many causes of this deficiency (Nettler 1975), but one factor of relevance to the study of crime is that the events we wish to explain are morally saturated. The legal classification of killing that has been described illustrates the intrusion of moral evaluation upon definition. The result is that we have no precise taxonomy of homicide. In succeeding pages we can, and shall, speak of styles of deadly quarrels where those styles are broadly conceived and defined only by fuzzy boundaries. But there is as yet no system of classifying mortal conflict that yields classes of lethal acts sufficiently *clear and narrow* as to permit development of a science of homicide. This point is illuminated by noting the criteria that have been nominated, and variously employed, for defining kinds of homicide.

Classifying the Killing

Attempts to define kinds of homicide are unsatisfactory because they mix, in no regular way, considerations of:

1. The number of killers involved in one "event."

2. The number of victims.

3. The relations between killers and their victims.

4. The circumstances of the homicide. This often includes reference to the presumed motives of the actors in the deadly drama.

5. The personal characteristics of killers and their victims. These characteristics are, in turn, used to assign blame or excuse.

6. The "responsibility" of the *killers* for their acts. This notion includes ideas concerning the sanity of the killers and whether they were acting voluntarily or under some kind of coercion, including that coercion vaguely titled "pressure."

"Pressures" themselves receive different definitions as when soldiers doing their duty are honored while tribesmen exercising their obligation to vendetta are indicted. "Pressure" is more easily recognized, and allowed as an excuse, when the crime is "out of character" than when it seems an expected act in continuation of a violent career. Thus children who kill their parents or siblings are often deemed less responsible than rational killers. One author calls them "the deadly innocents" (Gardiner 1976), indicating that they are "victims" of circumstance and, hence, less responsible than agents.[1]

7. The "responsibility" of the *victims* for their deaths. There *are* bullies who pick fights and sometimes get themselves killed, and we call such homicide "victim-precipitated." Evaluation of the victim's "deserts" becomes part of the classificatory schema.

8. The degree of impulse or plan that seems to characterize the killing. One has to add, "seems to characterize," because it will be argued (pp. 114–120) that some "impulsive" murders are events that end long histories of wishful thinking.

9. The reasons given by the survivors in the homicidal drama. These reasons serve best as justifications when they are phrased as idealistic intentions.

10. Effects of the homicide. Some killing is classified by what is achieved, or believed to have been achieved, by the mortal attack. As we shall see (p. 10), "justice" is one of these recommended effects.

11. Our approval or disapproval of killers, victims, and consequences. This evaluation varies with all the preceding considerations and it moves the location of causation, as we have noted (Volume One, Table 2.1).

12. Causal assignment. The causes that are adduced in explanation of homicide shift as we differentially assess killers, their victims, their histories, and the deadly circumstances.

This inventory of the morally infused criteria by which we classify homicide produces no taxonomy adequate for a science of mortal

---

[1] Disputes about who is a victim and who is an agent, who is responsible for his/her condition and action and who is not, are *moral* quarrels. They are moral debates even when the argument turns to science for resolution. The recourse to science asks knowledge to locate the causes of conduct, but the moral motive that asks the question itself affects the answer that will be deemed acceptable.

fighting. It leads readily, however, to a babel of recommendations, promises, and justifications of homicide. These verbalizations, when added to the history of deadly quarrels,[2] do not inspire confidence in the probability of unbroken peace, domestic or international.

AN ASSORTMENT OF DEADLY RECOMMENDATIONS, PROMISES, AND JUSTIFICATIONS[3]

Recommendation (No. 1): Kill the right people:

> There's nothing wrong with shooting people as long as they're the right people (Dirty Harry speaking in *Magnum Force* 1974).

Recommendation (No. 2): Kill the right people:

> I do not really see anything wrong with burning university professors. Some of them are criminals (The French existentialist philosopher Jean-Paul Sartre, *Encounter* 1973, p. 96).

Recommendation (No. 3): Kill the right people:

> It is not necessary for a black man to hate a white man, or to have any particular feelings about him at all, in order to realize that he must kill him (The American novelist James Baldwin 1972, p. 191).

Recommendation (No. 4): Kill the right people:

> I don't disagree with murder sometimes, especially political assassination. I'm not entirely upset by the Kennedy assassinations. In many ways two of the most dangerous men in the country were eliminated (The American "civil rights" attorney William Kunstler 1976).

---

[2] Some philosophers and some historians have equated history with human brutality. Thus Voltaire (1694–1778) wrote that, "History is little else than a picture of human crimes and misfortunes" (1767) and the historian Edward Gibbon (1737–1794) later added that history "is indeed little more than the register of the crimes, follies, and misfortunes of mankind" (1776–1788, Chapter 3).

These comments themselves express a prejudice that assumes a standard of peace from which to judge human activity. Against this assumption, it is not at all clear that human beings prefer lives without some violence. If we human beings did not like fighting so much, we would not pay so much to *be* in combat and to *witness* it.

[3] Reprinted, with additions and emendations, from the author's *Social Concerns* (1976:277–279) with permission of the publisher, McGraw-Hill Book Co.

Recommendation (No. 5): Kill the right people:

I'd like to burn you at the stake (Betty Friedan, American feminist, to Phyllis Schlafly in debate on the Equal Rights Amendment, *Newsweek* 1973).

Promises (No. 1): Peace

We are advocates of the abolition of war, we do not want war; but war can only be abolished through war, and in order to get rid of the gun it is necessary to take up the gun (Chairman Mao 1967, p. 35).

Promises (No. 2): Peace

We will have peace even if we have to fight for it (General Dwight Eisenhower, upon the conclusion of World War II 1946).

Promises (No. 3): Peace

When one group of clans finally decides to invite its enemies for a *gaingar* (a ritualistic clan battle), the people always say that this is a spear fight to end spear fights, so that from that time on there will be peace for all the clans and tribes. This is sincerely believed at the time, since it is an effort to stop clan feuds (Thomas 1937, p. 496, describing a "primitive" tribe).

Promises (No. 4): A better world

Run up and down Broad Street niggers, take the shit you want. Take their lives if need be, but get what you want, what you need. ... We must make our own World, man, our own world, and we can not do this unless the white man is dead. Let's get together and kill him, my man, let's get to gather the fruit of the sun, let's make a world we want black children to grow and learn in (Imamu Baraka, né LeRoi Jones 1972).

Justifications (No. 1): Assassination mitigated by industrial accidents:

In considering the death of Mr. LaPorte, you must also consider the deaths of construction workers in so-called accidents (Jacques Larue-Langlois defending the assassination of a government minister in Quebec, *Edmonton Journal* 1971).

Justifications (No. 2): Death for insult:

We'll kill Brian Davies for calling us murderers (Newfoundland harp-sealers vs. Davies and his animal "protectionists," cited by Levin 1977).

Justifications (No. 3): Killing for dignity:

One of the best guarantees to make a man a man is a gun in his hand (Landau 1961).

Justifications (No. 4): Killing for dignity:

At the level of individuals, violence is a cleansing force. It frees the native from his inferiority complex and from his despair and inaction; it makes him fearless and restores his self-respect (the psychiatrist Franz Fanon 1963, p. 73).

Justifications (No. 5): Unity of humanity:

After all, we are all one. Killing someone, therefore, is just like breaking off a piece of a cookie (Mass murderer Charles Manson, cited by Zaehner 1974, p. 57).

Justifications (No. 6): Good intentions:

To condemn Karl Armstrong is to condemn a whole anguished generation. His intentions were more significant than the unanticipated consequences of his actions (The historian Gabriel Kolko in defense of a murderous bomb-thrower at the University of Wisconsin, cited by Bickel 1974, p. 22).

Justifications (No. 7): Killing innocent people kills institutions:

It can of course be suggested that it takes little courage for two strong eighteen-year-old hoodlums, let us say, to beat in the brains of a candy-store keeper. . . . Still, courage of a sort is necessary, for one murders not only a weak fifty-year-old man but an institution as well, one violates private property, one enters into a new relation with the police and introduces a dangerous element into one's life (The American novelist Norman Mailer 1960, p. 312).

Justifications (No. 8): Deserts

You can prove that people need killing, but you can't prove that a horse needs to be stole (sic) (Richard "Racehorse" Haynes, 1980, a prominent attorney, successful in defending persons accused of murder).

Justifications (No. 9): Social change:

Nothing is ever done in this world until men are prepared to kill one another if it is not done (the character Undershaft in G.B. Shaw's play, *Major Barbara,* 1934, p. 497).

Justifications (No. 10): Killing for justice:

> To the question most commonly asked about the Eichmann trial: What good does it do? there is but one possible answer: It will do justice (the philosopher Hannah Arendt 1964, p. 254, justifying the trial and hanging of the Nazi Eichmann).

MORALS: ABSOLUTE, RELATIVE, DEFENSIVE, AND SUICIDAL

There is no end to justification of our actions, including our criminal actions. This sample of defenses of homicide illustrates only skimpily the variety of attitudes toward murder and our continuing ambivalence toward killing.

The ambivalence begins with the Judaic-Christian codes out of which Western laws and morals have evolved. For example, the biblical scholar Harmon (1952) tells us that:

> The Hebrew text of the Sixth (Fifth) Commandment is *You shall not kill.*
> ... The commandment is concerned with the protection of human life within the community of Israel, against destruction by fellow Israelites. The verb is not limited to murder in the criminal sense and may be used as unpremeditated killing (*Deuteronomy.* 4:42). It forbids all killing not explicitly authorized. This means that in Israelite society it did not forbid the slaying of animals, capital punishment, or the killing of enemies in war. It had no direct bearing, either, on suicide (p. 986, emphasis in the original).

In addition, Harmon (1953, p. 367) observes that, among the ancient Hebrews, "one might ... kill his slave [and] one was bound to kill in revenge for the murder of one's kin, whether the crime had been intentional or accidental."

Although Christians, and others, invoke the commandment, "Thou shalt not kill," as an *absolute,* they act and argue as if the commandment were a prescription *relative* to time, place, motive, and consequences. "Thou shalt not kill" is then translated as "Thou shalt not murder," and the classification of homicide as murder, or as something else, becomes again a matter of moral debate as well as legal definition.

Moral quarrels about the justice of homicide are interesting, but they go on without resolution. Philosophers have not been able to invent a moral principle that people can consistently practice, or even consistently preach, that would guide our attitude toward homicide (Devine 1979, James 1979). Thus we are not surprised to find that some people who *oppose* legally induced abortion *favor* capital punishment, and it is no longer news that some people who *oppose* capital punishment *favor* revolutionary killing.

Our ambivalence toward homicide has psychological and philosophical facets.

Psychological Correlates of Morals

Psychologists find that "kinds of people" select moral principles congenial to their personalities and their accompanying assumptions about the world. Moral character is a distinguishing feature of personality, just as is temperament, and there is some harmony between our feelings about ourselves and others, our cognitive maps of the social scene, and our morals. Thus Hogan (1973) shows that:

> There are clear-cut personality correlates of the disposition to adopt the *ethics of conscience* or [*the ethics of*] *responsibility*. . . . Persons who adopt the ethics of personal conscience . . . are independent, innovative, form-creating . . . impulsive, opportunistic, and irresponsible. . . . Persons whose moral judgments reflect the ethics of social responsibility . . . are reasonable, helpful, dependable . . . conventional, and resistant to change (p. 225, emphasis added).

These different personalities locate the causes of conduct in different places. Hogan and Dickstein (1972) find that, while each polar type of moral person is highly sensitive to injustice, those guided by the "ethics of conscience" assume that people are naturally good and corrupted only by social institutions which, in turn, are the source of injustice. On the other hand, those guided by the "ethics of responsibility" assume that people are naturally prone to evil, that institutions are required to restrain action, and that other people are the source of injustice.

These psychological facts affect philosophical quarrels.

Philosophical Questions About Morals

For centuries philosophers have wrestled with four overlapping questions about right action:

1. What is the nature of a moral code?

2. Which moral code, if any, do people follow, and how consistently?

3. Which moral code should people follow, and why?

4. What are the consequences of following one code rather than another?

The fact that debate on these questions persists, without resolution, underscores our emphasis of the ambivalent attitude human beings exhibit toward homicide. This fact illustrates the ambivalence and explains it. The *diversity* of justifications for killing and the many promises offered as consequences of killing indicate the lack of a principle universally prescribed, much less universally practiced, that defines the ethics of homicide.

Fortunately, description of criminal careers does not require development of a universal moral code. Here we need only note a quarrel that intrudes upon the interpretation of homicidal courses.

This is the quarrel between those who believe that a moral code does, or should, consist of absolute rules and those who believe that what is "right" does, and should, vary with circumstance. The first position holds a moral rule to be an *ultimate*. It is conceived as an end in itself, not to be evaluated by consequences or bent by expedience. The second position holds that a moral rule is always *context-bound*, and that it does and should change with conditions. The second attitude is that of "situation ethics" (Fletcher 1966).

Biologists and psychologists favor situation ethics when they view the action of living things as generated in a web of causes in which the activity of organisms "feeds back" to determine consequences for individuals and species. For example, the biologist Hardin (1977, p. 114) describes "situation ethics" as defining "the morality of an act . . . by the state of the system at the time the act is performed." He adds, "Ecology, a system-based view of the world, demands situational ethics."

Given this relative conception of how one should act, it appears that people adopt moral codes that are *suicidal* as well as codes that are *defensive*. The biologist is willing to consider that moral prescriptions that do not bend with circumstances sometimes defend their practitioners, but they also sometimes lead to extinction of their practitioners.

FOCUS

There are difficulties in accepting either an absolute or a relative attitude toward moral prescriptions. Discussion of these difficulties occupies other texts. But the fact that there are persisting troubles in describing "right" action—and, worse, in prescribing it—justifies limiting present attention to those homicides defined as murder, manslaughter, or infanticide by laws of the major world-states. Narrowing our attention selects only some of the circumstances of deadly fighting out of a large inventory of homicidal situations. Since there is no reliable taxonomy of lethal events—for the reasons noted on pages 5–7—we can best approximate a description of culpable killing by describing broadly the occasions on which it occurs. Describing the occasions will permit discussion of motives and satisfactions and will demonstrate, again, that different people can come to the same criminal end by different routes.

"Maps" of the social location of murder and manslaughter begin the description of deadly circumstances. From these pictures of homicide in the aggregate, we will then extract portraits of individual careers.

2 SOCIAL LOCATIONS OF HOMICIDE: **AGE, SEX, WORK, WEALTH**

Abstract • Age, sex, work, and wealth are four indicators of differences commonly employed to explain human action. • Age and sex differentials in violence are demonstrated in different societies and for a variety of physical attacks. ○ Young men are the most murderous people. ○ Sex and age ratios of violence fluctuate with cultural contexts. • Work and wealth are commonly considered to be determinants of behavior. ○ When work is viewed as those social arrangements called "economies," only a loose association is discovered between the "economic base" and homicide rates. ○ Within jurisdictions, poorer people tend to be more violent than richer people. "Social class" is correlated with some styles of homicide. ○ However, between jurisdictions and historically, no strong association appears between poverty and homicide. ○ Increasing national wealth does not necessarily reduce violence. Prosperous economies engage in mass violence as frequently as poor ones. ○ Within countries, income inequality is associated with murder rates, but what is measured as "income inequality" may also reflect cultural differences. ○ Countries that have engaged in large-scale wars experience more post-war homicide. • The chapter concludes that the possession of a quantity of wealth is less important as a cause of conduct than what one does to receive a portion of wealth. In short, economic condition is not to be confused with cultural condition.

SOCIOLOGISTS CHARACTERISTICALLY USE four major indicators of difference between people as both descriptive and explanatory tools.[1] These four markers are age, sex, work, and wealth. Age and sex are biologically rooted facts, but their significance for action is contingent upon the cultures in which they function. The same may be said of the meanings of work and wealth.

AGE, SEX, AND DEADLY QUARRELS

Deadly quarrels stand at one end of a continuum of fighting that ranges from the trading of insults, through rule-regulated battling in sports, to assaults that produce varying degrees of injury. In all modes

---

[1] Description is not necessarily explanation. What kind of description counts as an explanation depends on one's purposes.

of *physical* attack, males are more aggressive than females and young males in particular are the most dangerous human beings.[2]

This fact has been confirmed among many cultures and in many times, among children as well as adults. Differential proclivity to violence between the sexes has been observed in natural settings and in experimental ones, among primates as well as human beings. Sexual differences in violence occur in that playful fighting called "agonistic"—from the word's Greek roots in athletic and other contests—and they occur as well in the varieties of assault intended to humiliate, dominate, or injure others that sometimes end in death by accident or plan.

The difference in probability of physical attack is related to sex-hormonal balance (Hutt 1972, Levine 1966, 1971, Maccoby & Jacklin 1974, pp. 242–243). Among mammals, the male hormone, androgen, produces aggressive behavior. When natural or synthetic androgens are ingested by females, either in the uterine environment or after birth, they become more aggressive (Hart 1974, Money & Ehrhardt 1972, Quadagno et al. 1977, Reinisch & Karow 1977, Vandenberg 1978). This effect has been observed among girls whose mothers have suffered a genetic defect that yields the so-called "adrenogenital syndrome" or whose mothers have taken progestin-formulated medication to increase their fecundity—in both cases, mother's chemistry affects the female fetus and masculinizes it. The result is a "tomboy" who grows up "with typically masculine mannerisms and behavior patterns" (Eysenck & Nias 1978, p. 230).

These statements should not be over-interpreted. They do not mean that some females may not be more aggressive physically than some males, or that females may not attack by other means—as with the sulphurous tongue, in business, or through the law. Nor does any of this mean that women may not have murder in their hearts as

---

[2] This statement refers to probability of *direct physical* attack. "Dangerousness" in this context says nothing about the hazards to life generated indirectly by political leaders of either sex. It also says nothing about people who fight with other means than fists and guns, as in economic and litigious contests. For example, the possibility that one may fight with lawsuits is recognized in the crime of *barratry*. Barratry (from the Middle French for "combat," "fighting") is the crime of harassing another with unjust lawsuits. It is a crime difficult to prove, of course, and only a handful of men have ever been convicted of it. However, a woman, for the first time in the English-speaking world, has recently been convicted of barratry in Pittsburgh after filing about 20 suits in less than two years against her divorced husband (*Associated Press* 1979).

often as men. Of this last, we know nothing, but we do know something about fights between the sexes. For example, Scottish psychiatrists interviewed all patients treated for "parasuicide" (attempted suicide) in the Royal Infirmary, Edinburgh, during 1977–1978. They report that 16 percent of these unhappy people were women, of 20 to 40 years, living with a man. Among these women, slightly more than half said they had been involved in domestic violence and 88 percent of the women in these domestic brawls reported having been injured. But, at the same time, almost half of the women who reported injuries in these fights also described themselves as "excessively violent" (Oswald 1980). The physicians involved in this study contend that, if damage to *mental health* were included in the tally of "violence," the sex differential would be reduced.

In parallel with this Scottish finding, an American study of 2,143 married couples reports what might be called "homogamy in violence." That is, when it comes to "batting one another about," husbands and wives are equally likely to do the hitting (Straus 1980).

With allowances, then, for other modes of injury, it is fair to conclude only that males more frequently attack others *lethally* than do females.

Terman and Tyler (1954) provide an early summary of research on this matter, and their conclusions have been validated in studies by Omark, et al. (1973) in Ethiopia, Switzerland, and the United States; by Whiting and Pope (1973) in India, Kenya, Okinawa, Mexico, the Philippines, and the United States; by Elwin (1950) in India; and by Bohannon and his colleagues (1960) among seven African tribes. Given's (1977) careful analysis of historical documents notes that homicide in thirteenth century England "was an overwhelmingly male phenomenon" (p. 134), and surveys of research worldwide confirm this kind of finding (Goldberg 1973, Hamburg & van Lawick-Goodall 1973, Hutt 1972, Johnson 1972, Lunde 1973, Maccoby & Jacklin 1974, Chapter 7, Money & Ehrhardt 1972, van Lawick and van Lawick-Goodall 1971).

"Genderlect"

Men not only *do* more violence, they also *talk* more. Tallies of the topics of conversations and of the descriptive language used by men and women, boys and girls, indicate that males more frequently refer to hostility and destructive action than do females (Eble 1972, Gleser et al. 1959, Haas 1979).

AGE, SEX, AND SOCIAL CONTEXT

The biological facts of age and sex differences, like other biological differences, are always culturally embedded as they are converted into conduct. Biology is translated into action only through social sieves. Biology limits capacity and creates disposition, but social relations channel the expression of disposition. Males are disposed to greater violence than females, but social situations variously facilitate or inhibit manifestations of this biological given. This means that females in one culture may be more murderous than males in another (p. 60).

Social sifting of biological differences also means that age and sex distributions will vary in time and place with the kind of lethal attack that is prevalent. For example, where murders are disproportionately domestic, as they have been in recent times in England and Wales (Morris & Blom-Cooper 1964), the age of killers is higher than it is in countries like the United States where murder in recent years has been increasingly that of strangers as an accompaniment of robbery (Barnett et al. 1975, Block 1976, 1977, Sorrells 1977, Zimring 1979).

Sex ratios also vary with style of violence. While men are generally more physically dangerous than women, the proportions arrested and convicted for personal attacks fluctuate with the kind of violence. For example, allowing for differences in legal nomenclature, sex ratios of those arrested or convicted of selected violent crimes in recent years run in parallel for Canada, England-Wales, and the United States. Table 2.1 reports these similar sex ratios for roughly similar kinds of attack.

Generally, the risk of mortal assault is greatest among men who are "post-pubescent" but not yet "middle-aged"—men approximately between the ages of 14 and 40. It should be repeated, however, that the ratio of male to female attack moves with the social context, and it does so in ways that have been described but not adequately explained. Thus, in eighteenth century France, many of the reported murders and assaults occurred in family disputes concerning honor and property in which women played an important role (Castan 1971). The sex ratio in homicide varies, too, in settings of war, revolution, and terroristic activity when women become more active as killers (Zeldin 1977, p. 908).

Summary

In brief, the quantity and quality of deadly assault are not fixed by sex or age. Sex and age differentials in violence are culturally em-

Table 2.1   Distribution of Arrests or Convictions for Selected Violent Crimes by Sex: Canada,* England and Wales,** and the United States***

	Canada	England & Wales		United States
Forcible Rape[3]				
Male	99.8%	100%		99.1%
Female	0.2	0		0.9
Robbery				
Male	93.4	93.2		92.9
Female	6.6	6.8		7.1
Wounding[†]				
Male	81.6	92.5		86.9
Female	18.4	7.5		13.1
Murder and Manslaughter[††]		(Mur.)	(Mansl.)	
Male	87.7	97.4	80.5	85.1
Female	12.3	2.6	19.5	14.9

* Source: Statistics Canada 1979, Table 2, convictions.
** Source: Home Office 1978, Table 10, convictions.
*** Source: FBI 1977, Table 34, arrests.
† "Aggravated assault" in the United States.
†† "Culpable homicide," exclusive of "infanticide," in Canada. "Murder" and "manslaughter" reported separately for England and Wales.

[3] "Crime" is legally defined rather than primitively observed. What constitutes "forcible rape" and who may commit the crime are matters of definition. Thus some jurisdictions, but not all, permit females to be charged and convicted of "forcible rape" as "a principal . . . and [to] be punished equally with the actual perpetrator of the offense. To be an aider and abettor, it is immaterial that the person is disqualified from being the principal actor by reason of age, sex, condition, or class. A woman, a boy under the age of physical ability, or the husband of a female victim, who aids, abets, encourages, or assists in the commission of the crime may be convicted as a principal under statutes existing in many states" (Reiser & Warden 1972, p. 776).

Human beings also "rape" persons of their own sex, but such homosexual assault is called something else like "buggery," "sodomy," "defilement," or "indecent assault." As far as we know, homosexual attacks, like heterosexual ones, are also committed disproportionately by males. It would be interesting to know whether this holds true within prison populations where male sexual attacks are common and lesbian attacks at least not unheard of.

bedded; they move with time and place, but there is an apparent biological constant underlying cultural variations. The constant is reflected in persistent, differential sex ratios and age representations of homicidal offenders in widely separated cities and countries.

For such cities as:

Chicago (Voss & Hepburn 1968)
Columbus (Hamparian et al. 1978)
Detroit (Wilt & Bannon 1974)
Montreal (Tardiff 1966)
New York (Barnett et al. 1975, Burnham 1973, West 1968)
Philadelphia (Wolfgang 1958)

For such countries as:

Canada (Reed et al. 1978, Schloss & Giesbrecht 1972)
Denmark (Svalastoga 1956)
England, Wales, and Scotland (Gibson & Klein 1969, McClintock et al. 1963, Morris & Blom-Cooper 1963)
Finland (Verkko 1951)
India (Driver 1961, Elwin 1950)
Israel (Landau & Drapkin 1968)
Italy (Simondi 1970)
Kenya, Nigeria, and Uganda (Bohannon 1960)
Poland (Holyst 1967, 1969)
Sri Lanka (Jayewardene & Ranasinghe 1963, Strauss & Strauss 1953)
Uganda (Mushanga 1970)
USSR (Connor 1973)
USA (any annual FBI report)
48 preliterate societies in Africa, Asia, Oceania, and North and South America (Bacon et al. 1963)

It bears reminding that this biological constant is a theme that persists among wide variations in homicide rates, but that this theme should not be interpreted as the complete explanation of such variation. A consistent, yet varying, difference in group traits need not be a major cause of differential action.

This point is important because it has been popular among criminologists to attribute variations in crime rates to a "demographic factor" like age and to discount "real changes" in conduct. For example the *New York Times* (January 1, 1972), citing one of America's prominent criminologists, reported that "the experts who have precisely studied the homicide patterns in the United States over the years say that the real cause for the increase is demographic rather than social." Barnett and his colleagues (1975) tested this allegation with homicide data from America's 50 largest cities between 1964 and 1975 and found that "the changing age profile of the American people explains no more than ten percent of the increase in homicide since 1964."

To repeat, culture and opportunity expand or contract the exercise of biological differentials. This is particularly apparent with changes in the social roles of women.

Conditions of Convergence in Homicidal Sex Ratios

Approximations toward equality of sex roles are accompanied by a convergence, but not equality, of male and female murder rates. Conversely, the more sheltered the lives of women, the more they are "protected" by men and segregated from civic life, the greater the differential in favor of the homicidal activity of males. It is in "modernizing" countries, as opposed to the traditionally sex-segregated lands, that the proportions of men and women arrested for violent crimes move closer together (Adler 1975, Blum & Fisher 1978, Hoffman-Bustamente 1973).

Provocative, but inconclusive, tests of this "convergence hypothesis" have been conducted in a few industrialized countries. For example, Fox and Hartnagel (1979), working with the assumption that reproduction rates may stand as a sign of traditional female roles, find a *negative* relationship between "total fertility rate" and women's crime rates in Canada from 1931 through 1968. In parallel with this Canadian study, Lyster (1974) reports a significant *negative* correlation between homicide rates and fertility in the United States from 1900 through 1973. Lyster's study does not isolate the particular relationship between reproduction and *women's* homicidal activity. His data refer to general homicide rates and Lyster admits that he does not know what his finding means. He believes, however, that the relationship is not a "nonsense correlation." It would be a more pertinent test of the convergence hypothesis to note how women's arrests for murder and manslaughter varied with reproduction rates.

Sex Ratios Among Homicide Victims

Men are more likely than women to be killers and there is justice in the fact that victims are also more likely to be men. However, the probability of being a victim "because of" one's gender fluctuates. It fluctuates because killing is a social act. It involves more than one person. But it is a social act also in the sense that the perennial powers of age and sex work through social sieves to produce action. Social networks determine the occasions on which people meet with differing degrees of intimacy, expectation, and obligation. These social webs define duty, honor, insult, justice, and desert, all of which are ideas used to justify the appropriateness of homicide.

It follows, then, that victims are variables and that the occasions on which homicide occurs fluctuate. Thus, although males universally are more frequently killers than females, sex ratios of victims vary widely. For example, among the seven African tribes Bohannon and his associates (1960, p. 239) studied in Nigeria, Kenya, Tanzania, and Uganda, the proportions of female victims ranged from one-fifth to one-fourth in five tribes to 45 percent and 62 percent of the victims in two tribes.

In Israel between 1950 and 1964, about one-half of the Jewish homicide victims were women, but only one-third of the Arab homicide victims were women (Landau & Drapkin 1968).

For selected countries in Asia and Oceania, Ting and Tan (1969) report sex ratios of victims that run from 15 males to one female in the Philippines, to 8:1 in Thailand, 3.5:1 in Taiwan, 3.2:1 in Hong Kong, 1.9:1 in Japan, and 1:1 in Australia.

In Europe the proportions of female victims have ranged from less than 10 percent in Serbia, Bulgaria, and Italy (Verkko 1951), to between one-fourth and one-third in Denmark (Svalastoga 1956), Finland (Verkko 1951), Poland (Holyst 1967), and the USSR (Curtis 1974, p. 40).

Sex ratios of victims vary with kinds of homicide, of course. In Canada, about 60 percent of all female victims are killed in "domestic disturbances." This is more than double the proportion of men (about 27%) killed in family fights (Reed et al. 1978, p. 193). Put another way, Canadian domestic murders have female rather than male victims in the order of 1.3 to 1. On other homicidal occasions, however, men are victims about two-and-a-half times as frequently as women (Schloss & Giesbrecht 1972, Table 10).

In the United States, nearly two-thirds of criminal homicides involve men killing men. Homicides in which a man kills a woman or a woman kills a man are of about equal frequency (17.5 and 16.4 percent of the cases, respectively). Homicides with female killers and female victims are rare (3.8 percent) (Curtis 1974, Table 2–4.) If the probability of being murdered is calculated by controlling for race and place as well as for age and sex, other differences emerge. In New York city, for example, "blacks . . . are murdered at eight times the rate of whites, and males at four times the rate of females; thus—assuming no race-sex correlation—a *black male* born there has a murder probability roughly 32 times that of a *white female* (Barnett et al. 1975, p. 106, emphasis added).

These cross-cultural, and provisional, data point again toward the convergence hypothesis in that women seem more likely to be victims of homicide as their status approaches that of men. But the wide variation in the sexual composition of killers and victims is additional evidence of the many roads that lead to homicide. Some of these paths are described by the social environments in which wealth is produced and distributed.

WORK, WEALTH, AND HOMICIDE

Making a living or getting a living—the two processes are *not* the same (Bethell 1980, Nettler 1978, pp. 138–140)—occupies differing proportions of one's time. Work describes what we do to obtain wealth, and that kind of doing is believed to have significance for other facets of our lives. Work is assumed to affect careers through the kinds of social networks in which it is embedded, and these networks are commonly characterized as "economies."

Making a living is done with others. Even isolated shepherds sell their product and at some point must deal with other persons. The kinds of social relationships involved in an economy are presumed to affect significant aspects of our lives (Bonger 1969). However, economic arrangements are themselves intertwined with cultures so that it is difficult to ascertain the constraints upon action set by economies as opposed to those determined by social habits. A strict economic determinism is always suspect.

It is interesting, nevertheless, to observe how styles of work become associated with styles of life, and how styles of life may, in turn, be correlated with violence. For example, it is a commonplace to note that central cities in some countries tend to be more dangerous places than suburbs and rural areas (Ennis 1967, p. 23, Harries 1974). However, this generalization is immediately qualified by the reminder that cities, suburbs, rural areas, and the countries (cultures) in which they are located, are *not* of one kind. Even those residential districts called "neighborhoods" are *not* of one type (Kapsis 1979, Warren & Warren 1975). Finding differences among "neighborhoods" is important because such areas have been defined as similar in racial composition and income level. Difference means, then, that conduct is not well described—much less explained—by just those status-linked characteristics.

From this it follows that the popular opinion that rural areas are more peaceful than urban zones will be more or less valid depending on the social setting. It follows that human congregations of like size may differ greatly in their homicide rates as a function of the cultures in which wealth-making and wealth-getting occur.

For example, Canadian murder rates for years have been higher in the countryside than in the metropolis (Schloss & Giesbrecht 1972, p. 22). This experience differs from that of the United States where there is some relationship, albeit a weak one, between urbanization and rates of physical attack. The geographer Harries (1974) studied 189 Standard Metropolitan Statistical Areas (SMSAs)[4] to ascertain relations between conditions of population congregation and American "index crimes."[5] His calculations show that the numbers of people in an SMSA and the amount of population change—movement in and out—are positively, but modestly, correlated with assault and homicide rates. Low income levels and high proportions of black people in the SMSAs are also significantly associated with violent crime (Harries's Table 3.12), a finding reported earlier by Schuessler (1962). Contrary to popular assumption, unemployment is *negatively* correlated with violent crime in these urban districts, but Harries recognizes that "unemployment" is crudely measured (p. 51).

These kinds of findings are paralleled in Scotland where cities, burghs (towns), and rural counties differ greatly in crimes of violence. Glasgow, for example, is a much more violent city than Edinburgh, and some rural areas, like Sutherland, have a thinly scattered population and a low general crime rate coupled with a high rate of violent crime (Shields & Duncan 1964, pp. 50–51). Sutherland police attribute violence in their county to transient workers imported for hydroelectric projects.

Similar differences between communities of like size in the character and level of crime has been reported for Poland (Radzinowicz 1946) and Norway (Christie 1960). Wiers (1939) long ago noted that the logging counties in northern Michigan had higher delinquency rates than the agricultural counties in southern Michigan and in Israel the highest rate of delinquency, presumably including crimes of violence, has recently been recorded "in the rural region of the Jerusa-

---

[4] Standard Metropolitan Statistical Areas are counties or combinations of counties in the United States. This measure has been developed in an attempt to distinguish urban ways of life from rural conditions and, given the limits of city boundaries, is considered to be a more accurate unit of study than cities. However, SMSAs differ widely in density of population, and hence they are crude measures of urbanism (Bogue 1969, p. 531).

[5] "Index crimes" consist of eight serious offenses reported by the U.S. Federal Bureau of Investigation in its annual Uniform Crime Reports. The eight crimes are grouped as the violent crimes of murder, forcible rape, aggravated assault, robbery, and the property crimes of burglary, larceny-theft, and automobile theft, and arson.

lem area, whose population is composed entirely of 'new' immigrants" (Shoham 1966, p. 82).

Pockets of violence are found in isolated villages and deserts as they are in some central cities, and in situations in which differences in violence *cannot* be connected to the requirements of an economy. For example, Elwin (1950) describes differences in murder rates between tribes in India that have similar economies, but different modes of rearing their young. Elwin tells us that, "The Bison-horn Maria have long had a bad reputation for violence and drunkenness" (p. 37). They kill one another at a rate three to four times that of their provincial neighbors, the Ghotul Muria. Elwin's analysis of the "causes"—more accurately, the histories—of a sample of 100 homicides among the Maria reveals, again, the many roads to the same lethal end. Elwin groups the major causes (his Table 15, p. 51) as:

Alcohol	19%
Sex motives	17%
Family quarrels	16%
Quarrels over property	15%
Resentment at abuse or "word-magic"	9%
Robbery or accusation of robbery	8%
Revenge	6%
Suspicion of magic or witchcraft	5%
Insanity	5%

The many occasions for deadly quarrels are further illustrated in the research of anthropologists who have studied Mexican tribes with high homicide rates. Their research shows that similar economies may be associated with different murder rates, and different cultures with similar rates. For example, Friedrich (1962) and Nash (1967) report high rates of homicide in Mexican villages of different cultures—Tarascan and Mayan, respectively. During the 1950s and 1960s, people in these pueblos killed one another at an annual rate exceeding 250 per 100,000 population. Murder is so common that Nash refers to deadly fighting in the village she studied as "a way of life." The Tarascans and Mayans of Friedrich's and Nash's research kill to satisfy political ends and sometimes to settle quarrels about sexual and property rights.

The anthropologist Schwartz (1972) has tallied similar, high rates of homicide in a mestizo village in central Mexico. Her estimates yield murder rates that have ranged at different times from 250 to 800 per 100,000 population. In contrast with the observations of Friedrich and Nash, Schwartz notes that homicide in the mestizo community is characteristically a product of friendly drinking that moves from joking to insult. People are killed because they refuse a drink, because they try to leave a drunken all-night gambling party, and, as always, because of jealousy. The drunken homicides Schwartz reports are *not* the result of conflicts within the village and they do *not* produce conflict. They neither express smoldering hostility nor do they stimulate it, and they do not flow from "frustration." As might be expected in such a context, "only three of 32 murderers were jailed for very short periods . . . fines are commonly assessed and paid . . . in many cases charges are not pressed. Some cases are heard only in the village where they are treated mildly" (p. 155).

Schwartz's description of killing without conflict contrasts with other routes to homicide observed in varied economies where murder is motivated by struggles for property and power. In a rustic setting, this kind of tendency to homicide characterizes the knife- and gun-wielding men of North Yemen today (Vicker 1979).

Dealing in death can indeed be a way of life, as Nash puts it, and there are men whose concept of masculinity, as opposed to their work or economic status, demands pride, sensitivity to insult, and quickness in lethal response.

An Interpretation

Differences such as these are only loosely associated with differences in economies, with what people do for a living and the quality of life they make. These mortal differences are more strongly associated with preferred ways of being. For example, it is often noted that ethyl alcohol (booze) is one of the principal fuels of violence. For inexplicable reasons, some work has become associated with a culture that recommends consumption of booze as part of "the way to be." In North America, for example, heavy drinking is a tradition among workers with timber—from front office managers to loggers. A similar tradition is found among workers in other extractive industries. In these contexts, being "a man" means being tough, and being tough means being able to drink and fight. Being willing and able to drink and fight puts one on a course toward criminal assault and homicide. It also means that much fighting is not reported to officials and that some homicides appear as accidents (Morgenstern 1965).

Rural areas differ, therefore, in rates of violent crimes. Within Canada and the United States, for example, rates vary with the economy in that rural districts devoted to the extractive industries or to government-financed idleness are more violent than rural districts devoted to agriculture.

A corollary of this difference is that populations in agricultural areas are usually more settled than those in extractive zones. The migration of people is, in turn, a correlate of increased crime rates in general and increased violence in particular. As we saw (p. 23), Harries's (1974) American study reports "net population change," a measure of movement, to be associated with rates of assault and homicide. Similarly, Clinard and Abbott (1973) note how the migration of people from countrysides to cities in Africa is associated with the breakdown of tribal life, increased affluence, and increased crime, including wounding and murder.

These facts point toward an interpretation. The interpretation modifies economic determinism. It holds that there is nothing in the nature of logging, mining, or peasant agriculture—that is, in the work itself—that requires boozing and brawling. Drinking and fighting are culturally stimulated ways of behavior and the present interpretation places culture as mediator between the work one does and the conduct one prefers.

The repeated correlation of migration with crimes of violence suggests another conclusion. It is that the proclivity to attack is inhibited by morals transmitted through stable primary groups. Deterioration of primary group control is a major source of physical attack. It is not the only path to violence, of course.

Homicide and the Wealth of Persons

Students of social behavior look at other aspects of economies than the work people do. They also attend to the quantity and distribution of wealth.

Attention to wealth is encouraged by a major assumption and a major fact. The assumption is that voiced years ago by the singer Sophie Tucker who commented toward the end of her career, "I bin rich and I bin poor; rich is better."

This assumption is bolstered by a fact, the fact that good things go together. Insofar as we have been able to measure these matters, the perennial goods of health, happiness, and wealth appear together (Nettler 1976, pp. 22–28). Advantages cumulate, and so do disadvantages.[6]

Criminology notes this association as it observes that, in recent decades, within jurisdictions of which we have record, poorer

---

[6] Students of "justice" are concerned with the fairness of the process by which one virtue attracts another. For example, Shapiro (1974) notes that one good quality draws to it other good qualities and he calls such attributes "resource attractors." Thus people with high IQs gain a higher net return from each unit of education than do people with low IQs (Hause 1975, Turner 1978). Advantage accrues to advantage, and Shapiro and others (Deutsch 1979) ask whether this is fair or, "who merits merit?"

people attack one another physically at higher rates than do richer people. Violence that ranges from brawling to killing is disproportionately practiced by persons of lower social status in all localities for which we have contemporary data (Henry & Short 1954, Lalli & Turner 1968, Munford et al. 1976).

Furthermore, the social characteristics of people who are disproportionately involved in homicide are similar to the social characteristics of people who more often injure others physically without killing them (Peterson et al. 1962, Pittman & Handy 1964). Homicide is frequently, but not exclusively, an outcome of a career in fighting, and such careers are distributed unevenly in the social hierarchy.

The clustering of disadvantages associated with violence is indicated by correlations among indicators of "poor starts" and American homicide rates. Loftin (1980, Table 2) finds that marks of disadvantage are correlated with state homicide rates for 1959–1961 as follows:

.88 with percent of children living with one parent.
.84 with proportion of persons failing the armed forces' mental test.
.83 with infant mortality rates.
.77 with percent of the population that is illiterate.
.71 with percent of families with less than $1,000 income.

In addition, Loftin shows that some 12 indicators of low status are intertwined. They correlate highly, one with all others, a statistical phenomenon called "multicollinearity." The coefficients of determination [R^2] of each disadvantage or risk factor with all others, by states, are:

Low school completion	.99
Percent illiterate	.98
Armed forces test failures	.96
Percent poor	.95
Percent nonwhite	.91
Percent of children living with one parent	.90
Gini measure of income inequality	.89
Infant mortality rate	.86
Percent living in rural area	.80
Region [former Confederate state or other]	.79
Percent of population in ages 20-34	.60
Number of hospital beds per 100,000 population	.49

(Adapted, with emendations, from Loftin's Table 7).

In sum, a negative relationship between homicide and social status is reported repeatedly. Morselli (1879) and Ferri (1895) observed this in Italy decades ago and Franchini and Introna (1961) report a similar relationship in more recent times. French researchers have also noted a correlation between lower status and homicide in the nineteenth and twentieth centuries (Amiot et al. 1968, Aron 1973, Frégier 1840, Tarde 1890), and Given (1977) finds a similar correlation in thirteenth century England.

The negative association of deadly fighting with social position has been recorded among a variety of countries of differing economic "structure" on several continents. For example, in Denmark (Svalastoga 1956), England and Wales (Morris & Blom-Cooper 1963), Finland (Verkko 1951), Mexico (Bustamente & Bravo 1957), South Africa (Lamont 1961), the Soviet Union (Connor 1973), Sri Lanka (Jayewardene 1964, Wood 1961), and the United States (Bensing & Schroeder 1960, Brearley 1932).

Qualification

The reported inverse correlation between deadly dispute and social position is impressive for its contemporary continuity across cultures. However, this association should not be interpreted as fixed. It is better interpreted as a limited generalization rather than as an immutable connection. Historians are careful to point out that such correlations are subject to the corruption of data by definitions of crimes. Ideas about what constitutes "violence" and, in particular, what constitutes culpable homicide, change, and with changes in conceptions go changes in tallies.[7] Thus Zeldin (1977, p. 917) reports for nineteenth century France that "murder . . . did not inspire horror if it was committed in the name of the 'right to love,' and the phrase 'I shall kill him and I shall be acquitted' became an expletive of daily

---

[7] Variations in conceptions of violence are not just historical, of course. They are also contemporaneous. Thus many jurisdictions employ the idea of "extenuating circumstances" to distinguish manslaughter from murder. A circumstance that may reduce the gravity of killing from murder to manslaughter is "provocation," and "provocation" sufficient to diminish blame for homicide is defined as that which, in the language of the law, "a reasonable man [person]" could not resist. However, the kind of assault or insult that may be expected justifiably to provoke a "reasonable man" varies. For example, if a wife tells her husband that she has been sexually unfaithful, this is considered "provocation" in Kentucky, Mississippi, and South Carolina, but it is not "provocation" for the "reasonable man" in California, Georgia, or Iowa (Fiora-Gormally 1978, p. 136, n. 39).

conversation. Because of the clemency of juries, crimes of passion increased in this period, taking on an almost standard uniformity."

In addition, tallies of murder among ancient and medieval people are often unreliable and histories are selective in that they record the actions of prominent people more than the actions of common ones. If we allow for this selective bias, homicide does not appear historically only among the poor; it has also been a privilege of the rich (Tuchman 1978).

We do not assume, then, that the distribution of homicide among citizens of high and low status is immutable. On the contrary, there is historical reason to suppose that the social distribution of physical attack varies with the ill-described contexts in which human hierarchies perform. Persons of relatively higher income, schooling, and occupational prestige are not immune to mortal combat, and we note that "middle-class" (or, more accurately, middle-income) people become extraordinarily deadly when they become revolutionaries. As we shall see (pp. 240–252), such idealistic violence takes the ominous form of killing innocent people in contrast with much lower-class brawling that selects its victims among intimates or among those who have given insult.

Social Class and Homicidal Style

A class of persons or things is a group that has some features in common not shared with other persons or things. All classification involves questions of *criteria* of similarity and difference, of *how much similarity* justifies inclusion in a class, and of *how much overlap* is permitted. Given these questions, the idea of "social class" is necessarily open to debate. Nevertheless, sociologists and others frequently attend to "class" differences and mark them principally, but not solely, by wealth and such correlated attributes as schooling and occupational prestige. It then becomes interesting to record how these indicators are associated with conduct.

In the United States, where such things are frequently tallied, it is noted that rates of physical attack vary inversely with social status. But it is also noted that the *style* of homicide changes with socioeconomic position. Thus, Green and Wakefield (1979) report many features that distinguish "middle- and upper-class" killing from "lower-class" homicide, such as these:

1. The upper-class killer tends to be a white male, over thirty years old. In the lower-class, he tends to be a black male under thirty.
2. There are no ascertainable cases of victim-precipitated upper-class

homicide. By contrast, between one-fifth to one-third of lower-class homicides are deemed to have been victim-precipitated.[8]

3. Intra-familial homicides predominate in the upper-class cases. Domestic killing occurs three times as frequently among the rich as compared with the poor.

4. Homicide followed by suicide accounts for 27 percent of upper-class cases, but only 0.8 percent to 9 percent of lower-class cases.

5. The upper-class method of killing is seldom stabbing. It often involves shooting, although upper-class killers do not use guns in higher proportions than do lower-case offenders in southern states.

6. Alcohol is rarely involved in upper-class homicide. But more than one-half of lower-class homicides are alcohol-related.

7. Upper-class homicides, like lower-class killings, take place more frequently during evening hours—from 8 p.m. to 2 a.m. However, unlike lower-class homicides that increase on week ends, upper-class cases follow no daily pattern.

8. Upper-class killings are significantly more likely to occur at the victim's home than are killings in the lower-class (p. 180).

Homicide and National Wealth

History with its uncertainties reduces assurance that as people become richer they necessarily become less violent. The repeated negative correlation between social status and physical attack is, like other correlations, embedded in a web of causes, and the meaning of money for conduct varies with how wealth is produced and distributed. *Receiving* money is not the same process as *earning* it, and what one *does* to achieve status is an important moulder of conduct.

It follows that a correlation observed *within* societies among individuals cannot be converted into a rule applied to societies as a whole. From the correlates of individual position and behavior, it cannot be concluded that increasing the wealth of nations will reduce violence within them. Such a conversion commits *the fallacy of*

---

[8] Green and Wakefield are aware that the concept of "victim-precipitation" seems clear at some extremity as when witnesses of a homicide concur that the bully who started the fight "got what was comin' to 'im." But as we move away from such extreme cases of immediate and visible provocation toward cases in which provocation is prolonged and subtle, it becomes apparent that "victim-precipitation" may occur without its being noted by police and other recorders. Chapter 6 describes instances of less visible provocation that cumulates until the killer is stimulated beyond some threshold of tolerance.

composition,[9] the error of assuming that what is true of individuals (parts) will be true of the groups (wholes) they constitute.

Easterlin (1973) makes this point in discussing the relationship between wealth and happiness, and what he says about happiness can be applied to violence. Easterlin summarized data from 30 investigations conducted in 19 countries of more- and less-developed economies on the relation between reported happiness and income. He concludes that, *"In all societies, more money for the individual typically means more individual happiness. However, raising the incomes of all does not increase the happiness of all"* (p. 4, emphasis his).

The gap between changing economic conditions and behavior is evidence, again, of the limits of an economic determinism. The limits are set by the fact that cultures and interpretations intrude between environments and conduct. This fact leads to varied conceptions of "need" and "deprivation," terms that are frequently invoked in explanation of action.

Need: Absolute and Relative

A popular explanation of homicide sees its cause in a vaguely defined condition called "frustration." This concept is criticized in Chapter 12 (pp. 273–275), but the idea that frustration produces killing rests on the assumption that "need" is a major source of mortal combat.

Unfortunately for a science of action, "need" is as vaguely defined as "frustration." The *content* of things needed ranges across a broad spectrum of material and psychological necessities. Furthermore, "need" is sometimes conceived as an *absolute,* to be measured against some universal standard, and sometimes as *relative deprivation,* a psychological state induced by comparing oneself invidiously with others.

When need is defined in absolute terms, it suggests the hypothesis that poor countries will have higher homicide rates than rich ones and that better times will result in fewer killings. When need is de-

---

[9] Cohen and Nagel (1934, p. 377) define the fallacy of composition as reasoning "from the properties of elements or individuals to the properties of the wholes which they constitute. For the same word may have a different significance when applied to a totality than it has when applied to an element. Thus the fact that the soldiers of a given regiment are all 'strong' does not justify the conclusion that the regiment which they constitute is 'strong'."

fined in relative terms, however, no particular relationship can be specified between national standards of living, the distribution of wealth among the citizenry, feelings of frustration, and homicide. No particular association of these allegedly criminogenic factors can be predicated because relative deprivation is a psychological state, and such a sentiment varies as much with ideology as it does with reality. For some people, the better off they are, the worse they feel (Crosby 1976). There is no symmetry between what "society provides" and the deprivation people believe they suffer (Foa et al. 1976, Davis 1959, Gurr 1970, Runciman 1966, Thurow 1973, Townsend 1974).[10]

Given the gaps between objective necessity, subjective need, and other possible causes of killing, it is no surprise that attempted tallies of the relationships between national wealth and internecine fighting give mixed results. The mixed results point to no necessary relation between per caput[11] wealth and violence within states nor to any necessary relation between improved economic conditions and concord. There is evidence, however, that countries with greater inequalities in the distribution of income experience higher murder rates (p. 38).

Some Statistics

International homicide and income statistics are sufficiently unreliable and sufficiently affected by local political conditions that no one has attempted to compute a worldwide correlation between per caput wealth and murder rates. However, Wellford (1974) calculated the relationship for 75 countries as of 1967–1968. Using International Criminal Police Organization (Interpol) data, he found a slight negative correlation ($r = -.12$) between the per caput wealth of these lands and their murder rates. When Wellford combined measures of wealth per person, population size, and "political orientation," these

[10] Relative deprivation is experienced by comparing one's condition with that of persons immediately "above" one, rather than with those who are socially distant (Runciman 1966). Furthermore, the sense of being relatively deprived is not to be confused with a demand for equality. For Americans at least, "equality" means that "no one is above you," not that "no one is below you" (Sarat 1977).

The sense of relative deprivation varies, too, with *how* one achieves "justice." There is evidence that those who use *violent* means feel more satisfied than those who use nonviolent appeals (deCarufel & Schopler 1979).

[11] The common phrase, "per capita," is ungrammatical. "Capita" is the plural of "caput," Latin for "head." Rates of events *per person* refer to individuals, not aggregates, and the singular noun should be used.

indicators accounted for only two percent of the variance in homicide rates among these states.

Such a low association between material conditions and violence challenges the optimism voiced by many Western theorists during the late nineteenth and early twentieth centuries (Parrington 1930). Some intellectuals promoted the notion that "civilization," encouraged by the twin underwriters, science and technology, would reduce savagery in "undeveloped" lands as it had presumably done in more favored nations. Only a few decades ago writers compared the low homicide rates in Scandinavia and England with the higher rates in southern Europe and concluded that material "development" would reduce deadly disagreement. As recently as 1960, the American sociologist Daniel Bell observed that homicide rates in the United States are "lower today than [they were] twenty-five years ago" and that "kidnapping, the big bugaboo of the early thirties, has virtually disappeared" (pp. 139–140).

The optimism implicit in these observations has been disappointed by current events. During the 1960s and 1970s, the resurgence of violence within countries of widely different standards of living has damaged the easy assumption that national wealth alone produces domestic peace.

Homicide rates fluctuate independently of the wealth of nations. For example, Argentina, Uruguay, and Puerto Rico, all countries above the world poverty line, have higher reported homicide rates than many poorer states in Latin America, Africa, and Asia (Delury 1978). Mexico, a country of middling wealth by world standards, has notoriously high mortality from violent attacks, rates reported to be on the order of 30 murders per year per 100,000 population and, as we have seen, much higher in some districts. Politically inspired killing has raised homicide rates in such relatively affluent countries as Italy and Northern Ireland and has reduced the once-prosperous state of Lebanon to poverty. Between 1971 and 1977, for example, convictions for murder in Northern Ireland increased each year until the rate in 1977 was 18 times that of 1971. Manslaughter convictions rose five-fold during these years and wounding convictions more than doubled (Ingram 1978).

The United States experience is a model of discrepancies between national wealth, culture, and homicide. Long identified as one of the richest countries in the world, the United States has a parallel reputation for violence. It has had, and has, a homicide rate higher than that of many poor lands and many times that of countries of comparable wealth. For example, in recent years Japan and states of western Europe (Belgium, the Netherlands, Scandinavia, Switzerland) have had homicide rates ranging between 0.5 and 1.0 per 100,000 population (*Statistical Abstracts* 1974). Canada's rate is more than *double* these Japanese and European figures at 2.65 per 100,000 people (*Statistics Canada* 1979), and the American rate runs about *four times* the Canadian.

The contrast between crime rates in a rich, but homogeneous, society like Japan with rates in a rich, but heterogeneous, society like the United States is particularly illuminating. Tokyo, which is probably the world's largest city as of 1980 and one of the most densely packed, has the lowest reported rates of serious crimes of any metropolis. For example, in recent years, for every million residents, New York City has been recording around 11,000 robberies compared with Tokyo's 40. Per million people, New York City annually reports about 450 forcible rapes to Tokyo's 30, and over 200 murders to Tokyo's 20 (Charlé 1979, p. 50). While American crime rates have risen with affluence, Japan's rates have been declining (Vogel 1979). Cultural differences that allow greater social control in Japan than in the United States seem to account for the difference (Volume One, Chapter 6).

It is noteworthy that homicide—which is sometimes economically motivated, but which is also a "crime of passion"—increased in the United States during a period of general prosperity. Murder and manslaughter rates increased during years when a higher proportion of America's age-eligible population was in the work force than at any time in its history[12] (Drucker 1978, Malabre 1979), when *real* household income was constantly and significantly while the number of persons "in poverty" declined dramatically (Malabre 1979, Paglin 1979a), and when America's visible minorities gained higher per caput buying power than inhabitants of most other lands (Gilder 1979).

Data from registered death certificates in the United States show that homicide rates rose from 4.7 per 100,000 population in 1960 to 9.8 in 1973 and an estimated 10.3 in 1974 (Klebba 1975, p. 196). These figures represent the highest levels of mortal dispute in American history, rates that were only approximated in the trough of the

---

[12] We have already noted that "unemployment" has to be defined before it can be counted (Volume One, Chapter 4). The "unemployment" that is counted is in part a function of the numbers of people who deem themselves available for work. It is therefore no contradiction to find officially tabulated "unemployment" statistics high or rising at the same time that more people are working and more jobs are vacant (Bethell 1980, Brittan 1975, Clarkson & Meiners 1977, 1978, Drucker 1978, Friedman 1968, Meadows 1978, Seligman 1978a, 1978b).

Great Depression, 1933, when the homicide rate was 9.7 per 100,000 people (Klebba 1975, p. 195).

It has been popular to attribute much of this increase in American violence to changes in the age composition of the population (Wolfgang 1978). Since the most murderous people are young men, it has been assumed that the postwar "baby boom" might account for the increase in homicide. However, a careful analysis of changes in murder rates between 1963–1965 and 1971–1972 in the *fifty largest cities* in the United States demonstrates that "less than *one-tenth* of the actual rise in the national homicide rate since the 1960s can be explained by demographic changes" (Barnett et al. 1975, p. 98, emphasis added). These investigators show that homicide rates increased in every one of the fifty cities during the late 1960s and early 1970s. When these rates are adjusted to take account of variations in the age and ethnic composition of the cities—differences that make a difference in murder rates—it is found that the greatest increase in homicide has been in Detroit, Buffalo, and Honolulu. Detroit has been given the title of "murder capital of the world" because of this dramatic increase in its homicide rate and because its 1971–1972 rate was the highest among American cities. Its killing rate of 38.93 homicides for every 100,000 residents is probably the highest among urban centers in industrialized countries.

Barnett and his colleagues conclude that murder rates in American cities are higher than many people believe and that:

> At current . . . levels, a randomly-chosen baby born in a large American city has almost a two percent chance of dying by homicide; among males, the figure is three percent. Thus, an American boy born in 1974 is more likely to die by murder than an American soldier in World War II was to die in combat (p. 102). If current trends continue, it is not inconceivable that the homicide rate may surpass the individual death rates due to cirrhosis of the liver, arteriosclerosis, suicide, diabetes mellitus, diseases of early infancy, and, perhaps, pneumonia (and influenza), and motor vehicle accidents. This last possibility is made more probable by recent reduced speed limits, increased use of automobile safety devices, and disincentives to leisure driving due to higher petroleum costs. By 1969 . . . homicide had already surpassed motor vehicle accidents as the cause of death in ten of the cities. . . . (pp. 105–106).

Mass Violence and Economy

The relationship between the economic environment and homicide has thus far been described in terms of the legally defined crimes of murder and manslaughter, with some attention to such correlative crimes of violence as rape, robbery, and assault. There are other orders of violence, of course, that range from the clearly criminal to the legitimate and that involve large segments of a population. Studies of such large-scale fights, including wars between states, supplement our information about criminal homicide. They fill out the picture of the conditions under which human beings injure and kill one another. Such supplementary information confirms the present thesis that neither the amount of wealth nor conditions of its production explain much of the variation in deadly quarreling.

This thesis gains support from major studies of mass violence. Independently of one another, students in separate disciplines have studied dimensions of mass conflict—sociologists (Archer & Gartner 1976, Sorokin 1937), psychologists (Cattell 1949, 1950, Cattell et al. 1951, Cattell & Gorsuch 1965, Eckstein 1962), political scientists (Chadwick 1963, Rummel 1963, 1966, 1969, Tanter 1965, 1966, Wilkenfeld 1968), a professor of international law (Wright 1942), and a physicist-mathematician (Richardson 1960a, 1960b). Some of these investigators employed mathematical procedures (factor analysis) to ascertain whether there are patterns in fighting and common conditions of their production. As concerns our present interests, these studies show that:

1. Fighting abroad and fighting at home are largely independent dimensions of conflict. Countries that are peaceful internationally may be violent domestically, and vice versa. However, Archer and Gartner (1976) and Wilkenfeld (1968) provide exceptions to this conclusion.

2. Within countries, there is variety in mass violence. Some of it is spontaneous, as in riots, and some planned, as in revolutionary and subversive activity. Again, there seems to be little connection between the amount of turmoil (unplanned violence) within a society and the amount of guerrilla fighting (planned violence).

3. Human beings are *not* becoming more pacific. On the contrary, wars have become more frequent in recent times (Richardson 1960b, p. 142) with larger proportions of the resources and populations of belligerent states involved (Wright 1942, p. 248).

4. Prosperous societies are no more peaceful than poor ones, and prosperous times are no more peaceful than depressed times.

5. Democracies and republics are no more peaceful than autocracies and monarchies.

6. Between 1837 and 1937 (at least), rich, industrialized, and well-educated countries have engaged disproportionately in inter-state combat (Cattell 1950). They have also won a disproportionate share of Nobel prizes for science, literature, and peace (!).[13]

7. Archer and Gartner (1976) show that countries that go to war experience an increase in their postwar homicide rates. They demonstrate this with data from 110 states that participated since 1900 in 50 "nation-wars" as compared with the experience of 30 "control nations" that did not engage in war.

Archer and Gartner report that increases in postwar homicide rates within belligerent states "were pervasive, ... occurred after large wars and smaller wars, with several types of homicide rate indicators, in victorious as well as defeated nations, in nations with both improved and worsened postwar economies, among both men and women offenders, and among offenders of several age groups. Homicide rate increases occurred with particular consistency among nations with large numbers of combat deaths."

An Inference

International data on homicide are made questionable, of course, by differential reporting practices, some of which are fostered by totalitarian governments that themselves contribute to killings not counted as homicides (Chalidze 1977, Hollander 1973). Granting this qualification, the magnitude of the differences in national murder and manslaughter rates is sufficiently great, and sufficiently corroborated by observations other than official statistics, to permit an inference about the relationship between material welfare and violence within states. The inference is that neither the poverty nor the wealth of nations is a major determinant of the level of deadly dispute. Violence is differentially distributed *ecologically* (in social space within societies) in a way negatively correlated with standard of living, but violence is not associated *historically* (in time) or *comparatively* (across cultures) with the wealth of a people.

This means that homicide may as well be expected to increase in good economic times as in bad, and that there is no necessary connection between a country's being relatively poor and its being mur-

---

[13] The fact that the Nobel prize for peace goes so frequently to countries that wage war has led to the wry comment that this award is a grant for need rather than a recognition of achievement. The irony is justified by the further fact that Alfred Nobel (1833–1896), the patron of the prizes that bear his name, was a Swedish chemist who made much of his fortune from his invention of dynamite.

derous or relatively rich and its being peaceful. However, there may be a connection between the way in which wealth is *distributed* within countries and their murder rates.

Messner's Study

Messner (1980) collected reports of murder rates in 39 non-communist countries as of the early 1960's.[14] He then compared these with a measure of income inequality called the Gini ratio (Atkinson 1975). Since there is some evidence that rich states may distribute incomes more equally than poor states, Messner controlled for overall national wealth by using gross domestic product per caput as a measure of "economic development." Controls were also applied for population size, population density, and degree of urbanization, factors frequently mentioned as correlates of crime rates.

Messner finds a moderate correlation ($r = .40$) between income inequality and murder rate. This relationship is strengthened when one controls for the skewed distribution of homicide rates by assessing rates logarithmically. This is a mathematical conversion that "spreads out clustered values" and that "pulls in" extreme values toward the middle of a distribution (Tufte 1974, p. 108). Taking the logarithm of murder rates yields a correlation of .59 between such violence and income inequality.

In summary, Messner finds that a measure of the unequal distribution of income in 39 countries correlates more highly with their homicide rates than other national characteristics such as population size, population density, and per caput wealth, and that the Gini measure of inequality maintains this moderate association with murder rate when these other variables are controlled.

Messner recognizes that his results are tentative. They are subject to all the hazards of counting events in different places in different ways. This hazard affects not only tallies of crime, but also tallies of income. While the Gini index of inequality is frequently used, it has defects and there may be more sensitive measures (Allison 1978).

In addition, the age composition of the countries studied has not been controlled, and this is a factor which we have seen affects homicide rates. Last, income inequality is frequently associated with eth-

---

[14] The states included are Argentina, Australia, Ceylon, Chile, Colombia, Dahomey, Denmark, El Salvador, Fiji, Finland, France, West Germany, India, Iraq, Israel, Italy, Ivory Coast, Jamaica, Japan, South Korea, Lebanon, Madagascar, Malaya, Netherlands, Norway, Pakistan, Peru, Philippines, Puerto Rico, Senegal, Sierra Leone, Surinam, Sweden, Tanzania, Trinidad and Tobago, United Kingdom, United States, Venezuela, Zambia.

nic differences. Ethnic differences, in turn are associated with differential homicide rates *within* countries (pp. 47–62), and one does not know the extent to which differential distributions of income reflect the cultural heterogeneity of different lands.

SUMMARY

Observations of homicidal occasions confirm the thesis of "many roads" and disconfirm hypotheses that attribute murder and manslaughter to singular causes. Data challenge the popular journalistic view of violence—the opinion that "poverty causes crime" and that any procedure for reducing poverty will therefore reduce rates of personal attack. This opinion is widely disseminated as fact, but it commits the common error of confusing correlation with causation. It confuses sympathetic description with causal analysis.

"Social locations" are sites of differential activity. It is easy to translate locations into causes, but the temptation should be resisted and the conversion tested with comparative and experimental information. For example, hospitals are sites of high death rates, and so are some poorer neighborhoods. However, as van den Haag (1968, p. 283) points out, few people conclude from the first correlation that hospitals *cause* deaths and it is inappropriate to draw a parallel conclusion about poverty *causing* homicide. Those who leap to such an inference are forever disappointed as their meliorative programs fail and history refuses to unfold according to plan.

Sources of Error

Four possible sources of error confront those who would translate "poverty" into a cause of violence: (1) the error of confusing selection with causation; (2) the error of assuming a monolithic process in poverty; (3) the error of mistaking a covering concept for effective causes variously associated with it; and (4) the error of confusing an economic status with a cultural one.

1. Selection

The first source of error lies in the possibility that different social locations *select* different kinds of people. The casual arrow need not point in the preferred political direction, from "social position" to behavior. As Volume One, Chapter 7 indicated, it remains an open question whether social situations generate actions or whether kinds of people produce the situations in which different kinds of conduct are observed.

2. Multi-Dimensional Poverty

A second source of error is the assumption that "poverty" is one kind of status. In recent years, the thesis that there is a distinctive, worldwide "culture of poverty" has been advanced and disputed (Lewis 1959, 1966a, 1966b, Valentine 1968). However, even the inventor of the idea of a "culture of poverty" admits that "there are degrees of poverty and many kinds of poor people" (Lewis 1966b, p. xlviii).

We have seen that deprivation, one conception of poverty, is defined both absolutely and relatively. When deprivation is defined relatively, it does not refer to an economic condition but, rather, to a psychological one. In its psychological state, "poverty" does not refer to lack of money or to any specific standard of living (Waxman 1977, p. 107). To employ a psychological concept of poverty is to risk mistaking preference for need and contingency for determinant.

3. Contingency Versus Determinant

A third source of error is the confusion of a contingency with a determinant. To interpret a contingency as a determinant is tantamount to confusing a broad covering concept with the multiple and shifting *efficient causes* of conduct that may be included within the covering concept.

"Poverty" is a general term of this type. It refers to many conditions, not one. The varied correlates of these many conditions may include the efficient causes of differential action. In brief, if being "poor" is *not* one status, different kinds of behavior can be associated with any index of "poverty." To attend, then, to a social condition called "poverty" may blind one to the actual sources of conduct, correlated with, but masked by, such a covering concept.

4. Economic Status Is Not Cultural Status

The third error suggests a fourth. It is the mistake of confusing an economic status with a cultural one.

We have already noted that money makes a difference in our lives, but it makes a difference in constricting or allowing kinds of activities. However, within the limits of what money makes possible, *income does not cause conduct.*

This has long been recognized in the co-existence of "the honest poor and the depraved poor, the productive rich and the filthy rich" and in our repeated point that what one *does* to earn wealth is culturally more significant than how much wealth one has.

Nominating "poverty" as the cause of violence because it is an intra-state correlate of violence denies history, the persistence of cultures, and the mysteries of human preference.

The meaning of culture and the difference it makes is the concern of the next chapter.

3 SOCIAL LOCATIONS OF HOMICIDE: **CULTURES**

Abstract • "Culture" refers to learned ways of behaving transmitted within groups that have a sense of being "we." ○ This concept has been used to describe, and also to explain, the varied ways in which human aggregates respond to apparently similar circumstances. ○ Since each generation is born into a culture that is deemed to be *prior to, external to,* and *coercive of* individuals, the idea of "culture" has been employed as an *environmental* variable. ○ Ethnic groups are defined by cultural criteria. ○ Physical markers may be added to these criteria. ○ "Subcultures" refer to nations within states. • Ethnic differences in rates of violent crime are described for selected European countries, Israel, Canada, and the United States. ○ In advancing this description, the concept of "stereotype" is criticized. ○ Relationships between alcohol consumption and violence, and between ethnicity and alcohol abuse, are described. ○ "Ecological determinism" of violent crime is criticized and a resolution proposed. ○ Popular assumptions about the causes of ethnic differences in violence are challenged. In particular, "economic determinism" of violent crime is shown to provide an inadequate account of ethnic crime rates. • Explanation of the differential conduct of aggregates by reference to their "cultures" is vulnerable to circularity. Tautology is a term for this redundancy. ○ Circularity of such explanations may be reduced by detailed description, by adding social structures to cultures, and by adding social psychology to explanatory efforts. ○ Social scientists disagree about *how different* ethnic groups are, *how durable* the difference may be, and whether or not the difference is *rational.* ○ It is concluded that cultural differences exist and persist and that attention to these differences is useful for *descriptive* and *forecast* purposes. It is doubtful, however, whether attending to "cultures" increases *predictive* accuracy. We count on continuities; we can forecast without being able to predict.

HUMAN BEINGS DO NOT RESPOND in the same way to what seem to be similar situations. If they did, a science of human action would be simplified. It would be possible, then, to develop laws of behavior stating that, whenever people are in an X-type situation, they tend to do Y-type acts with such-and-such frequency.

Invention of such laws of conduct assumes, of course, that "X-type situations" and "Y-type acts" can be reliably identified. However, ignoring for the moment the difficulties in developing a taxonomy of conditions and actions such as were mentioned in Volume One, Chapter 4, human beings exhibit a wide range of conduct in apparently similar situations. There is no one-to-one connection between situation and action—for individuals or for aggregates.

This common observation occupies sociology, psychology, and anthropology, particularly that branch of anthropology known as ethnography or ethnology.[1] These studies document the fact of variation in response to situation and attempt to explain it.

Explanation has proceeded through the invention of the concept of *culture*. Culture refers to:

> . . . a way of life of a people who have a sense of common history, a sense of being a "we" as opposed to a "them," and who, usually, live within a bounded territory.
>
> In Eliot's phrase (1948, p. 57), "Culture is a peculiar way of thinking, feeling, and behaving." Culture describes the pattern of our lives together, a pattern that is discernible in our art; in our diet, dress, and customs; in our religion and values; in our obligations to each other; and in our language. Dialect, a distinctive way of using a language, is one of the most sensitive indicators of cultural membership (Nettler 1976, p. 91).

The concept of culture refers to *regulated* behavior that is learned, transmitted as tradition from generation to generation, and that is somewhat durable. The idea of culture is employed as an *environmental* variable. Human beings are "born into" groups, of varying extension and community, that already "have" a culture. In the conception of the French sociologist Emile Durkheim (1924, 1950), culture is *prior to, external to,* and *coercive of* the individual. Hence, it is assumed that cultural lessons are impressed upon us and constitute a social environment.[2]

The mechanism of cultural transmission is rooted in biology, but the lessons taught are something added to, and intertwined with, the genetic givens of any species.[3] These lessons, incidentally, are *not* re-

---

[1] *"Ethnography,* a branch of anthropology dealing with the scientific description of individual cultures."

"Ethnology, a branch of anthropology that analyzes cultures, esp. in regard to their historical development and similarities and dissimilarities between them" *(Random House Dictionary of the English Language).*

[2] The revolutionary government of the Ayatollah Khomeini in Iran confirms the common conception of cultures as environments. On July 12, 1979, this government continued its execution of various enemies by killing several prostitutes and a distributor of pornography. The Iranian state justified these executions as necessary "to clean the environment" (ABC News).

[3] Culturally acquired habits "intertwine" with genetic givens in reciprocal fashion. Differences in genetic disposition mean that some individuals need more training than others. At the same time, lessons acquired by training affect our genetically transmitted physiologies and alter activities of gut, gland, and heart (DiCara 1970, Gaito & Zavala 1964, N.E. Miller 1969).

stricted to *Homo sapiens;* such traditions also appear in birds and many mammals, particularly primates (Douglas-Hamilton 1975, Hockett 1973, p. 55).

Reference to behaviors as "cultural" says nothing, then, about their "refinement"; it only says that a way of acting has been "cultivated," that is, acquired through training. It follows that the "crude" behavior of one tribe may be the expected behavior of another and that violent ways of living may be traditional and valued.

ETHNICITY

When groups of people differ persistently and significantly in several domains of action, it has become convenient and conventional to say that these groups "have" different cultures. This statement is strengthened as human beings group themselves by patterns of learned preference and develop a "consciousness of kind," as Giddings (1911, p. 66) called it. Consciousness of kind is an appreciation of difference, a difference acknowledged by insiders and outsiders alike. A sense of being a distinct "people" is the hallmark of ethnicity. The word "ethnic" derives from the Greek *ethnos,* meaning "the nations." In its origins and in its popular application today, "nationality" refers to cultural distinctiveness rather than to citizenship.

Cultural difference is observable in psychic life—how people think and feel about their affiliations—and in behavior—how people differentially "do things." The doing includes a wide range of cultural indicators. It includes, for example, a people's selective congregation and intermarriage, their "proxemics" or preferred personal spacing (Hall 1959, Sommer 1969), their conceptions of the good life (Morris 1956), their characteristic gestures, postures, and pace (Efron 1941), their sense of time and its use (Banfield 1974, Jones 1976, Lamm et al. 1976), their music, dance, art, and religion, and, of course, their diet, dress, and dialect.

Physical differences—differences in size, shape, color, and hair covering—are also used as ethnic markers. Although there are dissenting opinions (Baker 1974, Coon 1962, Coon & Hunt 1966, Redfield 1957), most social scientists today do not believe that these racial indicators have any relevance to the culture one can learn. Nevertheless, physical indicators are used as correlative signs of cultural difference. The difference frequently becomes one, among many, of the justifications for disliking others and attacking them. For example, Isaacs (1975b, pp. 39–40) reports that:

> Between the Watutsi and the Hutu, who have been slaughtering each
> other in Rwanda and Burundi ever since they received their "indepen-

dence" from the Belgians, the major physical difference is between tallness and shortness, badges of group identity that can hardly be missed when the groups of killers from both sides seek each other out.

"One [Hutu] woman who arrived at a . . . hospital had had both her hands hacked off with a machete. That is a common reprisal, for when the short Hutu finds the tall Tutsi, they often cut off their legs at the ankles" [Isaacs is citing *The New York Times,* June 17, 1973].

With or without biological markers of ethnic difference, difference itself is a common occasion for dislike and, however, much the morality of scholars proposes tolerance, people continue to attack one another on ethnic grounds. At this writing, for example, the peoples of Southeast Asia are killing each other under cultural allegiances that represent continuities of ancient hostilities, although they may be justified by modern political ideologies. Vietnamese hate the Chinese among them and the Cambodians on their border. The feeling is reciprocated. Cambodians, in turn, dislike the Thais, and vice versa. The plight of thousands of refugees from the warfare in these countries is inexplicable to many Westerners who cannot distinguish one of these cultures from another. However, cultural differences that seem trivial to us are important to these distant others.

When ethnic differences are associated with differences in privilege—real or imagined—they become fuel for homicide. The difference is defined as unjust and "justice," variously conceived, is one of the ideals that stimulates and rationalizes mortal combat (Chapter 1). One observes the incendiary action of ideals correlated with cultures repeatedly in history and currently in lands as diverse as Afghanistan, Iran, Lebanon, Israel, Northern Ireland, Spain, Canada, the United States, and much of Africa. In this context, it deserves reminding that the National Socialist German Workers' Party (1918–1945), abbreviated from its German title to "Nazis," justified killing Jews for this familiar reason and that this justification was approved by numbers of citizens in Great Britain and North America.

Noting these facts says nothing about the justice of any of these struggles. "Justice" is itself a word with shifting meanings (Nettler 1979). The present point is that one can observe circumstances under which human beings kill one another, and their justifications of the homicide, without taking sides in these deadly quarrels.

The Idea of a Subculture: Nations Within States

History is a record of diverse peoples meeting. The encounters have been both hostile and friendly, egalitarian and dominating. However, it is only in recent times that large numbers of nations have come to be governed by single states as citizens with equal legal status.

A *state* is an agency with a monopoly of power, where the power is deemed to be legitimate[4] and is exercised over people resident within a demarcated territory. The modern state is not necessarily a nation. On the contrary, many contemporary states claim authority over the lives of citizens who define themselves, and are defined by others, as a distinct people. This applies, in differing degree, to Belgium, Brazil, Canada, France, Great Britain, India, Indonesia, Iran, Israel, Lebanon, the Republic of South Africa, Spain, the Soviet Union, Switzerland, Vietnam, the United States, and other lands.

Modern states differ, of course, in the degree of their cultural homogeneity. For example, Japan and Norway are culturally homogeneous in comparison with Canada and the United States. This makes governance easier in the first two countries than in the latter two. It affects the amount of conflict within these societies and the means of resolving conflict.

States that are cultural mosaics differ among themselves in the accommodation or discontent experienced by their ethnic groups. Switzerland seems like a model of accommodation compared with Lebanon. Changes in the distribution of power run in parallel with changes in ideas about the "best" way for diverse groups to live together under the laws of one state. In the 1920s, the New World ideal was assimilation, as expressed in the motto on American coins, *e. pluribus unum* (out of many, one).[5] In recent decades, the notion of culturally heterogeneous states as "melting pots" has been displaced by a "fever of ethnicity," as Alpert (1972) has termed it. Cultural difference today is used as an instrument in lobbying for privilege (Glazer

---

[4] Vagueness is unavoidable in defining a state as an agency exercising "legitimate" power since there is no rule by which to recognize what proportion of a population under a state's authority must accord it legitimacy before it is "legitimate enough."

[5] The ideal of many nations becoming one is in conflict with the ideal of maintaining cultural identity.

Identity refers to "remaining the same one ... under varying ... conditions" *(Random House Dictionary of the English Language). Integration* means to bring parts together to form a "whole." *Congregation* has roots in the Latin word, *grex,* a flock. It means "to come together, to assemble" *(Random House Dictionary of the English Language).*

It needs to be pointed out that there are different styles of congregation and that the congregation of diverse peoples can occur without their integration. It confounds both language and logic to aspire simultaneously for integration and the maintenance of cultural identity. The conflict between these ideals is assuaged by another ideal, that of tolerance.

& Moynihan 1975) and, in some cases, it leads to a demand for ethnic separation that provides yet another occasion for homicide.

The fact that people of different cultures may be citizens of the same state has led to the notion of "subcultures" (Arnold 1970). This idea refers to the possibility that people of diverse nationality may come to share *some* aspects of a common culture, particularly in an era of electronic communication. The notion of a subculture allows, then, for cultural overlap while retaining the possibility of cultural difference.

The degree of difference, and the indicators of it, are forever disputed. They are disputed despite the fact that degrees of common culture can be measured, as Almond and Verba (1963), Cattell (1949, 1950), Hsu (1953), McClelland (1961), and others have demonstrated.

Argument persists in part because the boundaries of cultures move with changing times so that there can be varying generation gaps as well as shifting differences in the cultures of "social classes," nations, and sects. Argument persists, too, out of ethicopolitical motivation. For example, socialists and communists refuse to accept ethnic differences as sources of conduct and prefer economic explanations. Thus the persistence of Gypsy poverty and segregation in Communist Hungary is an embarrassment to a regime that stresses the "class" origins of differential behaviors and denies aspirations for separate cultural identities. Programs of "reverse discrimination" have been attempted in Hungary with little effect on the lives of Gypsies, but with the effect of increasing hostility toward them on the part of Hungarians (Spivak 1979).

Different policies follow from assumptions about how different a subculture is and whether it is adaptive or autonomous. Viewing subcultures as only, or largely, adaptive interprets them as flexible responses to transient situations. Viewing subcultures as relatively autonomous interprets them as valuable in their own right and worth defending against situational changes.

Difficulties in employing the concepts of culture and subculture as explanatory tools will be discussed, pages 66–74, but illustration of possible cultural differences in the production of violent crimes is first required.

A SAMPLE OF ETHNIC DIFFERENCES IN VIOLENCE

Whenever peoples meet, they remark on their differences, rather than their similarities (Berelson & Steiner 1964, pp. 500–519). Differences in ethics and etiquette, civility and aggression are particularly noticeable (Anonymous 1942, Cuddihy 1974).

Discussion of these differences is unpleasant because comparison tends to be invidious, particularly when one is comparing the "good" and "bad" behaviors of "our people" and "their people." It is for this reason that some countries with histories of culture conflict, such as Canada and West Germany, do not publish statistics on the differential criminality of their ethnic groups. Such information is recoverable, however, from primary sources (Hawryluk 1979, p. 18).

The attempt to reduce division by ignoring ethnic differences in crime rates in official publications is morally motivated and one may thus approve the tactic. However, observing differences and their correlates is part of the descriptive job of the social studies and necessary in the explanatory work of accounting for human action.

European Experience

Comparative research has been stimulated by human migration and by questions about the "adjustment" of foreigners in host countries. For example, over the past two decades Switzerland has imported thousands of alien workers, over two-thirds of whom have come from Italy. This movement has been accompanied by hostility toward the migrants and by journalistic tales of their greater criminality. To test these stories Neumann (1963) compared the arrest records of Italian workers in the canton of Zurich during 1949, 1954, 1955, and 1960 with those of their Swiss hosts and found that, contrary to popular belief, the overall Italian crime rate was lower than that of Swiss nationals. Graven (1965) then summarized broader Swiss data and concluded, to the contrary, that criminality in general was somewhat higher among foreigners than among their hosts, but his study did not control for age and sex differentials.

Gillioz's (1967) research qualifies these earlier findings by noting that, while the overall criminality of aliens in Switzerland did not differ greatly from that of the resident population, *violent* crimes were committed disproportionately among migrant populations. Ferracuti (1968, p. 206) adds to Gillioz's finding the opinion that violent crimes among migrant workers may have increased in recent years as their numbers increased. Physical attacks among intimates in these mobile groups are, as Ferracuti puts it, "not infrequent [and] they are frequently not reported."

Similar reports of higher rates of personal attack within migrant ethnic groups have been given for Hungarians and Yugoslavs living in Sweden (Klemming 1967, Sveri 1966), for Italians in West Germany (Nann 1967) and Belgium (Liben 1963), for Algerians resident in France (Hirsch 1953), and for migrants from Africa and Mediterranean countries living in West Germany (Wenzky 1965). McClintock et al. (1963), Bottoms (1967), and Wallis and Maliphant (1967) note that immigrants to England from Commonwealth countries in Asia and the West Indies have conviction rates for violent crimes that range from two to three times the rates of the host population.

Some of these studies have not controlled for age and sex differentials in host and alien populations. However, Zimmermann (1966) compared conviction rates of males, 18 to 50 years of age, among four migratory ethnic groups in West Germany with rates for German men of the same age during 1965. Zimmermann discounted from his tabulation tourists, members of foreign armed forces, and criminals known to have operated as international professionals. With some interesting variations, Zimmermann confirms other European research in finding differentials in violent criminality among nationalities. Table 3.1 compares conviction rates of Italians, Greeks, Spaniards, and Turks with that of their German hosts where the host crime rate is set at 100. The table shows that Turkish men commit a disproportionate number of violent crimes—murder and attempted murder, minor and grave wounding, robbery, forcible rape, and sexual

Table 3.1 Ratios of Criminal Convictions Among Migrant Males in West Germany by Ethnicity to Convictions of German Males, Ages 18 to 50, 1965*

Crime	Germans	Italians	Greeks	Spaniards	Turks
All crimes	100	50	72	32	88
Murder	100	133	66	66	366
Attempted murder	100	133	183	83	517
Serious personal lesions	100	250	150	50	100
Lesions	100	112	139	75	287
Forcible rape	100	123	150	63	323
Crimes against the morality of children	100	163	115	63	160
Robbery	100	69	77	46	163
Theft	100	69	86	54	59
Fraud	100	23	38	11	50

* Adapted, with permission, from H.G. Zimmermann, 1966. "Die Kriminalität der ausländischern Arbeiter." *Kriminalistik,* 2:623–625.

abuse of children. With the exception of robbery, Italian men are also disproportionately violent. Greek men rank third in this tabulation, with less than proportional representation in robbery and murder, while Spaniards in West Germany are relatively immune to criminality in general and violent crime in particular.

Interpretation

Interpretation of data on the comparative criminality of ethnic groups is made difficult because some studies have not controlled for the age and sex composition of populations, the size of the migrant population relative to the host population, the length of time migrants have been in a host country, and whether the migrants are transient workers or permanent settlers.

Allowing for these difficulties, two interpretations have been given of ethnic differentials in criminality among migrants. Additional interpretations are advanced of ethnic differentials among residents (Chapter 4).

One explanation emphasizes *cultural continuity.* It views migrants as culture carriers who exhibit in a host country the patterns of behavior characteristic in the land of origin. For example, this kind of interpretation is readily available in accounting for the violent behavior of southern Italians as they move into northern Italy, Switzerland, and Germany (Franchini & Introna 1961, Introna 1963).

A second interpretation explains the violence of migrants as a *loss of cultural controls.* This interpretation notes that some migrants have low rates of violent crime in their homelands, but high rates as they lose their cultural connections by moving abroad. This is one explanation offered of the high crime rates of Irish migrants to England. Such mobile persons tend to be young men cut off from an Irish community. According to Gibbens and Ahrenfeldt (1966, p. 141), their main occupations in England tend to become "work and drink." The drinking may represent a cultural continuity, but armed robbery does not. In recent decades, some 20 percent of persons convicted of robbery in London were Irishmen, although they constituted only about 12 percent of the single male population between the ages of 15 and 40 (McClintock & Gibson 1961).

Irishmen in England have persistently exhibited higher rates of conviction and recidivism for serious crimes (Bottoms 1967, Lambert 1970). They have recently demonstrated yet another path to violence, that of terrorist murder for political objectives in England and Northern Ireland (Ingram 1978, Table 4.32).

Israeli Experience

The state of Israel, established in 1948, has experienced rapid population growth in succeeding years and, as with other countries where peoples meet, it has found differences in the rates at which its ethnic groups commit crimes.

Jews in Israel constitute about 89 percent of the population and are divided culturally into those of western origin—born in Europe or America or born in Israel of parents from Europe or America—and Jews of oriental origin—those born in Asia or Africa or born in Israel of parents from Asia and Africa (Landau & Drapkin 1968, p. 9). The non-Jewish population consists of three principal religious groups: Muslims, Christians, and Druses, with Muslims in the majority (70 percent).

Landau and Drapkin (1968, pp. 9–10) report that the non-Jewish minority has a rate of homicide *conviction and victimization* six times that of the Jewish population. Furthermore, *within* the convict population, the non-Jewish minority has been found guilty of murder and manslaughter at a rate six times that of the Jewish majority.

Within the Jewish population, differential violence is observed among those who are immigrants and, in particular, among immigrants of oriental origin. Jewish immigrants from oriental countries are convicted of homicide at a rate twice that of immigrants from western countries (Landau & Drapkin 1968, p. 11).

European and Israeli examples of national differences in proclivity to violence overlap the experience of ethnic groups in North America, but there are also some important differences. These differences suggest still other combinations of causes—other routes—leading to homicide. In North America some "native"[6] groups have higher homicide rates than some recent immigrants.

Canadian Experience

Native peoples in Canada—Indians, Inuit, and Metis—have for years been convicted of indictable crimes at rates in excess of their repre-

---

[6] "Native" is another abused word. It comes from the Latin meaning "to be born of." Calling North American Indians and Eskimos "native" means only that more generations of them have been born in the land of their residence. In no other sense are such people more "native" than a first-generation American, Canadian, or Mexican.

Inuit is now the preferred denomination of people formerly known as Eskimo. Metis are persons of mixed Indian and Caucasoid parentage.

sentation in the population. Throughout the country, but in western Canada in particular, these ethnic groups are overrepresented in jails and prisons. Although they constitute about 1.3 percent of the population of the four western provinces, the Yukon, and the Northwest Territories (*Statistics Canada* 1978), they constitute between 14 percent and 60 percent of the population of "correctional institutions,"[7] depending on the year and jurisdiction (Canadian Corrections Association 1967, Schmeiser et al. 1974).

Other differences are notable. For example, native women are more highly represented in the female inmate population than are native men among male inmates. In addition, native inmates serve shorter sentences than other offenders; they are more likely to have a previous record and a longer record of crimes against persons; and they have a higher recidivism rate than non-native convicts (Schmeiser et al. 1974, p. 81).

Nationwide, Canadian Indians constitute slightly more than one percent of the population, but, between 1946 and 1967, they were convicted of 6.1 percent of all *capital* murders (Chandler 1976, p. 216) and they contributed about 16 percent of all homicides (*Statistics Canada* 1976, Table 5.3).

Other disproportions in violence among ethnic groups in Canada are of lesser magnitude. Blacks, for example, represent 0.2 percent of the population and 2.4 percent of capital murder convictions. Ukrainians constitute 2.6 percent of the population and 5.8 percent of capital murder convictions (Chandler 1976, Pearson 1978, Table 4.19).

A high proportion of native crime is fueled with alcohol and is therefore violent (Schmeiser et al. 1974, p. 81). For example, unpublished data for the province of Alberta during the 1970s reveal that roughly 55 percent of homicides involved booze in the victim, the offender, or both (McNish 1979, p. 6). These data also show that, while Indians constitute less than one percent of the provincial population, they are charged with between 15 percent and 38 percent of all murders and manslaughters, varying with the year (McNish 1979, p. 4).

Much homicide occurs in the domestic arena and, among Canadian Caucasians, the victims are likely to be women in the order of three women for every two male victims. However, among non-Caucasian people, the sex ratio is about equal.

---

[7] It is difficult to write "correctional institutions" without placing the phrase in quotation marks. It may be that jails and prisons in North America are *intended* to correct criminals, but they don't do much of that.

Domestic battling is often saturated in alcohol. The relationship between ethnicity, alcohol consumption, and rates of violent attack deserve comment.

Alcohol and ethnicity

Indians in North America have a long and sad history of alcohol abuse. For example, of inmates in Alberta jails, two to three times as many Indians and Metis compared with Caucasoid[8] peoples are diagnosed as having drinking difficulties (Hagan 1977a). Levy and Kunitz (1974) report that the American Indian rate of alcoholic cirrhosis is more than two times the national average, that accidental deaths, a high portion of which are ethanol-related, are almost three times the national average, and that arrests for drunkenness far exceed the rates for all other ethnic groups.

It is unpleasant to note these facts and commenting on them often subjects one to the charge of "stereotyping" others and contributing to the "firewater myth." An assumption underwriting this charge is that stereotypes are mostly false, an assumption uncritically built into the definition of a stereotype by a generation of social psychologists. But, to the contrary, when consensual images of others are measured and tested against public data, they more frequently prove to be true than false (Haas 1979, LeVine 1966, Mackie 1973, Nettler 1970, pp. 29–30).

It is a debater's tactic to deny a thesis by alleging ugly motives for its proposal,[9] motives such as prejudice and stereotypy. This tactic is blunted, however, when members of an ethnic group themselves proclaim their difficulty and ask for help. Thus Indian chiefs in Canada have more than once asked for assistance in controlling the alco-

---

[8] Adjectives are to be preferred to nouns in describing racial groups. Nouns categorize too rigidly. They "lump" people and connote more homogeneity than is warranted. Adjectives, by contrast, suggest degrees of. ... Since "white" people are not of one physical kind, the adjectival form, "Caucasoid," is preferred to indicate a modal type with variation around it.

[9] This tactic commits the "genetic fallacy." This is the error of believing that the motives for uttering a proposition constitute evidence of the validity of that thesis. The *source* of a line of argument is *not,* of course, a test of its truth.

It is popular to commit the genetic fallacy because it is convenient. We commonly judge the truth of what people say by the virtues or vices of the proponents. This saves us from having to check every public thesis against evidence. We can then make up our minds without having to know much.

hol addiction that is, in their words, "destroying our people" (*Canadian Press* 1979).

The tragedy of this appeal is that, although hypotheses flourish, no one has an adequate explanation of the differential drinking habits of distinctive peoples. In addition, no one has a cure for alcohol abuse (Cahn 1970, Davidson 1974, Lloyd & Salzberg 1975, Orford & Edwards 1977, Parloff 1979, President's Commission 1978, Snyder 1958, Verden & Shatterly 1971).

As we have noted (Volume One, Chapter 8), the conceptual bias of social scientists emphasizes environments—cultures and structures—as the powerful causes of differential conduct. This bias places an intellectual taboo on looking elsewhere for possible causes as, for example, in physiologies. This taboo is applied with less force to the study of individual differences, but it is strongly applied against the possibility that ethnic groups may have genetically transmitted differential physiologies that have relevance for social behavior.[10]

We can soften the taboo as we observe hereditary disorders identifiable with particular physiological differences and markedly associated with ethnicity, as in the differential liability of Ashkenazic Jews to the crippling Tay-Sachs and Gaucher's diseases and of Congoid peoples to sickle-cell anemia (Goldsby 1971, Morton 1980, Singer 1953).[11] We can then ask whether there is any logical reason why inbreeding groups may not have evolved physiologies that differentially affect their vulnerability to alcohol, just as they have evolved differences affecting vulnerability to congenital malformations and disorders of taste and vision (Baker 1974, Blakeslee 1932, Chai 1967, Fox 1932, Klein & DeFries 1973, Niswander et al. 1975, Post 1962a, 1962b, 1965).

---

[10] A technique by which we often avoid thinking about unpleasant hypotheses is to attach a dirty name to a hated idea. In this case, the label is "racism." This label is sufficiently vague, emotional, and mind-closing that no *scientist* can use it (Goodrich 1977, Havender 1978).

Science requires exact concepts. Such precision is a condition of taxonomy, the foundation of science (see Volume One, Chapter 3).

Good law also needs precise terminology. For the purposes of developing knowledge and producing just laws, words must have stable and clear nuclei of meaning. They should point to reliably discernible conditions or events.

Common language, however, is saturated with words with high emotional content (Osgood et al. 1957). Such concepts have shifting kernels of meaning with wide auras of connotation. They *express* more than they *designate*. Emotionally expressive terms are useful for everyday evaluation and for political persuasion, but they are obstacles to clear thinking.

[11] Recognition of the ethnic genetics of certain diseases is supported by an extensive literature (Gold 1981, Goodman 1979, Goodman & Motulsky

"Alcoholism," however, is not one disease entity. This means that the state of alcohol dependence can be reached by more than one course (Pattison et al. 1977). Nevertheless, there is evidence of differential susceptibility to the addiction rooted in genetically transmitted physiologies (Goodwin 1976, *Lancet* 1979a, Lansky et al. 1978, Pattison et al. 1977, Rutstein & Veech 1978, Schuckit & Rayses 1979).

Some individuals are at greater risk of an inherited vulnerability to ethanol abuse as is demonstrated by comparisons of children of alcoholic parents reared by non-alcoholic, adoptive parents. Goodwin's research (1976, 1978, 1979) shows that:

1. Sons of alcoholic fathers who are reared by non-alcoholic, adoptive parents succumb to alcoholism about *four times* as frequently as men in control groups and they show an *earlier onset* of trouble with drinking.

2. Sons of alcoholic fathers have the *same rate* of alcohol abuse whether they are reared by their biological parents or by non-alcoholic, adoptive parents.

3. This vulnerability is male-linked.

Other studies in Europe and North America confirm these findings (Bohman 1978, Kopun & Propping 1977, Vesell 1972).

Studies of genetically based individual differences in susceptibility to alcoholism suggest, but they do not demonstrate, that there may be ethnic differences in vulnerability to drinking troubles. For example, Schaefer's summary (1979) of research on this topic indicates that Orientals and Jews, both of whom have low rates of alcoholism, exhibit physiological responses to ethanol that differentiate them from other groups. Orientals and Jews appear to be differentially sen-

1979, Goodman et al. 1980). It has led to the formation in the United States of a National Foundation for Jewish Genetic Diseases and to one of the largest biological research grants ever made (Rosenfeld 1981).

Individuals who resist the fact of ethnic genetics are fearful of the word, "race," its connotations, and its abuses. Some even argue that there is no such thing as a race.

"Race" has as clear, or unclear, a meaning as many other common concepts such as "social class." Concepts such as these refer to distributions of features of people by selected criteria. Such distributions always have overlaps, which is to say that boundaries are disputed. However, it is not necessary to reify concepts in order to assess their descriptive utility. If "race" refers to a group that is genetically distinct with respect to some characteristics, the word is thus-denotative. As Edwards (1981) puts it, "The objective evidence of genetic variety in health and disease cannot be interpreted except on the basis of those genetic similarities which, if races are allowed to exist, constitute a race."

sitive to alcohol. This sensitivity is correlated with high levels of acetaldehyde (AcH), the first metabolite of ethanol, with rapid metabolism of alcohol, and with discomfort upon its ingestion in quantity. Among Orientals there is a characteristic "flushing" of the skin associated with drinking, accompanied by dysphoria.

Studies of ethanol metabolism among North American Indians have not yielded clear results. This is partly a function of heterogeneity among the tribes compared and partly a function of different controls employed in assessing body fat, body fluid, and lean body mass. For example, research conducted in Alberta indicates that Indians and Inuit do not metabolize ethyl alcohol as rapidly as do Caucasoid peoples (Fenna et al. 1971, Gilbert 1976). However, this Canadian finding has been contradicted by studies among Indians in other regions of the Americas (Farris & Jones 1977, Reed et al. 1976, Zeiner et al. 1976). Nevertheless, evidence accumulates to suggest that differences in enzyme function are associated with tolerance for ethanol, that these differences are genetic, and that they vary among ethnic groups (Rosenfeld 1981).

Summary

The point of this comment is to broaden our conceptions of the possible multiple sources of differential conduct. It suggests the possibility of interactions between physiologies and cultures (Bryan 1963, Freedman 1971, 1974, Spielman et al. 1974).

American Experience

The United States is a large laboratory in which the effects of ethnic differences and population movement can be studied. However, given the poor tools of mass observation and the intrusion of political preference upon explanation, American studies have not led to singular interpretations of data.

For some years American sociologists promoted the idea that the cultural differences of migrants made no difference to their modes of adaptations in the New World. The prominent Chicago school of sociologists looked for uniformities in city development and uniformities in the "ecology"[12] of crime and delinquency. This school emphasized the causal power of "structures of opportunity" and of differential status provided by education and wealth.

[12] Sociologists who adopted the notion of "ecology" from biologists employed the term in a different sense from its current journalistic meaning. They defined "ecology" as the study of the spatial and temporal distribution of organisms and activities.

This emphasis is congenial to the "melting pot" picture of peoples meeting. It holds that since situations, rather than people, make for differences in conduct, most people will behave the same way in similar circumstances and will change uniformly as their conditions change. Assimilation is assumed to be a one-dimensional process. This opinion has been characteristically expressed by Shaw and McKay (1942, p. 162) who summarized their research on delinquency in urban areas by writing that "diverse racial, nativity, and national groups possess relatively similar rates of delinquents in similar social areas."

Demands for cultural autonomy have contributed to the decline of the assimilationist assumption and prescription. An early critic, Jonassen (1949), charged the Chicago school with the error of "ecological determinism," that is, of assuming that areas *cause* behaviors. In addition, Jonassen accused such determinists of suffering from a "professional ideology of social pathologists" that confuses democracy with uniformity and that refuses to acknowledge differences in cultures.

Another American sociologist, Toby (1950), seems to have resolved this debate by proposing that both *ethnic values* and *economic structures* be considered as sources of criminality. Toby suggested that "ethnic tradition is an intermediate structure between class position and the personality of the individual." According to Toby, ethnic traditions that foster the attitudes and skills required by legitimate careers in particular societies reduce proclivity to crime. On the other hand, those ethnic traditions that are less congruent with the requirements of a socioeconomic system are likely to be associated with higher crime rates.

Toby's thesis alerts us to the changing mixtures of causes that affect how human beings respond to one another. Ethnic values persist, but their persistence requires transmission. Situations make a difference, but they do not make the same difference to different people. Talents and tastes vary between groups with ethnic identities as they do among individuals—in fact, such variation is part of the *definition* "identity" and "individuality."

The meaning of the variation is subject to change, of course, with everything else that affects our lives. Nothing stands still, Heraclitus (535–475 B.C.) assured us, but nothing in human action changes with the uniformity that early sociologists hoped to find.

Violence and ethnicity, American style

Ethnic groups in America exhibit differentials in crime rates. They attack and kill people, usually "their own people," at different rates. This fact holds true after one controls for age and sex composition, socioeconomic position, and length of residence in the United States (Blue 1948, Forslund 1970, Moses 1970, Stephenson & Scarpitti 1968).

For example, Dutch, German, and Scandinavian settlers in the United States have had low crime rates in general, and particularly low rates for violent crimes. When some of these people have gathered in religious enclaves, as have the Mennonites and the Amish, their crime rates are especially low (Reckless 1967, pp. 472–475). Jewish immigrants and their children have also exhibited an immunity to violence. So, too, have migrants from the Orient, with some interesting variations. Japanese and Chinese settlers have remarkably low crime rates in comparison with the general population, a fact that challenges the glib supposition that racial visibility, prejudice, and discrimination are sufficient to explain criminality.

Apropos the popular hypothesis that "racism" is sufficient to cause crime, it bears reminding that no people in history has suffered as much hostility, expropriation, and murderous attack as have the Jews. It needs to be remembered, too, that Japanese residents in Canada and the United States—citizens and aliens alike—are the only minority in the annals of these new countries to have been excluded and imprisoned solely because of their national origin (Davis & Krauter 1971, tenBroek et al. 1968, Thomas 1952, Thomas et al. 1946).

The *ad hoc*[13] nature of many explanations of conduct is indicated here by the differential employment of hypotheses of frustration and discrimination as causes of violence. These hypotheses are employed selectively and sympathetically to account for the violent behavior of some groups, but not others, and their nullifying tests are ignored. Thus, *if* Japanese and Jews were excessively homicidal, then, after the fact, one could marshal "frustration and discrimination" as explanatory ideas. But, in the absence of such a fact, the supposedly violent effects of ethnic exclusion and unjust treatment are not tested against the relatively pacific behavior of these minorities. The negative results of such tests[14] demonstrate that segregation, discrimination, and exploitation—however these abused terms are defined—do not describe a clear path to robbery, rape, and murder.

---

[13] *Ad hoc* derives from the Latin, meaning "to this," that is, especially constructed. An *ad hoc* explanation is one invented for a particular case, but lacking in generality. One cannot use such plausible, but particular, themes as laws of action.

Another way to characterize *ad hoc* hypotheses is to regard them as unconstrained by facts. Such hypotheses do not satisfy the scientific quest for "simplicity," where simplicity is but one of the desiderata of the scientific enterprise and where simplicity refers to few "degrees of freedom" in fitting data to hypotheses. By contrast, *ad hoc* hypotheses are not "simple"; they

Comparative and historical studies suggest other routes to homicide. For example, although Oriental residents have generally had low crime rates in the United States, there has recently been a resurgence of violent crime among the Chinese. New migrants, principally from Hong Kong, have taken to extortion, robbery, and gang slaying. The killing gained prominence in 1977 when three men entered the Golden Dragon restaurant in San Francisco's Chinatown and sprayed it with bullets, killing five persons and wounding eleven. The internecine warfare continues (Harvey 1970, Peterson 1972, Wong, 1977).

This violent activity shows a continuity with old China practices. The Chinese secret society or tong (from the Chinese for "meeting place") has a history of providing welfare for its members while preying on outsiders. In keeping with the ideal of a fraternal organization, members are regarded as "brothers" and are "taken care of," a benevolence that includes loans of money, provision for widows, and free burial when that is necessary. In parallel with Sicilian "godfathers," Chinese chiefs are often selectively philanthropic, distributing their largesse to hospitals and other worthy causes out of proceeds from illegal traffic in drugs, gambling, and prostitution (Robertson 1978). Within the tong, loyalty is demanded and silence is bought with the rewards of membership and threat of death for "finks."

This experience contrasts with that of the Japanese in America and suggests that the social psychology of violence (Volume One, Chapters 5-7) involves more than the popularly nominated causes of poverty, crowding, and ethnic exclusion.

These causes have been particularly emphasized to account for the differential criminality of blacks in the United States. However, the history of black people in the Americas differs significantly from that of other minorities in that their migration was involuntary and their early status that of property rather than that of persons. Transition from slavery to freedom has been laborious and the process is a continuing enterprise. All interpretations, then, of the differential crime rates of blacks in the United States are made against this strikingly different history.

---

allow many "degrees of freedom" and are therefore easy to invent and difficult to falsify (Simon 1977, pp. 22–23, 32–33).

[14] All of us prefer information that supports our assumptions and we tend to ignore information that is neutral or negative. Of this, there is much evidence.

It is easier to understand a proposition that affirms than one that denies (Wason & Johnson-Laird 1972). In the social sciences there is a bias against publishing research that does not find "significant differences" in the direction of the hypotheses tested (Greenwald 1975, Rosenthal 1978, 1979, Smart 1964, Sterling 1959).

Black people[15] suffer from a disproportionately high crime rate that victimizes principally their own minority. The disproportion is more striking in attacks against persons than in offenses against property. Black rates of arrests and convictions for aggravated assault, robbery, rape, murder, and non-negligent manslaughter exceed those of the American population in general and other minority groups in particular, and the excess has been persistent rather than intermittent.

During 1977, for example, blacks represented about 12 percent of the American population, but they contributed 45 percent of murder victims and 51 percent of those arrested for murder and non-negligent manslaughter (FBI 1978, Table 35). In addition, 38.8 percent of those arrested for aggravated assault were black, 47.3 percent of those arrested for forcible rape, and 53 percent of those arrested for robbery (FBI 1978, Table 35).

These figures vary, of course, with locations, times, and sex and age composition. Wolfgang's (1958) study of criminal homicide in Philadelphia reported that nonwhite men aged 20 to 24 had a conviction rate more than 25 times that of white men of the same age. Ethnic differences in homicide in that city were of such an order that murder rates among *black women* were two to four times as great as those among *white men* (Wolfgang & Ferracuti 1967, p. 154).

In Chicago where sociologists have intensively analyzed data on homicide, the number of black men 15 to 24 years of age who were arrested for homicide increased more than threefold between 1965 and 1973 and the number of black murder victims increased more

---

[15] Names of ethnic groups vary in their precision. For example, Petersen (1969) has shown that one gets different tallies of "subnations" in Hawaii by employing different measures of their "membership." Agreement on criteria fluctuates. Andorrans do not have difficulty defining who they are, but Jews in the United States and Israel sometimes debate "who is a Jew."

"Black people" are not a homogeneous nation, nor were they so, or are they so, in Africa. Both "black" and the former denomination "Negro," which is still used by the FBI (1978), are sociological terms. These words are associated with racial features, but they are not identical to the anthropometric concept of race. In the Americas these words refer to cultural groups defined by "consciousness of kind." This means that socially, as well as racially, there are people of mixed provenience. Some are marginal, both physically and sociologically, and can pass back and forth between minorities and majorities.

Japanese in America recognize such marginality with the term "kibei," referring to one who has been reared in both Japan and the United States. Mexicans call their marginals "pochos," and blacks refer to their "white niggers." The in-group is always antagonistic toward people who are only partly members of the flock.

than fourfold. Within this homicidal age and sex category, blacks in Chicago die of homicide about 20 times as frequently as Caucasoids (Block 1975).

The proclivity of blacks to violent crime is not "washed out" by controlling for the commonly suggested factors of education, occupation, income, racial visibility, and prejudiced reporting. Silberman (1978) has had access to data on ethnic crime differentials not published in the FBI's *Uniform Crime Reports*. He compares black crime rates with those of Puerto Ricans in New York and with those of Mexican-Americans[16] in Arizona, California, Colorado, New Mexico, Texas, and Utah. Silberman reports that:

> As a group, New York's Puerto Ricans are poorer than its blacks. The median family income among Puerto Ricans is 20 percent below the black median, and the proportion of families officially classified as poor is half again as high. Puerto Rican New Yorkers have less education than blacks, and a larger proportion hold menial jobs (p. 119).

Blacks in New York are arrested for all violent crimes about three times as frequently as Hispanics and almost two times as frequently for homicide. Comparisons between black and Mexican-American crime rates in the Southwestern states where most Chicanos live reveal similar differences, differences that have persisted since the 1920s (Silberman 1978, p. 123). In San Diego during the 1970s, for example, blacks constituted about eight percent of the population and Mexican-Americans about 13 percent. Yet, relative to their numbers, blacks were arrested seven times as frequently for homicide, almost five times as often for forcible rape, and about eight times as frequently for robbery (Silberman 1978, p. 122).

Differences such as these cry for interpretation. However, interpretation is easier to give than it is to validate. Explanations of social

---

[16] As the preceding footnote suggests, the names minorities prefer for themselves change. James Baldwin (1972, p. 189) writes, "When I was young . . . it was an insult to be called black. The blacks have now taken over this once pejorative term and made it a rallying cry and a badge of honor and are teaching their children to be proud that they are black."

Mexican-Americans presently disagree as to their proper denomination. Silberman (1978, p. 121) shows that some younger ones prefer being known as Chicano while some older people hate the term. Some consider Mexican-American to be demeaning and prefer Hispanic, Hispanos, or Spanish-American, titles that associate them with the Conquistadores and disassociate them from the Indian admixture connoted by the term Mexican.

The various labels are used here as people seem to wish to be known and without prejudice to changing preferences in title.

behavior always carry political implications. In the political arena, locating causes of undesirable behaviors comes to mean assigning blame. It is therefore difficult to construct explanations that have the degree of detachment that science requires. Ethicopolitical sympathy intrudes[17] and affects even the work of scholars who label each other's motives when they disagree, just as do other prejudiced people (Alper et al. 1976, Clark 1977, Evans & Novak 1965, Wade 1976).

The Subculture Thesis

Crimes against persons differ from crimes against property in that it is easier to explain theft, and to justify it, as an "adaptive response" to constricting social structures, limited opportunities, and an unfair distribution of wealth. However, it strains the idea of "adaptation" to claim that the forcible rape, robbery, and killing of "one's own people" is a rational mode of responding to circumstances.

Homicide is sometimes an instrument of theft, of course, but it is too frequently expressive, rather than instrumental, to be accounted for in the same terms as larceny. There is an "economy" of rape, assault, and murder, but the satisfactions in this economy are more psychic than material and they therefore appear to be less rational than the gains from theft. Thus explanations based on "class conflict" seem less plausible when applied to the understanding of physical attack.

This explanatory vacuum has been entered, but not filled, with the thesis of the "subculture of violence." This theme has been given its most comprehensive statement by Wolfgang and Ferracuti (1967), but other sociologists and anthropologists have contributed to the idea (Banfield 1974, Downes 1966, Gastil 1971, Lewis 1959, 1961, Miller 1958, Morris 1957, Spinley 1964, Willmott 1966).

---

[17] Some scholars hold that "compassion" is a requisite of the scientific study of human beings. Thus Hockett (1973, pp. 122–123) argues that "For optimum results the study of man requires, in addition to a striving for objectivity, an ingredient which is of little or no importance in the study of other aspects of the world: *compassion*. . . . Compassion is not just a moral obligation, but also an observational instrument of great power" (emphasis his).

Since most of us live in a culture that values compassion, we are quick to claim it and loathe to deny its relevance to the objective study of *Homo sapiens*. However, honesty, another of our values, requires noting that Hockett's argument is an *obiter dictum*, an incidental opinion not binding upon the curious student. However much you and I protest our compassion (and who would deny it?), it is questionable whether this sentiment is a useful tool of observation or a blinder.

The proposal that subcultures cause violence is based on descriptions of the lessons in aggression transmitted from generation to generation within social classes, regions, or ethnic groups. Ethnographic studies document the value differentially violent people place on being tough, on responding quickly to insult, and on getting one's way here and now by force. Observers analyze folk tales and songs for their violent content and record violence-supporting rituals, such as baptismal gifts of guns from godfathers to godsons. In addition, scholars have noted the preference for carrying weapons and the frequency of fighting.

Variations

Sociologists have played variations on this theme. For example, Pettigrew and Spier (1962) attempt to account for ethnic differentials in homicide by showing that black rates are associated with the "general traditions of violence" in the American states in which they were born or in which they reside. These investigators allege that some portion of homicide among blacks reflects the violent tradition of "frontier culture" and is but an extension of this more pervasive social environment. Pettigrew and Spier also note that some portion of homicide among blacks is associated with a high rate of their migration to northern states. However, this effect holds true only when the Pettigrew-Spier "homicidal culture index" is held constant. Moreover, these researchers report a finding that runs counter to popular assumption: When their cultural index is controlled, black homicide rates are *positively* associated with their level of schooling.

Criticism

A difficulty with this research is that Pettigrew and Spier's index of "the culture of violence" is a poor one. It says nothing about the experience of persons. It tells us nothing about the extent to which people were exposed to such a culture or acquired it. Their index is an aggregate measure, not an individual one, and it therefore is a measure of unknown potency. One cannot tell from their study how long people lived in "the culture of violence" or how much of that culture they acquired. This investigation is another attest of the tendency to refer behaviors to environments with inadequate measures of these social climates.

Another variation

Silberman (1978) gives yet another interpretation to the general theme that cultural atmospheres induce homicide. He holds that people who have had violence done to them learn to be violent. "Violence," he writes, "is something black Americans learned in this country. They had many teachers; violence has been an intrinsic part of the black American experience from the start. . . . For most of their history in this country . . . blacks were victims, not initiators, of violence" (p. 123).

The history of violence against blacks in the United States is undeniable and exceeds the violence that has been less persistently applied there against Chinese, Japanese, Mexicans, and Indians. It is also true that *individuals* who have been violently treated often become violent themselves (Volume One, Chapter 6). Silberman's thesis is therefore plausible, but it suffers from a learning gap.

Criticism

Silberman is arguing that people of a current generation whose grandparents and great grandparents were victims of violence have somehow learned violent lessons from antecedents they have never known. Today's violent black youths have not themselves been victims of the historical violence Silberman describes. Nevertheless, they are supposed to have learned a criminogenic lesson from that history, a history they may or may not know and did not experience.[18]

To make his thesis hold, Silberman cuts history at a convenient place. Silberman, as opposed to some other scholars (e.g., Glazer & Moynihan 1963, p. 53), recognizes that slaves brought aspects of African culture to the New World, a theme now made popular by the book and the TV series, *Roots*. However, Silberman claims that, "A propensity to violence was *not* part of the cultural baggage black Americans carried with them from Africa; the homicide rate in black Africa is about the same as in western Europe, and well below the rate in either white or black America" (p. 123, emphasis added).

Unfortunately for Silberman's argument, the one authority he cites for this alleged fact (Bohannon 1960) uses data from a few tribes in what was once British East Africa whereas the majority of slaves were captured thousands of miles away in West Africa (Herskovits 1941,

---

[18] All causal analysis requires a cutting point. Without an agreed-upon stopping place, arguments about causes are subject to endless regress. There are always plausible "causes of the causes."

Physical science tries to cut the causal analysis with various rules, including the classic notion of "no action at a distance." Simon (1977, p. 52) suggests that, in the social sciences, the analogue to "no action at a distance" is "no influence without communication." Silberman's thesis violates this principle by proposing influence without communication.

Chapters 2–3). Furthermore, ethnography of tribes in the Niger and Congo river basins does not permit calculation of homicide rates now or 200 years ago. Population counts in themselves are difficult enough (Herskovits 1941, pp. 77–78).

Definitions of "cultures of violence" are an additional difficulty. There is no agreement whether criteria of violent cultures are to include deaths by magic, infanticide, and intertribal fights (Thomas 1937, Chapter 15). In the eighteenth century, many "wars" between African tribes were engaged to supply slave dealers—one tribe raiding another—and there is no tally of the deaths they produced directly or indirectly (Herskovits 1941, p. 35).

It is impossible to make sensible comparisons of homicide rates between those areas, those times, and Europe and the Americas, then and now. We do not know whether violence inflicted upon slaves or cultural continuity accounts for current American black violence, and we have no tools with which to assign weights to these possible causes.

Silberman's thesis suffers from a cultural Lamarckism,[19] the doctrine that the experience of our progenitors marks us today, that the humiliations our grandparents suffered have entered into our nurturing. This is possible, but it is possible *only if* rage is taught us in memory of the oppression of our forebears. And this lesson is, of course, available to almost all peoples. If histories alone had the violent effects Silberman claims, then Jews should be the most murderous of minorities.

A more likely account

Criticism calls for substitution and one will be suggested in the next chapter. The alternative account stresses efficient causes of conduct, rather than historical causes, and it rests upon a theory of human development.

---

[19] J.B.P.A. de M. Lamarck (1744–1829) was a French naturalist who invented the term, "biology," and who is considered to be the founder of invertebrate paleontology. He proposed a theory of the evolution of organisms that antedated the ideas of Darwin (1809–1882) and Wallace (1823–1913), but which proposed as its mechanism the doctrine of *the inheritance of acquired characteristics.* The development of a science of genetics invalidated the notion that abilities acquired by one generation are inherited by offspring.

Unless one adds to Silberman's thesis a training program for *each* generation, it too suffers from a defunct Lamarckism.

DOES "CULTURE" EXPLAIN CONDUCT?

We have discussed some facts about the distribution of deadly quarrels among aggregates and we have described the prevalent interpretation that places cultures between situations and actions. There are two major defects with the thesis of cultural determinism. One defect is logical; the other, pragmatic.

The Logic of Explanation by "Culture"

Explanations that describe a way of life and that show the coherence, the "fit," of one aspect of that way with the whole, with the "ethos," are plausible. They make sense and they satisfy. They satisfy by quieting curiosity. This satisfaction, when it is provided by portraits of cultures, is quite a different one from the satisfaction provided by knowledge that increases predictive power.

The concept of culture describes a range of variables that seem causally connected to the kind of event we are trying to explain. Thus we can describe traditions of "subcultures of violence" that make it plausible that this group, rather than that one, have high homicide rates. However, this expanded description of the ideas and practices of the violent tribe is but an enlarged picture of its aggressive ways. When "culture" is employed as an *explanatory* idea, rather than as a *descriptive* abstraction, it runs the risk of becoming a tautology.

Tautology

A *tautology* is a sentence that appears to be a proposition but is not. Philosophers of science refer to tautology as a statement that excludes no logical possibility. As Giere (1979, p. 16) puts it, a tautology holds true "no matter what the facts might be." Such statements are sometimes called "logical truths" or, better, "empty truths" as when one reports that, "Today is either Monday or some other day of the week" (Giere 1979, p. 15).

Tautology takes a more subtle form when it appears as a sentence in which the predicate is contained within the subject. It can be a definition in which the definiens (the defining element) is described by the definiendum (that which is to be defined). It can appear as a proposition in which what is substantively proposed is already known from definition of the thing being discussed. In short, a tautological sentence or dialogue is redundant. It appears as though information were being given, but none is. Thus:

An American mother: "You won't get bald if you don't lose your hair."

A baseball philosopher: "You can observe an awful lot just by watching."

A former mayor of Chicago: "He didn't get elected because he didn't get enough votes."

An American president: "When many men are out of work, you have unemployment."

A famous psychologist: "A good theory is the most practical thing of all."

A test for tautology is to reverse the subject and predicate and see whether it makes any difference to the meaning of the statement. With a tautology, the sentence is circular; it might as well begin where it ends.

Arguments and theories, as well as sentences, can be tautological. Theories, as strings of propositions, can be, and have been, invented that sound explanatory, but that only draw large descriptive circles on which the events of interest are but an arc. Thus to attempt to explain differential homicide rates by reference to a subculture of violence is to give illustrations of the violent teachings and violent practices of a people and then to "explain" their high murder and manslaughter by reference to these other spheres of aggression. This is tantamount to saying "Those people fight because they are hostile" or "They are murderous because they live violently."

These statements can be true, but they are usually deemed to be uninformative. How much they inform, or fail to inform, depends, again, on what one wants to *do* with this kind of explanation. However, before assessing the practical utility of descriptions of cultures, some ways of "saving" cultural explanations from circularity deserve comment.

Reducing Circularity in Subcultural Accounts

Three procedures have been used to make subcultural accounts seem less circular. One technique describes the way of life of a homicidal people in such detail that the "big picture" makes particular events plausible.

What is described can vary from elements that are directly linked to homicide, like a preference for carrying knives and guns, to elements that are more remotely associated, like child-rearing practices and vengeful religions.

Such detailed description often satisfies curiosity, we have said, but it also adds confidence to forecast. Knowing factors in a way of life that justify physical attack and that seem to cumulate tells us how people are likely to behave. This information provides a reasonable basis for self-protection. This is quite a different utility, however, from increasing predictive power (Volume One, Chapter 3).

A second way out of the tautology of subcultural description is to add another determinant of action to that description. The added determinant is often the *situation* in which the cultural practices operate. This explanatory device admits cultural differences and cultural continuities, but it goes on to show how these preferences meet with "social structures" to mould behavior. This, for example, is the resolution Toby (1950) proposed in the debate between structural determinists and their critics.

This resolution seems plausible as it is used to account for differences in theft and theft-motivated assault. It seems less relevant in explanation of ethnic differences in the number of deadly quarrels among acquaintances and loved ones.

A third procedure by which subcultural descriptions are made less circular is to add social psychology to the account. The sociopsychological task is to describe *how* cultural prescriptions "get inside" actors. Sociopsychological research attempts to isolate and weigh causes of conduct. It describes processes by which human beings are formed. As Volume One, Chapters 5–7, made clear, these processes are multiple and complex, rather than singular and uniform. The interactional complexity of these nominated causes reduces predictability of conduct.

Utilities of Subcultural Explanations

One can use descriptions of ways of life of a people to forecast actions of such aggregates. A forecast is always a probability statement, of course, but that is a characteristic of *all* statements about human action.

However, we are reminded that forecasts are *not* predictions, and that descriptions of subcultures are *not* adequate for predictive purposes. In turn, it is prediction, rather than forecast, that is required by interventionist public policy—if it would be rational.

A subcultural explanation, by itself, does not tell us *how* to break the "vicious circle" of violence begetting violence or *where* to break it. Prescriptions that are based on descriptions, rather than on causal explanations, devolve into morally motivated recommendations. Lacking scientific substance, descriptive theories move policy from that which might be effective toward that which is politically convenient or ideologically satisfying.

For example, proponents of the thesis of violent subcultures advocate "dispersing the members who share intense commitment to the violence value" (Wolfgang & Ferracuti 1967, p. 299). It is recommended that "the scattered units . . . be small. Housing projects and neighborhood areas should be small microcosms of the social hierarchy and value system of the central dominant culture" *(ibid.)*.

There are, of course, moral and political questions involved in prescribing the *forced* movement and congregation of people.[20] But, in addition to these ethicopolitical questions, a recommendation to disperse violent ethnic groups assumes more knowledge than we have. We do not know what mixture of violent people with pacific people will break down the culture of violence. Moreover, we do not know to what extent the violent ones may act as "culture carriers" and contaminate their hosts.

Difficulties

Social scientists who employ the idea of cultures and subcultures quarrel about three issues: (1) when to assign a people's conduct to their culture or to their situation; (2) how durable or malleable a way of life may be; and (3) whether the unpleasant behaviors of other people are rational, or otherwise justifiable.

1. Scholars have not been able to specify how much of a people's conduct is cultural—which means different *and* preferred—and how much is "merely" a reaction to circumstance. This difficulty is in part methodological—a function of inadequate tools of assessment—and in part moral.

The prevalent morality among social scientists favors equality, and not just "equality of opportunity," the once New World ideal, but equality of condition (Bereiter 1973, Coleman 1974, Della Fave 1974, Herrnstein 1973, Jencks et al. 1972, Keyfitz 1973, Nisbet 1974a, 1974b, 1975). This ideal makes it unpopular to recognize differences, particularly disagreeable differences, that bad actors may prefer.

The politics of equality finds it more congenial to attribute "unfortunate" differences to conditions than to cultures. This produces a

[20] The United States Department of Housing and Urban Development (HUD) recently discovered that residents' satisfaction with their housing is principally determined by satisfaction with neighbors which, in turn, is a function of their neighbors being similar to them. Surveys of residents in 37 housing developments found that "perceived similarity" outweighs other matters that might affect contentment such as size of the project and its density, whether it is a high- or low-rise site, and whether the manager does or does not reside on the grounds. The study's authors conclude that, "Presently available findings . . . suggest that mixing households having widely different moral beliefs, lifestyles, and education should be avoided within a single development" (Francescato et al. n.d., ca. 1979, p. ES–5).

schizoid element in the treatment of class and ethnic values—a tension between approval of the quest for "identity" (that is, difference) by minorities and disapproval of some of the behaviors, like lethal fighting, that may result from that difference.

Some sociologists who use the concept of culture therefore seem unable to decide whether it is culture that determines actions, or whether it is the structure to which a culture "adapts" that should be assigned causal importance, or whether it is some unspecified meeting of cultures with other environments that causes conduct. Researchers move back and forth across these causal locations in ways that seem more rhetorically convenient than factually grounded.

For example, the tension can be read in Curtis's policy recommendations following his study of *Violence, Race, and Culture* (1975, Chapter 10). Curtis concludes that "structural determinists" are correct in prescribing "enrichment via employment, manpower retraining, equal opportunity, black enterprise and income programs" as a remedy for the subculture of violence (p. 121). However, two pages later, Curtis takes the side of cultural determinists in arguing against the feasibility of gun-control legislation. "Those who maintain that gun control will reduce the homicide rate may not fully take into account non-white contracultural behavior," he writes. Citing favorably another investigator (Seitz 1972), Curtis contends that "gun control laws would not dissuade non-whites from carrying firearms because possession is such an integral part of a non-white culture of violence, one that would remain unchanged" (p. 123).

Uncertainty about how to use the idea of culture is apparent in much of the anthropological and sociological literature that moves from description to prescription. The tension is demonstrated again in Rossi's (1971) criticism of Banfield's thesis about the durability of "cultures of poverty." Rossi writes:

> There is no "lower class" in Banfield's sense. Indeed, there is little firm evidence that there are many people, black or white, who are permanently hedonistically present-oriented. The existing evidence is just as supportive of a theory that there are poor people, black and white, whose position in society is such that they might as well be hedonistically present-oriented since acting otherwise does little to improve their position (p. 820).

This paragraph is notable in that it argues in short compass (a) that subcultures are not *that* different; (b) that whatever difference there is, is not permanent; and (c) that, if there is difference, it is rational.

This leads to questions about the longevity of cultures and their rationality.

2. Cultural persistence and change are mysteries. We have no science that identifies the conditions of endurance and transformation. It will not do to refer cultural continuity and change to circumstances unless we can specify the contingencies that produce *particular* kinds of "adaptation." It will not do to make this referral for another reason: The concept of culture was invented not only to be descriptive, but also to account for *variations* in the action of aggregates in apparently similar circumstances.

No people and its ways endure forever, of course, but those who would correct the unpleasant actions of others are repeatedly surprised by the persistence of cultural habits. The durability of preferred ways of living within a variety of "social structures" has been recorded for many groups (Alpert 1972, Armor 1972, Glazer & Moynihan 1963, 1975, Glenn 1974–1975, Herskovits 1941, Howe 1976, Isaacs 1975a, 1975b, Jones 1972, Maas 1975, Metzger 1971, Novak 1972, Reed 1975, Spivak 1979, Sutherland 1975).

The uncertainties of cultural change under changing conditions are well expressed by a student of Jewish culture who concludes that: "Almost every planned change has brought about results different from those anticipated. The student of culture is therefore highly skeptical of too optimistic plans for controlled culture change" (Anonymous 1942, p. 260).

3. Denial of the durability of ethnic difference is bolstered by another argument, an argument central to the ideology of ethnography and sociology. It is the claim of *cultural relativism.* Cultural relativism deems the conduct of different groups to be equally "valid" which often translates, as in Rossi's paragraph, to equally rational.

Cultural relativism is an attitude that flows from and reinforces the egalitarianism which is, according to Jarvie (1967), "the fundamental metaphysical framework within which the tradition of social anthropology has arisen" (p. 76). Cultural relativists "see no rational justification for ranking societies morally, cognitively or culturally. The key argument . . . makes any relativism into a combined relativism regarding truth, morality, justice and everything else" (Jarvie 1975, p. 344).

Under this assumption, "people do the best they can." All are equally rational, given their circumstances. Therefore one might as well be a hasty hedonist, which includes being a prolific parent (Rainwater 1960, Sheehan 1976), since, it is said, acting differently does not help. By this logic, if some people are more murderous than others, then this way of living and its justifying ethic[21] are as rational as any other preferred mode. To *judge* another group's values is to be "ethnocentric," which means to be provincial ("hick"), ignorant, and probably immoral (Ladd 1973, p. 7).

Of course, no one can be a consistent cultural relativist *if* at the same time she or he claims scientific expertise or moral authority. Knowledge assumes standards of truth and error, however probabilistic and contingent these standards may be. Moral authority also assumes a moral ground.

Cultural relativism challenges both criteria of knowledge and criteria of morality. "The mores can make anything right," William Graham Sumner (1906) wrote, uttering one of sociology's grandest tautologies. The ethical relativism that is part of cultural relativism *logically* permits only silence in the face of other people's savagery, for "savagery," we are told, is culturally defined.

Logic bends with interest, however, and today's cultural relativists shrink from the ethical nihilism into which moral relativism leads them. They resist this conclusion to their premises particularly as they wish to be of use in making the world a better place. But such relativistic reformers are hoist because every action taken in the name of a better world assumes some moral foundation on which to base judgments of better and worse, and it is this foundation which relativism erodes.

The conflict between cultural relativism and moral prescription is illustrated in a document submitted by the American Anthropological Association (1947) to the United Nations Commission on Human Rights. This document claims three principles:

1. The individual realizes his personality through his culture, hence respect for individual differences entails a respect for cultural differences.

2. Respect for differences between cultures is validated by the scientific fact that no technique of qualitatively evaluating cultures has been discovered.

3. Standards and values are relative to the culture form which they derive so that any attempt to formulate postulates that grow out of the beliefs or moral codes of one culture must to that extent detract from the applicability of any Declaration of Human Rights to mankind as a whole.

---

[21] All nations and all individuals justify their preferences, particularly when they are challenged. Justifications are advanced even for those preferences which seem barbaric by others' standards. Among rational people, only the psychopath seems not to need justification, although he or she may *use* one without believing it (see Chapter 5).

The cultural relativism of the third paragraph contradicts the ethical recommendations of the first two paragraphs. "Respect" is a moral prescription. It too must be culture-bound. The idea of "human rights" is also a moral notion,[22] and one with only recent currency (Raphael 1967).

If there are no universal standards justifying "respect," "tolerance," and today's content of "human rights," then there is no reasoned foundation for "respecting" others' cultural differences—including such different preferences as those which build concentration camps or promote ethnic and class warfare.

The rationality of cultures

The appeal to the equal rationality of all ways of life is employed *selectively* as a justification of others' strange, and sometimes unpleasant, practices. It is a justification that masquerades as science. The masquerade is apparent because objective criteria of rationality—of efficiency—cannot be applied in assessing the value of culturally promoted modes of conduct. This includes even the value of survival since some groups, like some individuals, do not give supreme importance to living long and reproducing. The evidence is apparent in the habits of individuals and in the histories of peoples who practice suicidal ethics. Turnbull (1972) provides a tribal example. An American moralist makes the point explicit: "An ethic of survival, at the cost of other basic human values, is not worth the cost" (Callahan 1972, p. 494).

---

[22] I have argued elsewhere (Nettler 1978, p. 6) that " 'Right' is a word used to establish a moral claim upon a territory of behavior. It is doubtful that there are 'natural rights,' waiting somewhere out in Nature to be discovered. On the contrary, rights are only socially subscribed and competing claims for access to something of value."

The concept of "a right" is not to be found in ancient Greek thought or in the Bible. In Roman law, the term *jus* does *not* refer to "a right" as something belonging to an individual, but rather to an objective state of social affairs that is just (Raphael 1980). Today the notion of "rights" has two meanings: that of *liberty to do something* and that of a *claim to have something*. Raphael calls these "rights of action" and "rights of recipience."

Demands for both forms of rights constitute yet other occasions for homicide. For example, in 1975 the president of Somalia declared that, in keeping with the ideals of International Women's Year, women would henceforth enjoy equal rights of inheritance with men. When 12 Muslim religious leaders objected that such equality violated Koranic law, they were shot (Bauer & O'Sullivan 1977, p. 55).

Chapter 10 provides other instances of homicidal stimulation by ideals justified as "rights."

We have no calculus for measuring the relative rationality of cultures.

Conclusions

The notion of "culture" is useful for descriptive purposes. It may also be employed as a tentative basis of forecast. This concept is defective, however, for the more stringent scientific tests of prediction and control. It is defective because it lacks that specification of verified causes of action that a science of conduct requires.

It bears repeating that we can learn about individuals by observing the differential probabilities of actions (events) among aggregates. Prediction proceeds through classification, that is, through grouping. What is at issue here is *how* one defines aggregates.

Ethnic groups are self-defined. Others, of course, validate the definition. When aggregates are self- and other-nominated, as are ethnic groups, the criteria by which we recognize ethnicity may, or may not, encompass the criteria of similarity and difference that are relevant to the differential conduct to be explained. Self-nominated clusters may or may not allow one to discern *what* is similar or different within these aggregates that *produces* differential response to stimuli and differential proclivity to kinds of conduct.[23]

It is not that we never know anything about causal dispositions that vary with ethnicity. We have seen Volume One, Part II, that some kinds of causes are identifiable. The difficulty is that, for the prediction of acts that are *not* limited by, or determined by, a specific physiology—acts like killing people—the taxonomy provided by the concept of culture is too crude. We cannot state with assurance, therefore, what will happen to this group or that one when their living conditions change this way or that.

We count on continuities; we can forecast without being able to predict.

Forecast is aided by information about some of the conditions under which people are likely to be more and less violent. This is the topic of the next chapter.

---

[23] On the difficulties of discerning similarity and difference and some of the determinants of this perception, see Shepard and Arabie (1979), Tversky (1977), Tversky and Krantz (1969), and Williams et al. (1971).

4 CONTINGENCIES

Abstract • Aggression is normal. Love and hate are complementary emotions. Both are forms of attachment, not to be confused with indifference. • Movement from normal aggression to violent action depends on contingencies. ○ Contingencies are uncertain conditions and events upon which causes depend for their effects. ○ Contingencies of violence are categorized, for convenience, as failure to tvain, as specific training in violence, and as a family of disinhibitory influences. • Some demographic facts suggest the extent of failure to train as a source of violence. ○ In North America, and probably in the Western World, higher proportions of teenage women have become sexually active in recent decades. ○ Many young women who engage in heterosexual intercourse know little about the facts of reproduction and some don't care. ○ As a result, illegitimacy rates have increased. So, too, have the proportions of children reared in fatherless households. ○ Ethnic differences in sexual practices, reproductive style, illegitimacy, and fatherless households parallel the ethnic differences in violent crime discussed in Chapter 3. ○ Political objections to causal inference from demographic data are described. These objections take the form of seeking "causes of the causes." This search is criticized. • Another road to violence takes the course of specific training for attack. ○ Some moral codes indoctrinate in violence. ○ Societies with fragmented cultures produce quantities of deracinated individuals who not only lack training in altruism, but who also have had violent models as teachers.

AGGRESSION IS every normal person's possibility. The person who is incapable of anger is incapable of love.

To be a "fully functioning" human being is to feel both emotions, and it is a mark of defect when neither emotion is experienced or when only one, hatred, dominates. There is an *asymmetry* here since no person who loves escapes the possibility of hating—with the exception of hermits whose "love" does not count because it is aseptic. The asymmetry lies in the fact that it is possible to hate without ever having experienced the compensation of affection.

In brief, for most human beings, love and hate are complementary emotions. It is difficult to divorce them. It may be impossible to conceive of one without the other. But, in addition, these emotions are complementary in that both are *forms of attachment*. Hating is not the simple opposite of loving; it is indifference that opposes both sentiments. To be indifferent is to be detached.[1]

The empirical question asked of social scientists, then, is not why people are ever aggressive, but why some individuals and some groups are disproportionately lethally so. An answer requires specification of conditions that sift the causes of conduct. Description of such conditions indicates that the causes of action operate contingently.

The philosopher Giere (1979, p. 17) tells us that, "The important statements in science, the ones whose truth or falsity might be of some real concern, are all contingent statements." They are propositions that might be true, but they also retain the possibility of being false. Giere distinguishes such statements from sentences that can only be true or false as in Figure 4.1.

Figure 4.1 Categories of Statements*

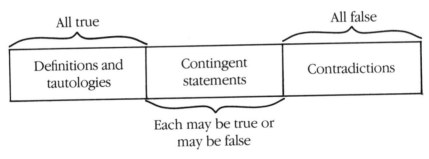

* Reproduced by permission from R.N. Giere, *Understanding Scientific Reasoning.* © 1979 by Holt, Rinehart, and Winston.

We can translate Giere's definition of a contingent statement to a definition of a contingent event. It is one that conceivably might or might not occur. A contingent event is one whose occurrence depends on other happenings that are not certain. Murder is a contingent event.

The causes of conduct outlined in Volume One all operate contingently. That is, they themselves are variously induced, and they pro-

---

[1] In the English language, indifference is often used synonymously with "disinterest" and "uninterest." However, as with many words, "disinterest" has more than one meaning. In law and the social studies, to be "disinterested" is *not* to be "uninterested," but, rather, to be unprejudiced, objective, fair. By contrast, to be "uninterested" is to be indifferent—not to care.

duce their effects not in a direct and linear fashion, but in a way that moves with situations. *Contingencies are the uncertainties upon which causes depend for their effects.*

Uncertainties include (a) the probability that a particular condition will or will not prevail and (b) the probability that any particular condition will itself be surrounded by this complex of facilitators or that complex of inhibitors.

We often think of "causes" as being necessary, but not sufficient, to do the work we have in mind. In this sense, contingencies are like "secondary causes." They function to allow a necessary agent to have its effect, or to reduce the effect of that specific cause, or to increase it. In the last instance, we speak of *synergism,* of causes that amplify one another so that their effects are strengthened. In synergistic situations, a particular effect may be "more than caused." It is not merely a metaphor to speak of "causal overkill."

To say, then, that violent acts are contingent outcomes is to say not only that their quantity and gravity vary with conditions, but also that the amount of variation in quantity and gravity fluctuates in a changing web of circumstance. The web of circumstance includes possibilities we can imagine but cannot foresee, and it includes possible causes whose strength depends on everything else that happens so that we have difficulty assigning weights to contingencies before they occur.

Categories of Contingencies

For convenience, the contingencies that channel homicidal careers can be grouped as conditions that limit training, as those that provide lessons in violence, and as disinhibitory influences. The first family of contingencies says that, if people receive no training toward consideration of others, they are more apt to grow up wild than pacific. The second category notes that some people receive specific lessons in violence. And the third set describes all those many contingencies that release once-learned inhibitions.

Learning never stops. Therefore, training and teaching can be disinhibitory as well as inhibitory and some of these releasers will be discussed in later chapters without assuming that the description is complete. In our discussion, disinhibition will be attributed to some major releasers—self-preservation, lust, loot, lunacy, and ideals—and to "the moral atmosphere." These stimulants to violence gather strength, in turn, from ethyl alcohol and cumulated insult.

These suggested categories of contingency are neither exhaustive nor exclusive. They overlap, which means that one condition allows another. Thus failure of parents to train permits peers to teach. Interaction among contingencies marks the difference between a linear and uniform causal process and a causal web. Careers seem better described as produced in a dense web of influences.

FAMILIES OF CONTINGENCIES

Some violence is a function of brain defect (Mark & Ervin 1970). This fact in itself tells us that the cerebral cortex operates to *inhibit* attack when the organism has been nurtured toward affiliation and against the expression of hostility. Conversely, this fact indicates that, without specific cerebral equipment, humans and other organisms behave ferociously.

Cerebral physiology is of interest in individual cases of homicidal rage, but it explains little of group difference. If, then, adequate neural functioning is assumed, some conditions can be described that facilitate violence for both individuals and aggregates. A first condition is lack of training in inhibition.

1. Failure to Train

The philosopher George Santayana (1863–1952) once wrote that, "Every generation is born as ignorant and wilful as the first man" (1953, p. 142).[2] This means that *Homo sapiens* is born only potentially human. If the potential is to be realized so that an infant develops into a recognizable "human being," nurturing is required. The training is a course in how-to-behave. It includes lessons in what to do and what not to do, and these prescriptions and proscriptions are obverse faces of the same coin. Behaving *this* way means that we do not behave *that* way. The training routine involves exercise in inhibition. It involves immersion in a culture that promotes restraint. Not everything is allowed; not all is to be expressed.

This is a theme that unites thousands of research reports on the psychology of aggression. The psychologists Margaret and Harry Harlow (1967) conclude that:

---

[2] Santayana is remembered as the philosopher who told us that people who know no history are doomed to repeat its mistakes. The rest of Santayana's (1953) comment about ignorant and wilful generations continues this idea:

> When tradition has lost its obvious fitness and numinous authority, eager minds will revert without knowing it to every false hope and blind alley that had tempted their predecessors long since buried under layer upon layer of ruins. And these eager minds may easily become leaders. . . . Thus the blind in extirpating the mad may plant a new madness (p. 142).

One of the most important functions of social learning in primates—and perhaps in all mammals and many other classes of animals as well—is the development of social patterns that will restrain and check potentially asocial behavior. These positive, learned social patterns must be established *before* negative, unlearned patterns emerge (p. 47, emphasis added).

Difficulties of civil life

The requirement that human beings be nurtured runs *counter* to the "greening" prescription to "let it all hang out" (Reich 1970). The requirement of socialization assumes with Sigmund Freud (1856–1939) that civilization is bought at the cost of "repression." Civilization is paid for through development of a sense of guilt (Freud 1958, p. 90). Guilt may be a burden and it may make us unhappy. But without the capacity to feel guilt, civil life is impossible.

Civil life is an orderly life among strangers. It contrasts with *tribal life* in which the order is taught by kinfolk and practiced among them. The difficulty in achieving civilization is the difficulty of nurturing human beings to behave circumspectly among people who are not their kin. The assumptions of civil life are that others have learned similar lessons and that there are others to teach these lessons to their offspring. As we shall see (pp. 81–88), these assumptions are sorely tried by some current demographic facts-of-life.

In Western cultures, the ideal of civil life aspires toward freedom with recognition that freedom rests on order. Order, in turn, means restriction. By contrast, disorder knows no pattern or boundary.

It may be a paradox that freedom *to do* certain things and to live a particular way requires *not* being free to do certain other things and live other ways. The paradox is assuaged by drawing a line between freedom and license. Freedom is bounded; license, unlimited. The tragedy of translating freedom into license is that when all are licentious, no one is free.

The paradox is appeased by another reminder: That every value exacts a price. Classical physics proclaimed that "nothing can be made out of nothing," and we can apply this dictum to social life. Nothing of value comes to us without a price in time and effort. Cost is an irrevocable feature of value. It is, indeed, part of the definition of value. The price of freedom in civil states is a pattern of inhibition that *orders* our lives together.

The connection between freedom and inhibition disappoints utopians who hope that social life may be possible without the constriction of ordered arrangements. This hope rests on a faith that human beings are "basically good" and that it is only "society" that, in Rousseau's words, "depraves and perverts" us. Jean Jacques Rousseau (1712–1778) voiced this faith in his *Émile* (1762) and some contemporary writers have adopted it. For example, the criminologist Quinney (1974) assures us that:

> Man is basically good. It is the institutions which oppress him that make for any shortcomings in man. Let man be free. Let him control his own institutions rather than be controlled by them. And he will be the good man that he is by the nature of his being" (p. 485).

A trouble with this faith is that the institutions that allegedly corrupt Man are human products. They have not been imposed upon us by mysterious forces from other planets. They have evolved out of *human* action and, in this sense, they *are* us.

Furthermore, to assume that "society" is to blame for our evil acts pardons us all. It is an assumption which, if disseminated and believed, excuses us from responsibility and opens doors to anarchy.

An additional trouble with the utopian faith is that we can never know how good or bad Man is "basically." Human beings from birth are dependent upon other human beings whose lives are already bound, more or less tightly, by institutions. We have no way of identifying a de-institutionalized "Basic Man."

Unconscious nurturing

The training required by social life need *not* be consciously engaged. Trainers and models need not be aware of what they are doing since they are practicing what they themselves have been trained to do. In stable, tribal groups, lessons are transmitted fairly smoothly because consistent trainers are on hand and because there is little competition from discrepant models. But in industrialized societies, depending on their size and ethnic heterogeneity, there are competitors vying with parents, and parents themselves are often so de-traditionalized that they are unsure which lessons, if any, to transmit or how to train their offspring.

Some significant proportion of children in Western Europe and North America grow up without being cultured. To be cultured means to be cared for, and to be cared for means not merely to be "provided for," but also to be trimmed into a distinctive moral shape. One does not become a moral agent without training any more than one becomes a gymnast without disciplined exercise. It is remarkable that some people who do not assume athletic expertise without training, assume moral motivation without practice.

Demographic facts

Some features of reproductive practices illustrate the possibility that large, heterogeneous, and free societies have the peculiar "problem"[3] of civilizing numbers of unwanted and un-nurtured children.

The status of bastardy is common—now as always. But the definition of "illegitimacy" changes and so, too, does the sociological significance of birth out of wedlock. To be illegitimate in societies where common law unions are themselves legitimated and fairly stable describes a different status from being illegitimate in the United States and Canada where a common characteristic of births out of wedlock is the transience of the union that produces the child. In these countries, high proportions of unmarried people copulate at early ages. Children result from an embarrassing number of these temporary encounters and their indoctrination is often left to hazard. Hazard means that rearing is no particular person's responsibility. It becomes dependent upon a succession of confusing models, serial "parents," and "welfare" institutions. Some statistics tell the story.

Heterosexual experience

A decade ago investigators asked a national sample of American female teenagers questions about their sexual practices (Kantner & Zelnik 1973, Zelnik & Kantner 1972, 1973). Among 4,611 women between 15 and 19 years of age, eight percent were or had been married. Of the 92 percent who had never been married, about 28 percent reported having had sexual intercourse. This proportion increases with age, of course, and varies with culture. While 14 percent of the 15-year-olds said they had had heterosexual experience, this proportion approaches one-half by age 19. Moreover, black girls report that they have had intercourse in greater numbers at earlier ages than white girls.

> For example, at age 15, about 11 percent of the whites and about 32 percent of the blacks have had intercourse; at 19, 40 percent of the whites and 81 percent of the blacks have had intercourse. Combining all age groups the proportion of blacks who have had intercourse is slightly

---

[3] "Problem" is placed in quotation marks because it is heedlessly used. It is popular in journalism and the social sciences to speak of "social problems" as though these troubles were puzzles that had solutions. Difficulties, of course, may have no solutions in the sense in which a mathematical problem has an answer or a chess question its resolution. What concerns us in social affairs is better conceived as "troubles" or "difficulties" because such conception disabuses us of faith in simple ways out (Nettler 1976, Chapter 1).

more than double the proportion of whites who have had intercourse (Zelnik & Kantner 1973, pp. 8-9).

In addition, it is significant that large numbers of young women have intercourse carelessly and without knowledge of contraception and the reproductive facts-of-life. Kantner and Zelnik (1973) find that:

> Of the sexually active 15-to-19-year-olds, 53 percent failed to use any kind of contraception the last time they had intercourse; and among the youngest group—those aged 15—the figure reaches 71 percent. The picture for consistent use is even worse. Less than 20 percent of sexually experienced 15-to-19-year-olds report that they "always" use some method to prevent conception during intercourse. A partial explanation of the low level of current use is the fact that a substantial number of those who have failed to use contraception believe that they cannot become pregnant (pp. 21-22).

In addition to those teenagers who incorrectly assumed that they could not become pregnant, a considerable proportion of the women interviewed either did not care whether they became pregnant or were trying to have a baby. Ethnic differences are again apparent: about one-eighth of the white girls gave these as their reasons for not taking precautions, while about one-fourth of the black girls so responded (Zelnik & Kantner, 1972, p. 370, table 15).

Sixty percent of these teenagers did not know which time of the menstrual cycle was the period of greatest reproductive risk (Kantner & Zelnik 1973, p. 21). The majority of these respondents believe that the time of menstruation is the time of greatest probability of pregnancy, and this false belief is also widespread among older women (Zelnik & Kantner 1972, p. 361).

Among teenagers who do *not* assume that the menses are the time of greatest risk of pregnancy, another false belief intrudes that distinguishes white girls from blacks. The black women disproportionately accepted the erroneous assumption that risk of pregnancy remains the same throughout the menstrual cycle.

In brief, many young women, and some older women, do not know the probabilities of pregnancy and some don't care.

Ethnic differentials in sexual practices are consistent through time and consistent whether data are gathered by asking women about their experiences or by observing who has illegitimate babies. For example, Zelnik and Kantner's (1972) survey finds that one-fifth of black teenagers who have never been married have been pregnant. This proportion is ten times that of white teenagers. If one restricts this comparison to young women who are what Zelnik and Kantner term "sexually active," the ethnic differential is reduced somewhat, but it remains substantial. Among "sexually active" girls, 40.8 percent of the blacks report that they have been pregnant compared to 10 percent of the whites. Moreover, among those who have been pregnant, 76.3 percent of the black women have had a child compared with 37.8 percent of the white women.

In a follow-up survey conducted in 1976, Zelnik, Kim, and Kantner (1979) found that:

1. Ten percent of American women become pregnant at least once before they are 17 years old. Twenty-five percent become pregnant at least once before they are 19 years old. Eighty percent of these pregnancies are "outside wedlock," although, of course, some proportion is followed by marriage.

2. Teenage women had become more "sexually active" in 1976 as compared with 1971.

3. Black women have *intercourse* earlier than white women and are more likely to become *pregnant* during their 'teens. These differences are reflected in the greater probability of *conception* and of *premarital conception* among black teenagers than among white teenagers. (Tables 4.1, 4.2, 4.3, and 4.4 tell the story.)

Illegitimacy

These survey data are seconded by figures on *illegitimacy*. 1940 was the first year in which complete statistics on American illegitimacy were available. Since that year, the *proportion* of all live births that are illegitimate has risen steadily in the United States and in Canada as well (Hartley 1975, Table 5; Ross & Sawhill 1975, p. 17).

Proportions are one thing, of course, and rates are another (Volume One, Chapter 4). For example, if legitimate birth rates decline, then the proportion of illegitimate births will increase without there being any change in the number of illegitimate babies. For this reason, demographers prefer to use rates of illegitimacy with the base of the rate the number of females in the fecund ages, 15 to 44, reduced to a constant of 1,000. This rate can, in turn, be refined by age and ethnicity.

Recent American experience shows declines in illegitimacy rates among older women and for second births. But illegitimacy rates among teenagers continue to rise (Ross & Sawhill 1975, pp. 17–18). Ethnic differences appear for both proportions and rates of illegitimacy. Among white women, the proportions of all live births that are illegitimate climbed from 1.8 percent in 1940 to 6.4 percent in 1973. Among black women, proportions increased from 13.6 percent in 1940 to 41.6 percent in 1973 (Ross & Sawhill 1975, Table 1–L).

Table 4.1   Estimated Percentage of Women Who Have Ever Had Intercourse by Exact Age x, Based on Combined Experience of Women Aged 15–19 in 1976 and in 1971, According to Race*

Age	Current Ages 15–19 in 1976			Current Ages 15–19 in 1971		
	Total	White	Black	Total	White	Black
12	0.0	0.0	0.0	0.0	0.0	0.0
13	1.7	1.1	4.8	1.2	0.9	2.9
14	3.7	2.6	10.3	2.7	2.1	6.7
15	9.2	7.1	22.4	5.7	4.4	13.7
16	19.9	16.8	39.1	11.9	9.7	26.1
17	33.9	30.0	58.1	24.2	20.7	46.7
18	47.7	43.6	73.0	37.1	32.5	65.6
19	63.3	60.2	82.8	55.2	51.3	80.1
Median Age at First Coitus	18.1	18.4	16.6	18.7	18.9	17.2

* Adapted from Zelnik, Kim, and Kantner. 1979. "Probabilities of Intercourse and Conception Among U.S. Teenage Women, 1971 and 1976." *Family Planning Perspectives,* 11:177–183. © 1979 by The Alan Guttmacher Institute. Reproduced with permission.

Table 4.3   Estimated Percentage of Sexually Active Women Who Have Ever Conceived by Exact Age x, Based on Combined Experience of Women Aged 15–19 in 1976 and in 1971, According to Race*

Age	Current Ages 15–19 in 1976			Current Ages 15–19 in 1971		
	Total	White	Black	Total	White	Black
15	18.6	14.9	25.8	17.8	11.5	30.5
16	24.2	20.3	34.6	30.6	24.7	44.6
17	30.0	26.4	41.6	34.6	30.7	46.1
18	35.2	32.3	46.3	40.3	36.5	52.7
19	40.1	37.4	53.4	43.5	38.6	64.5

* Adapted from Zelnik, Kim, and Kantner. 1979. "Probabilities of Intercourse and Conception Among U.S. Teenage Women, 1971 and 1976." *Family Planning Perspectives,* 11:177–183. © 1979 by The Alan Guttmacher Institute. Reproduced by permission.

Table 4.2   Estimated Percentage of Women Who Have Ever Had Premarital Intercourse by Exact Age x, Based on Combined Experience of Women Aged 15–19 in 1976 and in 1971, According to Race*

Age	Current Ages 15–19 in 1976			Current Ages 15–19 in 1971		
	Total	*White*	*Black*	*Total*	*White*	*Black*
12	0.0	0.0	0.0	0.0	0.0	0.0
13	1.7	1.1	4.8	1.2	0.9	2.9
14	3.7	2.6	10.3	2.7	2.1	6.7
15	9.1	7.0	22.4	5.5	4.3	13.7
16	19.6	16.4	38.9	11.1	8.8	26.7
17	33.1	29.1	58.0	21.9	18.1	46.1
18	46.5	42.2	72.9	33.7	28.7	63.7
19	59.4	55.8	81.1	47.5	42.6	78.1
Median Age	18.3	18.6	16.6	19.0	19.0	17.2

* Adapted from Zelnik, Kim, and Kantner. 1979. "Probabilities of Intercourse and Conception Among U.S. Teenage Women, 1971 and 1976." *Family Planning Perspectives,* 11:177–183. © 1979 by The Alan Guttmacher Institute. Reproduced by permission.

Table 4.4   Estimated Percentage of Premaritally Sexually Active Women Who Have Ever Had a Premarital Conception by Exact Age x, Based on Combined Experience of Women Aged 15–19 in 1976 and in 1971, According to Race*

Age	Current Ages 15–19 in 1976			Current Ages 15–19 in 1971		
	Total	*White*	*Black*	*Total*	*White*	*Black*
15	16.0	11.2	25.2	17.3	10.5	30.5
16	21.6	16.9	33.9	30.3	23.4	44.6
17	25.8	21.3	39.9	31.8	26.1	46.0
18	31.0	27.1	45.3	35.3	29.0	52.9
19	34.7	30.7	52.8	37.5	30.6	61.0

* Adapted from Zelnik, Kim, and Kantner. 1979. "Probabilities of Intercourse and Conception Among U.S. Teenage Women, 1971 and 1976." *Family Planning Perspectives,* 11:177–183. © 1979 by The Alan Guttmacher Institute. Reproduced by permission.

Illegitimacy rates show parallel ethnic differences, but the size of the difference varies from year to year. In 1940 there were 3.6 illegitimate births per 1,000 white women aged 15–44 and 35.6 such births among black women of comparable age. By 1973 these differential rates had become 11.9 for white women and 84.2 for black women (Ross & Sawhill 1975, Table 1–M).

The most recent census of American natality (Vital Statistics 1978) indicates that for 165 Standard Metropolitan Statistical Areas (SMSAs)[4] reporting for 1975 the ratio of illegitimate live births to every 1,000 legitimate live births was 74.0 for white mothers and 505.0 for black mothers.

Fatherless households

Another index of the nurturing environment is the number of households and the number of children with only one parent. It is now estimated that *more than one-third of all children* born in the United States will live some portion of their lives before age 16 in single-parent homes, usually with their mothers (Bumpass & Rindfuss 1979, Rindfuss & Bumpass 1977). Again, differences between the white and black experience are significant in accounting for differences in their violent crime rates. Larger proportions of black children will lack fathers during their formative years.

Before they are one year old, six percent of white children and 24 percent of black children will have lived with only one parent. By the time they are 10 years old, the proportions will have increased to 24 percent of the white youngsters and 52 percent of the blacks, and, by age 16, these proportions will have increased again to 33 percent and 59 percent, respectively (Rindfuss & Bumpass 1977).

These increases in the proportions of questionably nurtured children have occurred in parallel with increases in violent crimes. Between the mid-1950s and the late 1960s, Americans experienced a 55 percent increase in the proportion of *all* five-year-olds living with one parent. The increase has been even more dramatic for black children: 91 percent.

Table 4.5 shows a steady increase, with almost no reversals, in the proportions of American children, grouped in three-year-cohorts,

---

[4] Standard Metropolitan Statistical Areas are counties or combinations of counties in the United States. This counting unit has been developed in an attempt to distinguish urban ways of life from rural conditions. Since city boundaries no longer define urban limits, the SMSA is considered to be a more sensitive indicator of urbanism. However, SMSAs differ widely in density of population. They are therefore rather crude measures of urbanism (Bogue 1969, p. 531).

Table 4.5   Cumulative Proportion of Children Ever Experiencing a Disrupted Family*

Child's Year of Birth	Cumulative Proportion with Disrupted Family by Age (%)*																N Children
	1	2	3	4	5	6	7	8	9	10	11	12	13	14	15	16	
Total																	
1956–58	3	5	7	9	11	12	13	14	15	16	18	19	21	22	24	26	2,444
1959–61	5	6	8	9	11	13	14	16	18	19	21	23	24	25			3,045
1962–64	5	7	9	11	13	15	17	19	21								3,193
1965–67	5	8	11	13	15	17	20										2,865
1968–70	7	10	13	15	17	18	20										2,874
1971–73	8	12	15	17													2,424
White																	
1956–58	2	4	6	8	9	10	11	12	13	15	16	17	19	19	21	21	1,520
1959–61	3	5	7	8	9	11	12	14	16	17	18	20	21	22			1,857
1962–64	5	6	8	9	11	13	16	17	20								1,976
1965–67	4	7	9	11	13	15	18										1,720
1968–70	5	8	10	13	15	19											1,815
1971–73	6	10	13	14	18												1,505
Black																	
1956–58	12	16	18	20	22	24	27	30	31	33	35	37	42	47	48	51	924
1959–61	13	15	17	20	23	27	30	32	34	38	43	46	47	47			1,188
1962–64	12	15	18	21	23	27	29	32	34	36	36						1,217
1965–67	16	18	24	26	27	33	35										1,145
1968–70	23	29	33	37													1,059
1971–73	24	29															919

* Children born 1956–73 to ever-married mothers under the age of 30.

* Reprinted from Bumpass and Rindfuss, "Children's experience of marital disruption," *The American Journal of Sociology,* 85:49–65, Table 3, by permission of The University of Chicago Press. © 1979 by The University of Chicago.

who have ever experienced a disrupted family. Bumpass and Rind-fuss (1979, p. 57) note that, "The proportion experiencing a disrupted family by age two more than doubled, from 5% for the 1956–58 cohort to 12% for the 1971–73 cohort. The increase among whites was quite regular (from 4% to 10%), whereas among blacks there is a rather sudden increase for the two most recent cohorts."

Of course, many women who are not married at the time of delivery of their first child later marry, and many women who divorce remarry. But, again, there are differences between blacks and whites in these marital patterns. Black mothers spend considerably longer periods between marriages than do white mothers and they are also less likely ever to remarry. Ten years after the initial marital break-up, 84 percent of white mothers, but only 35 percent of black mothers, have remarried. Bumpass and Rindfuss (1978) conclude that the majority of black children and a large proportion of white children will, in coming years, spend part of their childhood living with only one parent. A high proportion of white children will then live in a second family as their mothers remarry, but the same will not be true of many black children.

Ethnic differences in sexual practices and reproductive patterns have been described at length because they parallel the ethnic differences in violent crimes reported in Chapter 3. It is proposed that one of the paths to violent acts is reproduction outside a social network that trains children.

Objection

Our hypothesis seems plausible, yet it remains convincing only by inference. Data on careless reproduction, illegitimacy, and family disruption do not *directly* tell us how offspring are reared. Observational studies are needed to test our inference, and there are few of these. Gilder (1978) and Sheehan (1976) provide two exemplary studies of individuals. But individual case studies can always be denied significance with the suggestion that such cases are unrepresentative.

In addition, we are reminded that a harmonious, single-parent household can be a better training environment than a discordant, intact household (Burchinal 1964, Goode 1956, Nye 1957). Some broken homes are more nurturing than some intact ones. Contingencies here include *how* a household is broken, at *what stage* in a child's life the break occurs, and *what kind of modeling relationship* succeeds the disrupted home. Furthermore, these contingencies work differently for boys and girls and vary in their effects with the sex of the parent with whom the child remains. For example, Toby (1957) shows that the broken home has a different effect upon girls and pre-adolescent boys from that which it has upon older boys. The impact is worse for girls and for the younger boys.

Such qualifications can be considered, but they do not override the reasonably inferred impact of unwed mothers and fatherless households upon child rearing. Everything we know about the correlates of illegitimacy in Great Britain, Canada, and the United States tells us that this status, in these countries at least, is not good for children, however much one may wish to qualify this conclusion with exceptional cases and lists of contingencies that make a difference. The correlates of North American illegitimacy are pathologies, not advantages: illegitimate children are more likely to experience poor health, to suffer psychological disturbance, to receive little schooling, and to contribute to unemployment rolls (Goode 1964, Hartley 1975, Krige 1936, Leighton 1955, Ross & Sawhill 1975, Schmitt 1956). These findings are not limited to North America. They are general for Western countries. Again, good things go together, and disadvantages cumulate.

Moreover, even legitimate offspring of *adolescent* parents suffer disadvantages. Card's (1977, 1978) longitudinal studies of the consequences of early childbearing show that children born to teenage parents are more likely than those born to older parents to be reared in single-parent households. With socioeconomic status held constant, these children have lower educational expectations and lower scores on tests of academic aptitude. Such children, in Card's samples, were disproportionately poor, black, and first-born. In addition, Card found that the offspring of teenage unions tended to repeat the practices of their parents by marrying early, reproducing early, and reproducing often.

A comparison

In accounting for the different criminal atmospheres of so-called "developed" countries, it should be noted that, while illegitimacy rates have increased in Canada and the United States since World War II, they have declined dramatically in Japan (Hartley 1970). By contrast with industrialized, but culturally homogeneous, countries such as Japan and Norway, the United States and Canada appear to be suffering from a "disease" of irresponsible reproduction that produces a significant quantity of unwanted children and untrained ones.

Quantity can be debated, but *fact* seems irrefutable. One road to rape, robbery, manslaughter, and murder is to breed children without provision for their training in civil habits.

Another objection

We remarked earlier that explanations of social behavior have political import. Explanations are seldom evaluated, then, merely on their evidence. They are also evaluated by the implications they carry for political action. The distinguished student of cities and minorities, Louis Wirth (1936), said it well:

> Since every assertion of a "fact" about the social world touches the interests of some individual or group, one cannot even call attention to the existence of certain "facts" without courting the objections of those whose very *raison d'être* in society rests upon a divergent interpretation of the "factual" situation (p. xvii).

Causes of causes

To cite "failure to train" as a road to violence is to nominate what Aristotle (384–322 B.C.) called an "efficient cause." It is the proximate agent; the last effective event in a conceivable chain or *web of causes.*

However, locating causes in the political arena is tantamount to assigning blame. A moral aura is cast around the allegedly scientific effort to ascertain the efficient causes of conditions that concern us. Argument, then, is inevitable.

Moreover, political preference selects particular "bad" things to be nominated as causes of the other "bad" things to be remedied. We are reminded that we suffer a "cognitive bias" that prefers evil causes of evil effects (Volume One, Chapter 8). It is rare, then, to hear a political faction claim that something "good"—like wealth and freedom—causes something "bad"—like crime.

Since the inventory of wrongs is endless and huge, partisanship, depending on its style, may divert attention from efficient causes to causes of the causes. The intention is to direct energies away from the proximate causes—now called "symptoms"—to more distant conditions that one wishes to change. In popular parlance, demand for attention to causes of the causes is termed getting to the "root causes."

The nominated "root causes" are usually evils in themselves and, hence, all persons of good will may want them changed in any event—whatever their effects upon violent crimes. But, whichever condition a political faction deems to be fundamental may not, in fact, be so. Distant causes of causes, when acted upon, have a way of producing unintended consequences so that one has no assurance that remedy of the alleged roots will transform reproductive practices, domestic arrangements, the training of children, and the production of crime.

An opinion

Nomination of "root causes" is performed sentimentally, without justification by any well-warranted theory of conduct. For example, there is no theory of human action or of homicide that justifies including "poor housing" as a cause of physical attack. By the standards of highly paid Western intellectuals, most of the world lives in "inadequate housing" *without* producing the deadly statistics of the United States. The same can be said of schools, jobs, and economic security. Few of us are willing to deny aspiration to more of these goods—although there are some modern Luddites[5] who would do so. But no theoretician of human action *knows how to produce* these goods for large numbers of people of diverse culture, and no theorist can guarantee that his or her proposals for changing these popular "root causes" will change the efficient causes of homicide in the desired direction.

Two points need to be discerned here. First, to say that "no one knows *how* to produce . . ." is *not* to say that no one knows the *conditions* of production. One can have "knowledge-about" without having "know-how." There is a difference between having information and having power, and there is a further difference between having knowledge and having *that knowledge* and *that know-how* which are efficiently applicable to a particular social concern (Nettler 1972, 1975).

The second point challenges the connection between the particular "root causes" nominated by any political faction, the instruments for uprooting those causes, and particular outcomes such as reduced rates of violent crimes.

An exercise in imagery

These points can be illuminated by imagining that one is the all-powerful and benevolent Ruler of Metropolis. Ruler reads Susan Sheehan's (1976) detailed portrait of *A Welfare Mother,* has sympathy for Mother's plight (if it is that), and concern lest her undisciplined

---

[5] Ned Ludd was a workman in 18th century England who destroyed knitting machines because he believed that they exploited workers. Between 1811 and 1816 some workmen who rioted in English industrial centers called themselves Luddites after their model. They systematically wrecked machinery as a way to improve their employment and wages.

nine children grow up to be "social problems." Ruler is advised about the "root causes" of welfare dependency and intercedes as popularly counselled. Ruler opens a suburban housing project available at low rent, provides clean schools with earnest teachers, and gives Mother a guaranteed X-thousand ducats a month plus free vocational guidance and "mental health" services.

No confirmed theory of human conduct can assure us that providing such benefits will change action in a desired direction.[6] To the contrary, what we think we know about causes of conduct suggests that the consequences one experiences when he or she *acts* do not have the same effect as gifts. Consequences that flow from effort differ from consequences that flow from status. People who do not believe this have never seen a "spoiled" child or adult.

Theories of human conduct that are to be applied to social policy must, at some stage, address the *efficient* causes of the kinds of activities they wish to influence. If the linkage between unpleasant conditions and efficient causes is loose—as it is—then remedying "root causes" will not have the desired effect. In our imaginary case, the most reasonable forecast is continuity of Mother and children in their present habits.

An additional hypothesis

Once we begin searching for causes of the causes, it is possible to look in other places than those preferred by most journalists and a considerable number of social scientists. We can, for example, examine the relationship between something valued and something abhorred. A risk of such inquiry that "runs against the grain" is, of course, ethicopolitical condemnation, usually accompanied by name-calling. Such condemnation does not invalidate a thesis, but it makes the proposal uncomfortable to utter.

George Gilder has been bold enough to provide such a hypothesis in his studies of changing male and female roles, family disruption, and the manufacture of poverty (1973, 1974, 1978, 1979a, 1981). Thus far, neither his research nor his thesis has been warmly welcomed by professional students of social life.

---

[6] A number of studies of varied quality have tested the degree to which money and better living conditions change conduct. Various "income maintenance" programs and housing projects have addressed the persistent question whether a "culture of poverty" has an independent existence or whether such a culture is only a rational response to a poor situation (Rainwater 1970, Spilerman & Elesh 1971).

Truth again seems to lie between these polar hypotheses. Research sug-

Gilder holds that "the rise of a welfare culture" has deprived men in America's "ghettoes" of the traditional role of head of household. "It is," he writes (1979b), "the decline of the male role as provider in ghetto communities that results in the emergence of a powerful criminal culture of young men. A father who is not providing adequately for his family cannot enforce his authority and probably will undermine the moral impact of all other authorities as well."

Gilder's thesis gains substance from two years spent interviewing inhabitants of racial enclaves in New York and South Carolina. Gilder draws a picture of their lives in a "non-fictional novel," *Visible Man* (1978), in which the career of a pseudonymous black man, "Sam Brewer," is traced. Reconstruction of the rationale and the sources of Brewer's life adds weight to inferences drawn from the gray tabulations of the preceding pages.

In brief, Brewer's career has lacked nurturance toward work and marriage. And, however much one may disdain these "twin chains" in favor of "liberation," work and marriage remain bonds of attachment to others that give purpose to living. In addition, Brewer lives in a social climate in which it is more rational in the short run *not* to work and *not* to marry and to have the pleasure of sex without responsibility for its product.

Gilder concludes:

> If all our women had leisure incomes that could support them better than our jobs, few of us could marry or stay married any more than Sam. Welfare to an uneducated lower-class man is wealth—wealth beyond the dreams of all the immigrants of our history, wealth beyond the ken of workers around the world. Illegal aliens swarm our shores, ignorant of the language, to earn the livings—the positions on the ladder up—that our own poor citizens disdain in order to qualify as fatherless, workless, disabled, impotent, lost (p. 243).
>
> Today, on Clinton Avenue [where Sam lives], the celebrations of marriage and reunion, the compassionate care of children, the faith and love of fathers, the dignity and strength of labor, all the rituals of family and community are dying out. In their place is a congeries of Human Resources Departments, Day Care Centers, Counseling Services, Welfare Of-

gests that "the poor" are *not* a homogeneous aggregate and that different kinds of poor people respond differently to a guaranteed income (Ternowetsky 1977a, 1977b, 1977c, 1979). Ternowetsky (1979, p. 16) concludes that "the jobless face a cluster of handicaps which affect the way they respond to income maintenance [and that] given the stability of their residual position in society, there is an obvious upper limit to which the poor can be expected to change."

fices, Food Stamp Registration Centers, and Medicaid Bureaus, all designed for one clear effect: to reward the people who manage not to marry or work. Yet work and marriage are the crucial ways that men grow up and become responsible citizens (1978, p. 246).

Gilder's thesis will not convince those whose "root causes" lie elsewhere. It will also not convince those who feel that "something must be done" whether or not a sound causal analysis supports the interventions they prefer. Political advocacy is not the friend of scientific inquiry and tensions in the political arena are not "problems" that have cost-free "solutions."

2. Lessons in Violence

Failure to nurture human beings describes one route to violent action. A parallel road, and one that sometimes merges with the first route, is marked with lessons that teach violence. Some of these lessons are barely visible because they are embedded in what we shall call "the moral atmosphere," but other lessons are clear in two extreme situations—where there are moral codes advocating violence and where de-cultured individuals practice violence so that their intimates and their children acquire a taste for it. The first teaching situation describes a preferred, institutionalized way of life that happens to be deadly. The second training regime occurs among deracinated individuals, jungle cats, who hate.

Violent cultures

Wolfgang and Ferracuti (1967) have given us shorthand accounts of some violent cultures. Their descriptions tell of patterned and preferred ways of living. The pattern is apparent in violent deeds, of course, but the actions are vindicated by beliefs about how a man should be and how the world works. For example, the "Barbaricino code," prevalent in the mountainous regions of Sardinia, prescribes vendetta. Indoctrination in the code "is almost total," say Wolfgang and Ferracuti, "for the Italian criminal code is accepted passively as a political, externally imposed necessity, but is discarded whenever it conflicts with the *barbaricino* code. The long history of this code is expressed in Sardinian folklore, and daily behavior is carefully regulated by its norms. For the Sardinian who breaks the code, violent death or escape are the only alternatives" (p. 279).

In the nearby district of Caserta, just north of Naples, villages inhabited by the Albanovesi have a well-earned reputation for violence that goes back to Roman times.[7] Wolfgang and.Ferracuti comment:

> A combination of ruthless vendetta practices . . . a high number of available weapons, and a largely shared and totally accepted code of honor, make violence an almost inevitable pattern of behavior which several repressive attempts by the police have failed to control. In the perception of the Albanovesi, weapons have an almost ritualistic value. A gun is a common gift of the godfather to the child at the time he is baptized. The community has lived in almost total isolation for centuries and even today is almost separate from the relatively peaceful surrounding area. . . . Outbreaks of violence appear to be spontaneous, caused by offenses that in nearby areas would be solved peacefully or go unnoticed.[7] The Albanovese *must* kill to redeem an offense. The common saying goes: "If you are slapped, you must wash the slap from your face." This means, as in Sardinia, that one should react to an offense with a more serious, more damaging offense, even to the point of causing a violent death. The person who does not exact revenge is considered inadequate and is ostracized. . . . Cultural transmission of violent values appears to be the only explanation .that fits the known facts about this puzzling area of unleashed violence in Southern Italy (pp. 281–282, emphasis theirs).

In brief, no sociologist has yet been able to find the causes of the causes of these violent preferences.

Hateful trainers

Some cultures administer lessons in violence, and approve of them. In other societies, however, the cultural system is fragmented and many inhabitants mature with little indoctrination in a patterned way of being. Such persons are de-tribalized, "culture-free," and they are left without boundaries to their possibilities. Since they have not been nurtured toward altruism, and since they have not themselves been appreciated, they grow up full of hate.

The difference between people who have been reared in violent cultures and alienated individuals in broken cultures is that moral codes tell the culturally violent when to be homicidal. By contrast, the deracinated individual knows no such direction. Hatred is diffuse and victims may be innocents. While the culturally violent kills only

---

[7] Upon my last visit to one of the villages of the Albanovesi, there was an apparently unplanned riot that destroyed the center of town. The "cause" of the joyful riot—and people *were* having angry fun—was the demotion of their football (soccer) team from B League to C League.

Incidentally, righteous anger *is* pleasurable, and so is the destruction it justifies.

those who have given insult, according to his code, the de-tribalized is insulted, potentially, by everyone. As in the model case of Charlie Manson (pp. 187–196), strangers may as well be killed as acquaintances.

Affluent economies in particular seem to breed a high proportion of such deracinated individuals, people with no altruistic connection to anyone. Repeatedly, to the point of boredom, psychiatrists and clinical psychologists in these countries are asked to examine "senseless murderers" who range in age from children to "mature" adults and whose lack of conscience has stimulated invention of such medically oriented titles as "psychopath" and "sociopath."

A common element in the background of such people is lack of pacific training combined with specific lessons in violence. For example, John Allen (1977), mugger, pimp, dope dealer, and armed robber, describes his criminal life as rewarding—until a police bullet in his spine paralyzed him. Allen writes:

> That's how it was. Somebody was always doing something in each family. If it wasn't the adults, say the mother or father, then it was the son or daughter. I was sticking up; one of my brothers was stealing; one of my sisters was bootlegging; one of my uncles wrote numbers; one of my grandmothers occasionally wrote numbers; and my grandfather bootlegged.
>
> In our neighborhood, the kids ran wild, and the adults were wild. It would be nothing for us to be on the front steps playing hide-and-seek and all of a sudden you hear bang, bang, bang, and people are shooting at each other in the street. And everybody ducking and hiding. This was normal (p. 1).

Violent lessons modeled by hateful fathers are repetitious. One of the last murderers to be executed in the United States, Gary Gilmore, leaves a history of the violence bred by hatred and nurtured by a heedless father and a doting mother who could see no wrong in Gilmore's early misdeeds.

By age 35, Gilmore had spent 23 years incarcerated in jails, prisons, and "reform schools." He was violent on the "inside" as he was out on the street, and more than one prison psychiatrist diagnosed him as a "classic sociopath," full of hate and free of conscience (Goldman et al. 1976). Gilmore once wrote his girl friend, Nicole:

> If I feel like murder, it doesn't necessarily matter who gets murdered. Murder is just a thing of itself, a rage, and rage is not reason, so what does it matter who? It vents a rage.

Descriptions such as these justify a common generalization: Parents who dislike their children produce violent ones.

A difference between tribes and societies is that, in tribes a higher proportion of children is wanted and cared for. Exact tallies are impossible, but tentative estimates in North America indicate that considerable numbers of children are nuisances at some time to many parents and that many children are actively disliked by one or both of their parents.

For example, interviews with large samples of American *married* mothers—exclusive of mothers who were either unmarried at delivery or who were not living with their spouses—reveal that, as of 1960–1965, about *one-fifth of all births* were not wanted by mothers, fathers, or both parents (Bumpass & Westoff 1970). A later report based on the National Survey of Family Growth in the United States estimates that *one-third* of births among married women during 1970–1972 were "unintended," a category that includes mistimed pregnancies as well as births that would have been unwanted at any time (Menken et al. 1978). Another estimate for 1972 tallies *35.4 percent* of all American pregnancies among married women as "unwanted" or "wanted later" (Weller 1978).

Mothers' statements that they or their husbands had not wanted some of their children are more frequently made by poor women, by black women, and by those who have had many children (Pohlman 1967). Bumpass and Westoff (1970) report that 36 percent of black births during 1960–1965 were *not* desired compared with 17 percent of white births.

The proportion of unwanted babies increases rapidly with birth order so that almost *one-third* of *all fourth* children and *one-half* of *all sixth* children are not wanted. For blacks, the corresponding proportions are nearly one-half and two-thirds.

Among all mothers defined as "poor" by the United States Social Security Administration, 40 percent of all births and 60 percent of all sixth- and higher-order births were unwanted.

Caution

There is always the possibility that unwanted babies may become wanted children, and there is a difference between not having wanted a child and disliking that child once it appears. However, these possibilities are balanced by Bumpass and Westoff's reminder that their mode of measurement probably *under*estimates the number of unwanted babies. In addition, underestimation is assured by surveys among *married* women. Much less is known about the pregnancies of unmarried women (Tietze 1979).

One can discount the results of surveys by some amount and yet agree with their significance—that an important proportion of children in North America may not be happily nurtured.

Repair

The significance of unwanted children is compounded by the fact that, after children have been rejected, *repairing* their hatred and violence is difficult. When rejecting parents attempt to control their hostile children, they usually resort to punishment. But all discipline, and particularly that called punishment, has different effects depending on the history of the relationship between trainer and child. We are more easily corrected by someone who loves us—where love has been demonstrated by deed rather than by word—than by someone who hates us. Hate is a strong word, of course, and there are many parents who dislike their children without hating them. Children, in turn, are sensitive to their parents' attitude toward them, even though they may not be able to articulate their awareness. Children's gestures, postures, relations with people, and their projective productions indicate that they can "read" their parents and sense when their parents find them "unsatisfactory."

In short, parents who neglect and reject their children are ineffective teachers when they wish to control their children. Punishment does not reduce aggression in unwanted children, but actually stimulates it (Eron et al. 1971).

3. Other Roads

Failure to train generations toward altruism and specific lessons in violence can be separate routes to murder and manslaughter. Unfortunately, they are frequently reinforcing conditions, one going with the other. These courses often run in parallel with other channels. Some people, having once learned tentative lessons that inhibit aggression, may be released from their inhibitions. The following chapters show that such release can be variously produced.

5 HOMICIDAL ROUTES: **SELF-DEFENSE**

Abstract • Heterogeneous, free societies provide competing moral lessons and diverse temptations to homicide. ○ Self-defense, love, lust, insult, loot, and ideals are persistent motives for homicide. ○ These motives sometimes combine with other causes of killing, as in the release provided by lunacy, by chemical agents (notably ethyl alcohol), and by moral atmospheres. • Self-defense is defined as a legal justification of homicide. ○ Self-defense is distinguished from self-preservation. ○ Examples illustrate the entanglement of legal judgment with moral attribution and the difficulties in applying legal definitions. • A people's sense of justice underwrites conceptions of justifiable homicide. This sense also defines the gravity of other styles of deadly disagreement.

LESSONS THAT WE THINK WE HAVE LEARNED are not necessarily learned well. In heterogeneous, free societies there are always countervailing lessons and disinhibitory situations. These lessons and these situations sometimes challenge acquired concepts of "what is right" and make what was once right seem less efficient than what we now "need to do," or want to do and may get away with.

We have agreed that moral codes prohibit only that which we are tempted to do. Temptation is a recurrent possibility. The homicidal temptation, like that toward other crime, is generated in a variety of situations by a variety of persistent desires. Self-preservation is one such motive; self-defense is another. Love and lust are additional universal appetites that open channels to homicide, sometimes in league with cumulated insult. Loot is a continuing reason for killing and sometimes combines with lust to produce death. But, of all the motives for murder, ideals are the most deadly. Ideals that promise a "better world," or that defend a present world, persistently serve as motivation and justification of mortal combat. It is probable that far more people have been killed idealistically than from the need to defend one's self, or out of erotic or mercenary motives, or because of repeated insult.

Contingencies

Self-preservation, self-defense, love and lust, insult, loot, and ideals provide persistent occasions for homicide. These motives, and their justifications, operate in social contexts and are subject, then, to the synergistic effects of other releasers. For example, some kinds of lunacy provide routes to homicide. In addition, chemical disinhibitors, like ethyl alcohol, sometimes work in combination with such homicidal desires as those stimulated by lust, loot, and insult. Finally, counter-lessons in the moral atmosphere operate as psychological disinhibitors and add their influence to persistent homicidal motives.

Describing these possibilities means, again, that there is no single route to homicide and no one type of killer. Recognizing these *contingencies* explains what seems to be inexplicable in the study of lives: How "straight" people can be bent.

We shall see that some of the most heinous homicides in recent decades have been committed by people who, for long periods of their lives, had none of the stigmata of moral deformity. These people run a psychological gamut from conventional bureaucrats who order genocide (Eichmann et al.) to "nice neighborhood kids" who end up sticking knives into strangers for "highs" (Manson's girls) or throwing bombs for "liberation" (Ulrike Meinhoff; Diane Oughton).

These contingent possibilities do not dispute continuity of personality; they reflect our earlier qualifications that persons function in situations and that learning is never-ending. What has been learned can be unlearned and what we are determines what we do through a sieve of social connections.

Some qualities of the social sieve that channel homicide will be described in this and following chapters. The descriptions cannot be exhaustive, of course, and they are only illustrative of lethal occasions.

THE JUSTIFICATION

Criminal law in Western countries grades homicide by morally defined degrees of gravity. As we have seen, moral judgment of gravity mixes considerations of relations between offender and victim, histories of both, and circumstances of the crime. The law excuses some kinds of homicide and allows reduced responsibility for others (pp. 3–4).

Self-defense is allowed as a justification of homicide, but the plea is circumscribed. The law resists opening the door to easy claims that a killing was defensive. At the outset, it distinguishes *self-defense* from *self-preservation*. In states whose laws have evolved with the Christian-Judaic tradition, the criminal law excuses homicide required to defend one's own life, but it does not normally excuse homicide required to preserve one's life.

R. v. *Dudley and Stevens*

The precedent derives from the 19th century case of *R.* v. *Dudley and Stevens* (McCormick 1962). Dudley and Stevens, along with two other men, were survivors of a shipwreck who had been adrift in the Atlantic for 20 days. After going eight days without food and five days without water, Dudley and Stevens killed the ship's cabin boy and ate him. They claimed that survival necessitated the homicide. But, in these circumstances, self-preservation was not deemed justification of homicide and the two were found guilty of murder.

Self-preservation grades into self-defense. What justifies homicide in the latter case, but not in the former, is the homicide *victim's threat* to the life of the person who kills her or him. The law recognizes provocation, and provocation excuses. Of course, this reasoning produces "hard cases" for decision. It not only requires definition of "provocation," but it also raises doubts whether self-preservation should excuse homicide in cases in which a victim is innocent and a killer has neither malice nor "choice" in producing homicide. For example, Morris and Blom-Cooper (1964, p. 289) suggest that possibility of "a mountaineer [who] loses his grip and so endangers the lives of others on the rope. . . . Would there not be a defense to one of those others deliberately cutting the rope rather than that all should perish?"

The answer to this question varies with jurisdiction. Uncertainty of the decision shows again that justice moves with a people's moral sense.

This moral sense allows self-defense as a justification of homicide, but narrowly defines it. A plea that homicide was justified by self-defense can be claimed when one is the victim of "an unprovoked attack" *or* when one becomes involved in a fight that "gets out of hand." Placing these qualifiers in quotation marks indicates that these aspects of a lethal occasion have to be defined rather than simply discovered.

With some variation by jurisdiction, defendants may claim justification of their violent response to others *if* defendants can show that:

1. They were unlawfully attacked.

2. They did not "provoke" the attack—provocation itself being defined by law as we have seen (p. 28, fn. 7).

3. The force used was not intended to cause death or "grievous bodily injury."

4. The force employed was "no more than necessary" to defend themselves.

5. They were under "reasonable apprehension" that they were threatened with death or grievous bodily harm.

6. They could not otherwise defend themselves.

Justification of assault or homicide in self-defense is also possible, varying by jurisdiction, if a fight had been started *without* the intent to cause death or grievous bodily harm and:

1. Force is used under "reasonable apprehension" of death or grievous bodily harm from the other's violence; and

2. In the belief, on reasonable grounds, that counter-force was necessary to preserve oneself from death or grievous bodily injury; and if

3. Defendant declined further conflict or retreated from it as far as possible before the necessity to defend himself/herself arose.

Intentions, circumstances, and justifications are difficult to determine by legal definitions or by psychological concepts. Gray areas persist and produce a continuum of "easy" and "hard" cases for juries and judges to decide. Here are some examples:

R. v. *Awad, 1957*

"Awad (29), a Somali, was attacked by Rees (age not reported) and six others in the street; Rees hit him on the head with a bottle, and one of the others produced a clasp-knife. Awad grapped the knife from him, opened it and showed it to the group in order to frighten them off. Cooze, the owner of the knife, attacked Awad and was wounded; then, as Rees tried to hit Awad again, he was stabbed. Rees died 10 days later.

"Awad pleaded self-defense and was found *not guilty at Glamorgan Assizes. . . .*" (Reprinted with permission, from Morris & Blom-Cooper 1964, p. 1 emphasis theirs)

R. v. *Hurdle, 1961*

"Betty Hurdle (30) was married to Roy (29) who was a bully, constantly beating her up and terrorizing her. One night, after she had returned from having, to her husband's knowledge, drinks with a man friend, he threatened her with a knife and came at her. She picked up another knife and he ran into it.

"*At Hampshire Assizes . . . Hurdle was acquitted of murder.* Mr. Justice Streatfeild described her as a woman of 'great character and courage'. She had stuck to her husband partly for the child's sake."

(Reprinted, with permission, from Morris & Blom-Cooper, pp. 193–194, emphasis theirs).

R. v. *Ward, 1978*

Karen Ward and James Wilson had lived together as husband and wife for some years. During their relationship, Wilson had beaten Ward many times. On the occasion of a last fight November 10, 1974, Ward killed Wilson by stabbing him repeatedly in the chest, with two of the wounds penetrating his heart.

A plea of self-defense was entered. The plea was denied, but Ward was convicted of manslaughter rather than murder. The jury's denial of the plea of self-defense was a response to the prosecutor's argument that Ward had "had ample time to get out of the apartment had she wanted, ample time to leave, but she didn't."

The judge's instruction to the jury interpreted Canadian law as justifying homicide by self-defense *only* "as a last resort" and "where there is no other reasonable means whereby a person can successfully retreat from the assault. The force used must be proportionate to the circumstances of the assault and must not exceed what is necessary to defend one's self or to prevent the attack."

Ward appealed her conviction on the ground that the judge's instruction omitted other grounds for a plea of self-defense. Canadian law *also* deems homicide justifiable if the defendant intended to cause death or grievous bodily harm under fear for her life and on the belief that she had no other way of preserving herself. The one section of the law does not exclude the other and Ward's appeal for a new trial was allowed.

The law of self-defense in English-speaking countries recognizes a subjective element in evaluating the circumstances of deadly quarrels and the "states of mind" of the accused (*R. v. Baxter,* 1975). The defendant "cannot be expected to weigh to a nicety the exact measure of necessary defensive action" (*Martin's Criminal Code* 1978, p. 36).

The Case of Francine Hughes, 1977

An American case similar to *Ward,* reveals how exculpation of homicide may be obtained by other procedures. Francine Hughes, a 30-year-old mother of four children, was charged in Lansing, Michigan, with killing her estranged husband, James, by setting fire to the room in which he was sleeping. Mrs. Hughes testified that she had been a long-suffering victim of physical and verbal abuse by her husband and that, given this history, the homicide occurred in a context in which, with good reason, she feared for her life.

Circuit court Judge Ray C. Hotchkiss denied a defense motion for direct acquittal on the grounds of justified self-defense. Mrs. Hughes's case went to trial at which a new plea was entered, that of "not guilty by reason of insanity."

This plea won freedom for the defendant after a period of psychiatric examination, but it did not secure the justice demanded by feminist activists who had hoped that this case might set a precedent. It was hoped that a "landmark ruling" would be established allowing a prima facie plea of self-defense where there was a history of repeated brutality (Jacoby 1977, *New York Times* 1977a, 1977b).

ON JUSTICE

The circumstances of the above cases, and the debates in the last two instances, demonstrate that there is a subjective element in assessing the "appropriateness" of defensive homicide. The propriety of homicide moves with a citizenry's sense of justice. It varies, then, with time and place, and it affects more than the definition of self-defense in justification of killing. It also affects the *gravity* assigned to different styles of homicide. This point is important because some journalists and some scholars assume that "murder is murder" and that each victim and each homicide ought to be equally valued.

The factual question is easier to resolve than the moral one. In fact, no society places an equal value on the lives of its members (Lowie 1940, Chs. 15–16, Reichard 1938, pp. 477–482, Thomas 1937, Chs. 13, 15). The fact that societies value certain lives above others is indicated by differential expenditures to save them (Rhoads 1978, Singer 1978), by the changing money values assigned them (Roth 1978, p. 239), and by the weighing of criminal penalties on scales that balance "qualities" of victims and offenders.

Equity is not equality, and these two ideals often conflict as principles of justice. The criminal law of independent states recognizes the difference by acknowledging circumstances that aggravate or mitigate condemnation of killing and that consequently attach degrees of culpability to homicide. These moral assessments are apparent in the written law, but they are also evident in the differential administration of the law.

A sense of justice cannot be assumed to be uniform across countries as large and culturally heterogeneous as Canada and the United States. It is probable that there are regional and ethnic variations in judging the gravity and "reasonableness" of different homicidal circumstances. Justice is not one concept and a sense of justice does not weigh crimes on a single scale (Nettler 1979).

For example, in Harris County (mostly Houston), Texas, about half of all homicides are "no-billed," that is, no bill of indictment is drawn against the killer (Lundsgaarde 1977). Grand juries in "space city" assess the circumstances of the crime, including the apparent impulsiveness with which it is committed and the relationship between the actors in the deadly drama. Killings in mortal quarrels between intimates are often deemed to have been "victim-precipitated," and Houstonians do not usually prosecute them. "The majority of homicide cases," Lundsgaarde writes, "are dismissed" (p. 42).

A parallel example of the differential evaluation of homicides is revealed by Zimring and his colleagues' (1976) study of the distribution of punishment for killing in Philadelphia. These investigators show that a moral judgment guides response to crime and that this judgment includes such considerations as the number killed, the number doing the killing, whether or not the homicide was part of another felony, proof of "malice," evidence of "intent," provocation by the victim, and the relationship and status of culprit and victim.

Zimring and his associates conclude that there are two prices for homicide in Philadelphia: "wholesale and retail." The wholesale price is paid for the majority of killings. These are homicides that prosecutors—and presumably the citizenry—wish to dispose of quickly, usually through plea bargaining and without a jury trial. The wholesale price is a prison sentence of two years or less. By contrast, a retail price is demanded for homicides that involve concurrent felonies or aggravating circumstances. Aggravating circumstances include the particular vulnerability of the victim or the wanton ("senseless") nature of the slaying. The retail price varies from 20 years to life imprisonment and the death sentence.

Zimring and his colleagues cannot discern a "rational theory of punishment" in this bimodal distribution of penalties. They say that they "cannot find the principle that justifies differences of ten-to-one within the general category of murder" (p. 242) and they conclude "not that [the American] system of justice is too lenient, or too severe; [but that] sadly it is both" (p. 252).

This complaint forgets that justice rests on moral foundations and that researchers' sense of justice need not be that of the people they study. In the Philadelphia data, a majority of homicide suspects whose killings were *not* associated with the commission of another felony were convicted of voluntary manslaughter or lesser crimes. Only three percent of "non-felony-murder" suspects were convicted of first degree murder. On the other hand, a majority of those suspected of killing *in the course of committing another felony* were convicted of first or second degree murder (Zimring et al. 1976, Tables I and V).

SUMMARY

In Western jurisdictions, we can discern some common principles of justice if we allow for local variations on these themes.

A first principle regards homicide "with malice aforethought" as more serious than homicides that seem to have been produced on impulse, in passion, or through negligence.

A second theme excuses assault and homicide in self-defense but, as we have seen, definitions of the "propriety" of defensive violence vary with time and place.

A third principle regards homicide committed in the course of another crime as more grave than deadly quarrels among acquaintances. This principle intertwines with yet another sense of justice—one that deems homicide between strangers as more serious than killing among intimates. These last two principles meet because most "felony murders" are also murders of strangers.

Noting these popular principles of justice does not evaluate them. It neither condemns nor defends them. We shall have occasion over and over to observe that justice is an idea, not an entity, and that conceptions of justice move with the morality that underwrites it (Nettler 1979). This conclusion becomes more apparent as we study the relationship between love, lust, ideals, and other motives in the generation of deadly disagreements.

6 HOMICIDAL ROUTES: **LOVE, SPURNED OR SPOILED**

Abstract • A significant proportion of all culpable homicides occurs among acquaintances and intimates. • Loving provides occasions for killing. ○ Love is distinguished from lust. ○ Jealousy is distinguished from envy. ○ Examples are given of homicides stimulated by love that has been spurned and love that has been spoiled. Insult characterizes both courses to homicide.

WITH COUNT BASIE'S BAND BEHIND HIM, Joe Turner sings, "That lovin' proposition goin' git somebody kill."

It is now common knowledge that "some significant proportion" of all homicides occurs between people who have known one another. The degree and quality of acquaintance varies, of course, but, as a rule-of-thumb, it can be assumed from recent experience in industrialized Western countries that between 40 and 60 percent of culpable homicides involve people who have been in a relationship initiated out of sexual attraction and associated with differing qualities of loving.

For example, Wolfgang (1957, Table 1) provides this classification of relationships between killers and their victims in Philadelphia from 1948 through 1952:

	Percent of Incidents
Relatively close friend	28.2
Family relationship	24.7
Acquaintance	13.5
Stranger	12.2
Paramour, mistress, prostitute	9.8
Sex rival	4.0
Enemy	2.9
Felon or police officer	1.1
Innocent bystander	1.1
Homosexual partner	0.6

Reed and his associates (1976, Table 3) classify Canadian homicides between 1961 and 1974 as involving the following relationships, with proportions varying by year:

	Percent of Incidents
Immediate family	24.9 to 31.7
Other kinship	4.4 to 4.5
Common-law family	7.2 to 7.9
Lover's quarrel and love triangle	5.2 to 6.5
Close acquaintance	7.5 to 8.3
Casual acquaintance	11.0 to 14.2
Business relationship	2.8 to 3.7
No known relationship	6.8 to 7.3
During commission of another criminal act	10.6 to 10.9
Unsolved	9.0 to 15.1

Statistics such as these illuminate some of the risks of the human connection. They draw parallels, while demonstrating differences between homicidal occasions in civil societies and those in tribal groupings. For example, the anthropologist Bohannon (1963, p. 298) reports for seven African tribes that "the vast majority of victims were kinsmen of their killers." A difference between civil aggregates and tribal ones is that civil societies provide a *greater variety* of occasion for homicide.

Among these occasions are intimacies that are *initiated* by the sexual bond. These intimacies include those in which there is a direct sexual connection between killer and victim and those in which the bonding is a *product* of a sexual connection, as when parents kill their children, children kill their parents, and children kill their siblings (Gardiner 1976).

The "lovin' proposition" starts with the sex drive. It may, of course, become independent of that urge. Conversely, sexual urgency moves people into erotic connections that are loveless. We are reminded that couples who are about to divorce seem to copulate as frequently as those in happier unions (Dickinson & Beam 1931, Terman 1938).

Love and Lust

The work stimulated by the sexual connection can be productive or destructive. It appears creative when channeled by institutions and foolish when liberated to impulse. The words we use to describe approved and disapproved uses of our sexuality indicate these opposed possibilities: "love" connotes altruism and is recommended; "lust" connotes egoism and is condemned.

Lust is a word that has a general meaning—that of wish, enthusiasm, appetite—and a more specific meaning—that of sexual desire. In both senses, lust, like love, provides occasions for killing.

Loving and lusting take many forms, of course. But, for convenience, the sexual bond may be considered to stimulate several, rather different courses toward murder.

One route is via the classic "crime of passion." This crime, in turn, may be reached by way of different paths. One course results in homicide because love has been spurned—with or without a rival on the scene. Another way to murder is marked by love that has proved to be defective because it has been unfaithful. Again, jealousy of a competitor may or may not characterize this career.

A rather different course to homicide is produced as affection turns to hatred through a history of insult. This passion is sometimes complicated by development of a new love that would replace the spoiled connection if only it could be severed. Homicide is sometimes attempted to cut the tie of a dead romance and to free a lover for a new one.

In sum, we are hoist. We do not do well without loving, but loving is hazardous. Battles between lovers are dangerous, and not only to the combatants. Police who respond to scenes of "domestic disturbance" are at risk of injury and death. In the United States during 1979, 40 percent of police officers killed in the line of duty were answering "house calls" to subdue fighting spouses or other lovers (Arenberg 1980). In Canada, the proportion of officers so killed is lower—in part due to the extraordinarily high number who die in airplane crashes during investigative work. Nevertheless, over the past 20 years, 14 percent of all Canadian police deaths during duty are attributed to responses to "domestic disputes" (Bentham 1980).

Pertinent to this dangerous duty, and indicative of the "meaning" of battles between lovers, it is not uncommon for policemen to be attacked by the woman they are trying to protect when they restrain her enraged man. Love can be simultaneously protective and hateful.

This chapter describes a sample of homicides generated by love spurned or spoiled. Another erotic route to murder is described in Chapter 7. It is the path paved with "loveless love," or lust. It is a style of killing that is often called "sex murder," meaning that sexual gratification has been linked to domination or submission, and these emotions, in turn, associated with brutality.

LOVE SPURNED: Killing for Love

"Love" is a glorious word. Most of us favor it and many institutions recommend it. However, as with most useful terms, "love" does not refer to one thing; it does not refer to one emotion or to one quality of the human connection. There is love tightly bound to erotic sensation and love quite remote from sexual urgency. There is love that respects the other's independence and love that absorbs the other. "Smother love" describes the latter variety of concern.

Not only are there qualities of love, but there are prices. As with all things valued, loving carries a cost. Life with love is exhilarating, but it is also risky because no price tag is hung on the loving relationship before it is engaged. One of the unforeseen possible costs is rejection.

Lovers invest their egos, as well as time and money, in the affectionate bond. Rejection of the investment hurts. It hurts whether or not a rival is on the scene. It is an injury in its own right.

We think that some people are more vulnerable to this injury than others. We call such people "insecure" or "overly dependent." But insecurity does not always wear a public face and in many "murders-for-love" we can only recognize the excessive dependence after the crime.

Recognition is made difficult because some degree of dependence is a mark of true love. This is the meaning of "caring." Thus there are few premonitory signs by which we can differentiate the dependency that is part of "normal" loving from the dependency that is so absorptive that one lover would rather kill, and perhaps die, than live without the other. After the killing, we can see that he or she "cared too much," but before the homicide some ill-fated lovers seem ideal.

EXAMPLE: *"Slain Student's Boyfriend Held: Campus Murder Aftermath"* (Jennings, *The San Francisco Chronicle,* September 7, 1979. Reproduced by permission).

> Funeral services for Catina Salarno will be held this morning in San Francisco at the same time that her boyfriend, Steven Burns, is being arraigned in a Stockton courtroom on a charge of murdering her at the University of Pacific Monday night.
>
> Burns, 18, the son of Lowell High School football coach Ed Burns, will appear in San Joaquin County Municipal Court at 10:45 a.m., 45 minutes after the beginning of services for Salarno at St. Stephen's Church.
>
> Stockton police said yesterday that young Burns admitted shooting Salarno in the back of the head after she told him that their four-year relationship was over.
>
> Burns, a top scholar and athlete at St. Ignatius High School in San Francisco last year, and Salarno, also 18, who graduated in June from Mercy High School here, had both enrolled at UOP last week.

Her father, Sunset District businessman Michael Salarno, said yesterday that his eldest daughter had been threatened by Burns in recent weeks whenever she attempted to break off their long relationship.

"He would say things to her like, 'I'm gonna get you,' or 'I'm gonna kill you.' But I just passed it off as kids' threats."

Regina Salarno, Catina's 17-year-old sister, said yesterday that young Burns had displayed a gun to Catina as recently as a week ago, telling her it showed how serious he was about not wanting to break up with her.

Students at St. Ignatius who knew Burns and footballed with him last year, described him . . . as a popular, outgoing young man who was an exceptional athlete and scholar.

"He was a big man on campus," said Chris Ottoboni, a senior and defensive tackle. "Everybody looked up to him."

Chris Stretch, a senior quarterback, said he often saw Burns and Salarno together and that she "always picked him up after football practice."

"They were a great team," he said of the two youngsters. Stretch said he never saw them argue. "She never flirted with anybody or anything like that. Everyone knew she was Steve's girl friend."

"It's unbelievable," said [school principal] James Kearney, who also lives near the Salarno and Burns families. "I knew both kids and of course I know Coach Burns real well."

"It's a neighborhood thing. We're all members of the same parish. Our kids went to school together. Steve Burns used to drive my kids home."

Lessons   One lesson to be learned from this tragedy is that the loving murderer wears no particular badge by which he or she can be recognized.

A second lesson is never to take threats lightly. Threats backed by displays of deadly instruments are all the more premonitory. To protect ourselves, we need no additional lethal cues.

A last lesson is that people who possess "non-sporting" guns and who, in addition, promise to kill with them, deserve to be "snitched upon." Snitching may violate one code of conduct, but it defends another.

Murderous Jealousy

Love that is spurned can trigger violence without a rival on the scene, as in the case of the San Francisco couple. However, a common form of "the crime of passion" involves jealousy.

Jealousy is a mixed emotion, a compound of anxiety, depression, suspicion, and hatred stimulated by the belief, *warranted or not,* that one is *losing* a loved person to a rival or rivals.

Jealousy is fueled by insecurity and insult. Because there can be a varied mixture of these fuels in the course of any loving career, the jealous killer can destroy a person with whom she or he is still in love or the killer can attack a person who was once loved but is now despised. Jealous murderers sometimes kill while still attached to the rejecting loved one and sometimes without attachment—as in cases in which love has been abused, worn away, and mocked with a final insult. The feeling of passionate attachment that kills is clearly expressed by one homicidal woman who justified her murdering by saying, "If I don't have him, no one will."

This is one meaning of "true love." It is the kind of love in which murder is often, but not always, followed by suicide (West 1965).

Premonitory cues are again difficult to read. They are difficult to read for outsiders who usually see only one face, the public one, of an erotic connection. And they are difficult to read by the victim-to-be because preliminary signs are being interpreted by a person who is also attached, or was attached, to the jealous lover. Emotion obscures vision.

Furthermore, interpretation depends on comparison, and comparison depends on the range of human relations one has experienced and the standards of normality against which cues are given meaning.

Allowing for these difficulties, dangerous jealousy is to be read in a lover's "excessive dependence" and "thin skin." "Thin skin" refers to sensitivity, to a lover's too-easy interpretation of any attention to another as a threat. Jealousy is also to be read in "flare-ups," in anger over slights that most of us think are trivial. The slights that injure a jealous person are any indication of diminished attention: a forgotten anniversary, a changed plan, dancing too long with another, and, even, pleasure in non-sexual activities that do not involve the jealous lover. Thus passionate lovers are sometimes jealous of their loved one's work or sport. These can be rivals as clearly as another person.

With any of these slights, the cue to danger is *repeated rage,* with or without tears, and with or without physical attack.

Jealousy Without Love

Insecurity and insult—the twin generators of jealousy—appear in varied balance. In the example of the San Francisco lovers, threatened loss was more important than insult, although withdrawal of affection is always wounding. But there is another form of jealousy in which insult dominates insecurity and in which the jealous lover is moved to murder, not so much by fear of losing a valued person, as by hatred of the rival who has demonstrated the treachery of someone who was once loved. This anger is mixed with hatred of the deceiving loved one. The treachery is a mockery.

The case of the wronged husband is classic. In the context of romantic love and "pair marriage" (Sumner 1906, pp. 374–375), to be made a cuckold is insulting. Some contemporary interpreters claim that the insult comes from a violation of male property rights in the female (Clark & Lewis 1977). This may be so in some instances, but the insult goes deeper than that of violated property. The insult is to pride, to one's dignity, to one's good sense in having trusted another who has proved faithless. The cuckold has been made foolish, and making a fool of a person is a universal occasion for killing.

Culture again directs blame. In some cultures, the wronged husband kills the offending rival, but spares his wife. In many tribes, however, adulterous wives are killed (Bohannon 1960), and in some cultures, enraged husbands kill both parties to his insult.

Murderous Envy

Jealousy is commonly confused with another deadly affliction, envy. The distinction is important and deserves mention at this point.

Dictionaries often make no distinction between jealousy and envy, but their differentiation is worthwhile because these lethal emotions have different sources and different ranges.

Jealousy is personal and its roots erotic. Its range is therefore limited. By contrast, envy is the "disinterested" resentment of the different and superior. Its range is expansive.

Envy is hatred of the other's advantage—whether or not one knows the other personally. The hated advantage can be that of wealth, of good looks, of achievement, and, even, of the other's happiness.

Envy is the wish to see the other "brought down"—whether or not this reduction adds to one's own advantage. In this sense, envy is "disinterested." Acting upon it produces nothing for the envious except the satisfaction of leveling the more fortunate person.

Envy is a persistent, universal emotion that every society attempts to control (Schoeck 1966). It is, in Schoeck's words, "the consuming desire that no one should have anything [that I do not have]. [It is] the destruction of pleasure in and for others, without deriving any sort of advantage from this" (p. 115).

Envy stimulates its own crimes, from "senseless" vandalism to "motiveless" murder. It differs from jealousy in that the jealous lover has, or had, an attachment to the person or thing he or she is losing. (One can be jealous, incidentally, of one's animal pets—as when they prefer a guest to their owner).

Example: Charles Manson

The envious killer hates difference and, in particular, the difference that betokens superiority. The mass murderer Charles Manson, about whom more will be said later, provides an example.

One night Charlie was cruising Sunset Boulevard with some of his "family." At a stop light Manson's jalopy pulled next to a fellow in an expensive, white sports car. The sports top was down, the engine revved its powerful tune, and the apparently rich driver (who knows his debts?) was lolling in a satisfied manner with his left arm draped over the door. This so infuriated Manson that he shouted to one of his aides, Tex Watson, "Gimme your gun. I'm gonna blow that son-ofabitches' head off."

The stop light turned green, the sports car sped off, and the victim-to-be may never know his luck. But the intended victim was an object of envy, not jealousy. The distinction is important because envy is a readily exploitable material in political movements. It is an emotion which, camouflaged by ideology, justifies irrational policies in public affairs as it does in private lives.

LOVE SPOILED: Cumulated Insult

Love takes yet another path to homicide than that of affection spurned. It is the course of eroded affection and accumulated insult. This road is paved with the contempt that familiarity often breeds, and is likely to breed, among those whose intimacy is not constrained by institutionalized etiquette.

Unless one assumes the mating of people perfectly matched in their tastes, all unions run the risk of erosion as different styles of living rub against one another. A traditional defense against this abrasion has been well-defined sex roles and an etiquette that accompanies such definition. Loss of any such tradition means the loss of manners that lubricate social relations. These losses, in turn, increase the possibility that people who once lusted for one another, and believed they loved, learn later that the taste for the other has soured. The souring is accompanied by complaint, bickering, and insult.

Individuals have different thresholds for insult, of course, and some murderous accumulations take years while others require only weeks or months. However, an interesting aspect of these killings through cumulated insult is that a seemingly trivial event works like "the final straw" to break restraint, that the murder is felt as a relief, and that little or no remorse is experienced by the relieved killer. Arthur Koestler's "Case of the Mace-Bearer" (1956) illustrates this path to homicide in one cultural setting. His story deserves recounting in full:

Example: "Case of the Mace-Bearer"

Donald Martin[1] was at the time a respectable and respected citizen of the age of fifty. He was Town Hall Superintendent and Mace-Bearer at the Borough of Notting Hill, and lived in a flat in the Town Hall called "caretaker's premises." On official occasions he walked behind the Mayor, carrying the mace in solemn procession. His wife Violet, also middle-aged, was working for the National Savings Association in the same Town Hall. They had one child, a pretty girl called Sally, aged seventeen.

On Wednesday, September 27th, 1950, Mr. and Mrs. Martin had lunch at an A.B.C. in Baker Street and, returning to caretaker's premises, had an argument. Martin tried to persuade Violet to give up her job so that she could spend more time in looking after their flat, and also that she should consult the Marriage Advice Bureau. Violet refused, whereupon Donald hit her on the head—the first time in his life that he had hit her—then, leaving her lying on the floor, went to the kitchen, took his razor out of its case, replaced the case neatly at right angles to his brush and comb on the shelf, went back to Violet, cut her throat, and when satisfied that she was dead, telephoned the police. When the police arrived, he was sitting at the top of the staircase waiting for them, perfectly composed. He remained equally composed while waiting for his trial and never revealed any real remorse for what he had done.

Donald was the third in a family of eleven children, of which ten survived. His father was a workman in the painting and decorating trade. His mother was a simple woman, who had led a very hard life. There was no hereditary mental disease in the family, and all of its members got on reasonably well in life. It is true that the father was said to have been a violent-tempered man who once broke the nose of one of his

---

[1] Reprinted by permission of A.D. Peters & Co., Ltd.
Koestler adds, "The facts of the case are as stated; the names of the participants have been altered to avoid distress to their families. 'Notting Hill Town Hall,' which does not exist, stands for the existing Town Hall of a London Borough" (p. 86).

daughters with a blow, but such incidents, alas, are not very exceptional in a hard-up, working-class family of that size.

Donald was a normal child, average in school, who got on well with his schoolmates and took an active part in all sports; he particularly excelled in boxing. According to his mother, he was always well behaved, never quarrelsome or violent; the only complaint about him was that he had been excessively "tidy and particular." Out of school hours he earned money for the family by polishing boots and selling newspapers. At fourteen, on leaving school, he held a job as a grocer's errand boy for twelve months, then another as a milkman for eighteen months. He subsequently worked in a rubber factory for a year, but did not like indoor work, and became a baker's roundsman.

At the age of nineteen, he enlisted in the Royal Tank Corps. He served altogether eighteen years in England, India and Egypt, reaching the rank of Sergeant and Acting Company Quartermaster-Sergeant. When he left the Army at the age of thirty-seven, his character was described as exemplary; he was awarded the long-service and good-conduct medal and granted a service pension. He then got employment at Notting Hill Town Hall, at first as a porter, and, during the next twelve years, gradually worked his way up to be Town Hall Superintendent and Mace-bearer.

A more decent and ordinary career could hardly be imagined. Yet Donald Martin bore a cross, part real, part imaginary, under whose weight he finally collapsed. He was, so to speak, a common-or-garden martyr of that commonplace Calvary: a marriage between incompatible partners.

He met Violet when he was twenty-two, while stationed with his Company in Dorset. She was at that time a laundry-maid. A year later he became engaged to her; another two years later they were married; another fortnight later, during their honeymoon, she infected him with syphilis.

He did not realize this at the time. He only found out about it eight years later, when he was stationed in India, and a medical examination revealed a syphilitic infection of the central nervous system. The date of the infection was then traced back to the appearance of a small genital ulcer a fortnight after his marriage, which he had noticed at the time but ignored as harmless. He received treatment in military hospitals in England, India and Egypt, over a period of more than two years, and was then reported cured.

The medical examination which led to the discovery of the disease was caused by an incident at the Army Barracks in Poona. This happened in the eighth year of their marriage, and one year after Violet had given birth to their daughter Sally. They were living in married quarters. Donald suspected that Violet, who had been sexually cold towards him from the beginning of their marriage, was committing adultery with a Company Sergeant. There was a quarrel, after which he stole a revolver from the Armoury, intending to shoot Violet, the baby and himself. Before he could do so, an officer and N.C.O. came to arrest him for taking the revolver and ammunition without authority. He was court-martialled, but pleaded that he could not remember what he was doing. He was sent for observation into hospital; where, in the course of a medical examination, he was discovered to be suffering from syphilitic meningo-encephalitis.

Yet the idea of shooting Violet, the baby and himself had already occurred to Donald prior to this discovery. What had been going on during those first eight years of their married life to drive him to this point? We only have a few glimpses of the idyll between Donald and Violet. One of them is provided by Donald's repeated complaints about her sexual coldness towards him, and by his description "how she would merely lie on her side and go on reading a book whilst he had sexual intercourse with her." But in the law of murder this debasement of a sacrament to an obscenity, this mortal offence to the male's pride, is not known as a provocation to a reasonable man.

Nothing could be more commonplace than the fact that during twenty-four years of their married life Donald loved Violet desperately and Violet treated Donald like dirt. He was not a lovable man. He was narrow-minded, vain, pedantic and egocentric, obsessed with tidiness, and respectable appearances; a hypochondriac, constantly afraid of microbes and infections. Yet he forgave her the honeymoon present she had given him, and forgave her all that she did to him during the sixteen years that followed his first impulse to do away with her and himself and their child; in return, she kept adding provocation to provocation, of a kind not mentioned in the law books.

He kept himself under control. Only twice during all these years did he lose his temper: the first time when he was twenty-nine and had a fight with a soldier who taunted him; the second time, three years later, on the occasion when he got hold of the revolver. His Army record describes him as an excellent N.C.O., a good driver and mechanic, and a man who could confidently be recommended for any position of trust.

He was thirty-seven when he left the Army and started work at the Town Hall. The next ten years or so, the life of Donald and Violet was outwardly uneventful. He had an excellent work record. After being appointed Town Hall caretaker, he was responsible for porters and domestic staff and managed them well, though occasionally he was inclined to employ Army Sergeant methods. During the war he was superintendent of the local A.R.P. office, and an active member of the Civil Defence Club, to which Violet often accompanied him for dances and whist drives. He took great pride in his functions as a Mace-bearer. He did not betray the inner strain under which he lived and which he held in check by a rigid, meticulous, indeed fanatical, observance of his civic duties—as a man with a broken spine carries his head held stiffly up by a metal harness.

Perhaps the only odd thing about him was the exaggerated seriousness, verging on obsession, with which he took his duties. Having once been reprimanded for forgetting to hoist the flag for Princess Elizabeth's birthday, he wrote a letter to Buckingham Palace, asking for a complete list of royal birthdays. When the time came to ask for an increase in salary, he sent an inquiry to a number of other caretakers at town halls regarding their salaries; then wrote a letter of seven closely covered foolscap pages to the Town Clerk, enumerating in detail all the important duties which he was called on to perform.

Since his main pride and obsession in life were order, discipline and tidiness, Violet, with the psychological insight that hatred provides, tormented him by being slatternly about their flat, never cooking a hot meal except once a week on Sunday, and turning caretaker's premises into a place of lewdness and abomination.

For by now the daughter, Sally, had become an attractive girl with an alarmingly developed temperament. At the age of seventeen, Sally had a "steady" named Horace, and besides him several sailor friends in the Merchant Navy. On one occasion, three of the sailors on different ships simultaneously applied for special leave to visit their fiancée, Sally Martin.

Horace, the civilian steady, was always hanging around caretaker's premises, and "carrying on" with Sally, with the consent and encouragement of Violet. This, of course, was a constant agony to Martin, the disciplinarian and prig; but he also had some additional reasons for loathing his daughter's young man. Horace had pimples on the back of his neck and Martin, who lived in horror of germs and infection, caught the pimples, so he thought, by washing out the sink after Horace had been there. On another occasion, he found a packet of contraceptives in Horace's pocket.

During the last year, the squalid cross became too heavy to bear. Donald believed that Violet and Sally were in alliance against him. At times they would "send him to Coventry" for several days on end. On one occasion they both left and were gone for a fortnight, leaving Donald to fend for himself in the flat. On several other occasions Violet left to stay with a sister, and threatened never to come back again. She knew that what he cherished most in life was his job at the Town Hall, and that if she left him he would lose it. She told him repeatedly that to sleep with him was repellent and distasteful to her, and encouraged him to have relations with other women. He tried this at the final stages, but it did not help.

Downstairs in the Town Hall he was still the strict and self-important Company Sergeant of Poona; upstairs at caretaker's premises he was virtually reduced to the state of an untouchable. In the Civil Defence Club he appeared, impeccably dressed, a paragon of respectability; in his sordid home he felt that he was drowning in dirt, pimples, contraceptives and fornications, real and imagined. He clutched at every straw. He implored Violet to give up her job because he thought that if she did so she would have more time to look after the flat, and all would be well. He sought advice from a doctor, who talked of sending him to a psychiatrist, and then all would be well. He sought advice from the Marriage Advice Bureau, and implored Violet to go there, because they would talk to her sensibly and all would be well.

About six weeks before the end, Violet again left him. She went to stay with her sister in Dorchester, and said she would never come back. Whilst she was away, Donald cleaned, painted and decorated the flat. Then he followed her to Dorchester and persuaded Violet to come back and "give it another chance." Donald's old mother, aged seventy-four, was invited to an egg-and-bacon tea to welcome Violet on her return, and the old woman felt that a real reconciliation had taken place. Then Sally, who had also been away, came back too, and then Horace, and the contraceptives, and the pimples.

He became so miserable that he could hardly eat. Some time before the end he developed a duodenal ulcer. He was operated on and put on a gastric diet—which he could not keep because Violet refused to cook for him. He then became suspicious, and later convinced, that Violet was having sexual relations with their daughter's young man.

The incidents of the last three days are as drab, ordinary and commonplace as the rest.

On Monday, September 25th, Donald is reported to have asked Sally to help him with Hoovering the flat, which she refused. There were a few words.

On Tuesday, September 26th, Donald called on a Mrs. Tiplady, Sanitary Inspector at Notting Hill Town Hall, and asked her to inspect his flat in her official capacity, to confirm that his wife was neglecting it. Mrs. Tiplady obliged and wrote a report.

On Wednesday, September 27th, he again called to see Mrs. Tiplady, excitedly waving a *Daily Mail,* in which a sensational article on the neglect of the homes of married women who went out to work had appeared. Then he called at Violet's office, asking her to give up her job. Then they had lunch at the A.B.C., Baker Street, and they had an argument. Then they went on to the flat and he asked her again to give up her job and to consult the Marriage Advice Bureau. She refused, threatened to leave him again and spoke to him, as he described it, "in a manner she had never done before." Considering the time they had spent together, it must have been quite some manner to speak in. Then he hit her for the first time in his life; and then a quarter-century of repressed hatred burst to the surface, and he fetched his razor and cut her throat. She must have resisted, because there were cuts on her hands and arms.

While awaiting his trial, he slept well and ate well, and said he felt much happier now that he was in prison. In his statements he was frank and co-operative and unhesitatingly volunteered information which was prejudicial to him. He only made one misleading statement, at an early interview, when he denied having ever been unfaithful to Violet. His only complaint about conditions in prison was that he could not keep his clothes as tidy as he would like to and as he always had done. He did not seem to be aware that he had committed a crime and seemed to have no sense of guilt. He said to one of his visitors that a girl with whom he used to go out before he met Violet, and whom he had not seen for many years, had written to him on reading about the case: this had led to an amorous correspondence and her visiting him in prison. He hoped that if acquitted he could marry her.

Donald was found guilty, but insane, and committed to a mental hospital "until cured."

Lessons   Donald did not know about continuities. He did not know that talk alone does not reform character. Like many children and some adults, he believed in the magic power of words to change events and personalities.

His case illustrates another point: that hypocrisy is a social lubricant. Hypocrisy reduces the friction produced by moral conflict (Warriner 1958).

In Donald's case, the moral conflict assuaged by hypocrisy was that expressed in the criminal law and its administration. The law did not wish to let him go scot-free, yet it sympathized with his plight. His plight made his murder "understandable," without making it justifiable. A way out of the moral conflict was to deem him "insane" and to restrain him for some convenient time. Since it is not known which "mental disease" he suffered from, it cannot be known how to cure him or how to recognize when he is cured.

7 HOMICIDAL ROUTES: **LUST**

Abstract • Our erotic physiologies stimulate affectionate union and reproduction, but they also stimulate aggression and destruction. ∘ The linkage of sexuality with brutality is more apparent in males than in females. ∘ Forcible rape is shown to be an assault with sexual tools, rather than a purely sex-satisfying act. ∘ Slang terms for the sexual act indicate the common connection of hostility with sexuality. • "Lust murders" are sometimes accidental and sometimes intentional. ∘ Kotzwarraism is a sexual practice that produces some accidental deaths. ∘ Necrophilia provides an example of lustful homicides that are sometimes accidental and sometimes purposive. ∘ Sadistic murders are intentional homicides that gratify hatred in association with sexual use and abuse of the victim. • Examples of lustful murders illuminate two conflicts in the administration of Western law. ∘ One conflict is that between regarding heinous killers as "sane" when they are not psychotic and regarding them as "sick" because of the nature of their crimes. ∘ Another conflict is that between freedom of the press and a defendant's right to a fair trial. • Debate about the influence of art upon manners is introduced. It is argued that sexual license in the arts operates as a moral anesthetic.

IF ONE CAN LOVE, one can hate. The emotions are linked conceptually and factually.

Freedom from this linkage is obtained only by those who move toward the near-death of indifference, a near-death that is observed in some kinds of psychosis in which the sufferer has lost capacity to feel affiliated to anyone. But, for those of us who remain "more alive," there is always the possibility that love will sour, that the souring will be accompanied by insult, and that insult will cumulate into a lethal explosion.

The love-hate connection has sexual roots, but our sexuality is also expressed without love or hate. It is an appetite that can be satisfied mechanically, *without* human association, and indifferently *with* human association. It is an appetite that is a source of both pleasure and misery and one that leads to both happy endings and sad ones. Our erotic physiologies stimulate affectionate union and reproduction, but they also stimulate aggression and destruction.

The conjunction of love and hate with erotic vitality is apparent in both men and women but, historically, males have exceeded females in their proclivity to kill "for love." Spurned love, and spoiled love, generate hatred in both sexes. However, in the male, the sexual drive is itself aggressive.

We have already noted that masculinity and femininity are not absolutely associated with the genital markers that define male and female (Volume One, Chapter 3). There is a continuum of masculinity and femininity such that some males are more feminine than some females, and some females are more masculine than some males. However, allowing for this overlap, it remains true that masculine sexuality is associated with physical vigor and the urge to dominate. The appetites are intertwined. Thus, the psychoanalyst Theodor Reik could claim that, "He who cannot bite cannot kiss."

The connection of male sexuality with physical aggression—with the ability to attack and with the pleasure of domination—is observed in literature, myth, and proverb, as it is in the clinic and bedroom. For example, Spaniards have a saying, "Un pene duro no tiene una consciencia." In the vernacular, this translates as, "A hard cock has no conscience."

Sexuality in its many forms challenges the morality that attempts to control it. Human beings are repeatedly astonished by the variety with which their sexuality is expressed and by the effort it elicits. Because "sex" has been a taboo topic, and because of its variable association with loving, we have been hesitant to acknowledge that erotic gratification is coupled with the pleasures of domination and submission. Domination and submission, in turn, are variously expressed as they yield sexual satisfaction. That is, there is more than one technique for inducing feelings of power and helplessness, superiority and inferiority, that stimulate sexual pleasure. Encyclopedias of sexual "psychopathies" provide details of these many techniques (Allen 1969, Gebhard et al. 1965, Janus et al. 1977, Karpman 1954, Krafft-Ebing 1935, Stekel 1929). Hence, it is necessary here only to record the connection between eroticism and brutality that underwrites a variety of homicides known as "lust murders." En route to this description, the connection between hostility and sexuality makes it appropriate to comment on rape.

A Note on Rape

It is now recognized that forcible rape, of both males and females, is not simply a "sexual crime" driven only by sexual need. Erotic feelings are involved, of course, but they are mixed with other emotions, so much so that one cannot say that the "primary motive" is erotic. Rape is not engaged solely in pursuit of orgasm and some proportion of rapists do not achieve it (West et al. 1978).

Forcible rape is best defined as an assault with sexual tools. It is a crime that gratifies hatred and feelings of power as well as the erotic appetite. Since sexual urgency and the "need" to express hatred and to feel powerful are variously produced, *there is no one type of person who rapes* (Chappell et al. 1977, Cohen et al. 1975, Gebhard et al. 1965, Groth 1979, Guttmacher & Weihofen 1952, Rada 1978).

For example, there are women who rape, with or without the assistance of men, and who are thrilled by the sight of other women being debased. Moreover, the linkage of sexual feelings with the satisfactions of domination and submission is indicated by the fact that a significant minority of women tell us, in private, that they have achieved sexual gratification by imagining themselves either glorified or humiliated. Fisher's (1973) interviews with 285 American *married* women, most of whom were white, Protestant, and in their early or mid-20s, revealed that:

> More than 75 percent . . . indicated that they have had at least one fantasy or image that recurred occasionally (but not frequently) during intercourse. When these fantasies were roughly categorized, it was found that about 40 percent involved scenes in which the woman was having a sexual contact or interchange with someone other than her husband. Within this category, more than half of the instances revolved about themes in which the woman perceived herself as being raped, sexually humiliated, or somehow sexually wicked. There were fantasies of being helplessly tied and having to submit to brutal rape, of being a cheap whore humiliated by men, and of having to expose one's genitals publicly in an embarrassing way. A number of the women fantasized that they were actresses on a stage and were performing sexually for an audience. Masochistic and exhibitionistic elements were strongly prominent in the fantasies. . . . Another interesting category (10 percent) of fantasy portrayed self as being a royal or superior figure (for example, goddess, princess) with special power or prestige (pp. 237–238).

Fisher's results are corroborated by studies that show a connection between sexual arousal in both males and females and power plays. For example, Malamuth et al. (1980) find that normal (non-rapist) persons are more sexually aroused by depictions of mutual sexuality between men and women than by stories depicting sexual assault. However, these investigators were "surprised" to find that stories of rape in which the female victim experiences involuntary orgasm were as sexually stimulating for both men and women as stories of consenting sexual relations. Moreover, men, but not women, are most aroused by pornography that depicts the female victim as experiencing involuntary orgasm *and pain.*

This finding fits results of other studies that indicate that many rapists justify their crimes by believing that their victims enjoy the act and by their interpretation of their victims' pain as pleasure (Clark & Lewis 1977, Gager & Schurr 1976). However, some fantasies reveal pleasure in giving sexual pain *without* the justification that the victim relishes the humiliation. Masters and Johnson (1979, pp. 178–179) report that the sexual fantasies of male homosexuals are more violent than those of male heterosexuals and that:

> Free-floating fantasies of forced sexual encounters were the second most frequently reported fantasies by homosexual male study subjects. In the forced sexual encounters men were imagined as victims almost as frequently as women. In all but one instance, the homosexual male subject played the role of rapist. The rapes were consistently fantasized as particularly repellent to the rapee, who usually was pictured as restrained and forced into sexual service by physical abuse such as whippings or beatings.

The frequent association of sexual satisfaction with violence and the increased publication of pornography (Malamuth & Spinner 1979) raise concern about the disinhibiting lessons taught by the media of mass communication. This issue is addressed in Chapter 12. Meanwhile, the search for one clear road to rape, or any guaranteed therapy of the rapist, seems futile (Groth 1979, Chapter 5).

Sources of sexual hostility

Studies of male rapists suggest that many, but not all such offenders, have had histories of rejection by women, beginning with their mothers. In addition, these offenders report histories that have reinforced their feelings of inferiority (Groth 1979, West et al. 1978).

Such reports are interesting, but they do not give us a clear picture of the production of a rapist since we do not know how many other men, similarly rejected by women, become hostile toward females. Nor do we know how many men who dislike women express their hostility—if they do so at all—in some other fashion than rape. That is, we do not know what else in a man's constitution or background turns his career toward rape rather than toward some other outlet for hostility.

We do know that parental rejection is universally associated with the unloved child's low self-esteem, hostility, and view of the world as a jungle—feelings that persist into the rejected child's adulthood (Rohner 1975). Such feelings mark one route to rape and lust murder, but we have no evidence that such a background *distinctively* produces such crimes. This means that we can describe such careers without explaining them.

Description of hostile courses toward sexual attacks notes that they sometimes appear as explosive responses to apparently trivial events ("triggers"). Such pent-up hatred is gratified by humiliating and defiling the victim, as exemplified by the cases of Ed Kemper and Tom Bean discussed on pages 132–138.

Women are not the only victims of male rapists, of course. Men rape men as well. The choice of victim indicates that a "free-floating" hostility, however it is generated, can attach itself to numerous classes of person. Victims of such violence are innocent of direct offense to the rapist, but they are *symbols* of classes of despised people who are interpreted by the rapist as responsible for his or her low status. These symbols can be people of opposite sex, or people of opposite sex and different race (Cleaver 1968), or people of same sex but different race (Carroll 1974, 1977; Davis n.d. ca. 1969).

For example, the study by the Assistant District Attorney for Philadelphia, Alan J. Davis (n.d.), reports in sordid detail sexual assaults—forcible buggery and forcible fellatio—among inmates in the Philadelphia prison system and Sheriff's vans from June 1, 1966 through July 31, 1968. Davis and associates interviewed 3,304 inmates and 561 prison employees and reviewed "hundreds of documents" describing sexual violence in the Philadelphia detention system. Davis finds that "virtually every slightly built young man admitted to prison" is approached sexually (p. 26) and that the majority of attacks (56%) involve black aggressors and white victims while none of the attacks involve white aggressors and black victims (pp. 34–35). This asymmetry in sexual assault across races reflects, in part, the higher proportion of black inmates in Philadelphia jails, but it also bespeaks ethnic hostility. Davis writes:

> It is clear that the conquest and degradation of the victim is a primary goal of the sexual aggressor. Investigators repeatedly encountered phrases such as "fight or fuck," "we're gonna take your manhood," . . . "we're gonna make a girl out of you." Some assaults recalled the custom in some ancient societies of castrating or buggering a defeated enemy.
>
> Sexual assaults, as opposed to truly consensual sexuality, are not primarily a function of sexual deprivation (p. 38).

Carroll's (1974) research on sexual attacks in a maximum security prison in a New England state confirms Davis's findings and notes that "black sexual aggression against whites is a common pattern in prisons, and is not dependent upon a black numerical majority in the population" (p. 4).

The Love-Hate Connection

This comment on forcible rape illuminates the various meanings that can be attached to sexual coupling and illustrates the power plays that are enacted with genital equipment. Some people think it a paradox that an act romantically associated with tenderness can also be an act brutally associated with degradation.

It may be a paradox, but it is nonetheless a fact that the "love act" can also be a "hate act." One need not be a Freudian to note that the slang terms for sexual congress are, *almost without exception,*[1] hostile expressions. "Screw you" does not mean "love you." "Up yours," and related phrases and their accompanying rude gestures, do not express affection and affiliation; they express defiance and derogation.

We need not know *why* this is so to recognize that it *is* so. There are, of course, biochemical grounds for this connection, but the fact that the sexual drive is intertwined with feelings of power and the pleasures of domination and submission means that assault and homicide can accompany the sexual act. The connection is sometimes accidental—as when sexual brutality "gets carried away" and results in death—and sometimes intentional—as in cases in which injury and even killing are planned parts of sexual gratification.

LUSTFUL DEATHS: Kotzwarraism

Deaths that occur during sexual play sometimes appear as accidents, sometimes as homicides, and sometimes as suicides. Definition depends upon inference, and inference depends upon cues at the mortal scene.

An example of lust-driven homicide that can receive these several interpretations is that which the psychiatrist Dietz (1978) has termed *Kotzwarraism.*

Kotzwarra was a Czech musician, regarded as one of the best bass players in 18th century Europe, who employed prostitutes to hang him for the sexual excitement induced by the debasement and the cerebral hypoxia (reduced flow of oxygen to the brain). During one of these "games," Kotzwarra died and the prostitute who had obligingly hung him, Susanna Hill, was charged with murder but acquitted and released with the court's definition of the death as "accidental manslaughter."

---

[1] The more venerable slang terms for copulation all express hostility. It is only in the last decade or so that the phrase, "to ball," entered street vocabulary. It is used both with and without hostile connotation.

Long before Kotzwarra's demise, it had been noted that cerebral hypoxia was associated with sexual excitement and both ancient civilizations and primitive tribes have practiced what Brittain (1968) calls "sexual asphyxia." Dietz's review of recent literature and his collection of cases show a variety of techniques employed, including hanging, strangulation, suffocation, compression, asphyxiation, and inhalation of gases deficient in oxygen. These techniques are used predominantly by men; only a few cases of female Kotzwarraism have been reported. Weisman (1965), for example, describes a woman who experienced unexpected orgasm during a suicide attempt and who thereafter adopted suffocation as a sexual stimulant. She later "graduated" to hiring male sexual partners to threaten and degrade her and partially to suffocate her.

The sexual asphyxias are practiced alone or with one or more partners. In a high proportion of male cases, these activities are associated with homosexual practices (transvestism, for example) and narcissism (the use of mirrors). For both sexes, Kotzwarraism is frequently employed along with other modes of degradation—for example, broken swizzle sticks piercing the nipples, metal clamps attached to the armpits, a wooden table leg inserted in the rectum, and so-called "golden or brown showers," i.e., being urinated or defecated upon (Dietz 1978, Janus et al. 1977).

News of varied sexual pleasures is spread by word and by film. Even cities like Edmonton, Canada—far removed from the reputed Sodoms of the world—have experienced Kotzwarra-style homicides within male homosexual circles where practices are transmitted by the gossip grapevine. In a recent Edmonton case, as in that of Kotzwarra himself, the court ruled death to have been accidental.

Motion pictures are increasingly prominent transmitters of bizarre sexual pastimes, many of them associated with violence. The current Japanese movie, *In the Realm of the Senses,* depicts a heterosexual couple that employs choking during intercourse, a practice that kills the man. Upon his death, his loved one cuts off his penis. This film is supposedly based on an actual incident in modern Japan and it illustrates yet again the common correlation between sexuality and brutality. We shall argue (pp. 259–267) that art of this nature is not innocent and that, however much one may value "freedom of expression," a price is paid for such exciting advertisement.

LUSTFUL DEATHS: Necrophilia

The sexual drive is expressed in combination with activities that are not physiologically required to achieve sexual satisfaction. The associations are assumed to have been learned, although investigators have not been able to specify learning situations that *distinctively* produce different tastes in sexual experience. But, however sexual preferences are acquired, it is also assumed that constitutional differences predispose individuals to learn one erotic lesson rather than another (Bell, Wienberg, Hammersmith 1981, Ehrenreich 1960, Fromm 1973, Stekel 1929).

Since sexual appetite is directed, principally but not exclusively, toward others, it is not surprising that erotic lives—in fantasy and in actuality—involve conceptions of one's self in relation to others. Feelings of personal worth are linked to preferred modes of sexual gratification. These feelings move on a gradient that runs from sexual play with forms of domination and submission toward sadism,[2] masochism[3] and homicide that is sometimes accidental and sometimes intentional.

In Kotzwarra-style deaths the pleasure-seeker is the victim. The deceased is a masochist. In other perversions,[4] however, the seeker is the killer. The homicide is sadistic and, again, may be accidental or intentional. Necrophilia provides an example.

Necrophilia is a rare disorder in which individuals show an abnormal fascination with death and its symbols (Brill 1941a, 1941b). Some necrophilia appears to be relatively nonsexual and is manifested by interest in corpses, funerals and cemeteries, and, at times, in the desire to dismember corpses. Such morbid interest has been reported principally among men, but one suspects that there may be women who also exhibit this attraction to death and the dead. However, sexual necrophilia—at least as it has been reported—seems to be an ex-

---

[2] "Sadism," like masochism, gets its name from an author, Donatien Alphonse Francois Sade (1740–1814), more commonly known as the Marquis de Sade. He wrote about people who achieved sexual satisfaction by being cruel.

[3] "Masochism" derives its title from Leopold von Sacher Masoch (1836–1895), an Austrian novelist who described characters who experienced sexual pleasure from being cruelly treated. The essence of masochism is the association of erotic gratification with being made submissive and being abused. Degrees of ill-treatment range from verbal humiliation and physical submission (bondage) to the enjoyment of a variety of pains, including spanking, whipping, piercing, cutting, and excruciating enemas.

[4] "Perversion" derives from the Latin meaning "a turning away from." In major religions, the "turning away" is from acts considered to be "natural," hence the phrase, common in law, "unnatural acts." However, modern psychology and psychiatry recognize that whatever exists in nature is "natural," although it may be abnormal. In present usage, "perversion" denotes practices that are rare and condemned by a particular social order.

clusively male preference. It involves sexual gratification through associations—actual or imagined—with mortuary objects or female corpses. For example, Stekel (1929) and Karpman (1954) describe men who are aroused by funerals, who masturbate in graveyards, and who enjoy intercourse with women who dress as corpses and pretend to be dead. Some sophisticated bawdy houses cater to this perversion.

A Career

As with other pleasures, necrophilia runs a course that is bent by contingencies. Continuity is observed, and it can be assumed, but forecasts are dimmed by our inability to foresee contingencies. Not all sadism leads to homicide, but its practice enlarges lethal risk.

Smith and Braun (1978) describe an instance recently tried in Canada. Their subject, D.P., age 36, admitted to the "partial strangulation of 20 women, the last of whom he finally murdered as he desecrated her body. He copulated with the body several times after her death" (p. 260).

D.P. claimed that he always had had "friends" and that "he had no difficulty securing a certain type of sexual partner . . . many of whom tolerated his abuse and even pleaded to live with him after he had assaulted them. . . . Of the 20 women D.P. assaulted, he claimed that only eight were assaulted against their will and without forewarning" (p. 262).

Smith and Braun report that:

> D.P. had been enuretic until age seven. He had been truant from school and had run away from home on at least ten occasions. He had been sadistic toward small animals and had attacked his stepsisters with knives and heavy pans. At age eleven he had nearly succeeded in cutting off his sister's finger.
>
> He had frequently witnessed his alcoholic father beating and strangling his stepmother. . . . His father stole money from the children to pay for his liquor, frequently threatened suicide, and once carried out one of these threats to a nearly successful conclusion.
>
> [D.P.'s adult life] became characterized by a pattern of alcoholism, petty crime, promiscuity, transient work history, and chronic sexual assault of women—always when under the effects of alcohol. When apprehended and during incarceration he constantly maintained a grubby and dirty appearance. At the time of evaluation he weighed 90 lbs. (40.5 kg.) and measured 5'6" (167.6 cm.) (p. 261). Police reports describing his underwear as saturated with black dirt, blood, and numerous hairs attested to his lack of personal hygiene (p. 264).

D.P. reported an impressive variety of sexual deviations. He had indulged in homosexual prostitution, sadism, masochism (erotic self-hanging), promiscuity, exhibitionism (made blue movies of himself), incestual fantasy and sexual molesting of one of his sisters, voyeurism, and necrophilia. He was frequently impotent with women and preferred either copulating with unconscious or "frozen" women, or masturbating to the accompaniment of sadistic fantasies" (p. 262).

Despite D.P.'s bizarre history and the number of pathological symptoms (insomnia, anxiety attacks, anorexia, suicidal behavior, depression, phobias, alcoholism, insensitivity to punishment, among others), detailed medical and neurological examination revealed no striking physiological abnormalities. Under Canadian law which employs a modified McNaghten (variously spelled as "M'Naghten" or "M'Naughton") test of "sanity," D.P. was adjudged "sane," that is, that he knew the nature and quality of his acts and that they were wrong. The examining psychiatrist (Smith) testified at his trial that D.P. "did not appear to have had any conscious intent to kill or physically hurt or injure his victim" and D.P. was convicted of manslaughter.

An opinion

In Western societies, saturated as they are with theories of human conduct, there is an inventory of explanations from which one can select an interpretation of D.P. Smith and Braun provide a brief summary of these explanations (p. 260). But none of these hypotheses, plausible as they may sound, permits a differential diagnosis, an assured prognosis, or a promise of cure.

"Therapy" is routinely recommended, but the treatment available does not assure cure (Nettler 1977). Given the hazards of forecasting the behavior of "dangerous" people from theories of their action (Volume Four, Chapter 4), the soundest recommendation is to contain D.P. until age dulls his appetite.

INTENTIONAL LUSTFUL DEATHS: Sadistic Murders

We have extensive biographies, and psychological and neurological records, of persons who kill as a pleasurable expression of long-brewed hatred. Of course, hostility may be generated *without* resulting in planned homicide and, conversely, we see instances of "unpremeditated homicide" committed by long-suffering spouses and by children who kill in an explosive outburst.[5] But, in contrast to such more spontaneous violence, sadistic killers *intend* murder. They kill with rage, but with rage that is often remarkably controlled—that is, aware of risks and, hence, effective.

Sadistic careers are marked early in their course by an intertwining of hatred with sexual fantasy. The sadist's hatred is expressed in mutilation of victims and by delight in using helpless bodies for sexual purposes. Sadistic murderers frequently have exhibited joy in cruelty from boyhood. Youthful anger is spent on such victims as cats, dogs, birds, and babies.

As far as we now know, sadistic killers are always men, and relatively young ones. Their histories show a similarity in that, by various routes, these men have come to hate their mothers and, by indirection, all women. They have no experience of a reciprocated loving relationship with a female. Characteristically, they have had no normal heterosexual relations and they feel that they might be impotent with a live woman. They often are.

These people grow up as "loners." They have few, if any, boyhood friends and they do not participate willingly in social or athletic activities in school. They are usually not aggressive toward teachers or their peers, and they frequently present the quiet demeanor of an "overcontrolled" person, as Megargee (1966) has described him. But their fantasies indulge the violence they would like to ventilate. Their fantasies combine images of brutality, domination, and sexual gratification. Masturbation is accompanied by images of debasing, cutting, and killing women.

For such men, the act of killing a woman is itself sexually stimulating. The preferred method is strangulation and it is often accompanied by ejaculation. Many sadistic murderers have sexual intercourse, in varied fashion, with the corpse before or after mutilating it.

These hate-filled men are sometimes caught after their first murder—usually by "luck" (p. 135)—but, if they are not apprehended, such sadistic killers are apt to repeat their crimes (Lunde 1975, p. 53).

The distinctive significance of sadistic killers is that they commit "butcher murders" without being psychotic. By legal standards, they are sane. By psychiatric standards, they are in touch with reality. They do not kill under the direction of a delusion, as do some assassins (pp. 163–168). They have no marked history of "mental illness," if by "mental illness" one means neurotic or psychotic manifestations

---

[5] See pp. 134–137 on the ambiguity of "planned and unplanned" crime.

or any "psychic" aberrations other than their sadistic daydreams and cruel acts.

Example: Ed Kemper

Ed Kemper was one of several mass murderers who, by coincidence we trust, made Santa Cruz, California, the scene of grisly crimes in the early 1970s.

Ed's parents separated when he was seven years old and Ed lived with his mother and two sisters. He grew to be a giant—6'9" and 280 pounds. He was always the biggest boy in his class and physically and socially awkward. Early on he exhibited sadistic tendencies. One of Kemper's examining psychiatrists, Donald Lunde (1975) describes his career:

> [As a child] Ed was fascinated with execution; he would stage his own execution in the form of a . . . "game" in which he had [his sister] lead him to a chair, blindfold him, and pull an imaginary lever, after which he would writhe about as if dying in a gas chamber. One Christmas [his sister] received a doll from her grandparents, and when she went to play with it later found the head and hands had been cut off. . . . Another time, she recalled teasing him about a second grade teacher whom she suspected he admired. She taunted him by saying "Why don't you go and kiss her," and was puzzled at his reply: "If I kiss her I would have to kill her first."
>
> Ed described himself as "a weapons freak" and recounted to me recurring fantasies of killing women, his mother in particular. Many times over the years he had, in fact, entered her bedroom at night carrying a weapon and had contemplated killing her.
>
> His first actual killings, however, were of animals. He tortured and killed cats. When Ed was 13, the family cat disappeared; his mother found it in the garbage can—decapitated and cut into pieces.
>
>   *   *   *
>
> In addition to his fantasies of killing his mother, Ed also imagined such things as killing everyone in town and having sexual relations with corpses. As a boy of 9, 10, or 11 he would sneak out of the house at night and from a distance stare at women walking down the street, fantasizing about his desire to love and be loved by them. Even at this early age, however, he felt that relationships with women would be impossible for him. The only kind of activity with women that he could fantasize, with any hope of success, was killing them.
>
> Years later he explained that he "felt very inadequate sexually and sensually and socially. . . . I couldn't follow through with the male end of the responsibility so my fantasies became . . . if I killed them, you

know, they couldn't reject me as a man. It was more or less making a doll out of a human being . . . and carrying out my fantasies with a doll, a living human doll."

Ed ran away from home when 13, hoping to go live with his father. But his father made it clear that Ed was not welcome and returned him to his mother. Since she was now finding Ed very difficult to handle and was also planning to remarry, she sent him, protesting and against his will, to live with his paternal grandparents on an isolated ranch in California. . . . Ed soon transferred his fantasies about his mother to his domineering grandmother, first shooting and then stabbing her repeatedly. Ed's grandfather was away at the time. Upon his return, Ed shot and killed him before he had a chance to enter the house and discover what had happened to his wife. Ed then telephoned his mother, told her what he had done, sat down, and waited for the police to arrive. . . .

Since he was a minor, Kemper was turned over to the California Youth Authority. . . . He spent 4 of the next 5 years in a maximum security mental hospital. . . . In 1969, when he was 21, he was . . . discharged to his mother, a disastrous situation from Kemper's point of view. (There were no psychiatrists or psychologists on the parole board, and in this particular case no consideration was given to psychiatric reports about Ed's feelings toward his mother.) Upon his release, he received no psychological or psychiatric treatment.

Repeated arguments with his mother again erupted, reviving his old fantasies about killing her. Substitute victims before had been dolls, cats, and finally his grandparents. Now his victims would be college girls. (His mother had moved to Santa Cruz, California, and was on the administrative staff of the University of California at Santa Cruz. A reserved parking sticker which she obtained for Ed's car gave him easy access to UCSC coeds.)

Between May 7, 1972, and April 21, 1973, Kemper killed eight women by shooting, stabbing, and strangulation. He acted out his childhood fantasies by cutting off limbs of the victims, attempting sexual relations with the corpses, and committing acts of cannibalism. The first six victims were young female hitchhikers. Despite his past record, police never suspected Kemper. In fact, Kemper associated regularly with the local police at a Santa Cruz bar. On April 21, 1973, the day before Easter, Kemper killed his mother and one of her friends. After decapitation, he cut out his mother's larynx and put it down the garbage disposal. "This seemed appropriate," he said, "as much as she'd bitched and screamed and yelled at me over the years."

He left an anonymous note in her apartment to taunt the police and drove off, fantasizing a nationwide manhunt for the "coed killer." He drove nonstop as far as Pueblo, Colorado, listening all the while for an "all-points bulletin" on the radio. After three days passed without any radio bulletins or newspaper headlines, Kemper called the Santa Cruz police to turn himself in. They told him to call back. He did, again and again, each time giving more details about the killings in an effort to impress them. Finally, he convinced them to have him arrested. When the police picked him up, he was waiting in a public phone booth.

Kemper was . . . sentenced to life imprisonment. He was found legally sane. . . . (Reproduced with permission from *Murder and Madness* by Donald T. Lunde. W.W. Norton & Company, Inc., New York, N.Y. Copyright © 1975, 1976 by Donald T. Lunde).

Lessons

A description of Ed's history and his feelings make his crimes plausible—after the fact. They do not make his crimes predictable.

Childhood cruelty to animals and people is premonitory, but, as Volume One, Figure 3.1, illustrates, an unknown proportion of cruel children do not become murderous adolescents.

There is not enough that is *distinctive* in Kemper's development (in his "environment," for example, or even in his attitudes) that can explain his crimes if, by explanation, we mean specification of necessary and sufficient causes. We can "account for" Ed's crimes only empathetically, or sympathetically, but not scientifically.

An additional lesson flows from Kemper's career. Sadistic killers do not wear emblems of their intent. There are no clearly visible stigmata. Girls who accept rides from such genial chaps cannot tell by looking at them whether they are "nice guys" or sadists.

Example: Tom Bean

In the early 1960s, an attractive young mother, whom we'll call Jane, moved from western Canada to Reno, Nevada. She moved to obtain a divorce—a difficult procedure at the time in Canada, but an easy process in Nevada. Reno also appealed to Jane because she had been an Olympic ski contestant and the Sierra Nevada above Reno offers a variety of winter resorts.

Jane's mother, herself an accomplished skier, moved nearby. Jane got a job as secretary-bookkeeper in an abattoir and quickly made new friends. She dated frequently and usually left her infant son with a baby-sitter who lived across town. If Jane was out late, it was her habit to leave her child overnight at the baby-sitter's and retrieve him the next day.

One Saturday morning after a date Jane did not show up at the baby-sitter's. The sitter 'phoned Jane's residence several times, received no answer, and became worried as the day wore on. She reported her anxiety to the police who drove to Jane's suite in a row of "town houses." Their rings and calls aroused no one in Jane's apartment, although police noted her baby-blue Triumph in the driveway. The officers aroused the housing superintendent and, with his passkey, opened Jane's door. The first man to enter almost stepped on a human heart. Jane's dismembered body was lying near her hope chest in the living room. She had received the "rapist's slash," cut from vulva to sternum.

The crime attracted international attention and the police began the required, but futile, interrogation of "all the men she had recently known." Her former husband was grilled. Suspects were traced as far away as European ski centers.

Reno is a 24-hour town and many of the dealers in its "gaming" (never "gambling") industry are women. With a "butcher-murderer" at large, women on swing and graveyard shifts were apprehensive about going to work. The press demanded action, but detectives and the district attorney's office were stumped. They had no idea where next to look for a suspect, but they were helped by "luck."

The culprit had committed a mistake, the kind of blunder that psychoanalysts interpret as "an unconscious cry to be caught." After the orgy, the killer had stolen Jane's clock-radio. Jane's mother, in making an inventory of the house, reported the loss to the police who began a routine sweep of pawn shops. They found Jane's radio in one of these shops ticketed to a "Tom Bean."

Tom turned out to be a 17-year-old high school youth of pleasant appearance and cooperative demeanor who readily agreed to go downtown for questioning. Arresting police did not think a nice-looking and apparently sane fellow like Tom could be their man and they were expecting some plausible explanation of the pawned radio. As they led Tom into the precinct building, the boy broke and ran, and the incredible began to seem possible.

Tom was living with his divorced father in a "trailer park." Tom's memory of his mother was that she was a "drunken bitch," and he blamed her for his parents' separation. This did not mean that Tom enjoyed his father, who was irritable, hostile, and no great friend to Tom. But, in the fashion we have seen so often, Tom transferred his hatred of his mother to all women.

Tom was a quiet boy in school. He was no brawler. He did average, or better, work and was respectful of his teachers who, of course, liked him. He did not participate in extracurricular activities and had no girl friends, but, then, he was young and well-behaved and such "symptoms" cannot be read with assurance. Besides, they are no one's business.

About a year before Jane's murder, Tom had been living with his father in Salt Lake City where he had one of the few dates in his life. His last date ended on a lover's lane where Tom began to choke the girl he was "loving." The girl screamed and fellows from nearby cars came to her assistance. Since Tom had a clean record, and since his father promised to leave town for a job in Reno, the juvenile court judge in Salt Lake City placed the boy on probation with the comforting proviso that he have a psychological examination in Reno's free clinic.

The examiner's record concludes with the judgment that "Tom is extremely dangerous." This judgment is based on cues which, as we know, can be premonitory without being predictive.

Tom's hostility, concealed under a passive exterior, was revealed in his "projections" on psychological instruments designed to "pull out" feelings about oneself and the world by indirection, rather than by interrogation. But, given the premises of our criminal law (one is innocent until proven guilty of a *criminal act*), and given the modest validity of the signs by which we forecast action (a high proportion of false positives occurs in relation to true positives), courts cannot contain potentially dangerous people on the judgment of a psychologist.

The trigger

On the night of Jane's death, Tom's father had come home from work, flipped his son a silver dollar, and told him to "get lost, go to a movie or somep'n. I got a dame comin' over."

The insult, and the repeated demonstration that women were sluts, triggered the latent hatred Tom felt for females. He decided to "kill myself a woman." He made a garotte of heavy wire with handles fashioned from halves of a clothespin. He put the garotte in his pocket and went out into the night looking for a woman to murder. He had walked for hours up and down streets and back alleys until, about one in the morning, he walked down the lane behind Jane's apartment. There he saw ladies' panties and hosiery on the clothesline. A woman must be inside. Tom went to the backdoor, tried it, found it unlocked, and crept quietly through the back porch and kitchen to a hallway with bedrooms on either side. He opened one door, saw a woman in bed, and moved silently across the hall to peer in the other bedroom. No one was there. With his way clear, Tom entered Jane's bedroom. He put the garotte around her neck and got astride her. Jane awakened with time only to cry, "Don't! My baby!"

Tom strangled his victim, had intercourse with the corpse, and then cut it open. He had never had a girl "all his own" and he now enjoyed possession. He took the body into the living room, put a record on the player, and danced with the corpse.

He noticed Jane's sports car in the driveway and thought it would be fun to take her for a ride—just like being on a date. The bloody condition of the body discouraged this idea, however, so Tom took a refreshing tour of the Sierra foothills by himself.

He returned to Jane's apartment and was going to dance again with the corpse. He set the body upright on a hope chest while he went to put a record on the machine. The body slumped over and this angered Tom. He then cut off some limbs, cut out her heart, and left.

On trial

At Tom's trial psychiatrists for the prosecution used the record of Tom's planfulness and his sensitivity to risk as evidence of his sanity. In Nevada, McNaughton's rule is the test of sanity and this means that a person is deemed to be legally sane if he knew the nature and quality of his act or that what he did was wrong (see pp. 149–150).

Tom passed this test of sanity, of course, but, in addition, he gave no sign of psychosis. He was in touch with reality. He suffered no delusions or hallucinations; he suffered only from hatred.

Despite such evidence, psychiatrists for the defense attempted to establish existence of an ill-defined "mental disorder" as cause of the killing on the ground that Tom had committed a "senseless" and brutal murder. According to the defense, the crime was so bizarre that it must in itself be indicative of a "disease."

"Do you mean to suggest," defense counsel asked a psychiatrist for the prosecution, "that a man could do what that boy has done and not be sick?"

Defense was arguing that heinous crimes must be caused by "mental disease" because the crime itself bespeaks such disorder. This reasoning defines the cause of an event by the nature of the event which the cause is supposed to explain. This is poor logic, but it makes for sympathetic argument.

Causes, of course, are assumed to be identifiable *independently* of the effects they are nominated to explain.

Defense attempts did not prevail. Tom was convicted of first degree murder and sentenced to hang. The state governor commuted this sentence to life imprisonment.

Lessons

1. Rage can seethe beneath a calm exterior. Again, we cannot assuredly identify a potential sadistic killer by his appearance.

2. Premonitory signs are warnings, but they are not guarantees. Safety rests in counting on continuity.

3. Lock your doors.

Example: The Moors Murders

Ian Brady, 27, and Myra Hindley, 23, were tried in April, 1966, in Chester, England, for the murders of a ten-year-old girl and two boys of 12 and 17 years. The case was dubbed "The Moors Murder Trial" because the killers buried their victims on the moors outside town.

Brady had the background that by now seems "classic" among sadistic killers. He was illegitimate and never knew his father. Although he was reared by an apparently affectionate foster-mother who treated him no differently from her own four children, he showed early signs of enjoying cruelty. By the time he was ten, he was torturing cats and burying them alive. A childhood acquaintance commented that, "The cats weren't worth bothering with after he'd finished with them. He always carried a flick-knife and was a great one for a carry-on" (cited by Johnson 1967, p. 76). This acquaintance remembers Brady well because Brady once tied him to a post, stacked newspapers around his feet, and set them on fire. The intended victim was able to slip his leash and escape.

Brady was of average intelligence, but uninterested in school. He was, like many sadists, a loner, unpopular, and poor at sports. He did show some musical gifts, however, and was interested in reading. He particularly liked to read about Nazis and cruelty.

He first appeared in court at age 13 for housebreaking. He was released on probation and back in court at age 14. He was again given probation but, this time, he was returned to his biological mother in the vain hope that "real" mothering would change him. When he was 16 he was convicted of more important thefts than previously and sent to a juvenile detention center.

It cannot be said that the "correctional institution" reformed Brady. Although he worked at legitimate jobs after his release, he continued to enjoy fantasies of cruelty associated with sexuality.

When he and Myra Hindley became lovers, he introduced her to the world of "kinky" sex. Brady and Hindley saturated themselves with pornography and used the "dirty" stories and pictures as sexual stimulants. They collected a large library of sadomasochistic books and, in their torture-killings, put into practice some of the ideas they had learned from the Marquis de Sade.

Hindley's teenage sister, Maureen, married David Smith, a man two years younger than herself. The two couples became close and partied together frequently. Smith himself had a record of criminal violence and Brady proselytized him and his wife for the pleasures of violent sexuality. Smith was an accomplice in at least one of the murders but, when Brady's activities seemed to be "getting out of hand," Smith and his wife called the police.

The pleasures that Brady and Hindley enjoyed, and wished to share with the Smiths, were to capture young prey, male or female, torture them, abuse them sexually, and to engage themselves in sexual play during or after the violence. Johnson (1967), who attended the trial, reports:

> On Boxing Day [1964], a man, or men, enticed Lesley Ann Downey into a van. She was stripped, gagged, photographed in pornographic poses, and then murdered. Hindley and Brady buried her naked on the moors, just as they had earlier buried the boy, John Kilbride. . . . During the tormenting of Lesley Ann Downey, a very pretty little girl, small for her age, Hindley and Brady took a tape-recording of her screams and pleas for mercy, fancifully concluding the performance with seasonal music—Jolly Old Saint Nicholas and Little Drummer Boy. The tape was played in the open court. It lasted over sixteen minutes (p. 14).

Hindley and Brady pleaded "not guilty." They were convicted of first degree murder and sentenced to life in prison. Their case raises the issue, to be addressed later (pp. 141–142), of the extent to which art, including pornography, influences action.

Example: Homosexual Lust Murder

On August 8, 1973, Elmer Wayne Henley, Jr., then 17, called Houston police to the home of 33-year-old Dean Corll to report that he had killed Corll in what later would be ruled to be self-defense. Under police questioning, which became the grounds for an unsuccessful appeal, Henley confessed to luring boys to Corll who tortured, raped, and killed them. Henley led police to the graves of 27 such victims. He was convicted for his part in the killing of six of these boys and sentenced to 594 years in prison.

Henley's history illustrates again the operation of *plausible, sufficient* causes of his conduct, none of which are *necessary* causes of his career.

Henley's parents were divorced. Before their separation, Henley's father had beaten him several times. After divorce, the father was himself charged with other assaults.

During the time of domestic troubles, Henley was involved in thefts and drug offenses and came to the attention of juvenile authorities. Henley's use of intoxicants expanded from booze and marijuana to hallucinogenic agents and acrylic sniffing.

Corll recruited Henley when the latter was 14 years old. Henley, in turn, brought some of his junior high school "mates" into the circle. The lure was dope, sex, and money. Corll paid Henley $200 for each boy brought to Corll's house or van and more "if they were good looking."

Victims were easy to find. Dropouts, runaways, and hitchikers provided a ready source. Corll and Henley would cruise in Corll's padded van with couch in back and pick up suitable hitchhikers. Henley acted as bait because, as he put it, "I had long hair and all and it was easier for me to talk with them" (Montgomery 1974a).

Conflicts

The trial of Henley illuminates two of the running debates about the management of justice in Western courts. One debate concerns the allocation of "responsibility." As might have been expected, Henley's defense tried to excuse him by arguing that he was not "responsible" for his acts. Pleas were entered that he was incompetent to stand trial and that he was "not guilty by reason of insanity." "Insanity" was attributed to the ingestion of psychedelic chemicals during the criminal episodes. It was argued that this rendered the accused less culpable than if he had been "in full possession of his senses." This tactic failed.

A second issue raised by this case is that of the conflict between demand for a "fair trial" and demand for a "free press." Journalists so publicized the case that venue was changed from Houston to San Antonio on the ground that Henley could not be judged fairly in his home town. However, upon removal of the trial, journalists again tried "to do their job," which included attempting to interview jurors' families. The trial became a major spectator attraction in San Antonio and this provoked the usual quarrel about whether "the media" create interest or merely reflect it (Montgomery 1974b). The sensational atmosphere led to a defense motion for a mistrial. Judge Preston H. Dial denied this motion and, in so doing, warned news personnel that attempts to talk with jurors or their families would make them liable to contempt of court. The conflict continues between the "right" to an unbiased trial and the "right" to publish news which normally includes more than facts.[6]

---

[6] Jacques Ellul's study of *Propaganda* (1965) demonstrates that all relevant facts about a "news item" can never be reported, much less assimilated by consumers of news, and that journalistic interpretation of events may distort them as much as it accurately reflects them. See, in particular, Ellul's pages 138–147.

ART AND LUST

The fact that some human beings associate sexual satisfaction with violent action is attested by art. In recent years, license to express everything has included freedom to produce and sell literature, motion pictures, and plays that associate sexuality with brutality. Competition in this lustful market has moved producers to become, as they put it, "more daring, creative, and explicit."

During the 1960s, for example, London theaters exhibited plays that depicted the torture of a priest, the pitchforking and beheading of an agricultural labourer, the kicking to death of a helpless old tramp, the eye-gouging of an elderly nobleman by the spurs of his enemy, the strangling of a nurse by her patient, and the torment and murder of a baby in a perambulator by a gang of louts, who roll it in its own excrement and then stone it to death (Brien 1965, Kitchin 1966, pp. 21–28).

The baby-killing play was written by Edward Bon and titled, "Saved." It aroused protests from many drama critics, but it was defended by its director, William Gaskill, who called it "a triumph to have these things put on the stage."

The "triumph" of sexually stimulating violence reaches a "new high" in the manufacture of "snuff movies." These are motion pictures that culminate in the planned killing ("snuffing") of the female as part of the sexual adventure. The killing is sometimes depicted with one male murderer and sometimes with a group of participants and their observers.

Attempts to censor such movies run into conflict with business interests in league with "liberal" ideals that claim a "right" to free expression. As we shall see (pp. 259–267), defenders of this right claim that there is no good evidence that such art encourages its imitation, but people in general doubt this (Baker & Ball 1969, p. 379, Martin 1977).

Lessons

Social movements that claim to be "liberating" are difficult to criticize because, in the Western context, "liberation" is a good word. It is also a vague word, and one cannot decide whether to favor any particular "liberation" until one knows who is to be freed to do what, with which probable consequences.

The general plea for "liberation" gains support from the cultural relativism which, we have noted (Volume One, Chapter 7), characterizes social science. Cultural relativism includes moral relativism. This produces a difficulty.

The trouble is that, if one assumes that "one moral code is as good as another," one destroys the foundation from which to evaluate courses of action. Even reference to likely consequences becomes irrelevant because consequences themselves are subject to moral interpretation and a persistently maintained relativism allows no ground for assessment of effects.

It is doubtful, of course, that any person who affiliates with others—and this *excludes* psychopathic "jungle cats"—can be a consistent moral relativist. Some moral foundation undergirds our relationships.

This comment is deserved because the demand for complete "sexual liberation," a demand peculiar to the Western world, is one with probable consequences. It is probable that advancing sexual license anesthetizes moral reflexes generally.

In reporting the Moors Murder Trial, Pamela Hansford Johnson (1967, p. 18) observes that:

> When the Nazis took on the government of Poland, they flooded the Polish bookstalls with pornography. This is a fact. Why did they do so? They did so on the theory that to make the individual conscious only of the need for personal sensation would make the social combination of forces more difficult. . . . The Nazis' scheme was the deliberate use of pornography to the ends of social castration. The theory was—and it is worth considering—that if you permit all things for self-gratification, you are likely to encourage withdrawal from any sort of corporate responsibility.

There are good reasons to assume that sexual depravity has moral consequences *beyond* the realm of the sexual. The good reasons for this assumption can be found in historical studies, in contemporary careers, and in the fact that *all* revolutionary societies attempt to build moral community and, in this process, *restrict* exercise of the sexual appetite.

No revolutionary movement is morally relativistic. Although Marxists argue, incorrectly, that morals only (merely) defend class interests, revolutionaries assume the relativity of others' morals but deny the relativity of their own.

The point

The point made in our discussion of lustful murder is that human sexuality is so saturated with feelings of dominance and submission, as well as with such other emotions as affection and sharing, that our sexuality can readily be channeled into violent satisfactions.

Sexual license operates as a disinhibitor. It releases one from the restriction of *other* moral lessons. It challenges *their* validity as well as the validity of sexual inhibition, and it is often used in league with "comforting chemicals" to demoralize one's prey.

This argument will be repeated when we discuss killing for ideals and the possible role of "moral atmospheres" in affecting rates of physical attack.

Careers in lustful homicide demonstrate that, with graduated practice, we can develop emotional calluses so that what used to offend us morally no longer produces an effect. The poet Alexander Pope (1688–1744) told us as much in his *Essay on Man* (1734):

> Vice is a monster of so frightful mien,
> As, to be hated, needs but to be seen;
> Yet seen too oft, familiar with her face,
> We first endure, then pity, then embrace.

8 HOMICIDAL ROUTES: **LUNACY**

Abstract • Sanity is a general term for mental health. As with all definitions of health, sanity rests on a conception of proper function. ◦ Lunacy is a non-specific term for mental disorder. ◦ The legal profession works with a more specific definition of mental disorder, that of insanity. ◦ Psychiatry and psychology, in attending to individual killers, work principally with concepts of psychosis and psychopathy. • The legal concept of insanity rests on moral assumptions. These assumptions affect objectives of the criminal law. ◦ Common objectives of the criminal law are to do justice, to protect "society" through deterrence, and to protect "society" by reinforcing a moral code. ◦ Satisfaction of these objectives is qualified by moral definitions of "responsibility." ◦ Tests of insanity attempt to apply these moral definitions in excusing "incompetent" individuals from culpability. • Two qualities of lunacy, in particular, provide channels to homicide: psychosis and psychopathy. ◦ Psychosis is defined. ◦ This definition has flexible boundaries. The boundaries move with group-support and competence. Strange beliefs are protected against the charge of lunacy when they are group-supported. They are open to the charge of lunacy as they are idiosyncratic and voiced by incompetent individuals. ◦ People who are psychotic are less than sound in different ways, in differing degrees, and in differing patterns. Impairment may be partial or total, episodic or chronic. ◦ Signs of paranoid schizophrenia and of paranoia are described. • Assassins are distinguished from terrorists. ◦ Some assassins suffer psychotic delusions. ◦ Examples of psychotic assassins include several murderers of American presidents. ◦ Borderline lunatics are also described as they behave murderously.

SOME MURDEROUS PEOPLE ARE CRAZY and the quality of their lunacy seems connected to their homicides either as cause to effect or as part of the content of their lunacy. This means that "homicidal maniacs" may be said to be *caused* to kill by their mental disorder—as jorunalists commonly assume—or that killing is but one facet of the complex of feeling and thinking that defines a particular lunacy. Whichever interpretation is given, the idea that some homicide is a function of insanity requires comments on being sane.

DEFINITIONS

Sanity is a general term. It has roots in Latin where to be sane is to be sound. It is to be healthy. The notion of "health," in turn, derives from ideas of being "whole."

These interchangeable terms rest on some conception of *proper function.* Whether one is speaking of mental health or physical health, "wholeness" and "soundness" imply that we agree on a definition of what the organ or animal ought to be able to do, that is, how it should function. As we shall see, this requirement is a source of difficulty when we attempt to define "sound minds" as opposed to sound bodies, organs, or machines.

From the basic notion of sanity, other words "spin off" to describe malfunctions of thoughts and feelings. "Crazy," "nuts," and "loony" are common words that are useful as evaluators despite their vague reference. In fact, it is vagueness that allows such terms to be useful as expressions of disapproval.[1]

"Loony" is a slang derivative from lunacy and lunatic. Lunacy (from *Luna,* the Roman goddess of the moon) used to refer to intermittent craziness associated with phases of the moon. With the decay of that causal notion, lunacy is employed today as a non-specific term for mental disorder.

The legal and psychiatric professions have attempted more precise definitions of sound mental functioning and, hence, of disorders of "the mind."[2] Law works with the idea of insanity. Psychiatry and psychology—when they attend to homicidal criminals—work principally, but not exclusively, with ideas of psychosis and psychopathy.

INSANITY

Insanity is a word in the popular vocabulary, but it has a special meaning as defined by law. At law it refers to "mental incompetence" where that incompetence is due to an *impairment* of "the mind" rather than to an age (infancy) at which the mind is deemed to be "not fully developed." The legal objective in excusing insane persons from accountability rests on moral assumptions.

---

[1] To call someone "nuts" or "loony" is to express disapproval, of course. But to call someone or something "crazy" may express approval as when one says, "I'm crazy about old Bogart movies" or "Darling, what a wonderful, crazy idea!"

[2] "Mind" is another vague word with questionable descriptive utility. When philosophers and psychologists attempt to define "the mind," they write about feeling, willing, sensing, thinking, and conscious doing. Thus Susanne Langer (1967) titles her study, *Mind: An Essay on Human Feeling,* and Gilbert Ryle (1949, p. 199) claims that "to talk of a person's mind . . . is to talk of the person's abilities, liabilities and inclinations to do and undergo certain sorts of things and of the doing and undergoing of these things in the ordinary world."

Moral Assumptions and Legal Objectives

The criminal law has evolved out of moral concerns. The morality that has shaped Western criminal law is Judaeo-Christian and this code conceives of most human beings as able to control their actions. This conception assumes, too, that people who are competent to control themselves in keeping with the code deserve praise as they do so and blame as they do not.

Blaming individuals who do not control themselves is believed to serve socially useful functions. These functions are objectives mentioned, in various mixtures, as justifying application of punitive[3] criminal law. Reasons commonly given for punishing criminals include arguments that (1) justice requires assigning blame; that (2) societal protection through deterrence requires punishment; and that (3) societal protection through moral reinforcement requires condemnation of offenders. These justifications are discussed in greater detail in Volume Four, but here a few comments are required.

1. Doing Justice

A common sense of justice requires that wrongs *not* go unnoticed. This sense of justice asks that wrongs be condemned, and condemned in a public ritual.

The oldest notion of criminal justice is that of *retribution*. Retribution means "to give in return." It is the moral demand that the harm a person does be returned to him or her in equal degree, if not in kind. It is a principle found in the laws of many cultures, notably in Mosaic and Roman law, and it is expressed in the code of the Babylonian King Hammurabi (1760 B.C.) that recommended "an eye for an eye, a tooth for a tooth."

Retribution is not to be confused with *revenge*. Retribution seeks to *balance* the pain returned to a wrongdoer against the harm she or he has done; revenge knows no balance. Retribution may be viewed as a state-imposed punishment that mollifies the common desire for revenge by substituting a more balanced return for the sometimes endless injury that revenge stimulates.

Retribution has been attempted in many societies through *restitution*. Restitution is the idea of restoring the balance between crim-

---

[3] Some modern defenders of criminal law justify its application as necessary to *rehabilitate* offenders. Such advocates do not agree whether punishment may "rehabilitate" certain classes of criminal. But, most frequently, those who justify control of individuals under the criminal law as part of a correctional program believe that their motives are not punitive. However, from the point of view of the offender who is to be forcibly reformed, rehabilitative efforts may seem like punishment. (See p. 153, fn. 6.)

inal and victim by having the criminal repay the costs of injury to the victim—or to the victim's surrogates such as relatives or "society." The criminal law of some countries recognizes restitution as a proper penalty and also as a possible means of rehabilitation. The Canadian Criminal Code, for example, allows restitution as a form of sentence, but it is a sentence that has rarely been applied. However, it is now being urged that restitution be more frequently used as a sentence and that property offenders in particular be given the option of working out their "debt" to their victims instead of going to prison (Katz et al. 1976, Nader 1975, Smith 1965).

2. Protecting by Deterring

A second justification of blaming and punishing assumes that societies may be protected from some amount of crime through the deterrent effect of governmentally applied pains. Legal imposition of punishment is believed to add a cost to crime in the hope that cost will outweigh reward and thus deter the present offender and others from similar crimes. When this assumption is employed to change the conduct of the person punished, the justification is that of *special or individual deterrence*. When the objective of punishing one offender is to inhibit others who might be tempted to commit similar crimes, the justification is that of *general deterrence*.

Kantian moralists regard punishing one person to deter another as evil since it uses one individual as an *instrument* to achieve results with others. Whether or not one adopts Kant's code, governments continue to *use* individuals. They use this individual as a lesson for that one, and they use individuals in other ways, some of which are called "service to the community."

Present purposes do not require detailed assessment of the deterrent effects of punishment. The library of research on this subject is large (Berns 1979, Blumstein et al. 1978, Cousineau 1976, Zimring & Hawkins 1973). The outcome of these many studies is that punishment, and its threat, *do inhibit* many people from committing many kinds of crime. All societies assume this. However, no one knows the *threshold* of pain required to deter particular individuals from committing specific crimes under various circumstances. No one can set an exact figure on the number of potential offenders inhibited by any particular threat from committing any particular crime. As we have seen (Volume One, Chapter 6), pains come in various dimensions—physical, psychological, financial—and neither the quality nor the quantity of a "pain" has the same impact upon different individuals. It follows that *judgment* of risk and the *value* placed upon an estimated risk also vary among individuals.

3. Protecting by Reinforcing Morals

A third justification for legally assigning responsibility is that it is a proper part of the ritual of determining punishment, where punishment is used to *symbolize* what we are for and what we are against. Here the state's punitive action is defended as required to maintain a moral sense against its challengers. The theater in which trial and condemnation of the criminal is acted out is believed to be educational; it is held to reinforce an always fragile conception of right and wrong.

Responsibility and Capacity

We need not elaborate on the philosophic disputes about these justifications of the criminal law. The point here is that the Judeao-Christian ethic that underwrites the law holds people "responsible" *only when* they are deemed to be "competent." Competence refers, again, to the ability to control one's actions. This, in turn, is believed to require ability to think and feel appropriately, ability to reason, ability to foresee the likely consequences of one's acts—ability, in short, *to know what one is doing.*

Infants, idiots, and lunatics are deemed to be incapable of knowing what they are doing. Consequently, they are excused from legal accountability.

There is little quarrel about definitions of infants and idiots. *Nonage* excuses "legal infants" (usually those under the age of seven) from culpability. However, the idea of *juvenile delinquency* extends this notion and limits the blameworthiness of young people (usually those from seven to 16 or 18 years of age) on the ground that they are not fully competent to control their behavior. The concept of juvenile delinquency is more controversial than definitions of idiocy and legal infancy. It is a classification peculiar to Western countries and some industrialized Oriental states, and a category *not* to be found in the laws of most Asian, Middle Eastern, and Latin countries (United Nations 1965a, 1965b).

Of all the definitions of incompetence, lunacy is the most difficult. Since lunacy is defined as "maladaptive or inappropriate functioning of the mind," quarrels ensue about who is crazy and who is sane, and how we can tell the difference. Legislators have attempted to establish rules with which to resolve the quarrel, but none of the rules satisfies all parties in this moral dispute.

TESTS OF INSANITY

The legal definition of insanity is an embarrassment to a profession which, like the law, depends so heavily upon the precision of its terms. The word "insane" is avoided by psychologists and psychiatrists, although legal tests of sanity seem as clear, or even more clear, than psychiatric judgments. Nevertheless, the law has looked to professional students of the mind for assistance in judging the competence of defendants. In the Netherlands, Denmark, Norway, and Sweden, the test of insanity is simply the testimony of psychiatrists. In Belgium, France, Italy, and Switzerland, the test is psychiatric opinion concerning the offender's ability to know what he was doing at the time of his or her crime and to control such behavior.

In Commonwealth countries and the United States, legislators have attempted to guide judges, juries, and psychiatrists by formulating specific tests to be used in assessing competence. The multiplicity of such tests need not be described here (see Nettler 1978, pp. 42–48), but a fundamental contest deserves comment. This is the contest between the relatively old *McNaughton rules* and a variety of more recent tests advanced through the "mental health" movement.

The McNaughton Rules

Daniel McNaughton[4] was a wood-worker from Glasgow who suffered from persistent, but vague, beliefs that "the Tories" were persecuting him. He traveled to London where, on January 20, 1843, he fired a shot at a man he believed to be the Prime Minister, Sir Robert Peel, but who was the Minister's secretary, Edward Drummond. Drummond died five days later and McNaughton was on trial by February 2, only 13 days after his attempted assassination of Peel. Medical testimony at the trial was such that the judge dismissed the charge and instructed the jury to find the defendant not guilty by reason of insanity. This decision aroused such expression of concern in the House of Lords and from Queen Victoria as to call for a judicial explication of the rules by which insanity was to be recognized. The McNaughton rules have influenced the legal definition of insanity in English-speaking countries for more than a century and have only recently been superseded by a variety of tests more congenial to psychiatrists and psychologists. The McNaughton rules state that:

> [E]very man is to be presumed to be sane, and . . . that to establish a defence on the ground of insanity, it must be clearly proved that, at the time of the committing of the act, the party accused was labouring under such a defect of reason, from disease of the mind, as not to know the na-

---

[4] McNaughton's name appears variously spelled in different documents, but it will be recognized as M'Naghten and M'Naughton.

ture and quality of the act he was doing; or if he did know it, that he did not know he was doing what was wrong (Goldstein 1967, p. 45).

Lawyers work with words and they are employed to argue what words mean. However, as one cynic put it after suffering from violated contracts, "Lawyers are paid to prove that clear language does not mean what it says."

Common words, of course, are seldom clear. They usually point to many referents and their meanings are obscured by their covering of emotional connotation. Thus each of the key terms in McNaughton's rules has been debated. "Disease of the mind" is vague. "Wrong" may mean morally so or legally so. "To know" means many things. Critics of the McNaughton rules claim that "knowing" is interpreted under those tests as referring only to intellectual comprehension. Such critics have wanted to add "emotional appreciation" of one's acts to the meaning of "knowing" what one is doing. In Canada, then, the "knowledge test" employed with the McNaughton rules has been broadened so that "the act must necessarily involve more than mere knowledge that the act is being committed; there must be an appreciation of the factors involved in the act and a mental capacity to measure and foresee the consequences of the violent conduct" (Royal Commission 1955, pp. 12–13).

Mental Health Tests

Criticism of the McNaughton rules has increased as psychiatry and psychology have grown in authority. With expanded ideas about mental health and mental disorder,[5] it has been recognized that, by the McNaughton tests, psychotic people could be declared sane. The American judge, Biggs (1955), has documented cases of this sort. For example, In People v. Willard, 1907, Willard was formally declared insane by a California court, but he became enraged at the commitment proceedings and killed a sheriff who tried to block his escape. Under McNaughton's rules, which applied at that time, Willard was judged to have known the nature and quality of his act and to have known that it was wrong, and he was hanged as a legally sane person despite a diagnosis of "alcoholic paranoia."

---

[5] "Mental disorder" is a better descriptive term than "mental disease" since, in many aberrations of thought and feeling, no specific disease agent can be discerned. In addition, if we regard extremely unpleasant and inefficient ideas and emotions as signs of mental disorder, rather than as symptoms of disease, we shall be less vulnerable to the false hope stimulated by the notion of "disease"—namely that, if crazy people are "sick," there must be doctors with cures.

It is now recognized that some psychotic individuals may be moved by beliefs which we regard as false, but which they believe to be true and over which they seem to have no control. When such a delusion can be shown to have caused a crime, some jurisdictions excuse the agent as incompetent. Canada, for example, adds the defense of *delusive incapacity* to McNaughton's rules in defining insanity (Duhamel 1962, sec. 16), but it qualifies this excuse by saying that "a person . . . shall *not* be acquitted on the ground of insanity *unless* the delusions caused him to believe in the existence of a state of things that, if it existed, would have justified or excused his act or omission" (emphasis added).

If individuals can be "incapacitated" by delusions, it is conceivable that they may be rendered incompetent by a variety of other disturbances of thought, feeling, and will. Thus, in 18 of the United States, an *irresistible impulse* or *control* test is employed. This test first uses the McNaughton criteria. If defendants are judged sane by those standards, *then* the irresistible impulse test may be invoked to ascertain whether the accused could have controlled their behavior even though they knew their acts were wrong.

Such a test opens the door to psychiatric dispute in which experts testifying for the prosecution battle with those testifying for the defense to the disrepute of "the mental sciences" (Hakeem 1958, Robinson 1980). At present, psychological tools are not available with which to distinguish reliably between behavior that is *uncontrollable* and behavior that is *uncontrolled.*

The Durham Rule

The door to psychiatric and legal debate is opened even wider by other attempts to excuse "mentally ill" people from accountability. For example, Judge David Bazelon wrote an opinion in the case of *Durham* v. *U.S.,* 1954, holding that "an accused is not criminally responsible if his unlawful act was the product of mental disease or mental defect." This opinion, known as *Durham's rule,* has been codified only in the District of Columbia, Maine, and the Virgin Islands.

Durham's rule has not been widely adopted because it is vague. It does *not* equate a "mental disease" with a psychosis. It provides no standard, therefore, by which to gauge the capacity of defendants to control their behavior. Judges and juries are left dependent upon the conflicting assessments of psychiatrists (Arthur 1969, Ash 1949, Goldberg & Werts 1966, Schmidt & Fonda 1956, Zigler & Phillips 1965). Vagueness of the notion of "mental disease" allows fuzzy diagnoses to be certified as evidence of a person's lack of responsibility—diagnoses such as "character defect" or "emotionally unstable personality."

In addition, this test encourages hollow explanations of disapproved conduct. The explanations are vacant because the behavior to be explained is used as an indicator of the "disease" that is supposed to have caused the behavior.

Calling evil deeds the product of "mental disease" mixes disapproval of conduct with "sympathetic understanding." This mixture permits circular reasoning in which *bizarre* crimes become, *in themselves,* proof of mental incompetence. The fact that a person "could have done that!" becomes in itself a sign of incapacity. The "logic" is that heinous crimes, according to the judge's standards, *must* betoken insanity—even when experts can find no psychosis or neurosis, and even when the defendant is McNaughton-sane, "knows" right from wrong, and "knew" what she or he was doing the night of the crime.

There *are* such offenders, as we saw in the preceding chapter. Excusing them as "incompetent" because their crimes seem "senseless" and brutal ignores the history of human cruelty and violates a common sense of justice.

The Brawner Rule

An additional difficulty with the Durham test occurs in attempting to establish that the crime was the *product* of mental disorder. To circumvent this difficulty, Judge Bazelon, presiding in *U.S.* v. *Brawner,* 1972, proposed that a defendant be deemed "not responsible" if, at the time of his crime, his "mental or emotional processes or behavior controls were impaired to such an extent that he cannot justly be held responsible for his act."

Under this proposal, psychiatrists would answer only one question: "What is [was] the nature of the impairment, if any, of the defendant's 'mental and emotional processes and behavior controls'?". Juries would then decide whether the described impairment "justly" excused the accused from criminal responsibility.

Persistent Difficulties

Legal and moral difficulties persist in the assignment of responsibility for one's acts. Moral philosophers have not been able to resolve the difficulties by providing a clear principle that would excuse some, or all, wrongdoers from public attention. What is sought is a philosophic tool with which to define sanity so that we will not condemn poor lunatics to hang *without,* at the same time, excusing every bad actor from accountability. The dilemma we confront was described by the British Chief Justice Hale over 300 years ago:

It is very difficult to define the indivisible line which divides perfect and partial insanity, but it must rest upon circumstances duly to be weighed and considered both by the judge and jury, lest on the one hand there be a kind of inhumanity towards the defects of human nature, or on the other side too great an indulgence given to great crimes (cited by Ormrod 1977, pp. 4-5).

This issue was supposed to have become less important with the abandonment of capital punishment. It persists, however, and the excuse of "mental incompetence" has spread from murder cases to apologies for assault, burglary, and robbery. Robinson (1980, p. 205) reports that 47 percent of insanity pleas over a dozen years in New York were entered for crimes other than homicide.

Questions about who is, or is not, responsible intrude upon debate about whether some criminals need "treatment"[6] rather than punishment, and, if treatment is recommended, of what it shall consist and how long it will be administered. The argument ultimately moves toward questioning whether anyone deserves punishment for any crime.

Some philosophers and psychologists are beginning to recognize that, after the fact of a bad act, something can be found "wrong" with everyone, and that ideas of psycho-social determinism simultaneously *broaden* the notion of incompetence and *obscure* the criteria of responsibility. For example, Robinson (1980) shows that intrusion of "mental health" definitions of accountability into the working of the law shifts the burden of proof from the defense to the prosecution. Under such conception of competence, defense counsel describes defendant's "peculiarities" and unpleasant childhood as evidence of "insanity" and the task is then laid upon the prosecution to prove that the defendant was sane when he committed his crimes. Given the sad stories that characterize many careers in crime, and

---

[6] "Treatment" is another popular word without clear referent. Activities carried on under this rubric vary from pacification by medication, to conditioning techniques, educational and vocational training, and the spectrum of "talking therapies."

Treatment is recommended, and justified, as being less punitive than punishment. But there is no guarantee that this is so—from the "patient's" point of view. There can be a "tyranny of treatment," as Outerbridge (1968) has called it, and as McMurphy found out in the *Cuckoo's Nest* (Kesey 1964). Helpers who prefer to "treat" offenders, rather than punish or restrain them, see more symptoms premonitory of bad action and favor *longer* incarceration (Cousineau & Veevers 1972, McNamara 1975). Morris (1966, p. 637) tells us that "the rehabilitative ideal [imparts] unfettered discretion. . . . The jailer in a white coat and with a doctorate remains a jailer—but with larger powers over his fellows."

given expanded notions of incompetence, this becomes an impossible burden. Robinson gives this example of a defendant who, by McNaughton's rules would have been judged sane, but who, by Alaska's law, was judged not guilty by reason of insanity:

> . . . in *Alto* v. *Alaska* . . . Alto stabbed his victim, raped her, and stole goods from her house—including her husband's boots, which he wore during his escape. He brought the stolen items to the nearby house of friends and there attempted to sell them. He asked to borrow a clean shirt, his own being soiled with the stains of his recent crime. He accounted for his possessions by saying that he intended to move away, and expressed the desire that his friends would buy the stolen stereo. The state established all of these facts and the defense challenged none of them. All the defense did was produce three "experts" and a sister who recalled her brother's nastiness on several occasions when he had been drinking. In addition, a friend of the Alto family told the court that Frank Alto had had an unhappy childhood dominated by quarrelsome parents. On the basis of his examination and "long experience," one of the "experts" concluded that the defendant suffered from "chronic undifferentiated schizophrenia" and that "it was probably in existence August 6, 1972, as well as 1973" (pp. 73-73).

Robinson doubts that justice can survive such dilution of the concept of responsibility. The classic image of Justice has her holding scales, to denote that the practice of fairness requires *balance*. What is to be balanced in allowing the insanity defense is, on the one hand, a determinism that excuses extreme defect, and might excuse everyone, and, on the other hand, a moral sense that regards law as expressive, protective, promissory, and educational.

We will meet these issues again in Volume Four. Here we need only note the qualities of lunacy that pave several of the roads to murder.

QUALITIES OF LUNACY

Homicidal qualities of craziness can best be described in extreme cases. Extremity makes for clarity. But descriptive categories become fuzzy, and they overlap, as lunacy approaches normalcy. Then we have to deal with a multiplicity of borderline cases, borderline because people are more and less sane, not all-or-none sane. Those whom we judge to be crazy need not be so all the way, in every way, every day.

A dangerous fact, and one that confounds official explicators of crime, is that murderous people can talk sense much of the time and seem daft only in departments. This fact is dangerous because some therapists of good will, and most lovers, are apt to discount the part-time lunacy in favor of the part-time sanity.

Understanding that qualities of craziness refer to distributions of activities, rather than to all-or-none categories, allows us to describe two extreme channels that lunacy takes to homicide and to remember that the channels overflow as they move toward normal streams of conduct. One course flows through psychosis; the other, through psychopathy. The first takes a course marked by "breaks with reality." The second is a channel marked by lack of empathy and conscience.

PSYCHOSIS

Questions about sanity depend on assumptions about reality. People who are judged to be "crazy" are not all judged to be crazy in the same way. Nor are they judged to be crazy all the way. There are degrees of being "out of it." However, the lunacy that is today called "psychosis" is recognized by three major criteria:

1. a grossly distorted conception of reality

2. moods, and swings of mood, that seem inappropriate to circumstance, and

3. marked inefficiency in getting along with others and caring for oneself.

Safety in Numbers

These criteria are notoriously shifty. The boundary between sense and nonsense is a fuzzy one. This means that all societies, and particularly modern, large aggregates, tolerate varieties of ambulatory lunatics who act upon a wide range of strange beliefs. *Organizing* in the name of such beliefs protects an individual advocate from the stigma of lunacy. Being solitary in one's imaginative utterances exposes one to the charge of being crazy.

The difference here is one of competence again. Groups that congeal around myths may have an internal coherence that is protective and that allows an accommodation with the external world. But an individual who is alone in seeing reality differently is apt to antagonize others and is apt to be inefficient in adjusting to the world of others—depending, of course, on *what* is strangely believed and *how* it is acted upon.

The connection between competence and conceptions of sanity means that successful people can utter silly ideas without being deemed crazy. The false beliefs of otherwise competent people may be respected or ignored—until they insult some targeted group. By contrast, the same ideas, when uttered by common folk, tend to be ignored rather than respected, and they become signs of lunacy when they intrude strikingly upon the peace of a community. For example, notions of conspiracy are a common part of the delusions that betoken psychosis (pp. 157–161). But, since there *are* conspiracies in the real world, the unproved stories of plots are at least listened to when told by successful people. A case in point is Henry Ford's dissemination through his newspaper, *The Dearborn Independent,* of *The Protocols of the Wise Men of Zion,* a document alleging an international plot among Jews to dominate the world. A five million dollar lawsuit charging libel and slander compelled Ford's public retraction of this story (*New York Times* 1921, 1922).

Delusion is a mark of lunacy, but which belief is deluded depends on which test of reality one accepts. The present point is that people who are otherwise competent in human relations can "get away with" silly ideas. As an illustration, Ben Stein (1979) records some of the beliefs of the writers and producers who manufacture America's television shows. Stein worked in the TV industry, conversed at length with many of these image-makers, and reports:

> Soon after I arrived in Los Angeles in the summer of 1976, I dined with three important producers and their wives at The Mandarin, a restaurant in Beverly Hills. When one of the producers learned I once worked for Nixon, he wanted to know about the international conspiracy for which Nixon was a cat's-paw. What could I tell him about it? No protestations of my ignorance were adequate. Everyone knew, the producer said, to the general agreement of the party, that there was a world conspiracy of bankers and financiers and certain other people, and if I did not know it, I was a fool.
>
> The conspiracy, according to the producer, was composed of representatives of "the eight families who rule the world." These families included the Rockefellers, the Rothschilds, the Hunts, the Pahlevis, the Krupps, the Thyssens, and others he would not name. These folks got together each year, I was told, and decided what the level of unemployment and inflation was going to be in all of the countries of the world, who would win each election of consequence, who would live and who would die, whether any wars had to be stopped or started, and so on.
>
> One of the first couples I met in Hollywood was a husband and wife who were both producers. They had worked out an entire scenario of how the world was run. It involves the presidents of the largest multinational corporations telling General Alexander Haig what they wanted done. Haig, in co-operation with several ex-Nazis, carried out their

wishes. The greatest triumph of this group, according to my friends, was to make their own creature, a Jewish Nazi, into the Secretary of State (pp. 131–133).

Flexible Boundaries

There is, then, a broad no-man's-land within which otherwise "sane" people may operate as part-time or part-of-the-way lunatics. However, beyond some flexible boundary, we recognize individuals who have "broken with reality." These are individuals who perceive what is not there and whose thoughts and feelings make them incompetent to judge how things are, or what goes with what, and who is or is not a danger to them.

It bears repeating that the criteria of inefficiency and distorted sense of reality are easier to apply to individuals than to groups and that they become more clear at an extremity. Sanity is not of one piece. People who are less than sound are unsound in different ways, in different degrees, and in differing patterns of episodic to chronic impairment.

Signs of Psychosis

The different ways in which people experience mental disorder have been grouped into two large families: the organic and functional psychoses. The first set includes disturbances associated with, and probably caused by, observable damage to brain tissue. The second category of disturbances does not involve such clearly discernible impairment of the nervous system, although it is assumed that a physiological defect is involved (Meehl 1962, 1973).

Within these large families of mental disorder, there are specific styles, of course. But the psychoses that are of interest to criminologists are those "functional" disorders identified as *schizophrenia of the paranoid type* and the more rare condition of *paranoia* which affects a more restricted aspect of personality.

The Paranoid Schizophrenic

"Schizophrenia" describes a variety of personalities that differ in degree of impairment.[7] The signs that indicate schizophrenia are given different weight, then, by different observers. There is agree-

---

[7] Degrees of impairment are implicit as well in other signs of disease and disorder—from arthritis to broken legs.

ment, however, that the schizophrene exhibits a range of anxieties, particularly as concerns relations with others.

The schizophrene distrusts and fears others. He assumes that others are likely to reject him and that people in general are more likely to be sources of pain than of pleasure. This schizoid attitude is frequently ambivalent. The schizophrene simultaneously wants to be appreciated, but believes he won't be. He feels himself to be unlovable and, one might add, for good reason—given his actions and his history. From this unpleasant experience, hatred flows.

Fear of others is associated, obviously, with an inability to have fun. Psychoanalysts term this defect *anhedonia* (Rado 1956, Rado & Daniels 1956). It is a marked inability to feel pleasure. Inability to find joy may be part of a generalized inability to feel emotion, pleasant or unpleasant, and, in such cases, psychologists refer to this incapacity as "flattened affect."

The schizophrene not only distrusts others and has little fun, but he also thinks in peculiar fashion. Of all the signs of schizophrenia, Meehl (1973, p. 138) regards this one as "the diagnostic bell ringer." Thought disorder alerts us to the schizophrene's "break with reality."

Disorders of thinking can take the form of inability to maintain a train of thought, loss of memory, or the manufacture of bizarre associations. We typically think people are "crazy" when they put ideas together in strange combinations:

> *Sufferer:* "What are we going to do about the three B's?"
> *Psychologist:* "The three B's?"
> *Sufferer:* "Yes, your office is on Bedford Drive, you have on a blue suit, and then there's Aunt Beulah."

Meehl (1973, p. 138) has invented the phrase, "cognitive slippage" to describe the milder forms of peculiar association. He gives this illustration:

> Patient experiences intense ambivalence, readily reports conscious hatred of family figures, is pananxious, subjects therapist to a long series of testing operations, is withdrawn, and says, "Naturally, I am growing my father's hair."

The schizophrene is called "paranoid" when disorders of thought and feeling take the form of delusions and hallucinations.

Hallucinations are perceptual disorders in which the "sick" person sees things, hears things, feels things, or smells and tastes things without "adequate" sensory stimulation. The rest of us do not see the pink elephants and other weird animals that the alcoholic perceives in his delirium. The rest of us do not hear the accusing voices that the psychotic assures us are speaking to her. And we see no "creepy, crawly bugs" that the sufferer from a tactile (haptic) hallucination feels on his flesh.

The essence of hallucination is error in perception where the error seems to be stimulated by the perceiver rather than by ambiguity in the thing perceived. Perceptual errors that result from ambiguities in the external field of stimulation are *illusions,* rather than hallucinations.

The psychotic does more than hallucinate, of course, and some psychotics do not hallucinate. Psychotics may *perceive* parts of the world incorrectly, but what is more important to their diagnosis is, to repeat, that they *conceive* of it incorrectly. Thought disorder is the hallmark of psychosis.[8]

Since thinking and feeling run in tandem, disturbances of thought are commonly associated with disturbances of mood. These swings in mood, like the hallucinations and strange ideas, are, again, more the product of the sufferer than of events around him or her.

In sum, people are called crazy when, at some extremity, they cannot "think straight." The crooked thinking sometimes takes the form of strange associations of ideas that the rest of us believe result in false conclusions. When false beliefs are assumed by a group of others whom we regard as ignorant, we title those beliefs *superstitions.* When false beliefs are maintained by an individual whose thinking seems immune to "good reason," we call such ideas *delusions.*

Delusions of paranoid persons vary in their complexity. Their content, however, involves a sense of powers unacknowledged by others and of persecution by those others who deny the paranoiac's "truth." For example:

> A paranoid patient firmly believes that he is the Redeemer and as such he can turn night into day, he can cure all the ills of mankind, he can recall all the events that have ever happened since the dawn of civilization, with the unaided eye he can read newsprint from a distance of several thousand miles (Hinsie & Campbell 1960, p. 189).

---

[8] The continuity of sanity-lunacy is illustrated by the fact that psychologists are aware that their own modes of thought may become pathological. The philosopher-psychologist Sigmund Koch (1981) describes signs of the "pathology of knowledge"—what he calls "epistemopathy"—within the psychological fraternity. Psychological theorizing becomes pathological, says Koch, when it succumbs to jargon and "word magic," "single-minded imperialism," and the "substitution of *program* for performance" (p. 258, emphasis his). It becomes pathological when it is divorced from common sense, personal experience, and utility.

Delusion may characterize a limited sphere of a person's thought or it may permeate a person's entire "philosophy." *Paranoia* refers to a condition in which an otherwise sane person develops an elaborate chain of associations in defense of a delusion, but where—outside the realm of the topic on which she or he is irrational—the paranoiac performs normally. The paranoiac characteristically works well as long as the "touchy topic" is not raised. But on that subject, the delusion persists—well fortified, certain of who the "enemies" are, and angry at the conspiracies of the hated others.

While a paranoiac may organize politically and thus harm others, the more immediate, physically dangerous lunatic is the paranoid schizophrenic. By degree, this person differs from the rest of us by:

> Being more nervous, tense, and excitable.
>
> Being exquisitely sensitive and alert to interpersonal cues.
>
> Acting and talking *self-referentially*, by which we mean that more acts of others are seen by our subject as directed toward him than you and I can perceive.
>
> Being suspicious and jealous.
>
> Demanding much of loved ones at the same time that he is critical of them for their obvious lack of appreciation of him.
>
> Talking with hate and behaving aggressively.
>
> Saying that he is rejected unfairly.
>
> Believing that people and the fates are against him.
>
> Talking more dirty sex than is "normal" and seeing more perversion in others.
>
> Being unreasonable.
>
> And, of course, talking and acting as though the social world were a jungle. (There is much of the jungle in our social lives, but the world is not *just* that.) (Nettler 1978, p. 273, emphasis in the original).

In such paranoid people, homicide is fueled by hatred and delusion. The delusion assumes that "those others"—Jews, Catholics, Nazis, Commies, or neighbors—are the source of personal difficulties and social ills, and that "those others," or some particular representative of them, is a menace to "good people" in general and the paranoid person in particular. McNaughton's delusion about "the Tories" is an example.

We have no tallies of the proportions of domestic murders committed by psychotic individuals. However, in forensic clinics one sees a sufficient number of battling spouses among whom one or both of the combatants suffers from paranoid thoughts and feelings to infer that some proportion of domestic injuries and killings are thus stimulated.

The paranoid schizophrenic remains, then, an unknown quantity in the production of damage between intimates. In the political arena, however, the deluded lunatic assumes importance as an assassin of prominent persons.

ASSASSINS

"Assassination" derives from the Arabic, *hashshashin,* eaters of hashish. According to legend, Muslim warriors were rewarded with cannabis for bravery in their attacks on Christian Crusaders from about 1090 to 1272 A.D. The word has evolved from this source and it has taken on special meaning in English. In the English lexicon assassination refers to premeditated killing, usually of a prominent person, for profit or ideals. The ideals may, of course, be "sound" ones or delusions.

In other European languages, the idea of "assassination" has no such connotation. In French, for example, the equivalent term, *assassinat,* means only "murder in the first degree" and it carries none of the special significance of the English word (Heppenstall 1972). For our purposes the word will be used in its English-language sense.

Types of Assassins, Terrorists, and Random Killers

For descriptive convenience, it seems useful to distinguish types of assassins and to note possible differences between assassins, terrorists, and "random killers."

Assassins kill particular persons. Terrorists kill indiscriminately—for a cause. Random killers murder people they do not know, and they do so either in the course of committing another felony, as in robbery or burglary, or out of a raging misanthropy that compensates for a failed life by ending others' lives.

Assassins select a particular individual as their victim. Sometimes these are hated individuals and sometimes they are loved ones. That is, assassins kill to eliminate enemies, but they also kill out of the warped wish to be the person they murder. For example, Mark David Chapman, the murderer of the Beatle, John Lennon, December 8, 1980, exhibited the latter form of lethal lunacy.

In his own way, Chapman was a "groupie." He identified with the Beatles, adopted their costume and coiffure, played guitar with rock combos, dabbled in "mind-bending" drugs as recommended by his idols, was "concerned" about "doing good" for people—children, in particular—and married an older woman of Japanese ancestry as had his hero, John Lennon. After he shot Lennon, Chapman commented, "I've got a good side and a bad side. The bad side is very small, but sometimes it takes over the good side and I do bad things" (Clarke 1980).

Chapman can be characterized as a lunatic, unsane but not insane. He suffered from a delusion without becoming a full-blown psychotic. His feet touched some ground of reality.

Terrorists, by contrast, tend to be more realistic. They kill anonymous others as part of their plan for power. The plan is to terrorize a government into submission according to the Chinese maxim, "Kill one, frighten ten thousand."

The distinction between an assassin and a terrorist is not fixed. Killers for ideals may operate today as assassins and tomorrow as terrorists. For example, the Irish assassin of Lord Mountbatten and his family had also operated as a terrorist. But functioning alternately as an assassin and a terrorist is the option of two kinds of killer who may sometimes reside in one body: the sane idealist and the psychopath. Such alternation is less frequently the option of the deluded schizophrene who is prone to assassinate rather than to terrorize.

Whether one distinguishes the sane idealist who kills from the psychopathic murderer depends more on moral judgment than on any objective criteria. When we agree with the ideals of the revolutionary or the reactionary killer, his or her violence is interpreted as the product of a "sound" mind. When we disapprove of those ideals we are more apt to notice the "cold-bloodedness" of the assassin and attribute his murders to psychopathy. There is no historical evidence, however, that allows us to distinguish the rational "coldness" that marks the idealistic killer from the rationality of the psychopath. Judgment of sanity moves, again, with notions of how a mind should function, and this judgment moves, too, with the amount of group support for the killer. There is defense in numbers against the charge of lunacy.

Acknowledging this shifting base for the assessment of killers, we may tentatively type assassins and would-be assassins in four categories *if* we recognize that the boundaries between these types are not firm and that any particular person may function across categories. To repeat, classifications move, and they move particularly as a killer's anger receives group support and ideological justification or as s/he remains a solo performer.

With this qualification, we can type assassins as deluded, as lonely "zeros," as psychopathic mercenaries, and as idealists.

Some assassins and failed assassins are clearly operating with a delusion. Others are lonely incompetents, "rebels without a cause," whose thoughts and feelings lack the systematic organization of a delusion, but whose thinking-feeling represent an inability to relate means to ends rationally. These are people who kill, or attempt to kill, prominent persons to assuage their own feelings of insignificance.

When a lonely "zero" attempts to kill a distinguished person in order to become a "somebody," this act has *a* rationality. In the era of electronic publicity, the killer's means are efficient for his or her ends, although we *may*[9] regard them as immoral.

A third category of assassin includes psychopathic mercenaries and a fourth includes idealists whose mental health is variously judged.

Delusion and Assassination

The psychiatrist Donald Hastings (1965) has evaluated the biographies of assassins and would-be assassins of American presidents. In the short history of the United States since its first presidency in 1789 to the present (1981), four presidents have been killed—Abraham Lincoln, James Garfield, William McKinley, and John Kennedy. Known attempts have been made to kill seven other presidents.

Hastings's study is limited to the four successful assassinations and to four of the unsuccessful ones—to nine persons in all (the unsuccessful attempt to kill President Harry Truman was made by two Puerto Rican nationalists). Hastings concludes that, with the exception of the Puerto Ricans, all the other killers and would-be killers suffered from degrees of paranoid schizophrenia.

The flavor of lethal delusion and the moving boundaries between lunatic belief and sound idealism are illustrated by extracts from Hastings's descriptions.

John Wilkes Booth, Assassin of President Abraham Lincoln, 14 April 1865

Booth was the ninth of ten children born of an illegitimate union between Junius Brutus Booth, an English actor, and an 18-year-old flower girl with whom the father "escaped" to the United States. Three sons of the senior Booth also established reputations as actors in America and, at the same time, accumulated reputations as "crazy."

---

[9] The qualification, "may" is necessary because some people side with the killer, as Chapter 1 demonstrated. Most recently, when the American President Reagan was shot, "[some] seventh-graders in Tulsa . . . cheered this TV shooting as they had J.R.'s on 'Dallas' a year ago and the occasional callers to radio phone-in shows [asserted] that Reagan got what he deserved" (Goldman 1981).

The father, acknowledged to have been one of the greatest actors of his time, "was psychotic in episodic bursts. In 1824 he was seized with a 'violent fit of insanity,' according to a newspaper account, and stabbed at a fellow actor, saying, 'I must cut somebody's throat today, and whom shall I take?'." (Hastings 1965, p. 96).

Kimmel (1940), a biographer of "the mad Booths," reports that John Wilkes Booth's parents treated him differently from his siblings. Kimmel notes that "To Edwin and his sisters [John] was a troublemaker and a vexation, but to his father and mother he was an exceptional child whom they petted for his bright appearance and fiery temperament. They could not keep up with his pranks, and he was allowed to run about like a wild colt."

John's father died when the boy was 14 and his mother continued to overindulge him. Hastings (1965, p. 97) describes John as a spoiled and cruel child:

> He was undisciplined, unmanageable, and intolerant of any authority but his own. He had a vicious streak; he shot dogs and cats for the sake of killing them and once shot a neighbor's pig that wandered into their yard. He was an excellent marksman. Any attempt to correct him frustrated him so badly that he might go into a tantrum. As a student he was only average, soon got bored, and had trouble with the self-discipline that schooling required. He went to several schools but did not accomplish the equivalent of a high school education.

During "the war between the states," Booth adopted the South and its cause. He joined a secret, pro-rebel society and was frequently involved in brawls with men who defended the North or denigrated the South. His brother, Edwin, wrote that John would go into "a patriotic froth" over the issue of secession and that he "was insane" on matters of slavery, states' rights, and the belief that Lincoln might become "King of America."

John Booth entered into a conspiracy with other Southern sympathizers to kill Lincoln and, as we know, assassinated the president during a performance at the Ford Theater. Booth fled the assassination scene and was hunted for twelve days before Union soldiers found his hideout. During Booth's flight, he wrote in his diary:

> I can never repent it, though we hated to kill. Our country owed all her troubles to him, and God simply made me the instrument of his punishment. . . . I bless the entire world. Have never hated or wronged anyone. This last was not a wrong, unless God deems it so, and it's with Him to damn or bless me (Donovan 1955, p. 288).

Booth was killed, either by his own bullet or that of a Union soldier, during his resistance to arrest. His dying words were, "Tell mother I died for my country. I have done what I thought was for the best."

Charles J. Guiteau, assassin of President James A. Garfield, 2 July 1881

Charles Guiteau is described as "a small, quick, nervous man who had a remarkably checkered career: lawyer, evangelist, insurance salesman, author, publisher, and swindler" (Hastings 1965, p. 157). He had a long history of psychotic behavior. He believed himself to be immortal and that God directed his actions. His lectures were often rambling and marked by that "cognitive slippage" characteristic of schizophrenes.

Under "divine direction," Guiteau long planned to kill President Garfield. He had several opportunities to do so, but was foiled by minor events: sultry weather or the fact that Mrs. Garfield was next to the president, looking appealing frail and worn. Guiteau finally assassinated Garfield in a railroad station, indicating again the vulnerability of prominent persons who must appear in crowds.

At his trial, Guiteau told the court, "I come here in the capacity of an agent of the Deity in this matter." He added, "I expect an act of God that will blow this court and jury out of that window if necessary" (Hastings 1965, p. 159).

Guiteau justified his assassination this way:

> I think of General Garfield's condition as a removal and not as an assassination. My idea simply stated was to remove as easily as possible Mr. James A. Garfield, a quiet and good-natured citizen of Ohio, who temporarily occupied the position of President of the United States, and substitute in his place Mr. Chester A. Arthur, of New York, a distinguished and highly estimable gentleman.
>
> Mr. Garfield I intended to quietly remove to Paradise (which is a great improvement on this world), while Mr. Arthur saved the Republic. . . . Not a soul in the universe knew of my purpose to remove the President. If it has failed I shall never attempt it again. My motive was purely political and patriotic, and I acted under divine pressure. It was the same kind of pressure that led Abraham to sacrifice his son Isaac. . . . The President's nomination was an act of God; his election was an act of God; his removal is an act of God. These three specific acts of the Deity may give the clergy a text (Alexander 1882, p. 36).

Guiteau was hung for his crime on 30 June, 1882. He went to his death reciting a poem he had written that morning and chanting, "Glory, Glory, Glory. . . ." Hastings contends that, had Guiteau been tried in today's climate of opinion, he would have been declared not guilty by reason of insanity.

A Borderline Case: Lee Harvey Oswald, Assassin of President John F. Kennedy, 22 November 1963

Delusions and other "breaks with reality" occur in degrees. Lunatics can be dangerous without being "full-blown" psychotics, and some killers espouse beliefs that are plausible, but untrue. Their thoughts are "wild" without being so disordered as to signal psychosis.

In paranoid personalities, conspiratorial ideas work in team with feelings of loneliness, neglect, and rejection to stimulate hatred and to justify it. One's nothingness is blamed on "the system" and one dreams of doing something that will make the world notice. The drastic deed will ventilate hostility, kill some hated symbol of the unjust "system," and, at the same time, aggrandize the assassin. Even a nobody can become a somebody by pulling a trigger and killing an important person.

Lee Harvey Oswald's career illustrates this theme. On November 22, 1963, Oswald fired three shots from his workplace in the Texas School Book Depository that killed President Kennedy and wounded the then governor of Texas, John Connally. Less than an hour later, Oswald killed policeman J.D. Tippitt who had stopped Oswald for questioning about the earlier shooting. These murders followed Oswald's alleged attempt in April to kill General Edwin A. Walker, whom Oswald believed to be a "fascist."

In contrast to fully deluded assassins who readily confess their crimes, and who sometimes do so with pride, Oswald maintained his innocence through two days of police interrogation. On November 24th, while Oswald was being led from police headquarters to the county jail, a Dallas bar owner, Jack Ruby, stepped out of the crowd of journalists and cameramen, and shot Oswald at point-blank range. This murder-upon-murder demonstrates again the conflict between the "rights" of journalists and the requirements of justice.

The story of Oswald's life parallels that of other losers. It is a story of floundering and of living without purpose. It is a story in which assassination fills the void of alienated existence.

Oswald was the third son born to a family of modest means. His father, Robert E. Lee Oswald, died when Lee was two months old. Lee spent some time in boarding school, but, for the most part, lived with his mother in various cities—New Orleans, Fort Worth, New York. He lived with his mother through her third marriage, a brief one, and by the time Lee was in junior high school, he exhibited characteristics of the schizoid personality.

He was vicious with children and he angered with little provocation. He is described by his teachers and classmates as "carrying a chip on his shoulder" and lacking self-control. His report cards show low grades, despite an average IQ. His teachers rated him as undependable, uncooperative, and truant. His truancy brought him to the attention of the New York Children's Court which referred him for psychiatric examination. Dr. Renatus Hartogs, chief psychiatrist at New York's Youth House for Boys, found Oswald to be an emotionally disturbed youngster who was isolated from others, suspicious and defiant toward authority, and sensitive and vengeful with his peers. In an interview after the killings, Dr. Hartogs reported that Oswald "saw himself as being singled out for rejection and frustration. . . . He also appeared to be preoccupied about his sexual identity and his future role as a male. He was guarded, secluded, and suspicious in his dealings with the psychiatrist" (Jackson 1964, p. 78).

Dr. Hartogs termed Oswald's view of the world "paranoid." He diagnosed Lee as suffering from "incipient schizophrenia," judged him to be potentially dangerous, and recommended institutional commitment. This recommendation was not acted upon.

When Oswald was 17 years old, he joined the United States Marine Corps where he demonstrated a continuity of his poor school record. He had no friends and was frequently in fights. He had difficulties with his officers, liked to "show them up," and was twice court-martialed. His section chief at Camp Pendleton remembered that, "He was good with a rifle, but he was such a hothead I was glad when he was finally shipped out for radar training. He was always having beefs with the guys." (Hastings 1965, p. 297).

Oswald's search for significance took him to Russia where he sought to renounce his American citizenship and become a Soviet subject. But his emotional instability and occupational incompetence were apparent in that "promised land" as they had been in the United States. He married a Russian girl, fathered a child, and became disillusioned with the Soviet Union. His wife, Marina, commented that "everybody hated him . . . even in Russia." Since he was still an American citizen, he effected a loan of $435.71 from the State Department and returned with his new family to the United States.

Oswald's poor work habits continued. In addition, he had frequent quarrels with his wife who used his sexual inadequacy as a weapon in their disputes (Hastings 1965, p. 301). Oswald compensated for his unsatisfactory life by becoming a Marxist. He saturated himself in

Leftist literature and dreamed of action. He bought a Mannlicher-Carcano rifle from a mail-order house to supplement his Smith and Wesson revolver. He nominated himself a one-man Fair Play for Cuba Committee and distributed handbills on the streets. He traveled to Mexico in an attempt to gain entry to Cuba. His efforts to gain importance as a revolutionary were as futile as his attempts to be competent as a husband and worker.

Oswald's claim to fame is that of assassin who, in Santayana's phrase (1951, p. 49), "blames the world for being himself ill fitted to live in it."

Other Occasions

Varieties of lunatics continue random killing and assassination. In Europe, Japan, and North America, all prominent persons are potential targets, but Americans, it seems, suffer disproportionately.

In 1965 the black civil rights leader, Malcolm X, was shot to death in New York City by three men. Circumstances of the shooting cast doubt on the guilt of those convicted and raise questions about the identity of his actual murderers.

On April 4, 1968, another black leader, Martin Luther King, Jr., was assassinated in Memphis by James Earl Ray who first confessed his guilt and later recanted his confession. Two months later in Los Angeles, Senator Robert Kennedy, the Democratic nominee for president, was killed "on television." The convicted murderer, Sirhan B. Sirhan, says he cannot recall doing the shooting. Circumstances are again clouded in that Sirhan's gun carried eight shots, but 10 cartridges were recovered from the murder scene.

On May 15, 1972, George Wallace, governor of Georgia and candidate for the Democratic presidential nomination, was shot by Arthur Bremer. Wallace survived the shooting, but he has been left paralyzed. Three years later two women tried on different occasions to kill President Gerald Ford. Lynette "Squeaky" Fromme, a former member of Charlie Manson's "family," failed in her assassination attempt in Sacramento September 5th. Two weeks later, in San Francisco, Sara Jane Moore tried without success to shoot President Ford.

American homicide in its many styles became of such concern that two magazines, *Newsweek* and *Time,* brought out cover stories on violence on the same day, March 23, 1981. One week after that publication, yet another lunatic shot another American president, Ronald Reagan.

The accused would-be assassin of President Reagan, 25-year-old John W. Hinckley, Jr., differs in interesting ways from many of the other solitary, successful and failed, murderers, but his psychic career parallels those of other unsane killers.

Hinckley differs from so-called "normal bad actors" in that he was not bred in misery. None of the environmental "bad things" routinely brought forth to explain lethal lunacy apply to John Hinckley, Jr.—no poverty, no boozing father and sluttish mother, no parental neglect or rejection.

Hinckley, Jr., is the son of a successful and devoted father, reared in an affluent setting, and nurtured in a loving, religious family. Social environment, a favorite causal site, cannot explain his lunacy. Constitutional difference does. Good families can produce bad seeds.

Starting in adolescence, Hinckley exhibited the withdrawal and loneliness, the apathy and anhedonia, that bespeak schizoid process. He became glum and purposeless. He enrolled in college without knowing why, attended irregularly, and, after seven years, completed no degree. He had no friends, male or female, and he lived in sloth. He was unhappy, depressed, and seedy. In 1978 he joined the American Nazi party, but he was dropped from membership one year later. He was rejected apparently because party rallies agitated him and he talked of the need for more dramatic exhibitions like "shooting people."

Hinckley's search for significance fixed on a teenage movie star, Jodie Foster, who had played the role of a 12-year-old prostitute in the 1976 film, "Taxi Driver." In that scenario, the taxi driver achieves fame by killing the whore's pimp. An hour before Hinckley set out to assassinate the president, he wrote a letter to his unrequited love explaining that he was "doing all of this for your sake. By sacrificing my freedom and possibly my life I hope to change your mind about me."

After Hinckley's unsuccessful attempt at murder—an attempt in which four men were shot—the usual gusher of explanations flowed through the media of mass information. These explanations locate causes in popular sites, but not necessarily in accurate ones. They reflect contemporary folk beliefs given the gloss of "science" in some academic departments.

Locating causes again

When a sufferer manifests obvious delusion, his doctors have little or no hesitancy in locating the cause of that conduct in the biochemical "wiring" of the actor. However, when a sufferer exhibits less obvious delusion, camouflaged by periods of lucidity and a passive exterior, then the locus of causation is moved more fashionably.

Thus a sociologist explains Hinckley's shooting of President Reagan and others as due to "all the frustrations created by our society" (Getschow & Schlender 1981). The American novelist Gore Vidal also nominates "bad environment" as the cause of assassination. Sirhan, the convicted killer of Robert Kennedy, is, according to Vidal, a product of the city in which he was reared, Pasadena, California. Interviewed by the German magazine, *Stern,* Vidal assigns causation this way:

> Sirhan grew up in Pasadena, a center of the John Birch Society, a center of radical right reactionaries, a despicable blot on this earth. The people of Pasadena are well-off. They hate the Jews, they hate the Negroes, the poor, the foreign. I find these to be really terrible people. Sirhan grew up in this atmosphere and I do not doubt that he heard many anti-Kennedy speeches. He simply accepted the way people in Pasadena think. He decided that Bobby Kennedy was evil and he killed him (cited by Buckley 1969, p. 124).

Psychoanalysts offer yet another causal site. They note that John Hinckley's mother is named "Jodie," as is the actress whom Hinckley loved and whose attention he sought through murder. These physicians then recount the Oedipus story as they observe that Hinckley's father and older brother were successful while he was not.

Criticism

The trouble with these explanations is that they can be plausible without being true. There is no evidence that society is "more frustrating" now than ever or that would-be assassins experience more frustration than others. Frustration—not having everything one wants—is a condition of life, and no one has an objective gauge of its powers in moving the actions of individuals or aggregates.

Political environments are moral atmospheres, of course, but Vidal's evil Pasadenans do not usually murder their political opponents and, since Sirhan was not one of the detested rich, white reactionaries, Vidal's explanation is a political screed without explanatory substance.

Similarly, references to the early family life of assassins do not point to distinctive features of murderous careers. Many individuals with similar experiences do not behave similarly. (See Volume One, Figure 3.2 again.)

"Bad starts" do not have uniformly bad consequences and, conversely, "good starts" do not determine good ends. Between environment and conduct, personality intervenes. The intervention is contingent, of course, and that is why Figure 3.2 says, in effect, that "not all who experience this, do that. . . ."

Constitutions Again

Lunacy of the schizoid type opens a possible path to assassination, but it does not determine that all paranoid people follow it. On this, it is advisable to think as physicians do about vulnerability to disease.

Medical scientists employ the term "diathesis" to refer to those constitutional differences that make individuals more and less prone to disease. *Diathesis is a constitutional predisposition.*

Predisposition is not all that is sufficient to produce a disorder nor does constitutional vulnerability chart an inevitable career for an illness. But the idea of a constitutional predisposition recognizes that not everyone whose body is invaded by a pathogenic bacillus "gets" the disease or runs its full course. Similarly, not everyone in the same environment "catches" the ideas, or other alleged motivants, that are "in the air."

Immunity is differential. It interacts with environment. Our small science of conduct does not permit fine weighing of the moving contributions of constitutions and particular environmental features in the life of a lunatic. It does tell us, however, where *not* to look when a career gives repeated signs of that difference in thinking-feeling called schizoid.

Paul Meehl (1962) presents a clear model for interpreting such lunatic lives. Meehl holds that accumulated evidence about that family of lunacy called "schizophrenia" suggests that people are born with differential disposition to the bizarre thoughts and feelings that characterize this aberration. Underwriting this disposition is a "neural integrative defect" that Meehl terms *schizotaxia* and "which is all that can properly be spoken of as inherited" (p. 830).

Schizotaxia is the physician's diathesis, applied to schizophrenia. Meehl then proposes that, given differing degrees of schizotaxia, the varied environments in which we are nurtured tend to generate a universally recognizable personality that he calls a *schizotype.* In the vernacular, such people are simply called "schizzy."

Meehl claims that becoming schizotypic is learned by schizotaxic individuals, but he also argues that, under all learning schemas we know, the transformation from genetic predisposition to personality type is highly probable.

However, not all schizotypes become lunatic to the same degree. If the social mirror is sound and if, Meehl writes:

the schizotaxic person also has the good fortune to inherit a low anxiety readiness, physical vigor, general resistance to stress and the like, he will remain a well-compensated "normal" schizotype, never manifesting symptoms of mental disease. He will be like the gout-prone male whose genes determine him to have an elevated blood uric acid titer, but who never develops clinical gout (p. 830).

This description of a causal web tells us several things: (1) It advises us to abandon the search for specific environmental agents of lunacy; (2) It tells us that schizoid personalities can be compensated (controlled) or activated; (3) It cautions against the assumption of assured cures through environmental manipulation and (4) It reminds us to count on continuities in careers.

Other Dimensions of Lunacy

The degrees of delusion that characterize paranoid pesonalities shade into beliefs that are called idealistic when they are group-supported visions of a better world. Whether these visions are realistic is always disputed and so, too, is the sanity of idealistic killers, as we shall see in Chapter 10.

However, lunacy moves along another dimension, a gradient on which the hostile and lonely feelings of the paranoid person shade into antisocial sentiments in individuals who differ from schizophrenes in their better grasp of reality. These legally sane, solitary murderers are often characterized as psychopaths. Their description is the work of the next chapter.

9 HOMICIDAL ROUTES:

PSYCHOPATHY

Abstract • The psychopathic personality is described. ○ Psychopathy is more congenial to some vocations than to others. ○ About one-third of male prison populations are diagnosed as psychopathic. These individuals differ from other inmates in several ways. They demonstrate a greater proclivity to violence and an earlier onset of criminal conduct. • Moral judgments affect the definition of psychopathic homicide. • Examples of psychopathic killers are provided. • Lessons are drawn from these illustrations, namely: ○ That attacks on a civil way of life are both flanking and frontal. ○ That the mass media are aids to psychopaths. ○ That the many roads from sanity to lunacy are continuous. There are no sharp breaks in the routes.

HOSTILITY AND HOMICIDE THAT ARE GROUP-SUPPORTED are defended against the charge of lunacy. By contrast, the hostility and homicidal activity of an individual are vulnerable to definition as crazy.

To be antisocial by oneself—without the protection of like-minded rebels or the protection of a socially valuable "creativity"—is to be liable to crime and liable to the accusation of mentally disordered criminality. This accusation will be made even though the murderous rebel is free of psychosis and legally sane. In such cases, we move the locus of "mental" disturbance from the zone called "thought" to that called "feeling," and we invent a new category of lunatic. This category consists of individuals who are in touch with reality, as everyone else sees it, but out of touch with morality. These moral lunatics are called psychopaths.

PSYCHOPATHIC PERSONALITY

It has long been noticed that some individuals who "know what's going on" consistently act in an antisocial manner and without sympathy for those they injure. J.C. Prichard (1835) believed this loss of empathy to be a moral disorder which, of course, it is, and he termed such lunacy "moral insanity" and "moral imbecility." Prichard's observations of morally obtuse persons was seconded by succeeding psychiatrists who noted individuals who were in touch with reality and who did not suffer the schizophrene's cognitive debilities, but who were excitable, impulsive, deceitful, and larcenous. Koch (1888) coined the phrase "psychopathic inferior" to describe such people and Adolf Meyer (1905) added the notion of "constitutional psychopathic inferiority." Meyer meant his addition to indicate that the disorder had an early onset and was chronic.

As with all descriptions of personalities, the notion of psychopathy has been disputed. The validity of such a type is questioned as one sees borderline cases, but the utility of this classification is greater as one describes extreme, or "pure," cases.

Current investigators assume that the word "psychopath" characterizes a discernible pattern of conduct and that it is not merely a semantic fiction (McCord & McCord 1964). The psychiatrist Cleckley (1964) provides a classic description. The combination of signs listed below constitute a psychosis, in Cleckley's opinion, because the emotional qualities expected in sane persons are deformed. They do not constitute a psychosis, however, if that term is reserved for people who conceive reality in idiosyncratic and ill-founded ways. In fact, Cleckley titles his work, *The Mask of Sanity,* precisely to indicate that these people appear sane because they are competent recognizers of reality. They are deemed to be a variety of lunatic, however, because they lack appropriate feeling for others. Cleckley's marks of the psychopath include:

1. Superficial charm and average or better intelligence.
2. Absence of delusions, hallucinations, and other "breaks with reality."
3. Lack of anxiety. The psychopath is not neurotic.
4. Unreliability.
5. Chronic lying. The psychopath may or may not be a "pathological liar," if that refers to one who does not know when she or he is lying. However, psychopaths constantly tell lies and they enjoy duping those who love them and other victims.
6. Inability to feel guilt or shame. Shame is embarrassment at having been caught; guilt is remorse for having done something immoral. The psychopath is "free" of both regrets.
7. Chronic antisocial behavior. Psychiatrists often speak of the psychopath's disobedience and disdain of authority as "inadequately motivated," by which they mean that it is not "idealistic." Antisocial idealism changes the diagnosis.
8. Poor judgment and inability to learn from experience. The psychopath pays for his antisocial action, but seems unable to modify his behavior to lessen the costs of his appetites.
9. Egocentricity. The psychopath is "all for herself" and unable to love. Loving can be dramatized and affection can be spoken, but the

psychopath's behavior indicates that affection for others is verbal, not emotional.

10. Poverty of affect. This sign is a generalized extension of the egocentricity. The psychopath feels no empathy, although she may protest it.

11. Failure to respond to kindness. The psychopath interprets others' altruism as a mark of the "sucker." Altruistic folly in those who meet the psychopath justifies his exploiting them. The psychopath's inability to appreciate kindness is part of his egocentricity and poverty of affect.

12. Wild, rude, and socially upsetting behavior. Alcohol often precipitates these "shows," but the psychopath sometimes "breaks things up" out of boredom with tranquillity.

13. Immunity to suicide. Psychopaths are not suicidal. On rare occasions, they may feign suicide, but these are only acts put on as part of the delights of deceit.

14. Impersonal sex life. For the psychopath, the sexual connection is trivial. It means little because human commitment means little. A psychopath's sexual activity may sometimes be bizarre, but this does not indicate passion or affection. It is, rather, an additional expression of his disdain for others.

15. Contracted time-frame. The psychopath is a "hasty hedonist" (my term). She lives in the present and follows no prudential plan for her life. The future is inconceivable; the present is all. Impulse is preferred to deliberation.

16. Poor work history. The description thus far is unsurprisingly associated with frequent job changes, unemployment while jobs are available, and inability to tolerate the normal "frustrations" of work.

17. Early signs. Psychopathic indicators appear early in life—usually by adolescence and no later than the early 20's. The early signs include truancy, vandalism, lying, fighting, stealing, and persistent rule-breaking at home, school, and the playing field.

Research confirms this descriptive configuration and shows that reliable diagnoses can be made from interviews and analyses of careers (Hare & Cox 1978). These diagnoses *narrow* the category called "antisocial personality disorder" and give the psychopath a distinctive "flavor."

Some investigators suggest a neural basis of the disorder (Elliott 1978, Sandler et al. 1978). But, whether or not a neurobiological foundation can be discriminated for psychopaths, several studies have demonstrated that psychopaths differ from neurotics and more normal actors in that they tend to choose present consequences of their decisions over delayed consequences, learn less from punishment, recover more quickly from stress, and show less anxiety and less anticipation of the unpleasant consequences of their acts (Dinitz et al. 1973, Hare 1966, 1968, Hetherington & Klinger 1964, House & Milligan 1976, Schachter & Latané 1964, Schmauk 1970, Siegel 1978, Waid 1976).

Psychopaths not only feel differently about themselves, other people, pleasure, and pain, but they also think differently. This is not surprising since we have agreed (p. 145) that "mental work" includes perceiving, feeling, and willing as well as conceiving the world through written or spoken symbols (Langer 1967, Ryle 1949). Whatever we mean by "thinking," it is not a disembodied activity. It is not something done only "in the head," but something performed by an organism with a specific physiology (McGuigan 1978). Thus studies that demonstrate a difference in the autonomic functioning of psychopaths run in parallel with studies that reveal differences in their cognitive practices. Psychopaths are less able than normal people to construe how others think and feel (Widom 1976, 1977). When they are given conceptual tasks, like running the Porteus Maze,[1] they are characteristically careless, rule-breaking, and, of course, error-making (Schalling & Rosen 1968).

This kind of character is temperamentally different from most of us, but this does not say that psychopathic attitudes may not be learned. Constitutional differences make some people better candidates than others for whatever predatory lessons are available in a cultural climate. This possibility acknowledges, then, that there may be peripheral, or secondary, psychopaths, as well as pure ones, and that moral atmospheres may move vulnerable individuals one way or the other. The idea here is analogous to the notion of vulnerability to disease; some individuals are more susceptible than others to a contagion.

Psychopathy and Work

By whatever process psychopaths are produced, they are better

---

[1] The Porteus Maze Tests are presumably "culture-free" measures of mental ability. They consist of a series of mazes, graduated in difficulty, that may be administered without verbal instruction. They may be constructed as line-drawings or as channels in wooden tablets. Subjects try to trace a route from entrance to exit of the mazes without crossing lines or lifting pencils or styluses. Porteus claims that his test is particularly suited to assess those facets of intelligence associated with social competence, such as foresight, diligence, and planning.

suited for some occupations, lawful and criminal, than for others. They are well adapted, for example, to lawful work as politicians,[2] as opposed to statesmen, to work as "yellow journalists," as opposed to responsible reporters, and to work as propagandists, as opposed to scholars.[3]

Among the criminal vocations, psychopaths are wonderfully fit for fraud (Volume Three, Chapter 3). Their capacity for lying and their ability to feign emotions they do not feel make con-games their forte. Psychopathy is not the only road to fraud, of course, but it is an easy route.

Psychopathy is also congenial to mercenary killing. A "hit man" is a psychopath by the very nature of his work. People who kill on hire can only do such work efficiently if they lack empathy for their victims.

Executioners, too, require some degree of psychopathy for their work. This is particularly true of those who work as individuals rather

[2] Politicians in democracies are stimulated, and often rewarded, for assuming the limited time-frame of the psychopath. Their interest is in getting elected, and re-elected. Maximizing votes requires attention to present issues rather than to the later effects of present policies. Nordhaus (1975) shows that this focus has two consequences: choice of policies that in the long run favor lower unemployment and higher inflation than is optimal and an electoral cycle that begins in austerity and ends in give-aways. Elster (1979, p. 61) calls the give-aways "potlatch," after the Kwakiutl custom of obligating others by one's generosity. Tufte (1978) provides data from Western democracies confirming the occurrence of this "psychopathic" practice among politicians. The practice is commonly called "buying the vote." It is illegal if done directly, but legal if done indirectly.

This note is descriptive, not moralistic, although one may draw a moral from it. This note suggests that what is rational in the short run may be irrational as a long-term policy. It suggests that economic decisions made for political reasons are usually poor economic decisions. The literature on this possibility is large. It may be sampled in Bauer and O'Sullivan, 1977, Cornuelle, 1968, Lichtheim, 1968, Lippmann, 1956, Rose and Peters, 1978, Shefter, 1977, and Shilling, 1979.

Volume Three, Chapter 3 demonstrates that tension between short-run and long-run rationality paves one road to fraud.

[3] Propagandists are not necessarily liars. Moreover, when they lie, that is not all that they do. A skillful propagandist knows that truth can be persuasive and that it is less risky than lying (Ellul 1965, pp. 52–61). A propagandist differs from a scholar, however, in the narrower focus of her truth-seeking and truth-telling. The scholar, by contrast, is dedicated to "whatsoever things are true," regardless of the political side truth may favor. The current status of the "social sciences" makes it problematic whether professors of the social studies wish to be propagandists, scholars, or some shifting mixture of both (Laue 1978, Nettler 1980).

than as members of groups like firing squads.[4] This requirement also applies more strongly as the execution is performed face-to-face rather than more impersonally as in pushing a button or throwing a switch that kills an unseen person. Recruitment for such work in Western countries faces the difficulty of finding "stable" killers rather than gleeful sadists as executioners. A recent newspaper headline notes that, "Illinois Needs Executioners" (*United Press International* 1980b). The Director of State Corrections, in announcing the job opening, specified that an aspiring executioner must be willing to remain anonymous, must be unrelated to the prisoner slated for execution, and must be "psychologically stable." The Director added, "It's an odd thing, but we're not looking for any nuts. I don't know yet how you determine a nut from a sane person, but we'll be working on it."

Psychopathy and Violence

We do not know the distribution of psychopaths by degrees of their difference and their locations in social settings. We do not know, therefore, whether they run a greater risk of conviction for crime or whether, in some social networks, their charm and persuasiveness might not defend them against the risk of arrest.

For example, women who become entangled with male psychopaths invariably tell stories of physical and emotional abuse, but they also have difficulty believing that they are being "suckered" and they often blame themselves for the beatings they take. Women who love such charmers are difficult to reform.

The point here, however, is that some unknown proportion of psychopaths prey on others without being convicted of crime. Still, it may be expected that a significant number of psychopaths of lesser talent might end up in prison and might have a history of violent crime.

Hare (1981) reports research with Canadian prison populations, some of whom were followed for 15 months to 11 years after original examination. With the use of a reliable and valid rating scale administered independently by two clinicians, Hare and his colleagues find that between 27 and 33 percent of white male inmates score sufficiently high as to merit the appellation, "psychopath."

---

[4] In Western lands where execution is taken more seriously than in some Eastern countries, the conscience of individuals in a firing squad is eased by the ritual of having one rifle loaded with a blank cartridge and assigned randomly. No one rifleman is certain, therefore, that his bullet caused death.

Inmates diagnosed as psychopathic differ, by degree, from other convicts in the following ways:

- They are more likely to have been convicted of armed robbery, assault, forcible seizure, and rape.
- They are more likely to have used a weapon in their crimes. They have been in more fights and have more often engaged in aggressive homosexual behavior.
- They have been convicted for their first serious crime at an earlier age, have more convictions, and have spent more time in prison.
- They are more likely to have used aliases.
- They have engaged in a greater variety of crimes with higher rates of recidivism.
- They more frequently escape from prison.

These men peak in criminal activity between ages 30 and 35 and "mature out" thereafter. Hare also notes that the quality of person-situation interaction differs for psychopaths. *With them, more of the action flows from their dispositions.*

In summary, within prison populations at least, these individuals have a significantly higher rate of commission of violent crimes. Furthermore, they are difficult, if not impossible, to wean from their wicked ways. *No one knows of a reliable cure of psychopathy.*

Four Early Signs

When attention turns from the "normal psychopath" to the "farther-out psychopath" who kills for pleasure, where the pleasure is the joy of exercised hatred, four early cues are often noted: sleepwalking, fire-setting, bed-wetting, and cruelty to animals. No one cue is a "sure sign," of course, but a repeated combination of any three of these abnormalities may be taken to be premonitory. Cruelty to animals is particularly indicative when it includes delight in mutilating the beast. Beheading is a favorite form of such domination.

MORALS MOVE BOUNDARIES

It is apparent that the concept of psychopathic homicide has foggy frontiers with idealistic killing, on one side, and psychotic killing, on the other. As we examine some psychopathic cases, it will be seen that the lunacy of their killing is not the lunacy of psychosis, if the sign of psychosis remains a "break with reality." While many killers called psychopathic do not exhibit the full spectrum of Cleckley's criteria, they have in common a "give-away" combination of characteristics: They know what they are doing, which is to say that they are legally sane, and they have no conscience about killing. Lack of conscience means that they feel neither shame nor guilt. They do not feel these emotions and they cannot feel them.

On another conceptual frontier, the gradient from psychopathic killer to idealistic terrorist runs through vaguely defined qualities of emotion and aspiration. The ideals with which terrorists justify their homicides do not deny the callousness with which they kill, and it is this lack of feeling for the victim that joins the solitary killer-for-profit with the solidary killer-for-ideals.

In comparing psychopaths with idealists, it is popular to say that their *motives* differ. This may be so, but it is more accurate to say that their *justifications* differ. As Ambrose Bierce commented (p. 2), this distinction is important for lawyers, but not for victims. Students of human behavior note, however, that it is easier to identify justifications—*reasons* given for actions—than it is to identify motives—the *causes* of those actions. As philosophers of the social scene, we avoid confusing the two. Moreover, as students interested in *describing* what people do, we need not take sides with killers on the justice of their murders. This dispassion frees us to observe that impersonal homicide, whether for profit or ideals or both, is comfortable work for the psychopath and a more difficult job for the rest of us.[5]

A SAMPLE OF PSYCHOPATHS

The flavor and variety of psychopathic damage can be illustrated by a few examples. The first case is from Yochelson and Samenow's work on *The Criminal Personality* (1976), a three-volume study full of psychopathic characters. Their convict *C–1* is estimated to have committed more than 64,000 crimes in his 31 years for which he was convicted only seven times. Yochelson and Samenow chronicle *C–1's* career thus:

PROPERTY CRIMES

Stealing beginning at age 5; at 7, stealing such things as knife at school, tobacco from father, and toy guns

---

[5] Some writers (Smith 1978) assume that a market economy distinctively produces and rewards psychopaths, but there is no tally comparing the proportions of psychopaths and their successes in capitalist and communist countries. There is defense again in numbers and in power. Depending on one's politics, the lying and killing that characterize totalitarian states may be deemed "defensively realistic" rather than psychopathic.

Organized a gang of thieves at age 9

Engaging in fraudulent practices at carnival at age 13

Had a "contract" to procure wine for other adolescents at age 13

Fraudulent magazine sales

Participated in arranging and carrying out illegal abortions

Fraudulent television repair service

Misrepresented self as foreign diplomat to get illegal supplies of heroin

Stole $4,000 worth of clothes and embezzled $3,000 cash in 18 days while working for a clothing store

Illegally wrote and cashed checks for $75-100 daily for 3 years, or about $25,000-30,000 per year

Stole check cashing and writing equipment and in 2½ days cashed $7,500 worth

Bank swindle using illegal and fraudulent securities involving $24,000

Stole negotiable securities, using these to get loan of $3,800

Impersonating a physician—writing fraudulent prescriptions, using some of these to obtain drugs, which he used himself or sold illegally

Extensive buying and selling of drugs

Theft of equipment from wife's place of business

Writing bad checks on wife's business account

Organized phony promotional and consulting firm

ASSAULT

At least three serious cases:

One man shot fatally

One man pistol-whipped

One man made paraplegic by C's deliberately running him down with a car

SEXUAL CRIMES

Numerous cases of carnal knowledge with underage girls

Procuring for government officials

Pimping at 15 for a madam from whom he received money and sex (Volume 1, pp. 221-222, reproduced with permission of the publisher).

Killing for Kicks: Charles Howard Schmid, Jr., 1966

Psychopaths find justification of their thoughts and deeds in the complicity of "normal" people. Howard "Smitty" Schmid's career illustrates this as does that of Winston Mosely to follow.

At 23 years of age, Smitty was convicted of murdering three teenage girls in Tucson, Arizona. Smitty had been a teenagers' hero around town. Journalists described him:

as someone to admire and emulate. He was different. He was Smitty, with mean, "beautiful" eyes and an interesting way of talking, and if he sometimes did weird things, at least he wasn't dull. He had his own house where he threw good parties, he wore crazy make-up, he was known at all the joints up and down Tucson's Speedway, and girls dyed their hair blond for him. Three of the girls who knew him . . . wound up dead in the desert outside of town (*Life* 1966, p. 19).

To this description, Moser (1966) adds:

He wore face make-up and dyed his hair. He habitually stuffed three or four inches of old rags and tin cans into the bottoms of his high-topped boots to make himself taller than his five-foot-three and stumbled about so awkwardly while walking that some people thought he had wooden feet. He pursed his lips and let his eyelids droop in order to emulate his idol, Elvis Presley. He bragged to girls that he knew 100 ways to make love, that he ran dope, that he was a Hell's Angel. He talked about being a rough customer in a fight (he was, though he was rarely in one), and he always carried in his pocket tiny bottles of salt and pepper, which he said he used to blind his opponents. He liked to use highfalutin language and had a favorite saying, "I can manifest my neurotical emotions, emancipate an epicureal instinct, and elaborate on my heterosexual tendencies."

He occasionally shocked even those who thought they knew him well. A friend says he once saw Smitty tie a string to the tail of his pet cat, swing it around his head and beat it bloody against a wall. Then he turned calmly and asked, "You feel compassion—why?"

Smitty's parents gave him money. He drove a good car, spent freely, and had "nice manners." He even seemed considerate and would, for example, send flowers to girls who were ill. The "consideration" expressed a bid for attention, of course, rather than concern for his friends.

Through his parents' generosity, Smitty acquired a cottage of his own where he could entertain. His friends were usually younger than he and he enjoyed impressing them with his "sophistication." On one day be bought two fake diamond rings and got "engaged" to two girls. He told buddies that he planned to put his girls to work and have them deposit their earnings in joint accounts with him. One of the girls did go to work in the business run by Smitty's parents. She deposited her earnings as instructed. When the joint account grew large enough, Smitty withdrew the money and bought himself a tape recorder.

Smitty's adventures escalated into killing "for no good reason" and bragging about it. He involved two 19-year-olds, Mary French and John Saunders, in one of his murders. Mary and John lured Alleen Rowe into Smitty's car and drove with her to the desert where she was beaten to death with a rock.

Smitty also talked at length about his murders with Richard "Richie" Bruns. However, Richie was in love with Kathy Morath, and he began to fear that Kathy was next on Smitty's murder list. Someone had cut the screen door on Kathy's house and a prowler had been seen. One night Richie blurted out the Smitty story to his grandmother who, of course, did not believe him. His grandmother's attempts to talk him out of this foolish idea enraged Richie who screamed at her, "The one time in my life when I need advice and what do I get?" With that, he called the police.

Mary French and John Saunders confessed to their parts in killing Alleen Rowe. Mary was sentenced to four to five years in prison and John to life imprisonment. Smitty was sentenced to death, with the sentence later commuted to life imprisonment.

The moral climate in which Smitty operated is both depicted and tested by the fact that, during his years of bragging about his crimes, no one snitched on him. At least six high school students told authorities after the trial that they had known of the murders. One of Smitty's friends added, "I didn't know he killed her [Alleen Rowe] and even if I had, I wouldn't have said anything. I wouldn't want to be a fink."

There are other ways to avoid "being a fink." One is not to recognize the crime that one is witnessing, as in the case of the 38 persons who heard Winston Moseley kill Catherine Genovese.

Winston Moseley, Catherine Genovese, and 38 Witnesses, 13 March, 1964

Catherine "Kitty" Genovese worked as bar manager in the New York City borough of Queens. About 3 a.m. on March 13th, Kitty drove home and parked her car near her apartment. As she left her car she noticed a man lurking nearby and she ran toward a police telephone box. Before she could get there, her assailant threw himself on her back and stabbed her several times. The Metropolitan Editor of *The New York Times,* A.M. Rosenthal (1964), describes the attack:

> She got as far as a street light in front of a bookstore before the man grabbed her. She screamed. Lights went on in the ten-story apartment

house at 82-67 Austin Street, which faces the bookstore. Windows slid open and voices punctured the early-morning stillness.

Miss Genovese screamed: "Oh, my God, he stabbed me! Please help me! Please help me!"

From one of the upper windows in the apartment house, a man called down: "Let that girl alone!"

The assailant looked up at him, shrugged and walked down Austin Street toward a white sedan parked a short distance away. Miss Genovese struggled to her feet.

Lights went out. The killer returned to Miss Genovese, now trying to make her way around the side of the building by the parking lot to get to her apartment. The assailant stabbed her again.

"I'm dying!" she shrieked. "I'm dying!"

Windows were opened again, and lights went on in many apartments. The assailant got into his car and drove away. Miss Genovese staggered to her feet. A city bus . . . passed. It was 3:35 a.m.

The assailant returned. By then, Miss Genovese had crawled to the back of the building, where the freshly painted brown doors to the apartment house held out hope of safety. The killer tried the first door; she wasn't there. At the second door, 82-62 Austin Street, he saw her slumped on the floor at the foot of the stairs. He stabbed her a third time—fatally.

It was 3:50 by the time the police received their first call from a man who was a neighbor of Miss Genovese. In two minutes they were at the scene. The neighbor, a seventy-year-old woman, and another woman were the only persons on the street. Nobody else came forward.

The man explained that he had called the police after much deliberation. He had phoned a friend in Nassau County for advice and then he had crossed the roof of the building to the apartment of the elderly woman to get her to make the call.

"I didn't want to get involved," he sheepishly told the police (Rosenthal 1964, pp. 33-37, reproduced by permission of *The New York Times*).

Rosenthal reports that at least 38 individuals witnessed the prolonged attack without calling the police.

Six days after Kitty's death, police arrested Winston Moseley for a daylight burglary. Under questioning, Moseley confessed to killing Miss Genovese and two other women, to setting fire to the genitals of one victim, to raping "four or five others," and to robbing and attempting to rape many more. He also admitted at least 40 burglaries.

Moseley, 29, was the father of three children, an accounting machine operator, a "middle-class" home-owner and church-goer. He was also a necrophiliac and he can be counted as a lust-murderer as well as a psychopath. But it is the psychopathy, the lack of conscience, that interests us here.

Moseley insisted to police and the examining psychiatrist that he felt no remorse for any of his crimes. He recalled that, after killing Catherine Genovese, he was at ease. He drove home, washed his German hunting knife, replaced it neatly in his tool box, and slept soundly.

When asked about his reaction to the shout from the window during his attack on Kitty, Moseley said, "I had a feeling that this man would close his window and go back to sleep, and sure enough he did" (*Time* 1964, p. 18).

In a fashion similar to that of Tom Bean (pp. 134–138), Moseley told the court that, "I just set out to find any girl that was unattended and I was going to kill her." Moseley's murders differ from that of Tom Bean, however, in their dispassion. Human beings can kill one another without hatred.

A jury unanimously sentenced Moseley to death and the courtroom audience burst into applause upon the announcement (Wainwright 1964). Judge J. Irwin Shapiro added, "I don't believe in capital punishment, but I must say I feel this may be improper when I see this monster. I wouldn't hesitate to pull the switch myself!" (*Time* 1964, p. 17).

Killing for Fun and Money: Dr. Maurice Petiot

On March 25, 1946, Dr. Maurice Petiot was guillotined for the murder of 26 persons. Two years earlier police had discovered in Dr. Petiot's Paris house 15 kilos of charred bones and 11 kilos of uncharred bones. They also found tons of the victims' clothing, a limepit, and a triangular room apparently equipped for torture ceremonies.

Dr. Petiot bragged that he had killed 63 people. His tally need not be accepted as exact, but his days of slaughtering coincided with a tide of carved-up corpses found adrift in the Seine.

Maurice Petiot graduated from an early career in crime in the region of Auxerre. As a child he was a sleep-walker and bed-wetter who delighted in torturing animals. He enjoyed dipping cats' paws in boiling water, for example.

By the time he was an adolescent he had moved into varieties of theft and showed himself to be inventive as a thief. He devised a technique for stealing letters from mailboxes with a glue-tipped stick. He was also suspected of arsons in his neighborhood.

Petiot became a physician in the town of Villeneuve-sur-Yonne where he was accused of many larcenies, including burglary, and one butcher-murder. Despite suspicions about his abnormal activities, Dr. Petiot's wit and charm made him popular and he was elected as Socialist mayor of his town. While in this post he was accused of pension fraud, a variety of other larcenies including siphoning electricity, drug-peddling, illegal abortion, and two murders.

Dr. Petiot met such accusations by calling them politically inspired. At other times he relied on the defense that he had been temporarily "sick." He had been briefly hospitalized for "emotional disorder."

In 1933 Dr. Petiot set up practice in Paris. He advertised his ability to "remove or relieve" almost everything—from skin spots and goiter to arthritis, depression, and senility. He invented an aphrodisiac suppository, a sure cure for constipation, a perpetual motion machine and, when World War II started, a silent, short-range, lethal weapon that was so secret it could not be demonstrated.

The war gave Dr. Petiot a grand opportunity to employ his persuasive powers and to satisfy his pleasure in fraud and homicide. The Nazi conquest of France resulted in the "disappearance" of thousands of people and the desire of many more to escape.

Dr. Petiot set himself up as a coordinator of escape routes for the French Resistance. His victims paid him a fee. They were instructed to remove all identifying marks from their clothing and to write letters to concerned intimates announcing their safe arrival in Argentina or some other refuge. They delivered themselves to Dr. Petiot's house with one suitcase into which they had crammed their most valuable and transportable possessions, jewelry preferred. They then allowed Dr. Petiot to give them an injection described as a vaccination required by the host country. The injection was, of course, their last purchase of immunity.

Thomas Maeder (1981) describes Dr. Petiot's trial that became a "social event" and at which the defendant gave a brilliant performance—humorous, mocking, scornful. At one point Petiot dramatized:

> I see it all now. The mad doctor with the syringe. It was a dark and rainy night. The wind howled under the eaves and rattled the windowpanes of the oak-panelled library. . . .

Lunacy comes in assorted packages, mixed with intelligence and lucidity. It need not be manifest in all departments of behavior.

The fact that lunacy can be part-time and the fact that humor, wit, and charm provide the "mask of sanity" make it difficult to believe in the cruelty that characterizes psychopathy.

A Borderline Case: Charles Manson and His "Family"

As we have seen (Chapter 1), sane people justify some kinds of homicide. What they call "senseless murder" is killing that lacks their common justifications. Common homicidal objectives that "make sense" include self-defense, honor, power, wealth, and ideals. People who engage in homicide that cannot be so justified seem lunatic. They seem particularly crazy when their killing is purely expressive.

Expressive homicide flows from demoralization. Since killing "for no good reason" is the ultimate violation of the commandment against homicide, it becomes the supreme test of freedom from morality.

Freedom from morality is one aspect of intellectual movements known as "irrationalism" (Gardiner 1967) and "nihilism" (Olson 1967). Irrationalism and nihilism have many faces—ideological, aesthetic, ethical, psychological, and political. In brief, these titles describe an amalgam of assumptions that claims the world to be disorderly, objectivity to be a "confidence trick," knowledge to be impossible, fine art to be merely what one likes, and morality, a matter of taste.

These philosophies assume that life has no purpose and that living is therefore of doubtful value. "Everything is up to us," existentialists claim, and the fundamental question becomes, "Why should we not commit suicide?" (Camus 1955).

In his *Beyond Good and Evil* (1907), Friedrich Nietzsche taught that conventional morality expresses unconscious forces in the psyche, forces in the form of sentiments such as affiliation, resentment, and fear. Freedom is to be found, then, by recognizing these sources and conquering them. The Nietzschean "Superman" transcends these "enslaving emotions" and moves beyond them to new values. Seeking the new values requires living in the present and acting on impulse. One challenges all codes of conduct, scratches where it itches, "does it" if it feels good, and indulges in meaningless behavior and absurd art as an expression of one's freedom from oppressive rules in the search for one's "true identity."

It was Nietzsche (1844–1900) who gave us those famous phrases, "God is dead; nothing is true, all is permitted."

From such assumptions it follows that absurdity is as sound as rationality, ugliness is beauty, and, in the words of the mad Hamlet, "there is nothing either good or bad, but thinking makes it so."

Any particular assumption of irrationalists and nihilists may be cogent, but these assumptions as a unit cannot be believed except at great expense. *To believe* an assumption is not merely to think it so, but to *think and act* as though it were so. Believing the irrationalist story opens doors to license.[6]

Philosophers debate whether denial of moral foundations necessarily demoralizes. "Necessarily" is a catch-word here and the argument ensues about the extent to which people become demoralized as they become skeptical of the grounding of conventional moral codes. This is a question the great novelist Feodor Dostoyevsky (1821–1881) wrestled with in his *Crime and Punishment* and *The Brothers Karamazov*. His conclusion was that doubt about the mythical sources of morals is destructive. Dostoyevsky's inference is substantiated by the lives of Charles Manson and his followers.

We characterize the Manson killers as psychopathic although some of the justifications uttered by these murderers border on the psychotic. It is impossible from this distance to ascertain whether some of Manson's utterances constitute delusions or con-jobs. Moreover, many actors were engaged in a series of homicides and all were judged to be legally sane. They were joined, however, by the common bond of moral idiocy. They lacked inhibitory conscience.

Horror Story

One Saturday morning in August, 1969, Winifred Chapman, a housekeeper in one of the homes overlooking Beverly Hills, California, arrived for work to find the front door ajar, blood splashed on the terrace and on the walls of the living room, a body on the lawn and another inside a car in the driveway. Mrs. Chapman ran to a neighbor's house screaming, "Murder, death, bodies, blood!" Police were called. They found three additional bodies and the word PIG printed in blood on the front door.

The invaded house was leased to the movie director, Roman Polanski, and his actress wife, Sharon Tate. While Polanski was in London on business, his wife had houseguests—the coffee heiress, Abigail Folger, and her lover, Voytek Frykowski. Tate, Folger, and Frykowski were three of the victims. In addition, Jay Sebring, a popular hair stylist and former lover of Sharon's, was visiting that night and he was a

---

[6] This argument raises an ancient issue: whether reason has a limited utility and whether myths that are, by definition, unprovable ought to be accepted because of their beneficial consequences. The French philosopher Blaise Pascal (1623–1662) phrased the issue as his famous "wager" (1955) about the utility of faith. His wager claims that it is reasonable, at some juncture, to stop reasoning.

This fascinating question runs beyond our present attention, but its convolutions can be read in Elster (1979).

fourth victim. The fifth victim was 18-year-old Steve Parent who had been to see an acquaintance, William Garretson, who lived in an apartment over the garage on the Polanski estate. Parent's body with four bullet wounds was discovered in his car.

Sharon Tate, eight months pregnant, had been stabbed 16 times. A rope had been looped around her neck, flung over a rafter in the ceiling, and looped again around the neck of Jay Sebring whose body lay a few feet away. Sebring had been stabbed seven times and shot once.

Abigail Folger had been stabbed 28 times and her friend, Frykowski, had been shot twice, hit over the head with a blunt instrument 13 times, and stabbed 51 times. Both Folger and Frykowski had been multiple drug users and MDA, a powerful intoxicant, was found in their blood samples. Cocaine and marijuana were found in Sebring's car and marijuana traces in Tate's bedroom. This finding led detectives to speculate that the killings were drug-related—either as part of an orgy or as part of a drug "burn," an argument with dealers over money or poor quality chemicals. Burglary was eliminated as a motive because money and jewelry were left on the victims.

The next night Leno LaBianca and his wife, Rosemary, were killed in their Los Feliz home, several miles from the Polanski residence. Leno had been multiply stabbed, the word WAR carved on his stomach, and a knife and fork jabbed into his body. His wife had been stabbed 41 times. The messages DEATH TO PIGS and RISE had been printed on the living room wall and HEALTER SKELTER (spelled that way) on the refrigerator door—all in blood. Three weeks earlier the body of Gary Hinman, a 34-year-old music teacher, had been found in his Topango Canyon cabin. The words POLITICAL PIGGY had been printed on the wall in his blood. Detectives were slow to see a connection.

Connections among these murders began to appear when Inyo County officers, some 200 miles from Los Angeles, raided a hippie hideout on the Barker Ranch near Death Valley. Their raid was based on charges of grand larceny and arson and resulted in the arrest of 24 men and women who regarded themselves as "The Manson Family." Their leader, Charles Manson, was a 34-year-old ex-convict, the son of a dissolute teenager, who, on the record, had been lying and stealing since he was 12 years old. Charlie had spent half his life in "correctional institutions," and, prior to his latest release in 1967, he had begged authorities to let him remain in prison because he felt he could not adjust to life outside (Bugliosi & Gentry 1974, p. 146).

Upon his release on parole, Charlie found the booming hippie cults a ready market for his talents. He learned to strum a guitar and had visions of becoming a composer. He wrote lyrics, one of which consisted only of the words, "you know, you know, you know. . . ."

Charlie called himself a "roving minstrel" and moved to the Haight-Ashbury district of San Francisco. There, among runaways, dopesters, and seekers after "meaning," Charlie became a magnet for young girls to whom he preached love and freedom, but whom he treated as inferiors. Men joined his tribe for the rewards of easy and varied sexuality, the excitement of hallucinogenic drugs and outrageous crime, and the comfort of community.

In keeping with irrationalist philosophy, Charlie taught his devotees that:

> No sense makes sense.
> Everything is only a thought.
> When you're free of ego, you're free of everything. Whatever you say is right for yourself.
> Fear is beautiful because fear is awareness.
> Death is beautiful because people fear death.
> Everything in the world belongs to everyone. Therefore, there can be no theft, but only a redistribution of property.

One of Charlie's songs says, "Cease to exist, just come and say you love me. As I say I love you or I should say I love Me (my love) in you."

Susan Atkins, one of The Family involved in the Hinman, Tate, and LaBianca murders, explained their "philosophy" to a jailmate:

> I wanted the world to know M [Manson]. It sure looks like they do now. There was a so called motive behind all this. It was to instill fear into the pigs and to bring on judgment day which is here now for all.
>
> In the word kill, the only thing that dies is the ego. All ego must die anyway, it is written. Yes, it could have been your house, it could have been my fathers house also. In killing someone phisally you are only releasing the soul. Life has no boundris and death is only an illusion. If you can believe in the second coming of Crist, M is he who has come to save.
>
> I know now it has all been perfect. Those people died not out of hate or anything ugly. I am not going to defend our beliefs. I am just telling you the way it is . . . love will still run forever (Cited by Bugliosi & Gentry 1974, p. 195; the spelling and punctuation are Susan's).

Charlie did not merely preach his lessons. He reinforced preachment with actions that erased inhibitions. He taught violation of all codes of decency and gave his pupils exercises in violation. He initiated girls with day-long sexual marathons and then ordered them into group sexual carnivals. He initiated one girl by buggering her in front of his disciples and he commanded every perversion he could think of. Public perversion indicated liberation from the middle-class morality which many of his followers had been tentatively taught. Drugs facilitated the liberation. One of Charlie's lead-killers, Susan Atkins, "reborn" as Sadie Mae Glutz and also known as Sexy Sadie, Sharon King, and other titles, had a baby boy whom she named Zezozose Zadfrack Glutz. Charlie helped deliver this baby and, when the infant was a few months old, Susan began fellating him before the tribe. Inhibition was dead.

Charlie moved his Family to a deserted movie set, the Spahn Ranch, near Los Angeles. He sent his devotees out on "garbage runs"—food-gathering forays—and on "creepy-crawly," fun burglaries. He had his followers cadge money from their parents and panhandle on the streets.

Charlie increasingly felt his powers. He ordered the killing of Gary Hinman because Hinman would not give him money he was thought to have inherited. Charlie hated the world that had found him useless, and the racial riots of the 1960s stimulated his hope that blacks and whites would kill each other off so that a new world could be created from zero. Charlie adopted the slogan HELTER SKELTER from a Beatles' tune as a symbol of the chaos he hoped to start. Moving his Family to the Barker Ranch was part of preparation for the war to come. Killing was practice for revolution.

The LaBiancas died because their house had been entered in previous "creepy crawly" adventures. Tate and her friends died because the Polanski house had belonged to Terry Melcher, a producer of TV shows and recordings, who had once listened to Charlie's singing and had refused to record him. Charlie had not known that Melcher had moved from the house that his gang invaded.

The full story of Charlie and his Family has been recorded by their prosecutor in the Tate and LaBianca trials, Vincent Bugliosi (with Gentry 1974). However, the devastation of conscience is best described by Susan Atkins's conversation with a jailmate and by some of the Family's trial testimony.

Susan bragged to another inmate, Ronnie Howard, about killing Sharon Tate:

> As Ronnie understood it, two other people held Sharon while, to quote Susan, "I proceeded to stab her."
>
> "It felt so good the first time I stabbed her, and when she screamed at me it did something to me, sent a rush through me, and I stabbed her again."

Ronnie asked where. Susan replied in the chest, not the stomach.

"How many times?"

"I don't remember. I just kept stabbing her until she stopped screaming."

Ronnie knew a little bit about the subject, having once stabbed her ex-husband. "Did it feel sort of like a pillow?"

"Yeah," Susan replied, pleased that Ronnie understood. "It was just like going into nothing, going into air." But the killing itself was something else. "It's like a sexual release," Susan told her. "Especially when you see the blood spurting out. It's better than a climax" (Bugliosi & Gentry 1974, p. 95).

At her trial, Susan testified:

She was holding Sharon Tate and "Tex" came back and he looked at her and he said, 'Kill her.' And I killed her. . . . And I just stabbed her and she fell, and I stabbed her again. I don't know how many times I stabbed her. . . ." Sharon begged for the life of her baby, and "I told her, 'Shut up. I don't want to hear it'."

Q. "Miss Atkins, were any of these people killed as a result of any personal hate or animosity that you had toward them?"

A. "No."

Q. "Did you have any feeling toward them at all, any emotional feeling toward any of these people—Sharon Tate, Voytek Frykowski, Abigail Folger, Jay Sebring, Steven Parent?"

A. "I didn't know any of them. How could I have felt any emotion without knowing them?" Fitzgerald asked Susan if she considered these mercy killings.

A. "No. As a matter of fact, I believe I told Sharon Tate I didn't have any mercy for her."

Susan went on to explain that she knew what she was doing "was right when I was doing it." She knew this because, when you do the right thing, "it feels good."

Q. "How could it be right to kill somebody?"

A. "How could it not be right when it is done with love?"

Q. "Did you ever feel any remorse?"

A. "Remorse? For doing what was right to me?"

Q. "Did you ever feel sorry?"

A. "Sorry for doing what was right to me? I have no guilt in me." (Bugliosi & Gentry 1974, pp. 426–428).

Susan added, "What I did was what I did with those people, and that is what I did."

Q. "Just one of those things, seven dead bodies?"

A. "No big thing."

. . . "So killing seven people is just business as usual, no big deal, is that right, Sadie?"

A. "It wasn't at the time. It was just there to do."

I asked her how she felt about the victims. She responded, "They didn't even look like people. . . . I didn't relate to Sharon Tate as being anything but a store mannequin."

Q. "You have never heard a store mannequin talk, have you, Sadie?"

A. "No, sir. But she just sounded like an IBM machine. . . . She kept begging and pleading and pleading and begging, and I got sick of listening to her, so I stabbed her."

Q. "And the more she screamed, the more you stabbed, Sadie?"

A. "Yes. So?"

Q. "And you looked at her and you said, 'Look, bitch, I have no mercy for you.' Is that right, Sadie?"

A. "That's right. That's what I said then." (Bugliosi & Gentry 1974, pp. 429-430).

Patricia "Katie" Krenwinkel, another member of the Family, testified:

. . . describing life at Spahn Ranch, she said: "We were just like wood nymphs and wood creatures. We would run through the woods with flowers in our hair, and Charlie would have a small flute. . . ."

On the murder of Abigail Folger: "And I had a knife in my hands, and she took off running, and she ran—she ran out through the back door, one I never even touched, I mean, nobody got fingerprints because I never touched that door . . . and I stabbed her and I kept stabbing her."

Q. "What did you feel after you stabbed her?"

A. "Nothing—I mean, like what is there to describe? It was just there, and it's like it was right."

On the mutilation of Leno LaBianca: After murdering Rosemary, Katie remembered seeing Leno lying on the floor in the living room. She flashed, "You won't be sending your son off to war," and "I guess I put WAR on the man's chest. And then I guess I had a fork in my hands, and I put it in his stomach . . . and I went and wrote on the walls . . ." (Bugliosi & Gentry 1974, pp. 430-431).

Leslie Van Houten, another of Manson's killers, testified about the La-Bianca murders:

Q. "Leslie, do you feel sorrow or shame or a sense of guilt for having participated in the death of Mrs. LaBianca?"

A. [Pause]

> Q. "Let me go one by one. Do you feel sorrowful about it; sorry; un-happy?"
>
> You could almost feel the chill in the courtroom when Leslie answered: "Sorry is only a five-letter word. It can't bring back anything."
>
> Q. "I am trying, Leslie, to discover how you feel about it."
>
> A. "What can I feel? It has happened. She is gone."
>
> Q. "Do you wish that it hadn't happened?"
>
> A. "I never wish anything to be done over another way. That is a foolish thought. It never will happen that way. You can't undo something that is done."
>
> Q. "Do you feel as if you wanted to cry for what happened?"
>
> A. "Cry? For her death? If I cry for death, it is for death itself. She is not the only person who has died."
>
> Q. "Do you think about it from time to time?"
>
> A. "Only when I am in the courtroom" (Bugliosi & Gentry 1974, pp. 432–433).

In keeping with his pupils, Manson himself expressed a similar casual attitude toward killing and dying. "Death was only a thought," he claimed and added, "I could kill everyone without blinking an eye."

When Bugliosi (1974, p. 378) asked him why he felt this way, Manson replied, "Because you've been killing me for years." He went on to say that "he had no conscience, that everything was only a thought."

Manson testified in his own defense. He took a line commonly employed by criminal lawyers and some philosophers: That others commit worse crimes and that he and his homicidal companions were *products* rather than agents. The latter, deterministic argument is one frequently used by attorneys: If all behavior is caused, how can anyone be blamed? This is an argument that is selectively applied and inconsistently maintained. In addition to these points, Manson's defense ventilated his hatred of a "society" that found him useless. Manson spoke for more than one hour:

> There has been a lot of charges and a lot of things said about me and brought against the co-defendants in this case, of which a lot could be cleared up and clarified.
>
> I never went to school, so I never growed up to read and write too good, so I have stayed in jail and I have stayed stupid, and I have stayed a child while I have watched your world grow up, and then I look at the things that you do and I don't understand. . . .
>
> You eat meat and you kill things that are better than you are, and then you say how bad, and even killers, your children are. *You* made your children what they are. . . .

These children that come at you with knives, they are your children. You taught them. I didn't teach them. I just tried to help them stand up.

Most of the people at the ranch that you call the Family were just people that you did not want, people that were alongside the road, that their parents had kicked out, that did not want to go to Juvenile Hall. So I did the best I could and I took them up on my garbage dump and I told them this: that in love there is no wrong. . . .

I told them that anything they do for their brothers and sisters is good if they do it with a good thought. . . .

I was working at cleaning up my house, something that Nixon should have been doing. He should have been on the side of the road, picking up his children, but he wasn't. He was in the White House, sending them off to war. . . .

I don't understand you, but I don't try. I don't try to judge nobody. I know that the only person I can judge is me. . . . But I know this: that in your hearts and your own souls, you are as much responsible for the Vietnam war as I am for killing these people. . . .

I can't judge any of you. I have no malice against you and no ribbons for you. But I think it is high time that you all start looking at yourselves, and judging the lie that you live in.

I can't dislike you, but I will say this to you: you haven't got long before you are all going to kill yourselves, because you are all crazy. And you can project it back at me . . . but I am only what lives inside each and every one of you.

My father is the jailhouse. My father is your system. . . . I am only what you made me. I am only a reflection of you.

I have ate out of your garbage cans to stay out of jail. I have wore your second-hand clothes. . . . I have done my best to get along in your world and now you want to kill me, and I look at you, and then I say to myself, You want to kill *me?* Ha! I'm already dead, have been all my life. I've spent twenty-three years in tombs that you built.

Sometimes I think about giving it back to you; sometimes I think about just jumping on you and letting you shoot me. . . . If I could, I would jerk this microphone off and beat your brains out with it, because that is what you deserve, that is what you deserve. . . .

If I could get angry at you, I would try to kill every one of you. If that's guilt, I accept it. . . .

These children, everything they done, they done for the love of their brother. . . . These children [indicating the female defendants] were finding themselves. What they did, if they did whatever they did, is up to them. They will have to explain that to you. . . .

It's all your fear. You look for something to project it on, and you pick out a little old scroungy nobody that eats out of a garbage can, and that nobody wants, that was kicked out of the penitentiary, that has been dragged through every hellhole that you can think of, and you drag him and put him in a courtroom.

You expect to break me? Impossible! You broke me years ago. You killed me years ago. . . .

Helter Skelter? It means confusion, literally. Helter Skelter is confusion. Confusion is coming down around you fast. If you can't see the confusion coming down around you fast, you can call it what you wish.

Conspiracy? Is it a conspiracy that the music is telling the youth to rise up against the establishment because the establishment is rapidly destroying things? Is that a conspiracy?

The music speaks to you every day, but you are too deaf, dumb, and blind to even listen to the music. . . .

It is not my conspiracy. It is not my music. I hear what it relates. It says "Rise," it says "Kill."

Why blame it on me? I didn't write the music.

I don't think like you people. You people put importance on your lives. Well, my life has never been important to anyone. . . .

I haven't got any guilt about anything because I have never been able to see any wrong. . . . I have always said: Do what your love tells you, and I do what my love tells me. . . . Is it *my* fault that your children do what *you* do?

What about your children? You say there are just a few?

There are many, many more, coming in the same direction.

They are running in the streets—and they are coming right at you (Bugliosi & Gentry 1974, pp. 388–392, emphasis in the original. Reproduced by permission of the publisher, W.W. Norton & Co.).

Conviction

Manson and three of his female assistants were tried together. During the trial other devotees held vigils in the streets before the courthouse and "campaign" buttons appeared urging FREE THE MANSON FOUR. In a separate trial one of Manson's male aides was also indicted for first-degree murder. All five defendants were convicted and sentenced to death. Upon hearing Charlie's sentence, his co-defendants shouted:

Krenwinkel: "You have just judged yourselves."
Atkins: "Better lock your doors and watch your own kids."
Van Houten: "Your whole system is a game. You blind, stupid people. Your children will turn against you" (Bugliosi & Gentry 1974, p. 455).

Opinions such as these were not limited to The Family. During the trial, and immediately after, the "underground" press expressed ambivalence about Manson. He was alternately described as a hero, a martyr, and as a symptom of a "sick society." Rebels, of course, were attracted to Manson's violation of all codes. The terrorist Bernardine Dohrn, a leader of the Weathermen,[7] praised The Family's butcher.[*] "Dig it!" she exclaimed. "First they killed the pigs, then they ate dinner in the same room with them, then they even shoved forks in their stomachs. Wild!" (cited by Powers 1971, p. 168).

In milder fashion, a young district attorney, who successfully defended Family member Lynette "Squeaky" Fromme against murder and armed robbery charges, said he would like to write a book "about the beauty I've seen in that group—their opposition to war, their truthfulness, and their generosity" (Bugliosi & Gentry 1974, p. 488). Squeaky is now serving a life term for the attempted assassination of former American President Gerald Ford.

Manson, one of his male aides and his three co-defendants, were sentenced to death. In 1972 the California Supreme Court abolished the death penalty and the Manson Family's sentences were commuted to life imprisonment. In 1978 Manson applied for parole and was refused.

Charlie is now 45 years old and living in a segregated cell in the California Medical Facility at Vacaville where he receives weekly fanmail from people who want to join his Family (*United Press International* 1980c). *Famous cruelty attracts followers.*

LESSONS

We can draw other lessons from the careers of psychopathic killers:

1. Civil life is acquired. It represents a thin crust of custom over a volcano of aggression.

Psychopathic behavior is stimulated by breaks in customary restraints. "Sanity is always, in one degree or another, an act of will; insanity an act of letting go," Schickel writes (1972, p. 108).

Breaks in customary inhibition are induced by challenges to every facet of a civilization: Its art as well as its morals, its epistemology as well as its myths, its mode of reproduction as well as its mode of production. Barbaric attack is both frontal and flanking.

Civil life is never secure. It must always be renewed; its lessons must be taught again and again.

---

[7] The Weathermen took their name from a song, "Nowhere Man," made famous by *The Beatles.* The lyric praises the "Weatherman" who rips up the motherland, trashes, bombs, and kills "pigs."

As women became prominent in this group, it changed its name to Weatherpeople and The Weather Underground.

2. In the age of repetitive visual presentation of shocking "news," the media of mass communication are corrosive of moral continuity. They constitute a source of gratification for all the "losers" who can attain instant attention by attempted assassination. Journalists become accomplices to psychopathic outrage. The fame that television bestows on psychopaths provides apprenticeship for psychopaths-in-training. Arthur Bremer, who tried to kill presidential candidate George Wallace, complained to reporters of the burden of being a "star." "It's lonely at the top," he said.

3. The many roads from sanity to lunacy are continuous. There are no sharp breaks in the routes.

Difficulties in ascertaining where sanity ends and lunacy begins are further illustrated by the varieties of idealistic killer described in the next chapters.

10 HOMICIDAL ROUTES: **KILLING FOR WEALTH AND POWER**

Abstract • The most commonly traveled route to homicide is that leading to wealth and power. ○ Power is the ability to control others. ○ Having power is satisfying in itself, but it is a satisfaction allied with other desires, including those for wealth, pride, independence, identity, and community. ○ This mixture of satisfactions, plus the varying numbers of people involved in killing for wealth and power, plus the differing justifications given for such homicide, make all taxonomies of deadly quarrels imperfect. • A dilemma of killing for wealth and power is that violence gets results, but the results are seldom precisely those that had been desired. ○ The slippage between homicidal ideals and homicidal results does not betoken an end to killing for wealth and power. ○ No such end is probable because *some* benefits derive from mass homicide, no one has scales on which to balance those benefits against costs, and the historical record does not promise peace. • Studies of large-scale homicide for wealth and power reveal dimensions of such fighting. Internal and external dimensions are distinguished. • Correlates of warring do not reveal readily manipulable causes of killing that might guarantee peace. • It is concluded that: ○ A prime role of government is to keep the domestic peace. ○ Quantities of homicide describe continuities ○ Narrow interests produce limited fights; broad interests (ideals) encourage more destructive fights. ○ It cannot be assumed that the horror of war makes it improbable.

OF THE MANY ROADS TO HOMICIDE, the most commonly traveled route is that leading to wealth and power. Wealth and power are separable desires, yet they tend to run in tandem. One appetite can be satisfied independently of the other and we note instances of tyrants who love their power without luxuriating in wealth. But it is also true that wealth gives power, and power, wealth, and the two motives are frequently mixed as lethal fuel in individual careers and social movements.

Meaning of Power

Power is the ability to control others. It is the ability to have one's way even against the resistance of others. It is a motive in its own right; people seek it for the very pleasure of having it.

Pleasure in power derives not merely from the respect that power brings,[1] but also, and more strikingly, from the ability to produce changes in others. For example, in their own minor ways robbers and rapists tell us of the satisfaction they feel as they see fear in their victims' eyes. Some have likened the thrill of domination to the heroin "rush," an intense pleasure deemed comparable to orgasm or a sky dive or surfing a "tube."

The leader who controls millions of subjects may experience no greater "rush" than the robber, but joy in domination is both a personality variable—some seeking it more than others—and a constant feature of human nature.

A recent American Secretary of State called power an "aphrodisiac" and the Marquis de Sade would have agreed (Gorer 1962). However, other personalities have called power different things. Thus the Greek Cynic Diogenes (ca. 412–323 B.C.) thought power was a distraction. When a contemporaneous Man of Power, Alexander the Great, offered the philosopher any gift, the Cynic asked only that Alexander stand out of his sunlight.

Desire for wealth and power varies, then, with individuals, but persists as a cause of death. Within societies, and between societies, contests for wealth and power motivate homicide to a far greater extent than the loving, lusting, and lunacy we have discussed.

SATISFACTIONS AND JUSTIFICATIONS

Contests for wealth and power satisfy a running mixture of supplementary appetites. This means that occasions for deadly political struggles, and justifications of them, are varied and endless. Killing for wealth and power is not a "problem" for which there is a "solution." Homicide of this nature is better conceived as a recurring difficulty with which statesmen, intellectuals, and their publics wrestle.

In any particular fighter or group of warriors, a medley of motives and justifying ideas is at work, and at work in varied proportion. It is this changeable mixture of desires and their justifications that makes it impossible to classify homicide neatly, as Chapter 1 showed.

---

[1] Even children demonstrate the appetite for power and the adulation that power attracts. Bandura's (1962) experiments show that children choose as models to be imitated those other children whose energies make them leaders and successful. *Successful* leadership is followed "regardless of the form of behavior . . . employed to obtain the rewarding outcome" (p. 235).

In short, aggression that succeeds is copied.

Some homicide, for example, is directly instrumental, a tool with which one takes another's wealth, as in banditry and some war. It is also a tool with which one obtains power and protects it, as in gang fights, labor disputes, police actions, and revolutions.

In comparison with these uses, other routes to homicide appear to be less directly instrumental until we enlarge our vision and recognize that lust for power is variously packaged. For example, it is expressed, and justified, as the demand for autonomy, the right to rule one's own life. It is expressed, and justified, as pride. And, in the largest and most popular package, aspiration to power is rationalized by claims for "justice," where justice takes many forms (Nettler 1979).

Killing for justice translates homicide as "execution" rather than as "murder." This is a translation that appeals to groups that regard themselves as legitimate possessors of moral authority. Thus both governments-in-power and revolutionary challengers of that power refer to their killing of enemies as homicides rationalized by their sense of justice, a sense that fluctuates between demands for revenge, retribution,[2] deterrence, and submission.

Demand for a justice that promises violence is also stimulated by calls for continuity of ethnic identity—that is, the right to survive as a different population. This claim intertwines, in turn, with demands for new distributions of wealth and power.

In addition to these mixed motives, gaining power in a struggle is an impressive way of satisfying the need for community. Whether or not we approve of the fact, conflict reinforces community sentiment (Coser 1956). *Affiliation feeds on a sense of difference in conflict with others.*

This sentiment is exhibited in relatively innocent contests as it is in deadly combat. We observe stimulation of affiliation in sporting events, and not just in contact sports. For example, when America's individualistic chess player, Bobby Fischer, met Russia's team-supported Grandmaster, Boris Spassky, in what has been called *The Chess Match of the Century* (Roberts et al. 1972), Soviet writers claimed that the contest would show the superiority of "Socialist Man." (Fischer won).

Contestants do not battle alone. Spectators align themselves with combatants to dominate outsiders and to be "Number One." Community spirit is expressed in the theme songs of proud competitors who chant, "We Are Family!" And Our Family is distinguished from

---

[2] As noted in Volume Four, Chapter 1, revenge is to be distinguished from retribution.

Theirs by speech and dress, by gesture and posture and way of walking, by tattoos, hair-styles, hand-shakes, and other emblems of difference. Domination is the ultimate test of difference and its worth. A modern example illustrates a persistent phenomenon: Human beings value difference and enjoy combat.

Example: The Delights of Difference (Excerpts from Trillin & Koren 1978)

In the forties, the sort of tough teenagers who belonged to neighborhood gangs in East L.A. were called pachucos—identified by their zoot suits and their long key chains and their inclination to do violence to anyone who found himself in the wrong neighborhood. Pachucos used to lower their cars, sometimes by simply tossing bags of cement into the trunks. Tough teen-agers in East L.A. still belong to neighborhood gangs—often the same gangs their fathers or even grandfathers belonged to—and they still lower their cars. In East L.A., gang members are now called cholos rather than pachucos. Their customary outfit now consists of stiffly starched khakis or dungarees, a white T-shirt, a plaid Pendleton shirt worn as a jacket, and a watch cap or a small-brimmed pork-pie or a headband. They refer to themselves as *vatos locos,* or crazy guys, and to their life as *la vida loca.* Someone who leads *la vida loca* sees himself as defiant and fatalistic and willing to face the most horrifying dangers—dangers from police or other gangs or hard drugs or prison—without flinching. The cholo style of dress is derived largely from prison clothing. A cholo who has been in prison may wear, in addition to elaborate tattoos on his arms, a single teardrop tattoo on his cheek as a sort of battle stripe. Cholos are known for their ferocity. Gangs normally account for at least seventy murders in Los Angeles a year—and it is said that a true *vato loco* shows his pride and defiance by walking rather than running from the death scene. Some cholos drive their lowered cars sitting low in the seat—grim-faced, both hands on the tiny steering wheel, hat pulled low over the eyes. Esteban Veloz, a former gang member . . . remembers his gang meetings ending ritualistically with the *vatos* climbing into their lowriders and forming a caravan that slowly patrolled the boundaries of the neighborhood—like a male wolf marking off his territory. . . . Cholos in East L.A. tend to think of car clubbers as just short of sissies—people who have stolen the lowriding style from *vatos locos* and then gussied it up, using money they may even have got from their parents. "Let me tell you, they're a hundred per cent different from us," a *vato* from the East L.A. barrio that is known as Big Hazard said recently. "They were never raised like us, to suffer like us. They might have a beef, all they do is maybe beat on each other's cars. They ain't been through what we've been through."

"Why are your cars low?" a member of Chicano's Pride, a San Jose car club, was asked recently. "Whose cars are high?" he answered. . . . Going slow has to do with being observed—a cholo being seen as ominous, perhaps, or a car clubber being seen as suave. "You got pride. You got a nice ride," a member of Chicano's Pride . . . said recently. "You show off. They check it out. They say. 'That's the way. Look at that. That's sharp to the bone. That dude's got a bad ride'." (by Calvin Trillin, in *The New Yorker;* © 1978. Reprinted by permission).

Local yet historical

This example is local, but it should not be interpreted, therefore, as trivial. It represents historical continuity. It betokens a fact, not altered by one's personal preference, that great numbers of human beings value toughness, cruelty, treachery, and violence. Circumstances change, and styles of contest for wealth and power, but modern observers find what historians have long noted—that, in John Dryden's (1700) words, "nothing is lost out of nature, though everything is altered."

For example, the anthropologist Chagnon (1977) goes to South America, lives among the Yanomamö, and dubs them "the fierce people." He early discovers their parallel of *la vida loca,* that "to get along with them . . . I had to become like them: sly, aggressive, and intimidating" (p. 9). As Chagnon learned to be fierce, his status rose.

Chagnon's story is but one of the many similar descriptions provided by ethnographers of today's urban gangs (Miller 1958, Thompson 1966), by students of "the subculture of violence" (Wolfgang & Ferracuti 1967), by records of ancient and modern terrorism (Chapter 11), and by the persistence of piracy. The "macho" spirit lives, and its vitality is not denied by our inability to explain its sources. Nor is the reality of this spirit denied by the fact that some ideals contest the violent ethic. The contest only bespeaks our ambivalence toward homicide, remarked at the beginning of this discussion.

Deadly Difference

Some moralists hope that we will become One World, a world in which all are equal and in which differences, if they are noticed at all, will be occasions for appreciation rather than dislike. This ideal is an ancient one and human beings today seem no closer to realizing it than they were 2,000 years ago. Historically and contemporaneously, human beings seek "identity," and they achieve it by being "this way" rather than "that way."

"Why are your cars low?"
"Whose cars are high?"

Difference is a common occasion for dislike. Put the other way, we find it easier to like people who appear to be similar to us (Byrne & Griffitt 1966). Conversely, people whom we like are thought to be similar to us (Berkowitz & Goranson 1964, Fiedler et al. 1952, Lundy 1956).

Birds of a feather do flock together. When we observe how people choose people—in situations as far-ranging as how individuals seat themselves in strange rooms to how friends are selected—the unsurprising finding is that we select associates who give *apparent* indication of their similarity to us and who are also *objectively* similar (Evans 1962, Chapter 4, Lundberg & Dickson 1952, Sommer 1969). In short, the assumptions we make about our similarities and differences are not just works of imagination. They have an accuracy. For example, Byrne and Griffitt (1966) show that actual similarity of belief is associated with attraction to strangers, and that what is true of adults is also true of children.

Preference for "our own kind of people" and dislike of difference provide occasions for deadly quarrels. Differences in tastes can become deadly by themselves, without the aid of other differences. That is, dislike of difference can be an independent motive. But it can also be linked to other motives and strengthened by them. Thus differences in identities that are associated with differences in wealth and power stimulate homicide. This kind of reinforced homicide is particularly prone to moral justification. It is seen as a struggle for justice, and idealistic killing of this sort is likely to be most lethal and most difficult to control by compromise and "sweet reason."

IMPERFECT CLASSIFICATION OF STRUGGLES FOR WEALTH AND POWER

We can conveniently analyze homicidal struggles for wealth and power as generated by the desire for others' property and privilege, the responsive desire to keep what one has against others' claims, and the desire to change a present distribution of wealth and power and the rules for acquiring them.

This grouping does not allow a clean classification of killing, however, because these three sets of motives come in assorted packages. They are "packed," for example, with different justifications, justifications that range from private miseries[3] to ideals of "justice." Justice, in turn, does not refer to one state of affairs (Nettler 1979) and different conceptions of what is fair provide additional occasions for mortal strife. Classification is further complicated by the fact that homicidal justifications are given by people of varying degrees of sanity and we judge some homicidal action as more rational than others. In addition, our evaluation of the exercise of these major motives varies with the numbers of persons involved. Actions to acquire others' wealth and power seem least just and most criminal when initiated by solitary individuals or small groups and most just and least criminal when exercised by large numbers. For example, in India and Burma where homicidal gangs have been given such titles as thugs, dacoits, criminal tribes, and terrorists, Richardson (1960b, p. 114) notes that:

> The Inspector-General of Police for the Punjab, P.L. Order, remarked in his report for 1939, p. 4: "Murders by single men acting alone are less than half as numerous as murders by several men acting in unison as a group. The single murderer is often hanged, while the group murderer almost invariably escapes the death penalty."

Last, large-scale homicide that succeeds is evaluated differently from that which fails, and the judgments of success and failure themselves change with the times and with our affiliations. As the historian R.C. Dudley (1977) puts it, "Small crimes may have a reason, but large crimes have a philosophy."

We conclude that *intrusion of justification upon description prevents a clean taxonomy of morally saturated acts.* Thus The Mafia is an example of "organized crime" for some criminologists, but General Motors and The Exxon Corporation are examples of "organized

---

[3] Private miseries are readily converted into political issues. Freudian psychologists believe this and other scholars have demonstrated consistent correlations between personalities and their politics (Costantini & Craik 1980, DiRenzo 1974, Elms 1976, Glad 1973, Greenstein 1969, Helson 1980, Hermann 1977, Lasswell 1977, Schoenberger 1968).

The conversion of private troubles into social problems is not often stated so frankly as it was by one of the leaders of Berlin's Free University *Kommune I.* During that university's time of troubles in the 1960s, Dieter Kunzelmann told journalists, "I do not study. I do not work. I have trouble with my orgasm, and I wish the public to be informed of this" (cited by Becker 1977, p. 35).

Kunzelmann's translation of individual defect into social problem illuminates the risk of following the advice of the popular sociologist C. Wright Mills (1959, p. 187) who urged that "the social scientist [ought] continually to translate personal troubles into public issues."

crime" for Ralph Nader (1974). Thus "violence" becomes "force" when it is employed by our police against others' demands, but "force" becomes "violence" when we disapprove its use (Blumenthal 1972, Blumenthal et al. 1972, Blumenthal et al. 1975). Thus "robbery" of "bad guys" by "good guys" becomes "social banditry" (Hobsbawm 1969). Thus the affluence of capitalist countries becomes "consumption violence" and "consumption terrorism" in the dialect of European revolutionaries (Becker 1977). Thus one group's "terrorist" becomes another group's "freedom fighter," and yesterday's successful "terrorist" becomes today's Prime Minister.

Political interests stretch words to give different meanings to similar acts according to our approval or disapproval of sources and consequences. This repeatedly noted fact loosens all classifications of crime. Killing for wealth and power is given different titles depending upon some observer's judgment of the legitimacy of the claims of the fighters. Evaluation of the justice of contestants moves the boundaries of acts called crimes, and, particularly so, when those acts include killing in the name of ideals.

Illustrations abound. Providing illustrations takes no sides in the deadly struggles. Our purpose is descriptive, and descriptive of the fact that public opinion moves with "whose ox is gored." It also moves with propaganda, with the writing and re-writing of history, and with the attribution of success or failure to homicidal social movements.

Example: An Exercise in Imagery—by the French Historian Jacques Ellul (1979)

Let us begin by taking a perhaps extreme example of the justice of opinion. How can justice be administered to the Hitler regime? To be sure, all that was said against him was true and entirely deserved. But let us ask what would have happened if Hitler had won. We then would never have heard anything of Hitler's concentration camps, the massacres, or the experiments on human beings. Instead, Stalin's crimes of 1945 would have been discovered, and he would have been considered a war criminal. The Russians would have been charged with genocide because of their concentration camps, their massacres in the Baltic countries, the Ukraine, and Rumania. (Let us remember that of the 100,000 German soldiers captured at Stalingrad and deported from there, less than 5,000 returned—all the rest died in Russian camps!) In victory, Hitlerism would have softened progressively, after having liquidated all the elements to be liquidated—such as communism. And ten years later the moderation of the chiefs, who by then would have relaxed their hold, would have been admired. Historically, the struggle between races rather than the class struggle would have then taken first place. The Nazi doctrine would have been deepened and broadened, eminent philosophers such as Heidegger would have made their contribution to it, and Marxism would have ceased to preoccupy the intellectuals. Christians, after having been violently opposed to the Nazi doctrine, would have progressively doubted the need to oppose Hitlerism, in the same way they came to doubt the need to oppose Marxism, which surely no longer ruffles the Christian conscience. And, thanks to propaganda, because people would have known little of communism except its crimes—nothing of its love of justice, nothing of economic progress in the Soviet Union—and because people would have been submersed perpetually in National Socialist ideology, the latter would have appeared perfectly just at the end of ten years, and the well-known Nazi crimes would have been forgotten.

This extreme example—and the changes in attitude toward communism between 1939 and 1950 are probably sufficient to make such description reasonable—reminds us that the concept of justice in public opinion is subject to extreme fluctuation, indecision, and variation according to circumstances, even while giving itself the strongest doctrinal assurances (pp. 240-241).

Example: From Terrorist to Prime Minister

In 1977 Menahem Begin became Prime Minister of Israel. His "tough" view of the world has a history that started with a childhood in Eastern Europe where Jews were systematically despised and brutalized. During the 1920 Russo-Polish war, Begin witnessed pogroms and, when Hitler promised extermination as a "solution to the Jewish problem," Begin took the threat seriously. He takes similar threats seriously today.

As a young man, Begin joined a militant faction within the Zionist movement known as B'rit Trumpeldor, abbreviated as Betar, and he served in executive positions with this group in Czechoslovakia and Poland. This organization called for "direct action" to establish the Jewish state in Palestine promised by the British Balfour Declaration of 1917 and the League of Nations' Mandate.

During World War I, the British conquered the area of the Middle East that included a territory of shifting boundaries known as Palestine (from ancient Philistia). In 1920 the League of Nations accorded the British government control of this area which included the present state of Jordan. The terms of the League's "mandate" called for establishment of a Jewish "homeland" in that zone to be set up with due regard for non-Jewish Palestinians.

Conflict was immediate, and it continues, between Arab, Christian, and Jewish claimants to this religiously significant, but small piece of arid land. At the height of Hitler's power, the British government issued an edict (the White Paper of 1939) proposing a single Palestinian state in their mandated territory that would have been predominantly Arab. At the same time, the White Paper limited Jewish immigration into Palestine and proposed stopping it entirely in 1944.

Begin was then commander of the Polish Betar and he led mass demonstrations outside the British embassy in Warsaw that resulted in his arrest and imprisonment for several months. He was released just before the Germans overran Poland, and he fled with his family and other Betar members to Lithuania.

In 1940 the Soviet Union conquered Lithuania and Begin was again arrested, but this time as a threat to Soviet rule. He was sentenced to eight years at hard labor in an Arctic prison camp. However, when Germany attacked Russia in 1941, Begin and other Polish prisoners were released to form a Polish army. Begin's unit was sent to the Transjordan, now Jordan, and this lucky move allowed Begin to enter Jerusalem where he became leader of a paramilitary faction, the Irgun Zwai Leumi (National Fighting Organization).

When the British tried to restrict Jewish immigration into Palestine, the Irgun began a campaign of sabotage against the British and the British responded with stringent "police action."

Begin was forced into hiding and did so by adopting a series of aliases that included being a law student, a Talmudic scholar, and a physician. All the while he directed a fighting force of about 2,000 persons in attacks on the British. These attacks were designed to reduce British prestige, to make their governance expensive, and to convince the British that the Irgun could conduct raids at will. The encyclopedia, *Current Biography* (1977), notes:

> Begin planned and directed a guerrilla campaign against the British that has become something of a classic in the annals of wars of liberation. At the same time, he gained a reputation for ruthlessness and was condemned as a terrorist by the British and, after the collapse of the united fighting front in August 1946, by the official leadership of the Palestinian Jewish community. David Ben-Gurion, who became the first Prime Minister of Israel, once went so far as to publicly condemn Begin as a fascist.

In 1946 the Irgun bombed headquarters of the territorial government in Jerusalem's King David Hotel. Civilians were killed in this attack, but the Irgun absolved itself of culpability by claiming that its warnings were ignored and that, contrary to other, current terrorist groups, the killing of innocents was not one of its tactics.

The Irgun's guerrilla activity ended with the United Nation's partition of Palestine in 1947 and the outbreak of the Arab-Israeli war of 1948. In this fashion, one version of terrorism became "normal war."

DILEMMA: RESULTS—WITH AND WITHOUT FULFILLMENT

Every violent defender of a present power, and every violent claimant to a future power, believes that his or her career in homicide will be vindicated by good consequences. Thus Menahem Begin. Thus Fidel Castro who, in 1953, stood before a military tribunal in Santiago de Cuba charged with grave crimes. In his defense, Castro shouted, "Condemn me. History will absolve me" (Mullin 1980). Thirty years before Castro's appeal to history, Adolf Hitler gave the same justification. Hitler's first attempt in 1923 to overthrow the German republic failed and he and nine conspirators were tried for treason. In his closing speech to the court, Hitler argued:

> It is not you, gentlemen, who pass judgment on us. That judgment is spoken by the eternal court of history. What judgment you will hand down, I know. But that court will not ask us: "Did you commit high treason, or did you not?" That court will judge us . . . as Germans who wanted only the good of their own people and Fatherland; who wanted to fight and die. You may pronounce us guilty a thousand times over, but the goddess of the eternal court of history will smile and tear to tatters the brief of the State Prosecutor and the sentence of this court. For she acquits us (cited by Bullock 1962, pp. 119–120).

History, like God, is commonly alleged to be on Our Side. Success is deemed to prove it.

Success excuses much, but not everything. Moreover, no success can be counted on to endure. Success and failure are evaluated against a span of time; they are differentially appreciated with time as well as with competing criteria of justice.

As students, we need not take sides in any particular deadly struggle to note a persistent dilemma in killing for ideals. One horn of the dilemma is that violence gets results. From the viewpoint of the homicidal idealist, it does good. The other horn of the dilemma is that no result can be guaranteed.

A German proverb says, "The broth is never eaten as hot as it is cooked." There is always slippage between the promise that justifies killing, "one last time," and the social product of mass homicide. No revolution—from the great French Revolution of the eighteenth century to the present—has achieved what it promised.

The same Fidel Castro who promised his people "liberty and happiness," the chance to earn their bread honestly without having to emigrate in search of a decent livelihood, and a standard of living "soon" to be higher than that in either the USA or the USSR (Castro 1959, p. 32) finds himself, 20 years after his successful revolution, with thousands of "his people" fleeing the once richest country in Latin America (Halperin 1974, Thomas 1971).[4] Castro's farewell to these freedom-seekers was to call them "delinquents, homosexuals, lumpen-proletarians, anti-social and parasitical elements and bums" (*Economist* 1980, Mullin 1980).

An Inference

If there is slippage between homicidal ideals and results, there are also degrees of that slippage. Success and failure in violent struggles are seldom all-or-none matters; they are usually matters of more-and-less.

Wars are won and lost, but not always cleanly. Power shifts, but evaluation of the consequences of these changes depends on a judge's ideology, place, and time.

Because there is a varying gap between homicidal ideals and their consequences, it cannot be assumed that human beings will note this slippage and cease engaging in deadly struggles for wealth and power. One assurance of the continuity of combat is that we cannot tell in advance whether promises will become realities, and we quarrel about each other's judgment of what is possible. A related guarantor of the continuity of mortal contests for power is that no one has an exact scale on which to weigh the consequences of any fight. Consequences range from changes in the supply of food to changes in liberty, health, and happiness. There is no expert who can assign objective weights to these many results of political battles. In addition, assessment of consequences varies, of course, with the time-span employed.

---

[4] The Cuban economy is a disaster despite infusions of "more economic aid per caput than any nation on earth" (Gall 1971, p. 56). Hugh Thomas (1979, p. 611), author of a major history of Cuba, notes that ". . . poor countries do not realise that the rich countries can be ruined by bad government or over-government as much as poor ones can be starved by neglect. Cuba, a country which now puts itself forward as a leader of the 'underdeveloped' world, is actually a good example of a rich country gone to seed and then to revolution, not of a poor one which has never had a chance. . . . Cuba had railways before most of Europe, a steam engine before the US, and more televisions in 1958 than Italy did."

A third reason for assuming continuity of homicidal contests rests on history. The only *empirical* procedure for judging probabilities of future events is to read the record of human action. This record does not promise peace. We conclude that there can be no *reasoned* end to killing for ideals.

Many questions flow from this inference, including such questions as these:

- Does research show a way out of the homicidal dilemmas of power?
- Are there satisfactory explanations of individual careers in homicidal power-seeking?
- When political ideals fail, why do they?

We shall address the first question in the following pages.

STUDIES OF LARGE-SCALE HOMICIDES FOR WEALTH AND POWER

Academic curiosity and the desire for peace have stimulated study of the occasions on which human beings organize to kill one another. A justification of such research has been the hope that, if some "significant variable" could be isolated as the cause of violence between aggregates, then we could do something to control it.

This hope is part of a prevalent ideology that sees science translate into technology that "solves problems." It is a hope that follows the medical model in which diagnosis of a disease and description of its etiology lead to cure. However, research on the causes of mass conflict do not support this optimistic model when it is applied to mortal struggle.

Varieties of Mass Fighting

Chapter 1 noted that we give different titles to homicides depending on the numbers of people involved and the legitimacy accorded their claims to power. We observe, then, that some deadly quarrels occur *within* states where a government claiming a monopoly of power is challenged, as in civil or revolutionary combat. Such internal fighting is itself called different names depending, again, on how many people are engaged in the contest, how planful they appear to be, and how legitimate their demands seem. These internal struggles range from political assassination, to riot, to terrorism of varying popularity, to guerrilla warfare and rebellion. A first fact derived from studies of mass homicide is that domestic and international battles have different sources.

Scholars who have counted mass conflict within and between states have isolated dimensions of the deadly conflicts. A "dimension" represents a number of antagonistic acts that are highly correlated with each other. Statistical techniques, such as factor analysis, permit the identification of dimensions among a large number of variables and permit us to find out how such variables are clustered.

For example, Rummel (1969) summarized research on the dimensions of mass fighting for modern states through 1964. His survey indicates that domestic violence and international wars are separate dimensions of combat. Rummel concludes, *"There are no common conditions or causes of domestic- and foreign-conflict behavior"* (p. 226, emphasis his).

This means that some states experience much internal conflict but little foreign fighting while other countries have little domestic turmoil but much external conflict. This conclusion also means that still other political bodies suffer relatively high amounts of both internal and external violence, while a fourth group of states has little of either kind of conflict.

Not only are internal and external conflicts different kinds of homicidal occasion, but the internal type of struggle itself reveals styles of fighting that range from relatively unplanned and spontaneous rioting (the "turmoil" dimension) to terrorism and guerrilla war (the "internal war" dimension). The fact that there are such clusters of combat means that countries that experience much internal turmoil need not suffer revolution and that those states that have much guerrilla fighting need not experience "turmoil."

Wars Within and Between States

Killing for wealth and power, justified as killing for ideals, provides occasions for the greatest amount of homicide. When these occasions involve "enough" people, they are called wars. A war is a collective fight in which elimination of the enemy is the objective if that opponent will not otherwise submit to our wishes. A war is an organized struggle among groups of individuals who regard themselves as *politically independent* and *morally justified* in asserting their will violently.

There are qualities of such warring, of course. For purposes of counting their mortal consequences, it is important to discriminate between wars between sovereign states and those internal wars called revolutionary.

The distinction is important because wars between countries have relatively determinable beginnings and endings. We can date starts and stops of interstate wars and estimate the homicides occurring between those dates. However, in revolutionary struggles, the killing continues *after* the overthrow of a once-dominant power. The revolution has to be consolidated. A revolutionary ideology demands devotion; it tolerates no disagreement. But there are always persons who are remnants of the old order and persons who disagree with the new order. For such dissidents who will not be "re-educated," revolutionary ideologies endorse extermination, and the extermination extends to enemies outside the "liberated" country as well as to those inside it. It is easier, therefore, to estimate the deaths and casualties from interstate wars than it is to count the mortal costs of a revolution.

For example, the demographer Petersen (1969, Chapter 17) notes that the numbers of deaths attributed to the Maoist revolution in China range in the *millions,* but vary greatly depending on whether one is counting only "direct victims," those killed outright as "enemies of the people," or adding to that number those deaths above normal expectation that seem assignable to the power struggle. Allowing for such variations, Walker (1955) reports estimates of mortality from the Communist revolution in China from the first Civil War (1927–1936) to 1950 that run from a low of *34 million* deaths to a high of *64 million.*

Similarly high figures are given as the human cost of introducing Soviet Communism. Conquest (1968) puts the estimates at between *35 and 45 million* lives lost in the Soviet enterprise and Petersen's (1969, p. 664) population estimates are in accord with Conquest's.

Wars Between States

Revolutionary governments do not publish statistics about the mortal costs of their successes and all tallies of battlefield casualties are subject to error. However, we can learn something about the occasions of wars and their homicidal consequences from historical records if we employ this information as yielding broad estimates of the magnitude of fights. This has been done by three large-scale studies of interstate wars and by some minor investigations.

The three major studies were conducted by a sociologist (Sorokin 1937–1941), by a professor of international law (Wright 1942), and by a physicist-mathematician (Richardson 1960a, 1960b).

Sorokin counted "all recorded, major interstate wars" from 500 B.C. to 1925 A.D. in the histories of Greece, Rome, Austria, Germany, England, France, the Netherlands, Spain, Italy, Russia, Poland, and Lithuania." He tallied 967 such conflicts or *an average of one war every two or three years* among these Western countries. The proportions of years during which each state was at war, for any part of a year, vary from a low of 28 percent for Germany to a high of 67 percent for Spain. It cannot be said from such a record that war has been an abnormality among civilized nations.

Wright took all of history and traces of prehistory for his scope. His work reports on the fragmentary evidence of organized fighting among preliterate people and on the more detailed records since the fifteenth century. Table 10.1 gives his tally of the number of battles in which "important states" engaged from 1480 to 1941. By Wright's count, formal fighting appears, again, to be a common experience rather than some kind of deviant behavior.

Richardson's studies attempt to fit mathematical models to the data of deadly quarrels. His research assumes that "an essential characteristic of a war may be said to be casualties" (Richardson 1960b, p. 5). But, since wounds vary from the slight to the severe, Richardson chose to tabulate only *mortalities* since, in his words, "deaths are more alike, and therefore more reliable as statistical evidence" (*ibid.*).

Richardson then classifies his object of interest—intentionally induced deaths—by their *magnitude*. That is, he groups wars by the amount of killing as "the logarithm to the base ten of the number of people who died because of that quarrel" (1960b, p. 6).

The advantage of such a logarithmic scale is that it groups deaths by their numbers in large categories. It allows, thereby, for a range of error in tallies. One can "give or take" some differences in reported fatalities for a particular conflict without disturbing the *rank order* of such battles.

Richardson's scale runs a range "from 0 for a murder involving only one death . . . to 7.4 for World War II" (1960b, p. 6). His search of criminal statistics and histories for the entire world between 1820 and 1949 yields the following tally of mortal fights grouped by numbers of deaths:

I.   *Magnitudes in the range 7 ± ½*
      (from over 3,000,000 deaths to more than 31,000,000 deaths)
      Two Conflicts: World Wars I and II
II.   *Magnitudes in the range 6 ± ½*
      (from over 300,000 to more than 3,000,000 deaths)
      Seven Conflicts
III. *Magnitudes in the range 5 ± ½*
      (from over 30,000 deaths to more than 300,000 deaths)
      36 Conflicts

IV. Magnitudes in the range 4 $\pm$ ½
   (from over 3,000 deaths to more than 31,000 deaths)
   70 Conflicts

Below the fourth rank of fatal conflicts enumeration fades into estimates based on questionable counting. Richardson's list of deadly quarrels in the range 3 $\pm$ ½ and less is offered only as tentative and as a stimulus to inquiry. However, *the smaller the scope of mortal fighting, the more numerous the battles.*

For example, Richardson (1960b) counts some of these "small-sized" wars of the past 500 years—those with more than 300 fatalities but less than 3,200—and finds "over 170 military campaigns by the United States; over 100 international, and 300 domestic, conflicts of this size in Latin America; and *in the twentieth century before World War II,* over 70 campaigns by Great Britain and over 500 by all countries" (p. 73, emphasis added).

Findings

Before the present century was *half* over, it was already the bloodiest century in history in absolute numbers of homicides produced by organized bands of human beings (Sorokin 1937, p. 487). The fighting continues. It continues with such persistence against efforts to transfer conflicts from battlefields to negotiating tables that Carl and Shelley Mydans (1968) have been able aptly to title the period since the end of World War II,[5] "the violent peace."

We are concerned, then, to find out what seems to be associated with war in the hope that we might change those conditions. Unfortunately for this concern, studies of the varieties of war tell us more surely what is *not* so than what is. They more readily disprove common assumptions about the occasions of mass deadly fighting than they illuminate the path to peace. The *negations* may be outlined as follows:

1. There is no evidence that human beings are becoming more pacific.

This negation puts it mildly. Actually, the historical record points to a tendency for wars to be more frequent in recent times (Richard-

---

[5] At the outset of what has come to be known as World War II, President Franklin Delano Roosevelt asked for suggestions for names of that war. He wanted a title other than Number Two because numbering great wars implies that there might be Numbers Three, Four, and on. Obviously, he received no suggestion that took hold.

Table 10.1 Number of Battles Engaged in by Principal European Powers, by Decades, 1480–1940[*][†]

Decade	Great Britain	France	Spain	Austria	Prussia	Russia	Turkey	Netherlands	Denmark	Sweden	Participations by these states[‡]	Battles within modern civilization
1480–89	2	1	4	0			2				9	5
1490–99	1	2	2	2			1				8	4
Total	3	3	6	2			3				17	9
1500–09	0	3	3	0		0	0	0	0	0	6	3
1510–19	4	4	0	0		1	3	0	0	0	12	8
1520–29	0	2	2	4		0	3	0	2	2	15	10
1530–39	0	1	5	0		0	1	0	0	0	7	8
1540–49	8	1	1	2		0	0	0	0	0	12	10
1550–59	3	3	1	1		0	1	0	0	0	9	7
1560–69	2	5	5	0		1	4	4	0	0	21	14
1570–79	1	1	13	0		0	1	12	0	0	28	16
1580–89	4	2	5	0		0	0	2	0	0	13	7
1590–99	1	1	1	1		0	1	2	0	1	8	4
Total	23	23	36	8		2	14	20	2	3	131	87
1600–09	2	0	1	0		0	0	1	0	0	4	3
1610–19	0	0	0	0		1	0	0	3	4	8	4
1620–29	1	1	8	12		0	1	2	4	2	31	19
1630–39	0	18	16	27		0	0	1	0	22	84	39
1640–49	4	25	17	14		0	0	1	2	11	74	36
1650–59	10	5	4	1		1	8	10	2	4	45	27
1660–69	4	3	4	5		0	30	4	0	0	30	19
1670–79	5	27	13	9		0	2	16	4	4	80	35
1680–89	2	4	2	23		0	21	0	0	0	52	27
1690–99	10	20	10	11		1	10	13	0	0	75	30
Total	38	103	75	108		3	52	48	15	47	483	239

1710–19	10	18	15	34		5	10	15	4	7	118	49
1720–29	0	0	0	0		0	0	0	0	0	0	0
1730–39	0	10	7	28		7	18	0	0	0	70	35
1740–49	17	47	14	52	15	2	0	16	0	2	165	77
1750–59	28	32	0	31	38	4	0	0	0	2	136	71
1760–69	15	16	0	19	27	8	2	0	0	2	89	43
1770–79	11	3	0	2	2	14	14	0	0	0	46	27
1780–89	20	15	4	5	0	8	7	1	0	3	63	30
1790–99	46	284	24	179	32	36	11	42	0	5	659	336
Total	186	501	102	407	114	101	62	110	5	45	1,633	781
1800–09	26	177	32	88	31	26	10	0	1	3	394	188
1810–19	35	178	42	34	64	93	11	2	0	3	462	189
1820–29	1	1	0	0	0	14	17	0	0	0	33	17
1830–39	0	0	0	0	0	6	5	0	0	0	11	12
1840–49	1	1	0	27	3	10	1	0	3	0	46	37
1850–59	6	12	0	5	0	12	10	0	3	0	48	17
1860–69	0	0	0	17	21	0	0	0	4	0	42	79
1870–79	0	53	0	0	53	26	26	0	0	0	158	92
1880–89	0	0	0	0	0	0	0	0	0	0	0	2
1890–99	10	0	4	0	0	0	1	0	0	0	15	18
Total	79	422	78	171	172	187	81	2	11	6	1,209	651
1900–09	8	0	0	0	0	18	0	0	0	0	26	18
1910–19	218	81	7	117	310	213	137	0	0	0	1,083	662
1920–29	0	0	0	0	0	11	5	0	0	0	16	17
1930–40	3	3	100	0	20	2	0	1	0	0	129	195
Total	229	84	107	117	330	244	142	1	0	0	1,254	892
Grand total	558	1,136	404	807	616	537	354	181	33	101	4,727	2,659

* Reprinted from *A Study of War* by Quincy Wright by permission of The University of Chicago Press. From Volume 1, Table 22. © 1942 by The University of Chicago Press.

† Participation in battles by one of these states prior to its active relationship to the modern family of nations is not counted in this table.

‡ The figures in this column are usually greater than thelast column because in most cases at least two of these powers participated in a single battle, although, in case of civil wars, only one participation by the state is counted. Where the figures in the last column are greater, it is because states in the modern family of nations other than the European states here listed were the participants in a considerable number of battles of the decade.

son 1960b, p. 142), for a larger proportion of the resources and the populations of belligerent states to be involved, and, in Wright's (1942) words, for warring now to be "more intense, more extended, more costly . . . and less functional, less intentional, less directable, and less legal" (p. 248).

2. There is no sign that wars are more readily controlled now than formerly.

Both Richardson and Wright demonstrate that it is increasingly difficult for states to remain neutral in wartime and that, as the number of combatants increases, more neutrals are drawn into the conflict. Fighting is contagious.

3. It cannot be assumed that some nations are characteristically more belligerent than others.

4. It cannot be assumed that any one religion, even one that preaches peace, practices pacifism more than another. Christians are no more pacific than infidels.

5. There is no evidence that democracies and republics are more peaceful than autocracies and monarchies.

6. There is no evidence that prosperous societies are more peaceful than poor ones or that periods of prosperity reduce fighting.

There is also no evidence that the relative wealth and poverty of neighbors explains much of the warring. Richardson, for example, finds little of the killing to have been occasioned by "class conflict." For large-scale homicides of a magnitude greater than 3.5 on Richardson's scale, economic issues represent an estimated 29 percent of the "direct causes" of war (1960b, p. 210).

7. It cannot be assumed that a shared religion or a common language or a bond of citizenship reduces deadly quarrels.

Although religious similarities have little relevance for war or peace, Richardson finds that religious differences, particularly those between Christians and Muslims, have stimulated homicide.

8. It cannot be assumed that being "neighbors" makes for peace.

On the contrary, warring increases in proportion to the number of states with which a country shares frontiers. Fights over territory loom large as an occasion for combat.

9. Extensive studies of war do not support the hope that "enlightenment" produces peace.

A widespread assumption holds that "education" or "understanding," variously and vaguely defined, pacifies humanity. This assumption fails when it meets facts. Cattell (1950) looked at clusters of the characteristics of states that waged more and less war between 1837 and 1937. He found that countries that frequently go to war engage in a high number of political disputes with other countries, thus lending support to von Clausewitz's (1977) dictum that "war is . . . a true political instrument, a continuation of political activity by other means."

In addition, the more belligerent states write a disproportionately large number of treaties. They also have a high ratio of tertiary to primary occupations; that is, they are bureaucratized, industrialized countvies. It is the major powers that are disproportionately involved in wars (Small & Singer 1970). These fighting states are territorially expansive. They have big governmentw, and they win a disproportionate number of Nobel prizes in science, literature, and (supreme irony!) peace. In short, they are "civilized."

An Affirmation

These many negations do not support a faith in progress toward peace nor do they point to any remedy for war in aspects of social life that are readily manipulable.

According to Richardson's study, the one factor correlated with peacefulness is the length of time people have shared a common government. The longer a citizenry has been united under one rule, the less likely it is to have engaged in fatal conflicts.

Richardson considered this finding to carry a promise of peace, if anything does. It must be noted, however, that this correlation does *not* allow the causal conclusion that *creating* a government produces peace. All that this association says is that, when people have lived together under one authority—however that living together may have *evolved*—there has been a tendency for them to kill one another less frequently and less extensively.

CONCLUSIONS

Research on mass conflict and its correlates, when mixed with historical studies, allows some additional conclusions:

1. Government Pacifies

One inference is the unsurprising information that government controls belligerence. This is its first reason for being—*to rule*, that is, to serve as umpire applying the code of the game we have agreed to play.

This fact does not tell us how to achieve peace, however, since it does not specify the conditions under which individuals agree to play this game rather than that one. Against the hope that *creating* a government will produce peace, we are reminded that the consensus that makes governing possible *evolves* and that its *evolution* includes the possibility of its *dissolution*. No government is permanent and neither is any peace.

2. Quantities of Homicide Describe Continuities

A second conclusion suggests continuities between large-scale and small-scale killing. The continuities have been variously measured. For example, Richardson (1960b, Chapter 4) shows that a curve can be drawn relating the frequency of fights to their mortality. This slightly bent curve indicates that infrequent struggles produce more deaths while frequent struggles produce fewer deaths and that there is an unbroken continuity across the range of deadly quarrels categorized by their frequency and their mortal efficiency.

Another aspect of continuity is noted in the contagion of violence. The contagion has been measured in many ways. It has been recorded, for example, in short-term modeling. Watching violence induces it. Anyone who has participated in "contact" sports, or observed spectators at such contests, has noticed how "the adrenalin flows" so that even outsiders to a struggle engage in the teeth-baring, shadow-boxing, and sometimes real fighting that they are witnessing. This common observation has been authenticated by laboratory studies (Berkowitz & Macaulay 1971, Comstock 1975, Geen & Stonner 1974, Goldstein & Arms 1971, Hartmann 1969, Lovaas 1961, McCarthy et al. 1975, Mussen & Rutherford 1961, Soares & Soares 1969, Walters et al. 1962, Wheeler & Caggiula 1966, Wilkins et al. 1974). Publicity given to bizarre crimes stimulates their imitation (Berkowitz & Macaulay 1971)

Another repeatedly noted aspect of the contagion of violence is that children who have been brutally treated tend to become brutal (Eron et al. 1971, Farrington 1978).

Contagion is also demonstrated by the fact that violent times produce violent acts. This is not a tautology; it is a statement of the continuity of homicide across dimensions of magnitudes of violence. For example, the causal web in which behavior is generated may be described as a "moral atmosphere" (Chapter 12). One part of that atmosphere is indicated by living in countries that go to war. Archer and Gartner (1976) have compiled a *Comparative Crime Dats File* that includes time-series rates of homicide during this century for more than 100 governments. From these data Archer and Gartner tallied changes in domestic homicide rates experienced by 50 states that engaged in what the investigators call "nation-wars" against changes in "internal" homicide rates experienced by 30 control countries that had not engaged in such wars. Substantial postwar increases in domestic homicide rates are found among those countries that had gone to war. Archer and Gartner report that "these increases were pervasive . . . [they] occurred after large wars and smaller wars, with several types of homicide rate indicators, in victorious as well as defeated nations, in nations with both improved and worsened postwar economies, among both men and women . . . and among offenders of several age groups" (p. 937).

3. Narrow Interests = Limited Fights; Broad Interests (e.g., Ideals) = More Destructive Fights

This thesis is illustrated by the deadly differences between killings by gangsters, who have narrow interests, and killings by more idealistic murderers.

Gangsters, like other varieties of criminals, are not of one piece. Some specialize—as "hit men," for example—but many graduate from petty thieving to enterprises that range from the illegal, to the legal but shady, to the perfectly legitimate (Mack & Kerner 1974). There is an apprenticeship in "organized crime" as there is in other occupations.

The essence of a mobster, however, is his willingness to enforce his "business" with violence. Other businessmen who regard themselves as "legitimate" may be tempted into a variety of frauds (Volume three, Chapter 3), and the gangster has no compunction about such modes of money-making, but the defining difference between that species of thief called a gangster and the so-called "white-collar" criminal is the mobster's rational use of homicide and its threat as an instrument of enterprise.

Gangsters' businesses thrive on a few devices. One is the provision of products and services that are illegal, but for which there is a relatively inflexible demand. Thus American laws prohibiting the manufacture and distribution of alcoholic beverages during the 1920s provided a huge market for gangland. A second preferred line of work is that of extortion—which includes "loan-sharking" and making "suckers" pay for "protection" where, of course, one is being protected against the gangster himself. And a third form of gangland enterprise involves a variety of frauds.

Now, in all these gang-controlled enterprises, the fights that occur are for limited objectives: a labor monopoly, a trucking service, or an exclusive territory for the distribution of "drugs," slot machines, and whores. The killing, then, is numerically minor compared with the mortality incurred in fights for broader interests. For example, in New

York City during the height of the "gangster era," 1930 to 1950, there were 242 known gangland slayings, almost 80 percent of them during the 1930s (Block 1980). Despite the motion picture publicity given such assassinations, they produce a low annual homicide rate when compared with those terroristic activities that graduate into guerrilla fighting and the many styles of war (Chapter 11).

Kenneth Waltz (1959) concludes from his study of mass conflict that, "Wars undertaken on a narrow calculation of state interest are almost certain to be less damaging than those inspired by a supposedly selfless idealism" (p. 114). On this, he cites the historian A.J.P. Taylor who remarked, "Bismarck fought 'necessary' wars and killed thousands; the idealism of the twentieth century fought two 'just' wars and killed millions."

Statements such as these do not condemn any particular ideal. They do not even condemn idealism. There are only a commentary on our condition. This commentary acknowledges, however, that some philosophers believe that *all* killing for ideals is absurd. The witty Anatole France (1844–1924) argued that, "To die for an idea is to place a pretty high price upon conjecture" (cited by Peter 1977, p. 259). And Simone Weil (1946, p. 72) wrote that, "If one analyses the . . . words and slogans which, throughout human history, have inspired the combined spirit of sacrifice and cruelty, they turn out to be equally empty [and] every empty abstraction has its faction."

We may translate Weil as saying that ideals that motivate mass action have to be encapsulated in shorthand symbols. These symbols function as icons; they represent images, "pictures in the head," of what we revere and despise. The symbols take many forms. We see them in flags, colors, emblems (swastikas, crosses, stars). We hear them in sounds (anthems, chants, prayers), and read them in gestures (clenched fists, extended arms), and in the names we call ourselves and others. All these serve as unifying banners behind which we group. They serve as abbreviated images of what our tribe is for and against. They work like tom-toms to stir feelings that generate action.

It must be remembered—against the grain of much psychological theorizing—that *feelings* are primary stimulants. We do not usually think and then feel in responding to our environments, but, in reverse, we usually feel and then act—with or without the rationalizing comforts of verbalizable "thoughts." As Zajonc (1980, p. 172) puts it, "People do not get married or divorced, commit murder or suicide, or lay down their lives for freedom upon a detailed cognitive analysis of the pros and cons of their actions."

In this vein, Weil is arguing that the emotions stirred by impassioned images obscure particular empirical objectives of mass action.

In short, Weil is saying that the icons, the grand abstractions, that promote allegiance and motivate homicide are apt to be empty of empirical content.

Whether Weil is correct—or, better, when and to what extent she is correct—is the subject of other studies than the present one.

4. Multiple Causes of Homicide Allow Changing Combinations of the Causes of Any Mortal Struggle

Only unphilosophical observers of the social scene think that any particular kind of human action has a singular cause. All the rest of us assume that human action is generated in a dense web of causes so that isolating *the* cause, or a few causes, of deadly quarrels is not a task to be accomplished by any definitive investigation or by any precise mathematical equation.

We cover our ignorance of causes by appealing to "chance" or "luck." But the ignorance that is concealed by this appeal evades the possibility that the events we wish to explain may have grand causes *and* small ones. The small causes, in turn, can operate as "triggers" or as multipliers. It is conceivable, then, that a small cause that escapes our notice may produce a large effect. In the words of a geophysicist, "We cannot be certain that the flutter of a moth's wing may not precipitate a hurricane."

In addition, a multiplicity of small causes, each one of which has only a minute effect, may combine in sufficient numbers and patterns to produce a strong effect.

These possibilities mean that deadly contests, including wars, need not have one set of causes. These possibilities mean, too, that there can be *changing combinations* of the causes of large- and small-scale homicides. There are many roads to mortal combat—whether the killing is one-on-one or en masse.

5. The Assumption That the Horror of War Now Makes It Less Likely Is a Hope Without Basis in the Historical Record

It does not matter whether you and I *hope* that the increased horror of war makes it less probable. The present point is that this hope is an old one. Every advance in war technology has brought forth the same assumption—that horror makes war "unthinkable" and therefore impossible. Thus far, each renewal of this ancient assumption has been disconfirmed (Rapoport 1974). For example, there is evidence today that the Soviet Union has considered the costs of a nuclear war and found them acceptable (Douglass & Hoeber 1979).

One student of Soviet society (Pipes 1980, p. 36) believes that, given the objectives of Communist policy, "the reduction of the United States . . . is as essential to the Soviet Union as the elimination of Carthage was to Rome."

In the present time of "violent peace," the prospects of a world without war remain remote. Western civilization is under attack from internal and external enemies. The attack produces many questions, including questions about the psychological characteristics of those internal enemies called "terrorists," the prediction of "dangerousness," the causes of violence, and the promise of utopias. The next chapters address these issues.

11 TERRORISM **Abstract** • The quest

for wealth and power is often justified by utopian visions. The combination generates a particular kind of homicide called "terrorism." • Terrorism refers to the conscious use of cruelty and killing to spread fear through a population as an instrument of power. ○ The practice of hurting others, or threatening to hurt them, is a general means of getting one's way with others. • Terrorism carries this general principle to a murderous conclusion. • Generality of this principle makes it difficult to agree on a definition of terrorism. • Six characteristics are suggested in an attempted definition of terrorism: "No rules," "No innocents," "Economy," "Publicity and provocation," "Individual therapy," and "Varied objectives." • Moral assessment of terrorist activity moves causal assignment among situations, purposes, philosophies, and personalities. ○ Complications of causal assignment are illustrated by two terrorist careers: that of Giangi and that of Diana. ○ Academic attribution of terrorism to violent ideas is questioned. The text asks: "How much difference do ideas make, for which acts, at what juncture in a career, for which kinds of people, in which situations?" ○ It is argued that individuals are selective consumers of ideas. • Concern with terrorism leads to consideration of responses to it. It is indicated that: ○ Democracies are more vulnerable than totalitarian states to terrorism. ○ Remedying terrorists' grievances may not reduce terrorism. ○ Terrorism that succeeds escalates. ○ Justice and societal protection require application of force to combat violence. ○ In democracies, citizens tend to agree about the causes of terrorism and recommended response to it.

IF ONE ASSUMES THAT ALL PERSONAL TROUBLES ought to be translated into social problems, violence is justified. If, in addition, one assumes "metaphysical guilt"—the notion that "being human" entails being responsible for every wrong in the world—then "he who is not with us is against us" and no one is innocent.

The poet John Donne's (1572–1631) preachment that "No man is an *Iland,* intire of it selfe" and the philosopher Karl Jaspers's (1883–1969) idea of guilt—that allowing injustice anywhere makes one an accomplice to the wrong—these notions justify indiscriminate killing.

If, to these assumptions, one adds the belief that the imperfections of a present world are to be remedied by the creation of a better world, then all things are permitted. Producing present pain is justified by the promise of future gain. "Hell must precede Paradise" (Rapoport 1977, p. 55), and the quest for utopia becomes a stimulus to homicide.

The perennial pursuit of wealth and power, in league with utopian vision, generates a particular kind of homicide called "terrorism." *Terrorism refers to the conscious use of cruelty and killing to spread fear through a population as an instrument of power.*

Generality

Terrorism carries to a violent extreme a widely practiced principle: That of hurting others, or promising them pain, in order to get one's way with them. In mild forms, the principle is demonstrated whenever one uses punishment as a mechanism of control:

> *Parent:* "You can't go to the show unless you finish your homework."
> *Judge:* "The penalty for violation of copyright is $10,000."
> *Striker:* "Cross that picket line, scab, and see what happens."
> *OPEC:* "Settle the Palestinian issue or suffer a cutback in oil deliveries."

There is no end to quarrels about which applications of this principle are legitimate and which illegitimate. Boundaries of legitimacy move. The concept of "crime" attempts to define a limit to this popular practice. But we recognize that there is a gradient of the judged rightness of applying force in the control of others. Parental control of children is recommended; government control of citizens is disputed—from one category of action to another.

We mark off illegitimate applications of this general principle by calling such disapproved use of force particular names. Blackmail and extortion, for example, constitute "unfair" employment of a widely used strategy. Yet both are common devices that range in gravity from mild threats to grand harms. "Terrorism" carries the general principle to a murderous conclusion.

Because the notion of "crime" derives from ideas of "wrong," definition of "terrorism," *as a crime,* varies with moral assessment of the rightness of the cause for which one kills. We are returned to the ambivalence that characterizes attitudes toward homicide (p. 11). As Winegarten (1974, p. 61) puts it, "Where terrorism is concerned, each person draws the line where it suits him."

For example, the French philosopher Maurice Merleau-Ponty (1908–1961), a phenomenologist and revisionist Marxist, claims that idealistic killing is not murder "so long as you do not kill for personal gain, so long as you kill 'without pleasure,' and so long as you risk your own life. . . ." (cited by Winegarten, *ibid.*). For Merleau-Ponty, these conditions transform a murderer into a hero or a martyr.

Since morals move the boundaries of definitions, it is no surprise that the United Nations' *Ad Hoc Committee on International Terrorism* (1973) was unable to define what it was organized to combat. Lacking definition, the United Nations has been unable to agree on measures that might cope with this popular form of homicide. Since "wars of liberation" employ terror, and since "good governments" must deal violently with terrorists, it has been impossible to agree on whose cruelty should be prohibited or how.

Distinctions are blurred by moral evaluation of the killing. Thus the Palestine Liberation Organization (PLO) does not consider its massacres of Jews to be "terrorism." Yasir Arafat, the PLO leader, told the Viennese journal *Arbeiterzeitung* (9 July, 1979) that, if the PLO is considered terroristic, then "Washington and De Gaulle were also terrorists." And the American President, Jimmy Carter, added his voice to the confusion by drawing an analogy between the PLO's violent struggle for a homeland and the unarmed American civil rights movement (Wistrich 1980, p. 41).

It is true that power fortified by terror may be exercised in the name of a government that regards itself as legitimate or in the name of revolutionaries who would become the government. Modern use of the idea of terrorism comes to us from the French Revolution and its Jacobin dictatorship that instituted a "reign of terror" during the early 1790s as a weapon with which to inhibit opposition. However, the practice of homicide and its threat as an instrument of power is as old as recorded history. Today, reference of the term, "terrorism," has spread from the violence employed by a state to maintain control of a populace to violence employed by rebel organizations and even single individuals in their fights with incumbent governments. If one counts as "terrorism" only attacks on a state by individuals and small bands of rebels, such attacks in the Western world increased from 206 in 1972 to 2,662 in 1979 (Manor 1980, p. 20).

Without taking sides in these many struggles for justice in its many forms, we can describe a common ground among persons and acts most generally deemed to be terroristic.

CHARACTERISTICS OF TERRORISM

The essence of terrorism is the calculated stimulation of fear through cruelty, killing, or the threat of both as a means by which to obtain or maintain power. From this core additional attributes follow.

1. No Rules

Terrorism differs from most wars and police actions in that terrorists consciously violate all conventions that might restrict their cruelty and killing. By contrast, soldiers and police personnel are held accountable to operate within certain rules of the fight. These rules, like all rules, are subject to violation and change. There is nothing in logic or history to prevent obliteration of the distinction between rule-regulated policing and warring and unrestricted terrorism. In fact, the demographer Petersen (1979, pp. 175–176) believes that the twentieth century has "ushered in . . . an era of totalitarian wars" that erases all limits to killing. "In the two world wars," he writes, "regulations of various kinds were successively abrogated—concerning places (for example, open cities), concerning weapons (tanks, poison gas, atomic bombs), concerning forms (declaration of war, treatment of prisoners), and concerning values (setting limits to the spoliation of property or of persons)."

Allowing, then, for the possibility that "civil" warring may degenerate toward unregulated homicide, what has distinguished terrorists is their *explicit rejection of moral limitations upon their violence.*

Terrorists discipline themselves to be free of guilt. Atrocities are recommended as a test of commitment and as an exercise in will. Thus one of the fathers of modern anarchism, S.G. Nechaev (1847–1882), wrote a *Revolutionary Catechism* (1869) in which he proposes that:

> We recognize no other activity but the work of extermination, but we admit that the forms in which this activity will show itself will be extremely varied—poison, the knife, the rope, etc. In this struggle revolution sanctifies everything alike.
>
> For [the revolutionary] morality is everything which contributes to the triumph of the revolution. Immoral and criminal is everything that stands in his way.
>
> Tyrannical toward himself, he must be tyrannical toward others. All the soft and tender affections arising from kinship, friendship, and love, all gratitude and even all honor must be obliterated, and in their place there must be the cold and single-minded passion for the work of revolution. . . . Night and day he must have but one thought, one aim—merciless destruction. Aiming cold-bloodedly and indefatigably toward this end, he must be ready to destroy himself and destroy with his own hands everyone who stands in his way.
>
> The revolutionary . . . lives in this world only because he has faith in its speedy and total destruction. He is not a revolutionary if he feels any

sympathy for this world. He must not hesitate to destroy any position, any place, or any man in this world—all must be equally detested by him. All the worse for him if he has parents, friends, and loved ones; he is no longer a revolutionary if they can stay his hand (Reproduced as an Appendix in Rapoport 1971).

Nechaev's first and only violent act as a terrorist was to organize "a collective ritual murder" (Rapoport 1977, p. 57). This incident has been preserved in Dostoyevski's novel, *The Possessed* (1871), and practice in moral callousness continues among contemporary rebels.

Thus Jerry Rubin (1970) exhorted students at Kent State University: "Until you people are prepared to kill your parents, you aren't ready for the revolution." More recently Japanese police arrested a unit of the revolutionary Japanese Red Army. Eight of the 14 members of this unit had been tortured and murdered *by their comrades* for offenses indicating a "bourgeois mentality." Rapoport (1977, p. 57) comments:

> One member had put her child in paddipads [diapers], a second wore lipstick, and a third had risked death when ordered to swerve his speeding truck in order to avoid hitting an animal. When questioned about the appropriateness of the discipline, the survivors who were murderers, said the main purpose was to overcome the sense of shame and to help them become worthy revolutionary leaders!

2. No Innocents

About 100 years ago a French anarchist, Emile Henry, threw a bomb into a café crowded with clerks, workmen, and small shopkeepers. At his trial Henry argued that, "There are no innocent people."

Terrorists assume that their fight against an "unjust system" includes a fight against all people within that system who do not side with them. It follows from this assumption, and from the preceding one about "no holds being barred," that there are no innocents.

Therefore, children can be quite consciously killed as in Palestinian attacks against the Israeli communes at Maalot and Kiryat Shemona, 1975. Therefore, Protestants in Northern Ireland have murdered Roman Catholics at random in reprisal for IRA bombings. (These contemporary pogroms have been given the euphemistic title, "Paddy-bopping"). Therefore, during their Algerian struggle, French colonists organized "Arab hunts" in which they killed every Moslem they saw (Henissart 1970). Therefore, what starts as a focused war can become an indiscriminate terror as illustrated by the battles between the Indonesian government and its Communist enemies. During this conflict in 1965, an estimated half a million people were killed.

Communists began the slaughter with an attempted coup in which Indonesian military men were captured, some shot on sight, and some taken to a training field known as the Crocodile Hole. Coggin and Moser (1968) witnessed some of the killing and report that:

> [At the Hole] young members of the Communist women's organization performed a diabolic rite, castrating live cats and cutting them to pieces, and then dancing naked, drugged with narcotics, before the captured generals. Afterward they mutilated the generals with small sharp knives and gouged out their eyes.
>
> News of this obscene brutality spread quickly through the islands and the reaction was swift and ferocious ... [With the army's encouragement] the Indonesian people took up their swordlike *parangs* and throwing-knives and entered the slaughter. On every island, in every town and village they simply ran amok, killing not only Communists but their families and friends, as well as Chinese moneylenders and men who were said to be atheists or whom they envied for their landholdings or who were simply, for one reason or another, out of popular favor—in all, perhaps one out of every two hundred citizens (p. 380).

Moser interviewed some of the participants and he tells us that:

> On Bali, this most beautiful of islands, the Balinese proved capable of the most exquisite cruelty. When they attacked the Communists, "it was like watching kids torture a cat," said one of the few Westerners who lived there during the killings. In Denpasar, students beat a classmate to death with stones. Around Negara, where Communists had dug graves for their intended victims, the reprisal took a toll of thousands of party members who wound up buried in the same holes that they had prepared.
>
> What kind of people are these who participated in such a slaughter? ... Let us look at one who is a fair choice of many I have talked to. ... He is Hasan Hasri, a gentle-looking man of thirty ... a devout Moslem. ... Last December ... when the army began bringing Communist prisoners down to Djumpai beach and distributing them to the villagers, Hasan felt the call of Allah. And so he took the sharp *parang* he had made from the leaf of an automobile spring and began to haunt the beach.
>
> Hasan was usually given two or three [prisoners] for himself. He led his Communists down to the beach where local farmers had dug the long pits, one and a half meters deep. ... The prisoners were seated on the edge of the pit, their thumbs tied securely behind their backs. Hasan

shouted, *"Allah U Akbar, Allah U Akbar*—In the name of God." Then he began to chop. Hasan could usually sever the head in a single chop, he said. But sometimes at night he would miss in the dark and hit only a glancing blow into the head or neck. Then the prisoner screamed until Hasan finished him off.

Often he would chat with the men before killing them. He had nothing against them personally, he said. But they were Communists. . . . They were atheists, and Hasan was only carrying out the will of Allah.

The first time he killed, Hasan was a little upset, he said. But after a while he settled down and then he acquired a thirst for the chopping.

Why did the Indonesians destroy the Communists so mercilessly? Nothing can completely explain their ferocity, but they did have many grievances. . . . Yet it would be a mistake to think that all killings had genuine political motivation. Out in the countryside of Bali, people had no more conception of Communist ideology than they had of high finance.

The smiling young boys who bring flowers to tourists and guide them through the Balinese temple of Besakih bashed in the heads of three local Communists one night just outside the temple gates. When I asked their leader . . . if he understood the difference between Communist aims and the aims of his own party, the Nationalist Party, he replied: "No, I just work here at the temple, I do not understand about politics." Did he hate the Communists? "No, I did not hate them," the boy said. Why *did* he kill them, then? "Some authorities just came by one day and said to get rid of them," the boy answered with a shy, pleasant smile. "And so we did" (pp. 383–386, emphasis his). (Reproduced from "Indonesia runs amok, 1965–1966" by Dan Coggin and Donald Moser in C. & S. Mydans (eds.), *The Violent Peace.* New York: Atheneum. © 1968 by Time, Inc. Reprinted with permission.)

Obedience to authority is only one of the many routes to indiscriminate homicide and many terrorists take to the murder of anonymous others with different motives and different satisfactions. "Open societies" are particularly vulnerable to the spread of terrorism because models of violent political actors are increasingly presented by word of mouth and television to audiences that contain unknown numbers of individuals whose lack of personal purpose can be channeled into the camaraderie and excitement of righteous killing.

Righteous homicide justifies killing innocents, or denying that victims who happen "to get in the way" are innocent. Sam Melville provides an example.

Melville came to be known as the "Mad Bomber of Manhattan," a man who translated his personal deficiencies into attacks on "the system" that he thought was the source of his troubles. He achieved some fame among American Leftists as one of the prisoners killed during the riot in the Attica prison. Melville's associate, Jane Alpert (1972), writes:

> He put almost no care into the Marine Midland [bank] bombing. To judge from what he told me later, he merely assembled a bomb, timed it to go off at 1 a.m., stuck it in a briefcase and wandered down to the financial district to find a good target. It never occurred to him that people might be working in the building when the bomb went off and, as it happened, a night shift of mostly female typists and clerks was working on two floors of the building during the explosion. . . . It was mostly luck that the worst that happened was slight injuries to ten or twelve people. Sam had earlier rationalized the possibility of injuring people, in a theoretical discussion, by comparing his activities to those of the NLF and the Algerians who had carried out revolutionary terrorism in which not only the powerful but also "innocent bystanders" were injured or killed (p. 29)

The quotation marks around "innocent bystanders" are Alpert's. They indicate that the innocents are *not* to be so construed.

The appeal to a "theoretical discussion" also deserves comment. It is an attempt to elevate irrational damage into idealistic injury. Appeal to "theory" here bespeaks a schizoid tension that characterizies many terrorists. They are torn between "knowing what they are doing" and the emotional satisfaction of daring-doing with little or no thought.

3. Economy

The rationale of terrorism is that expressed by an anonymous Chinese general: "Kill one, frighten ten thousand." According to one student of terrorism (Clutterbuck 1978, p. 43), the era of electronic communication increases this ratio so that it may be: "Kill one, frighten ten million."

Whatever the range of terrorist influence, there is an economy to it. It is to achieve grand results from the small investment of lives.

4. Publicity and Provocation

Terrorists seek publicity and publicity encourages terrorism. Their acts partake of what the Russian anarchist Peter Kropotkin (1842–1921) called "propaganda by the deed."

Well publicized violence advertises the terrorist's cause. It gives terrorists a forum that they could not otherwise purchase. For example, the Palestinians who killed eleven members of the Israeli Olympic team in Munich knew that their act would have a television audience in the hundreds of millions, some portion of which would learn of the Palestinian cause and might sympathize with it.

Propaganda for the terrorist's side is aided by provoking the state into violent response to terrorist challenge. It is conscious terrorist strategy to incite the governments they attack so as to demonstrate the justice of the rebel's cause. A Cypriot fighter put it this way: "We are provoking you to beat us so that our cries reach their [the world's] ears" (Durrell 1957, p. 224).

Carlos Marighella, the strategist of urban guerrilla warfare, went further than to urge provocation for publicity. He recommended provocation as an instrument that allegedly would convert "moderates" to the revolutionary side and divide a country into armed camps. Marighella's popular *Minimanual of the Urban Guerrilla* (1971) proposes that:

> It is necessary to turn political crisis into armed conflict by performing violent actions that will force those in power to transform the military situation in the country into a political situation. That will alienate the masses, who, from then on, will revolt against the army and the police and blame them for this state of things.

In Brazil, where Marighella was killed, the guerrilla campaign worked partly as Carlos had prophesied: it provoked a backlash. But the backlash did not have the consequences Marighella had promised. The historian Robert Moss (1972a, p. 43) describes these results:

> The regimes of Marshal Costa e Silva and General Garrastazú Médici . . . flooded the streets with troops, collected intelligence by mass detention and very rough interrogation techniques (including the widespread use of torture), and forced the guerrillas to confront the security forces in open gun-battles that they were bound to lose. The Brazilian guerrillas lost three celebrated leaders in succession. . . . The backlash put paid to the guerrillas.

This strategy of terrorism continues. It is the ploy of compelling the "strong" to attack the "weak" so as to gain sympathy for the "underdog." It is a device that works poorly against authoritarian governments and better against democratic states. The strategy puts democratic governments in a predicament: They are "damned if they do, and damned if they don't." If they exercise restraint in response to terrorism, they permit its success. If they respond violently to terrorism, they provide material for revolutionary propaganda.

The worst response of a government—and the best from the terrorist's point of view—is vacillating action, action that allows rebels some freedom from penalty but that sometimes violates this policy of restraint and provides publicity for those who are attacking the state.

5. Individual Therapy

It has long been remarked that fighting is fun and that commitment to a fighting group is exhilarating. Engaging in battle gives purpose to life, and all the more so to lives that are meaningless.

Part of the pleasure in collective struggle derives from the relief of boredom. At the conclusion of the second World War, Winston Churchill was asked whether he found his life a bit flat. "Well," he replied, "you can't expect to have a war all the time."

Warriors ancient and modern have commented on "the comradeship in danger and delight in destruction" (Gray 1959, p. 29). A German soldier expressed his pleasure this way:

> The great moment had come. The curtain of fire lifted from the front trenches. We stood up.
>
> With a mixture of feelings, evoked by bloodthirstiness, rage, and intoxication, we moved in step, ponderously but irresistibly, toward the enemy lines. I was well ahead of the company, followed by Vinke and a one-year veteran named Haake. My right hand embraced the shaft of my pistol, my left a riding stick of bamboo cane. I was boiling with a mad rage, which had taken hold of me and all the others in an incomprehensible fashion. The overwhelming wish to kill gave wings to my feet. Rage pressed bitter tears from my eyes.
>
> The monstrous desire for annihilation, which hovers over the battlefield, thickened the brains of the men and submerged them in a red fog. We called to each other in sobs and stammered disconnected sentences. A neutral observer might have perhaps believed that we were seized by an excess of happiness (Ernst Juenger, from his World War I diary, as cited by Gray 1959, p. 52).

In some unknown proportion of cases, revolutionaries are attracted to violence as a remedy for their own purposeless lives. Thus Rapoport (1977, p. 55) notes that, in the University of California, "Perpetually overcrowded psychiatric facilities emptied during Berkeley's revolutionary days. Never did life seem more interesting or worthwhile." Placards exclaimed: "Revolution: The Highest Trip of All" and "Revolution Is Joy."

It is repeatedly noted in industrial countries that terrorism attracts the privileged young rather than the "working class" in whose name violence is exercised. Some observers find this difficult to understand. However, it is inexplicable only to those who assume, incorrectly, that discontent arises *necessarily* from poverty, and that contentment follows *necessarily* from wealth and freedom. To the contrary, the privileges of freedom and affluence are not enough to provide "spiritual satisfaction." Such advantages, cut loose from a moral mooring, produce boredom, a sense of the meaninglessness of life, and the temptation to blame the world for one's emptiness. "Poor, rich kids" are "suckers" for utopias.

Organized fighting is therefore personal therapy for some psychically distressed individuals. It is not the only source of terrorism, of course.

6. Varied Objectives

The immediate aim of a terrorist is to exercise power and to get more of it. However, what power will be used for—if terror succeeds—is variously conceived and often vaguely conceived.

Some groups, like the PLO, the IRA, the FLQ, and the Basque and Catalan fronts, have nationalistic goals. They want separate states for their nations.

Regardless of one's sympathy or distaste for these objectives, these goals are empirical. Such objectives are specifiable and achievable. Terrorism in such cases may be rational—whether or not it is considered to be moral.

Other groups, like the Red Army of Japan and the Red Brigades of Italy, seek a worldwide revolution that will destroy "bourgeois society" and usher in a communist utopia. Such more internationally oriented groups communicate with one another and, when tactically convenient, with nationalistic fronts. For example, in 1978 a congress of such groups met in Beirut. Delegates represented the PLO, IRA, the Red Army Faction (West Germany), the Montoneros (Argentina), Japan's Red Army Group, Italy's Red Brigades, and the Basque Socialist Separatist Group (ETA).

The terrorism of universalistic, revolutionary groups is demi-rational. Overthrowing a government is possible, of course, and this part of the revolutionary work may be rational. But creation of a utopia is another matter, and faith in this revolutionary assumption is irrational.

Both nationalistic and universalistic terrorists receive support—financial and military—from the Soviet Union, East Germany, Libya, and Cuba (Alexander 1976, Demaris 1977, Horner 1980, Munger 1977, Smith 1976, Sterling 1978, 1981). According to the American General George Keegan "over 150,000 full-time Soviet military intelligence officers, including KGB and military personnel, are involved in the training of foreign terrorists. The estimated expenditure for these operations by the Soviet Union amounts to about half a billion dollars annually, and 75 percent of this effort has been directed toward operations around the Persian Gulf" (Manor 1980, p. 21).

As an illustration, Thomas McMahon, the Irish terrorist convicted of killing Lord Louis Mountbatten by blowing up his boat, was trained in remote-controlled bomb-making in Libya under Russian supervision (*Daily Mail,* cited by *Encounter* 1980, p. 25). McMahon's bombing of Mountbatten's boat also killed the 82-year-old Dowager Lady Brabourne, a 15-year-old crewman, and Mountbatten's 14-year-old grandson. In addition, McMahon is suspected of arranging the massacre of 18 British soldiers a few hours after bombing Mountbatten's boat. McMahon's priest explained that this terrorist "is . . . working with love for his country. He wants a united Ireland and as far as he is concerned he was fighting the forces of evil" (*Daily Telegraph,* cited by *Encounter* 1980, p. 25).

New bands of terrorists, as well as some old ones, continue to be trained in Communist satellite countries, such as South Yemen (Horner 1980). For example, the newly formed Dutch Red Resistance Front receives its military lessons in that country.

Communist states are not the only supporters of terrorism, of course, although they provide the greatest assistance. Recent American administrations have given aid to foreign powers that have employed terror as an instrument of control. National loyalists in Canada and the United States send funds to the IRA. British subjects funnel money to the PLO via Jordan. The World Council of Churches gives financial support to a select number of terrorist groups, a fact that provides another commentary on ambivalence toward homicide and conditional pacifism (Lefever 1979, Norman 1979).

Nationalistic and revolutionary bands do most of the killing called terroristic. However, they are emulated by a number of other gangs that lack clear ideas, have no program, and that seem motivated principally by personal disaffection, boredom, and envy. Examples are the Symbionese Liberation Army and the Baader-Meinhof gang. When such groups talk about their objectives, their goals are typically stated in language that is either obscure or contradictory. Words are used as signal drums, with little attention to their referents, and words with possible referents are used to express contradictory objectives. Thus the Weather Underground declares that it is opposed to "rising prices, loss of jobs, [and] a lower standard of living," but, at the same time, it is also opposed to "the dominant values of conformity, materialism, and security" (Biskind & Weiss 1975, p. 43).

Insofar as these groups lack empirical goals as ends of their violence, their action is non-rational.[1] Insofar as their objectives are obscure or contradictory, no means can be appropriate, and their action is lunatic.

Concerning the rationality of terrorism, Brian Jenkins (1981) counted one facet of such action—the seizure of foreign embassies. Jenkins tallied 48 such attacks between 1971 and mid-1980, half of which occurred in the last two years of the decade. Terrorists made demands of some sort in 36 of the embassy captures. These were fully met in six cases and partially met in five incidents. Thus measured, the success rate is not high, and it drops as government resistance increases. However, a major motive of the terrorists is publicity, quite apart from the satisfaction of particular demands, and this objective is realized by the attack and with the assistance of the news media. Furthermore, of the estimated 326 terrorists involved in these assaults, 216 got away scot-free.

The variety of objectives that characterizes terrorists indicates that, as with other categories of homicide, terrorism is approached by many roads. This means, in turn, that more than one kind of person travels these diverse routes.

EXPLAINING TERRORISTS: SITUATIONS, PURPOSES, PHILOSOPHIES, PERSONALITIES

To say that there are many roads to terrorism is to say that there are many causes of such activity. Categories of causes nominated to ex-

---

[1] Being rational, irrational, and non-rational are distinct ideas.

To act rationally is "to know what one is doing." This means that one knows what she or he wants, the objective is empirical, and means are efficient.

To act irrationally is to employ inappropriate means to achieve empirical goals. The idea of irrational action carries with it the notion that the irrationality is caused by a deviation from clear thinking, a deviation that is induced by emotion.

To act in a non-rational manner is to act in any other way than rationally or irrationally. This residual definition is applied to two kinds of acts: (1) to expressive activity—that done for its own sake—and, more commonly, to (2) instrumental acts taken in the name of non-empirical goals. Non-empirical goals are objectives that cannot be achieved or that cannot be *known* to have been achieved. By this definition, striving to get to Heaven is non-rational as is trying to obtain "the greatest good for the greatest number."

plain terrorists include actors' situations, their purposes, their philosophies, and their personalities.

As Volume One, Chapter 2 indicated, choice of these causal categories moves with moral assessment of actors and their acts. Moral assessment of terrorists involves judgment of the justice-injustice of their situation, of the goodness of their avowed ends, the appropriateness of their means, and the amount of group support they receive.

For example, if we talk to denizens of a refugee camp who have been reared as descendants of some displaced nation, their fight to establish a territory that is to be ruled by their own people is likely to be deemed "understandable"—that is, a rational response to a situation and a just response. The locus of causation in such instances is commonly placed in circumstance and in actor's purpose in changing that circumstance. In such cases, there is little tendency to attribute causation to peculiar ideas or distinctive personalities.

However, if the terrorist is deviant, if she or he has less support of a people claiming national identity, then explanation of the terrorist moves from situation and purpose to unusual ideas and personalities.

In sum, the more popular the terrorism, the more likely that its cause will be attributed to circumstance and purpose. The more unpopular the terrorism, the more likely that its cause will be attributed to peculiar philosophy and personality.

Science and Policy

Different causal assignment justifies different social policy. To the extent to which assignment has been influenced by moral considerations, we may expect such causal location to be less than scientific. A scientific diagnosis of causation would be one based on data, where the data had been organized as confirmed hypothesis, and subjected to the test of improved forecast or predictive accuracy.

An assessment of the relative powers of the nominated causes of terrorism has not been made. We do not know whether predictive power is increased most by viewing the causes of violent action as people's circumstances, or as people's interpretations of their circumstances, or as the personalities brought to competing interpretations of situations.

As earlier chapters indicated, we assume that some combination of these sources of conduct would increase our predictive power and, hence, our wisdom. But we have as yet no science that tells us how to weigh these possible contributory causes. And we have no science, in part, because we have no taxonomy of situations, or ideas, or personalities that improves upon "historical judgment" or "good sense" in the forecast of terrorism. It is for these reasons that we have emphasized the themes of many roads and contingent continuities.

Lacking a science of human conduct, we debate. Aspects of the debate, as applied to the explanation of terrorists, illuminate difficulties in explaining human action and promote prudence in assigning causes.

The debate is joined by noting that, *after* the fact of an act, situations can always be interpreted so as to make conduct "understandable." But such plausibility does not denote correct nomination of causes. Moreover, *before* the fact, situations alone seldom explain actions. This is to say that many people in apparently similar circumstances behave differently.[2]

The fact of differential response to similar circumstance moves assignment of causation from situations alone to kinds of people and their ideas. In psychology, attention is paid principally to kinds of people. In sociology and social psychology, more attention is paid to people's ideas.

Ideas are variously titled "attitudes," "perceptions," "expectations," and "definitions of the situation," but whichever title is applied, what is measured in evaluating these causes is people's verbal performance, oral or graphic. The most popular research tool employed by social psychologists is the question.

Deficiencies of asking people questions as a means of probing their *motives* have been mentioned in Volume One, Chapter 2. Deficiencies of asking people questions as a means of finding *facts* about them have also been widely discussed (Nettler 1978a, pp. 107–117). But here we wish to raise a different, and difficult, issue.

The present issue is not whether ideas make a difference or whether ideas are to be known by what people write and say. That is granted. Ideas influence actions and all of us assume *some* effects of propaganda and education.

The interesting question is this: *How much difference do ideas make, for which acts, at what juncture in a career, for which kinds of people, in which situations?*

To ask this question is to recognize that individuals *differentially select* ideas as interpretations of their situations and as guides to action. It is to recognize the possibility that personalities differentially "consume" beliefs from among the variety available in civil societies.

---

[2] Ascertaining similarity and difference in persons, situations, and acts is the difficulty of taxonomy that impedes a science of human action.

And last, it is to recognize that ideas may be *accompaniments* of acts, or *rationalizations* of acts, as well as the *causes* of acts.[3]

Description of two careers in terrorism will illustrate these points.

Examples: On Beliefs, Tempers, and Consequences—Searching for Causes of Careers

Giangi

Giangiacomo Feltrinelli ("Giangi" to his friends) was a son of the rich who flipped from the fascist faith in the 1940s to the communist faith in the 1950s and 1960s. Today he is a martyr—among the European Left. He was killed, presumably by accident, while attempting to connect Milan's network of electric utilities to a charge of dynamite. The distinguished journalist, Luigi Barzini (1972), describes Giangi's course:

> Long ago, when I married his widowed mother Giannalisa, I was Giangiacomo Feltrinelli's stepfather for seven or eight years; and I tried to do what I could for his education, to understand how his mind worked and, up to a point, to guide his studies, until the family's separation and the divorce in 1949. No previous experience in my life helped me with all this, and perhaps I was not particularly well suited to it. As the son of a writer and editor, brought up on books and with a juvenile penchant for irreverent paradox, I came from a life of wandering journalism, and I was myself a rebel against the academic, bourgeois, provincial conventions of Italian life. So I felt uneasy in a grand house full of servants, regulated and staffed like a small court. Perhaps my influence (or the lack of any real influence from me) helped just a little to take Giangi, with such ideas as motivated him, to his death that night in March at the foot of a pylon in the misty countryside near Milan.
>
> Soon after my marriage, in May 1940, I was arrested on Mussolini's orders and condemned to exile. Bocchini, the chief of police, had admired and been grateful to my father who had been as open-hearted as a child. At the Versailles conference in 1919, my father (then special diplomatic correspondent of the *Corriere della Sera*), had a gold-topped walking stick stolen; and, in the whole of the great city of Paris, he turned to

---

[3] In lay thinking and cognitive psychology it is popular to assume that ideas are the engine of action. Sometimes they may be. However, a more fair phrasing of the question asks, "Under what conditions are ideas causal?" and "How powerful are ideas as generators of acts?" For example, Cramer (1980, p. 167) shows that as regards "planning" to have children, "plans generally seem to be consequences more than determinants of behavior."

the modest policeman attached to the Italian delegation and asked him to find it. This was the young Bocchini, who was so moved and amused by this ingenuous sign of confidence from a famous man that he considered himself at his disposal ever after. And so, twenty-one years later, after I had been condemned, Bocchini chose a comfortable, pleasant place in which to exile me, unknown to Mussolini: Amalfi.

When Mussolini asked him where he had sent me, he looked him straight in the eye and said, without lying: *"Provincia di Salerno, Duce!"* (My father told me this). The province includes Eboli, Battipaglia, and many other isolated and disagreeable places, where more eminent men than myself were sent. Later I realised that Bocchini had not really done me much of a favour. The fact that I spent most of my exile in a tourist paradise has always prevented me from being thought a martyr of the fascist regime.

Giangi was with me in Amalfi, and so were his sister and his mother, in that summer of 1940, and I taught him to sail; this was an enthusiasm that stayed with him all his life. Later he became an expert skipper (he had got the necessary diploma, the only diploma he ever had, I think). . . .

I saw to his studies, first, in Milan. We lived at San Siro, the horse-racing compound, next to the stable that had been Gualino's and near the one where Luchina Visconti lived with his thoroughbreds; and later, in 1943–44, we moved to Porto Santo Stefano, where we waited for the Allied advance under constant air-raids. A few days before the liberation, we managed to get to Rome in a dramatic flight, Giangi and his mother and sister, my own two very small girls, and myself, on a truck with dubious German documents, travelling all night with a *Wehrmacht* military column. In order to stop him missing the school year I gave him lessons in Latin, Greek, English and philosophy, going back over school-work I had long forgotten. This meant that I spent a few hours each day with him.

Perhaps I was a poor teacher, perhaps I lacked whatever it is that makes a good stepfather, perhaps Giangiacomo was an inattentive, rebellious and hostile pupil, or perhaps we simply didn't get on, since we were profoundly unlike; but whatever the reason, the fact remains that I don't think I taught him anything lasting. In the early days in Milan he was an ardent fascist. He wore the uniform of a mounted *avanguardista,* the youth military organisation, and papered the house with posters singing the *Duce's* praises, announcing the inevitable victory of the Axis, and celebrating the imminent conquest of *irredente* Nice, Tunisia, Savoy and Corsica. If he had caught me listening to foreign broadcast I'm sure he would have denounced me without a qualm; and so his mother and I used to lock ourselves into a small study when the broadcasts began.

Later a gardener converted him to the Revolution, and he embraced his new faith with the same blind fanaticism. He was the kind of man, quite commonly found in Italy, who can pass from one extreme movement to another that is its exact opposite, so long as it is illiberal and mythological—never stopping to consider the ideas (which may be boring and over-earnest, because they promise no instant miracles, merely hard work) of the liberal middle-class revolutions, of freedom achieved with difficulty and daily defended, a freedom which allows people to face problems and solve them gradually, and which tolerates, indeed defuses and makes use of, whatever is valid in dissident and heretical movements.

What the gardener taught him was surely not Marxism and Leninism but a utopian-socialist enthusiasm, which, when the revolutionary situation ripened, was to prepare the great blood-letting: political purges and quick killings similar to those Giangi had approved and dreamed of earlier, when he wore his black shirt. It was hard for me, who believed in reason, to cope with this kind of romantic apocalypse. It was clear that we could scarcely understand each other.

I was baffled. Only later did I understand why a boy like Giangi could gravitate to an extreme Left Wing proletarian party immediately after the War. He was not alone. There were many others, including Alberto Pirelli's oldest son, Giovanni. A few had possibly made a conscious choice: some were finding explanations and consolations for the collapse of their youthful dreams of an Italian victory; others were in revolt against the suffocating Buddenbrooks atmosphere of their families, frightened of the name they bore and the terrible burden of wealth; still others were terrified of the coming revolution, and joined the other side before it was too late. . . .

The extreme Left was, come to think of it, the best solution to many a rich boy's problem. It freed them from the strictures and conventions of the bourgeois life and gravely offended their parents (it was, in a way, the contemporary equivalent to marrying a ballerina or chorus girl). It surrounded them with admiring friends (for some reason, the revolutionary movements shelter a multitude of snobs, both intellectual and worldly, among them the most avid name-droppers of all). It gave them instant self-esteem and notoriety (everybody talked about a millionaire's son who had joined the Party, nobody knew the names of the diligent boys who studied hard to prepare themselves for running the family business).

In 1944, I persuaded him not to go into the *maquis* (the partisans of the Argentario, where we were living, were led by an escaped Soviet prisoner, a formidable character) but to wait for the arrival of the Italian liberation army in Rome before joining up to fight the Nazis and Fascists in a way that would be more rational and effective. He was not happy about it, of course, because by nature he preferred adventurous, risky solutions, in war as well as in revolution, to disciplined armies or parties led by logic and technical skill. However, he went along and fought with honour as a volunteer until the liberation of the North.

We lost sight of each other after 1947, when his mother and I parted. He had been accepted by the Communist Party, had a humble job organising workers at Sesto San Giovanni, an industrial suburb of Milan, was busy preparing for the *revoluzione imminente,* and had found his first love among the girl comrades. It was Togliatti who took him away from all this, guessing the advantages which the Milanese boy, with his huge personal fortune, could offer the working-class movement.

He sent Eugenio Reale to him, a learned Neapolitan intellectual who has now left the Party; Reale surrounded him with serious Marxist intellectuals, and got him to collect, all over Europe, the very rare documents on the origins of the working-class movement which today belong to the Giangiacomo Feltrinelli Institute. The Institute later published important studies, monographs and translations, which became steadily more popular and sold in increasing numbers; until Giangi one day decided to set up a separate publishing firm and to make use of the success which the Party guaranteed among the militants.

It was clear to anyone who knew him that he would leave the Party as soon as he felt its discipline, its control, its restrictions, and as soon as he realised that it was not quite an organisation of *terroristi e dinamitardi* ... strewing the streets with its enemies' corpses; but that it was, rather, a large, prudent, even erudite movement which had benefited from the setbacks of the last fifty years in so many European countries and intended to win by avoiding ... a catastrophic civil war.

Little by little, ever more to the Left, ever more adventurous, ever more rebellious in the face of any control, he spent an increasing part of his fortune, and brought all his activities into line with his ideas and his hopes. His fortune soon was (and still is) in serious jeopardy. Debts recently ran into thousands of millions of lire. The publishing firm had its isolated spurts of success (it published *The Leopard* and *Dr. Zhivago*) but it usually lost ... about 400 million lire a year. ... In the last few years Giangi was ... forced to dispose of shares and to sell large tracts of land in the centre of Milan, which had been in the family for generations. ...

I lost track of him for many years. I saw his mother only when necessary. ... His sister Antonella was married in Paris. I felt no desire to see him; we had little to say to each other. I have always had a particular horror of people dominated by irrational devils, like medieval *indemoniati,* and I cringe in front of drunks. Emotional, frenetic, uncontrolled communists or fascists gave me the same sensations. I also always disliked rich boys surrounded by courtiers. We met casually once in a while and usually exchanged polite conversation. We never talked politics, books, or publishing.

The next-to-last time I saw him ... he attacked me violently [concerning nationalisation of the electrical industry, but] I said nothing because there was no point in trying to sort out his ideas and mixed sentiments.

The question everyone has been asking is: even if it is clear why a millionaire boy joins the Communist Party in times of confusion, how on earth does he give up everything, his fortune, peace, family happiness, success, and in the end, tragically, even life itself, in order to destroy society—the society that created (among many other things that may be more useful) the millions from which millionaires prosper?

There is, of course, no single answer. There are many, and here are some of them.

Blood, first of all. The family comes from Desenzano on Lake Garda. . . . They were small traders. . . . They grew rich on trade between the Veneto and Austria. . . . In the last century the family tended to be pro-Austrian. The Feltrinellis owned huge estates and rented others, all over the old Empire, in places that peace treaties later expropriated from Austria. . . . Giangi spent most of his childhood on the Austrian estate at Moessna, speaking German (he had German governesses) and wearing *lederhosen.* . . . The family doctors and dentists were always in Vienna, as Italians could not be trusted. . . . All this meant that Giangi did not inherit from his forbears the love of the Italian state and the ideas of liberty that were quite naturally taught to the descendants of the 19th-century patriots. Like many children of Bourbon legitimists in Naples, or *Papalini* in Rome, a century ago, he continued without quite realising it the fight against a liberal, unified, and independent Italy, but from a position on the Left. . . . There was, however, a vein of rebellious extravagance and independence in his forbears and in his uncles (two of whom committed suicide) as well as the tendency, common to both millionaries and revolutionary leaders, to think that laws are useful for keeping others in their place but that such restraints did not apply to them.

Education In the early years of his life, he was always isolated from others of his own age, and in the charge of stern German governesses and strict tutors, like a prince of the blood royal in olden times. . . . From his lonely and harshly disciplined childhood, surrounded by the rather servile affection of servants, he inherited a curious incapacity to tolerate any form of control, to distinguish between people, or to behave as if others were his equals. He would be deferential with superiors and arrogant with inferiors, was seldom courteous and matter-of-fact with his peers. He ended by preferring always the company of the illiterate, the fanatic, and those who were in some way dependent upon him.[4]

Money had a great influence on him. Easy millions give weak men who inherit them a sense of exaltation comparable with the effect produced by certain drugs. They feel as if they are allowed to do anything, and nothing can stop them—not the opinion of others, or the penal code, or the rules of normal life. (In traffic Giangi disliked stopping at red lights.) The only thing that sometimes deters is the fear of losing their millions and the power and immunity that go with them. But Giangi did not fear this, first of all because his resources were enormous and seemed inexhaustible, and he deluded himself that he could always get over his losses, but also because he thought he was carrying on the biggest speculative manoeuvre ever, one which he felt was a sure thing. He believed his position of power would be immensely reinforced—and that of all the other rich destroyed—on the day he returned to Italy at the head of the revolution, the Italian Fidel Castro.

Without realising it, he had retained many of the attitudes of the 19th-century rich. He was overbearing with servants and employees; treated writers with ill-concealed contempt; dismissed Giorgio Bassani, the novelist, who was at one time editor of the Feltrinelli publishing house, like an unsatisfactory footman (after forcing open the drawers of his desk and reading his private letters); and, like many millionaires, was capable of curious acts of avarice. He financed seditious clandestine movements, but did it so meanly, checking all the accounts and stalling on payments. In a way he was a caricature mirror-image of the old-fashioned plutocrat within the context of the dynamite-toting Left, the *Sinistra dinamitarda*.

Like many rich men—in fact, like his uncle Tonino who used to pay hard-up aristocrats small salaries in order to have them round him at the club, laughing at his jokes—he was an easy victim of flatterers. Togliatti, a rather subtle man, realised this, and so did the talented young Communist intellectuals who guided his first political and publishing efforts. Yet as soon as he felt he was being influenced, guided and exploited, he turned on them like a capricious prince, banishing one-time favourites and choosing new ones. But he also liked meeting the snobbish rich, like himself; he mixed with smart radical-chic millionaires, men who despised the masses as he did, who thought them something they could

---

[4] This mixture is not uncommon among men who have been harshly reared. Sadism and masochism can function in one personality. Such persons are "either at your feet or at your throat."

play with, pushing them Left or Right, whichever seemed the most likely to be to their own advantage.

Perhaps the best way of comprehending him is to consider other people who resemble him. He was like the great Russian textile industrialist who employed the engineer Skriabin (alias Molotov) and the engineer Krassin, at the beginning of the century; who financed Lenin, *Iskra* and *Pravda* for years; and after the Revolution hanged himself in a hotel room in Cannes, perhaps having concluded that his money had now served its purpose. Curiously, Giangi also recalls, in some ways, Howard Hughes, the notorious American millionaire who lives in a world apart, surrounded by secrecy and served by sycophants, courtiers and employees, whom he likes to believe are as faithful as slaves.

But perhaps the character he is most like is the Count of Monte Cristo. Giangi had the same immense wealth, the same passion for mystery, the same dizzying sense of being all-powerful and above ordinary men, the sense of being able to decide their fate in order to bring about justice and to avenge wrongs. He liked best playing the Count of Monte Cristo in poor, backward and disorganised places, where injustice was most obvious and most burning, in Bolivia, Cuba, or Sardinia, where he was by contrast more powerful than ever, where he could all the more easily impose his will.

It doesn't much matter whether Giangi died as a victim of a secret plot or through an accident when he was connecting Milan's network of electric wires to a charge of dynamite. Political fanatics of both Left and Right always like the explanation of a secret plot. . . . The probability is that some loose electric contact (the pylon was broken and there might have been a leak to the ground) exploded the charges under him, while he was working some twenty feet above the ground. Giangi died, in any case, for his ideas (and it doesn't even matter at this stage, whether they were right, realisable, or demented). One cannot fail to respect his sacrifice.

I embrace the boy I tried to teach about Thales of Miletus all those years ago, thinking of all the serious, useful things he might have done, with his energy and his money, if he had managed to find peace within himself. But history may prove me wrong. . . . (Reprinted, with permission, from L. Barzini, "Feltrinelli." © 1972 by *Encounter*, 39:35–40).

Argument

It is popular to say, as does Barzini, that such people "die for their ideas." This kind of statement suggests that their ideas were their motives. In short, it suggests that ideas *caused* their actions.

A contrary view assumes that careers are produced in a dense web of causes rather than by some simple, linear process in which A causes B, B produces C, and on.[5] In a *web of causes,* ideas play a varied role, but most often they are themselves accompaniments, or effects, of other, more powerful determinants of conduct. This assumption can be strengthened by asking a series of questions.

1. As we review Giangi's career, even in such outline as Barzini provides, can we ascertain whether Giangi's beliefs came first or last in the causal chain? Were his ideas the most powerful of the causes of his terrorism, or were they epiphenomena, "an additional symptom arising during the course of a malady"?[6]

Were Giangi's beliefs necessary, sufficient, neither, or both? Would any other set of apocalyptic notions have served Giangi's "psychic needs" as well? Is this not suggested by his conversion from one authoritarianism to another? How is it that a gardener's "education" impressed Giangi, but not the "education" provided by his literate stepfather?

2. Would it be more accurate to say that Giangi died *of his personality* than that he died *for his ideas?* Would it be more accurate in the sense of improving foresight about his acts?

3. Do beliefs of the nature described—beliefs that justify violent lust for power—require a fertile field in which to germinate? Do such social "fields" differ in their propensity to such violent thoughts? And how important is the "field" as compared with the "seeds" of such crimes that may lie in temperament and training? Are we all equally vulnerable?

4. If one wished to prevent production of Giangi-type delinquents, or to reform them, should one begin by treating their ideas, their situations, or their training?

A Personal Opinion   An attack on the ideas of some unpleasant person is, by itself, futile. We often say, "No one wins an argument." At any rate, no one wins a debate about articles of *faith.*

"Brainwashing" sometimes works, but "brainwashing" is not just a therapy of the thoughts. It represents a change in reinforcement. It would attack Giangi's "condition" by taking away his riches and his friends and placing him in a distant environment—an Israeli kibbutz or a Siberian work camp—where the consequences of Giangi's every

---

[5] See Chapters 2 and 8 in Volume One, and Chapters 9 and 12 of this Volume, on styles of causation and their political palatability.

[6] This is one of the definitions of "epiphenomenon" provided by the *Random House Dictionary of the English Language,* 1966, reproduced by permission of Random House, Inc., publisher.

act would have a different pattern of results from those he experienced in Milan. Along with this alteration, Giangi's "helper" would provide new ideas, a revised view of Giangi's world which would "explain" to Giangi how his new role was right.

This kind of conversion does not rely on the power of ideas alone, but on the power of circumstance and conditioning to change behavior, with altered ideas as an accompaniment.

This argument is extended by the story of a woman bomber, a biography that illustrates the weakness of ideas alone, and the strength of personality and peer-stimulated reinforcement, in generating action.

Diana

Diana Oughton was 28 years old when she and three companions blew themselves up in a Greenwich Village townhouse while preparing two 50-pound cases of dynamite for Weatherman bombings. Diana's great grandfather had founded the Boy Scouts of America and her own background was "square," and rich, Middle American. On the surface at least, she had a model childhood. After her death her revolutionary ardor seemed inexplicable, out of joint with her "socialization."[7]

Diana's temperament was sensitive to injustice; her times were violent. She was in college during the politicization of American campuses, a movement justified by the Viet Nam war. Her personal sympathies and the moral climate in which they were nurtured turned her toward revolution. She met Bill Ayers, then a leader of Students for a Democratic Society, and they became engaged until their "consciousness was raised" to see that marriage was a bourgeois institution that had to be destroyed.

Diana and Bill reinforced one another in their political commitment. Participation in social movements is characteristically assisted by the erotic bond. Most of us need to love someone and, of course, we select loved ones from among those with whom we associate. The sexual connection operates, then, as both a stimulus to group affiliation and as a reinforcer of that affiliation. People get

---

[7] One might assume, however, that she was "spoiled." To be "spoiled" is *to be given* without learning the conditions that make the gifts possible. It is to assume that the benefits of a civilization that have accrued through effort are "natural," constant, and one's "right" by virtue of one's birth. It is a characteristic of Ortega's "mass-man" (1932) "to believe that the material and social organisation, placed at [his] disposition like the air, is of the same origin. . . ." (p. 64).

"turned on" to ideas—and, in particular, to political ideas—not just by the clarity and cogency of their philosophies, but also, and more strikingly, by attraction to those who express the ideas.

Political ideas are not autonomous, not powerful in their own right. They are more and less congenial to personalities, and to personalities-in-situations. Personalities select companions, companions reinforce ideas with love and other rewards, and the circle of causes narrows.

Bill Ayers's background paralleled Diana's. He was the son of a Chicago corporation president who was also a trustee of Northwestern University. When Ayers was asked what the Weatherman program was, he replied:

> "Kill all the rich people . . . break up their cars and apartments."
> "But aren't your parents rich?", he was asked.
> "Yeah," Ayers said. "Bring the revolution home, kill your parents, that's where it's really at" (cited by Lasky 1972, p. 20).

Lasky goes on to say that Diana was devoted to children, but:

> . . . with a childishness of her own which verged on ideological temper tantrums. After Bryn Mawr, she went to Germany, and then to Guatemala, and then to Ann Arbor to teach in the "permissive" Children's Community School on Hill Street. If it was Tuesday, it was Che; if Friday, then A.S. Neill. But if the tots were "allowed to do what they liked when they liked," how and when would they get around to learning the alphabet? Some parents became concerned, but Diana only wondered "if learning the alphabet was really all that important. . . ." The Negro families seceded. For Diana . . . trying to help mankind was a bitter trial. As her biographer puts it, "Bill and Diana were committed to helping the black children, but rejected the terms on which the black parents wanted their children to be helped. . . ." They always wanted it their own way, it being the only way they knew, and they clung touchingly to the petulance of arrested adolescence.

If one acknowledges that Diana, Bill, and their comrades were rich and "educated" while the Manson Family was neither (pp. 187–197), there is much else in the lives of these tribes that runs in parallel. The parallel suggests that political ideas *caused* Weathermen's conduct as much as vengeful notions *caused* the psychopathy of the Manson Family—which is to say, not much.

Thomas Powers (1971, pp. 143–145) writes about Diana's group in terms reminiscent of the Manson clan:

> . . . Life in the collectives took on a frenzied, brutal, savage air as the Weathermen tried to root out their fear of violence, their sexual inhibi-

tions, their sense of themselves as individuals and all their "bourgeois hangups" about privacy, cleanliness, politeness, tolerance and humor.

Weathermen felt that movement people had failed in the past because they were not totally dedicated to the revolution. They intended to exorcise every error in thinking, feeling or behavior: CRITICISM—SELF CRITICISM—TRANSFORMATION. In practice this meant long meetings in which individuals would analyze themselves for deviation from correct thinking or from mistakes in their practice. The self-criticism would be followed by criticism of the individual by the group, an often cruel process. On the basis of criticism and self-criticism the individual was expected to transform himself.

The purpose of this self-transformation was to end their sense of themselves as private individuals with private lives, and to make themselves into "tools of the revolution." Every action, every thought, every word was to be judged only by its political utility: POLITICS IN COMMAND. Every personal resource, spiritual, physical and financial, was to be devoted to the cause: EVERYTHING FOR THE REVOLUTION.

Daily life in the communes centered on criticism sessions, karate, and rifle practice, and political actions designed to sharpen the members' ability to behave as a coherent group. In practice EVERYTHING FOR THE REVOLUTION meant nothing for anything else. As a result, the collectives turned into foul sties where beds went unmade, food rotted on unwashed plates, toilets jammed, dirty clothes piled up in corners.

The emotional atmosphere inside the collectives, barricaded behind windows covered with chicken wire (to keep out bombs) and double-locked doors (to keep out police), was savage and neurotic. On one occasion Diana's collective killed, cooked, and ate a tomcat. On another they went on a tombstone-smashing rampage through a local graveyard.

The smashing of monogamy meant, in practice, communal sexual relations. In some instances homosexuality and lesbianism were involved, occasionally by order of the collective when it was thought that an individual was not being honest about latent sexual tendencies. Some collectives even planned to raise money by prostitution, both male and female.

Most of the time alcohol, tobacco and drugs were forbidden, but during one period collectives took LSD together, but on direct orders from the Weather Bureau in Chicago, for the double purpose of breaking down their old sense of themselves as individuals . . . and of weeding out suspected police informers.

Every expenditure was a matter for group decision and Diana's dividend checks went into the common fund, as did all other monies. Collectives imposed foodless days on themselves when they needed to save money for bail or other purposes. Sometimes they stayed awake for two-

and three-day periods in order to discipline themselves for the hardships they would face as members of the Red Army.

Inside the collectives the Weathermen were cruel to themselves and each other. Hurt feelings and smouldering grudges poisoned the atmosphere. Suffering themselves, people tended to attack each other with increasing violence. Individuals were sometimes attacked so brutally in group criticism sessions they were left whimpering and speechless. Individuals who seemed to hold back some part of themselves were subject to harsh psychological assault; if they persisted they were sometimes purged. Everyone was overtired and underfed, nervous and fearful. People became stiff and unnatural, afraid they would be attacked for the slightest error, a deliberate process which sometimes hid a desire literally to *destroy*. . . . (Reprinted, with permission, From Thomas Powers, *Diana: The Making of a Terrorist*, pages 143–145. © 1971 by Thomas Powers. Reprinted by permission of the Karan Hitzig Agency).

Summary: On Ideas and Acts

The role of ideas in careers such as these deserves recapitulation. The summary has relevance for policy.

Thinking is part of acting, not something independent of it. Thinking proceeds whether we will it or not. It is a physiological product that persists even when we are asleep.

Reasoning is an effort to discipline thinking. In Aaron's words (1971, p. 175), "The function of reason is to bring the constraint of knowledge to bear upon the spontaneity of thought."

We reason with ideas. *Ideas* are structured patterns of the thought process, embodied in words and other symbols. We like to think of "ideas" as only those thoughts expressed in—or expressible as—sentences, but images, those "pictures in the head", also serve as ideas.

Ideas can be independent of actions, but not of physiologies. Only physiologies can produce ideas. But, of course, we need not act on the ideas that pass across "the screens in our minds."

If a metaphor may be forgiven, one might say that physiologies *select* those ideas that are congenial to their working. And their working includes—depends upon—their neurology, their biochemistry, and their histories. Histories, we have seen, include *how* one was trained and *what* one was taught.

The point of this note is that individuals are *not* empty vessels that can be filled with any content of idea. Individuals are selective appreciators of their worlds, and the selection is a function of biochemical individuality mixed with experience.

Experience is important, but it consists of more than just "grabbing an idea."

Some conclusions and recommendations follow.

RESPONDING TO TERROR

The last two decades have been notable in the number of violent challenges advanced against the legitimacy of state power. These challenges are largely domestic products; they come from within societies whose governments attempt to rule over groups with conflicting interests. These challenges have increasingly employed terror as a tactic and have stimulated debate about proper response. Some conclusions from recent research are relevant to policy.

1. Democracies are more vulnerable than totalitarian states to terrorism. Insofar as we have tallies of those raids called terrorist, it is apparent that their preferred targets are democracies and poorly organized authoritarian regimes (Beichman 1978, Laqueur 1976, 1977, 1978, Liston 1977, Wilkinson 1977). Totalitarian states are remarkably free of terrorism.[8] This fact, in itself, says something about the *validity* of terrorists' complaints and about the *conditions* that deter terrorism.

2. Remedying terrorists' grievances may not reduce terrorism. It cannot be assumed that the condemnations uttered by terrorists represent the causes of their activity. There is no one-to-one corre-

---

[8] "Authoritarian" and "totalitarian" governments deserve distinction, a distinction which is, of course, a matter of degree. Authoritarian states are those in which political power is concentrated and intolerant of opposition. Under authoritarian regimes, large segments of activity are left free and the government may pay little attention, for example, to planning the economy, influencing the family, or regulating religion. Mexico is a modern example.

By contrast, totalitarian states are characterized by the intended domination of *all* spheres of social life (Friedrich 1969). Modern totalitarian states differ from older autocracies and, of course, from heterocracies, by six features. They possess:

1. An ideology that justifies state intrusion into all aspects of social life.
2. A single party committed to this ideology, administered by a small cadre, and usually led by one person, a dictator.
3. A fully developed, armed, and intrusive secret police that functions outside the boundaries of Western "due process."
4. A monopoly of mass communication, including, of course, education.
5. A monopoly of force, including all weaponry.
6. A monopoly of the economy, including central planning of production and distribution.

In Curzio Malaparte's words (1964, p. 203), totalitarianism refers to "a state in which everything that isn't forbidden is compulsory."

spondence between "legitimate grievances"—as most citizens conceive of such (see point #5 below)—and the production of terrorism.

Terrorists would like to have power, and one of their complaints is their lack of power, but this is not a grievance most governments can, or will, recognize as legitimate. Apart from this "deprivation," satisfaction of other of terrorists' demands probably will not reduce their violence. Since terrorism that succeeds escalates (point #3), "good governments" are torn between responding to violent assaults upon them as crimes or as expressions of grievances that require remedy.

From the recent record, it is easier to negotiate with "ordinary criminals" when they riot than with "idealistic criminals," a function, again, of it being easier to satisfy limited objectives than grand ones.

3. Terrorism that succeeds escalates. It escalates by *imitation,* a contagion from one cell of disaffected people to another, and by *repetition,* a return to violence by the successfully violent.

Murray (1980) notes, for example, that Italy's middle-class, "intellectual" terrorists recruit followers from among the petty criminals they meet in jails. These small-time crooks, "unemployed, restless, ignorant [and] young [find themselves] suddenly supplied with organizational support, money, and a political philosophy [and it becomes] easy for them to make the transition from a life of personal crime to one devoted to the higher cause of bringing down by force the social order they despise" (Murray 1980, p. 85).

Not all people are rational calculators, weighing the costs of their actions against their prices, but there is sufficient rationality in terrorists, as in other criminals, that we may expect a high probability of quick and severe punishment to deter some enthusiasts from throwing bombs. Capital punishment has a short-term deterrent effect on homicide (Phillips 1980b). However, long-term effects are less evident, and less evident among idealistic and group-supported killers than among those whose objectives are more immediately material and individual.

Conversely, where penalties are improbable and slight, terrorism is encouraged. For example, Beichman (1978, p. 21) observes that:

> Of 146 international terrorists arrested by West European governments before 1975, 140 were released. No apprehended terrorist has been executed in a western democracy in the 1970s. Between 1970 and 1975, less than 20 percent of captured international terrorists actually served their prison terms, and the *average* sentence was only 18 months. Much of the risk for terrorists has been eliminated (emphasis his).

It is estimated that "about 80 percent of terrorist attacks [during the 1970s] succeeded either in gaining freedom for imprisoned comrades or in obtaining substantial ransom or in achieving publicity" (Manor 1980, p. 20).

4. Both societal protection and justice require the application of legitimate violence (i.e., force) to combat illegitimate force (i.e., violence).

During the 1970s terrorists abroad killed five American ambassadors. They did so without penalty and, in at least one case, under the supervision of Soviet "advisers" (Shaplen 1980, p. 52). In Italy the Red Brigades, led by a former professor of sociology, assassinated the Prime Minister, Aldo Moro. Such murders have been accompanied by an increase in the kidnapping of business and political executives in Europe and North and South America. The kidnapping is used, of course, as an instrument of extortion where the object of extortion is money, the release from prison of fellow terrorists, or both. Belatedly, governments and private corporations have taken defensive action. In Canada and the United States investment in private security services jumped 50 percent in 1979 over the preceding year. In addition to bodyguards, such protective services now include "private planes and bullet-proof cars with gun ports, electronic tracking units, and concealed tear-gas canisters" (*Wall Street Journal* 1979).

Some observers fear the spread of terrorist activity and the increased capability of terrorist weaponry (Burnham 1978). William Schlamm, editor of the Munich magazine, *Zeitbühne,* "considers the possibility that German terrorists might get hold of a nuclear device, make it into a time-bomb, hide it in a large German city, and then begin to blackmail in a way that will make all previous attempts seem like a parlour game" (Mann 1978, p. 87).

The possibility is sufficiently real that the United States now has a special team (NEST) equipped to respond to atom-bomb alarms. Such apprehension is justified by the fact that nuclear plants have difficulty accounting for all the weapons-grade material they handle. Some of this is stolen. Emshwiller (1980) reports that, in 1979, "an employe at a General Electric Co. plant in North Carolina stole 150 pounds of uranium intended for use in nuclear reactors and tried to ransom it for $100,000."

The 20th century has been so full of horrible surprises as to make nuclear blackmail seem but another in a chain of crises. The possibility moves some scholars to advocate greater vigilance and greater penalty for terrorism. For example, Beichman (1978, p. 23) proposes that:

> The terrorist who attacks the innocent must know in advance that a drumhead court-martial will follow his apprehension; and execution, his conviction. There can be no forgiving the literal killer of the literal innocent. . . . No opponent of capital punishment I know of opposes killing an enemy in wartime or the firing squad for the spy.

Democracies are divided between "under-reacting" and "over-reacting" (Wilkinson 1977). One can always recommend avoiding these extremes, but both terms are vague and it is easier to judge over- and under-reaction after an incident than before it.

In Western countries, some portion of "the intelligentsia" suffers from *The Stockholm Syndrome.* This is the phenomenon of victims learning to love their exploiters, a reaction so titled upon evidence that some women in a Stockholm hostage-taking extortion had intercourse with their captors. Against this "disease," Laqueur (1976, p. 105) argues that:

> Psychiatrists, social workers, and clergymen are the terrorist's next-best friends. They are eager to advise, to assuage, and to mediate, and their offer to help should always be accepted by the terrorist. These men and women of good will think they know more than others about the mysteries of the human soul and that they have the compassion required for understanding the feelings of "desperate men." But a detailed study of the human psyche is hardly needed to understand the terrorist phenomenon; its basic techniques have been known to every self-respecting gangster throughout history. . . . If governments did not give in to terrorist demands, there would be no terror.

As measured by surveys, public opinion in the West supports Laqueur's thesis.

5. In democracies, citizens tend to agree about the causes of terrorism and recommended response to it. De Boer (1979) provides a summary of polls on this topic:

- Citizens in the United States (90%) and in Great Britain (85%) agree that political kidnapping and bombing are "serious problems."
- The farther from home the violence, the less sure people are whether it constitutes "terrorism."
- People say that they are willing to submit to censorship and to suffer a dimunition of their civil liberties to combat terrorism.
- There is a high degree of agreement about the "causes" of terrorism. Citizens name as causes news coverage, "soft" policies in response to violence, and terrorists' success.
- Majorities in the British Isles, Canada, and the United States favor capital punishment of terrorists.

In response to our violent times, citizens ask difficult questions about the prediction of dangerousness in individuals and the causes of outrageous homicides. These issues have been touched upon during our description of the many roads to deadly quarrels. The next chapter provides a summary statement while Volume Four, Chapter 4 discusses the work of predicting individual violence.

12 VIOLENCE AND MORAL ATMOSPHERE

Abstract • It is more sensible to assume that individual and societal careers are generated in a dense web of causes than by singular factors. The complex of causes may be conveniently designated "the moral atmosphere." ○ This assumption poses difficulties for research that attempts to explain what has happened and predict what will happen. ○ Research difficulties are illustrated by two major American studies: one of "violence," the other of "obscenity." ○ Some unsurprising conclusions—truisms—are described as flowing from these, and other, studies. ○ These studies illuminate limitations of social science as policy science. These limitations derive from addressing *vague questions* for which the *content* of causes and effects is narrowed by availability of data, for which *the nature of the causal system* is unknown, and for which the *values* to be assigned probabilities are unspecified. These four limitations work in concert to assure that recommended policies will have unintended consequences. • It is concluded that spheres of moral activity, such as the sexual and the violent, interact. Their separation is artificial. ○ Art both reflects and affects the moral atmosphere and reveals an association between interest in the sexual and interest in the violent. ○ Display art provides one example. • Some threads in the causal web are described. ○ Such description does not assume that pleasant conditions have only good consequences or that unpleasant events are the only source of evil consequences. ○ The present description assumes that "civilization is bought at the cost of repression." ○ Three main routes lead to homicide "within societies," as distinct from wars between societies. These routes are culturally prescribed occasions for killing, money-and-power-making occasions, and disinhibiting influences. Each of these major avenues has tributaries. ○ Among the disinhibiting influences in contemporary rich countries, we note frustration, relative deprivation, the entitlement theme, philosophies of ethical relativism and nihilism, useless youth, and fragmented families. ○ Additional disinhibiting influences derive from market forces, residential and occupational mobility, and increased use of a spectrum of comforting chemicals.

LOOKING BACK WE ARE OFTEN AMAZED at our own behavior and hard put to explain it. If this is true of our individual careers, it is even more true of the careers of societies.

Knowing *what* happened, or is happening, is one difficulty. Finding out *why* is an even more difficult matter. And knowing *how-to,* when one wishes to correct the *what,* is the most troublesome of all problems put to knowledge. Knowing how rests, of course, on knowing why—at least if one is to act rationally rather than super-stitiously. But we have seen that listing the causes of "what happened" is forever disputed. Guaranteeing what *will* happen, if only we follow Policy-X rather than Policy-Y, is even more in contention.

Dispute is generated and justified by the possible impact of multiple causes upon the events that interest us. In the present context of concern with the many occasions of homicide, it seems useful to attribute changes in quantity and quality of these occasions to a dense web of causes that may be termed "the moral atmosphere."

Moral atmosphere is a convenient phrase for that host of conceivable influences that channel careers. These influences include models who teach and train. These models may be acquaintances or distant images. We can be influenced by seeing them, hearing them, or reading about them. Their effects may be intended or not. Models—parents and peers, heroes and heroines—need not know what they are doing in order to produce effects in others.

Influences in the moral atmosphere also include consequences that occur when we act. These consequences may be "natural" or purposive. They seem "natural" when they are the probable results of the social system in which we function, without any particular agent having intended that consequence. But consequences are also attached to our acts purposefully, by some other actor or set of actors who intends to guide our behavior by manipulating its consequences.

Research Difficulties

The possible impact upon careers of moral models and of the consequences that follow from actions is everywhere admitted. Every tribe rears its young with this assumption, whether or not it can articulate this premise. But, in modern "mass societies," the range of these possible influences, and their powers, are unknown. Governments and curious individuals who would like to guide careers toward happier endings ask social research to weigh the relative impact of moral influences. In response to this request, a huge inventory of research has accumulated on the effects upon careers of families, finances, schools, opportunities, personalities, and massively distributed messages. These investigations are interesting, but they are not always informative.

Research discovers and manufactures data. Data are facts, but they are not necessarily organized in such a manner as to provide knowledge. Data may be as organized as a telephone directory, for example, and this list is informative, but it is not knowledge-generating *until* the information is so systematized as to allow us to use it to produce distinctive results. "Distinctive results" means different from what one could have done or would have predicted without that knowledge.

The data of much policy research are less than knowledge-bearing because the boundaries and styles of the causal systems within which the alleged influences operate are not known. Moreover, the system of influences upon careers is usually conceived as sparse. There are political reasons for this in that it is easier to recommend change of a few causes than of many, interacting causes. But, if we reject a simple picture of the social system and assume, instead, that the moral atmosphere is dense, then weighing the relative effects of changing influences becomes difficult.

USING SOCIAL SCIENCE TO JUDGE MORAL EFFECTS

During one time of troubles in the United States, the American executive established two National Commissions—one to study "The Causes and Prevention of Violence" and the other to study the effects of "Obscenity and Pornography."[1] The reports of these independent commissions and their investigative "task forces" overlap in that both commissions were concerned with the possible impact of the mass media upon behavior and both addressed some common violent crimes where "sex crimes" and violent crimes intersect.

Details of these studies and criticism of them can be read else-

---

[1] "Obscenity" and "pornography" are notoriously difficult to define.

Obscenity usually refers to communications that a "community"—and that is itself a vague term—regards as disgusting. The disapproval is expressed chiefly in regard to display of two human functions: excretion and sexual activity.

Pornography derives from Greek roots referring to literature about whores. Many dictionaries therefore give overlapping definitions of these two terms. For example, the *Random House Dictionary of the English Language* (1966) defines pornography as "obscene literature, art, or photography, having little or no artistic merit."

Both terms concern "matters of taste." Aesthetics influences moral judgment, and vice versa. This is apparent in a definition that includes "artistic merit" as one of the criteria of that which should, or should not, be disgusting. It is apparent, too, when we ask people to judge "obscenity." Observers are more likely to judge an act "obscene" when it is performed by ugly people than by pretty ones (Higgins & Katzman 1969, Katzman 1970).

where (Bogart 1980, Cline 1974, Comstock et al. 1972, Comstock & Rubinstein 1972a, 1972b, Dienstbier 1977, Surgeon General 1972, Short 1969, Wolfgang et al. 1969, Wilson 1974). What concerns us here is the attempt to employ social science to identify, and to assign a power to, possible causal elements working in a probably dense moral atmosphere.

These Commissions began their respective jobs from different sides of a question. The Violence Commission, as it came to be called, was asked, "What *causes* some categories of events?" The Pornography Commission was asked, "What *effects* do obscenity and pornography have?" Despite these approaches from opposite ends of a causal question, many critics expected consistency in the evaluation of massively distributed messages upon human behavior, with the proviso that the same quantity of message may affect different segments of behavior differently. Doing violence is *not* identical with doing sex. However, it is ordinarily assumed that people's conceptions of their worlds and their consequent responses to those worlds are influenced by repeated images transmitted verbally and pictorially. It is on this assumption—which we can always question and qualify—that minority groups form "anti-defamation" leagues, that "consumer advocates" contest some advertising, that federal communications commissions require "balanced" political propaganda, and that almost[2] everyone urges censorship of someone or something.

However, with a few dissenting opinions, the two commissions disagreed about the probable effects of messages upon behavior. The Violence Commission concluded that "Violence in television programs can and does have adverse effects upon audiences—particularly child audiences." The Pornography Commission concluded that there was no evidence that "the sale, exhibition, or distribution of sexual materials" hurt consenting adults. It did recommend prohibition of sale of certain sexual materials to children and prohibition of "the public display of sexually explicit pictorial materials." However, the two sociologists on this commission favored removal of all legal restrictions on allegedly obscene materials.

---

[2] The qualification, "almost," has to be added since no one has a tally of how many people would censor some expressions *if* they had the power and *if* we could observe them unobtrusively. If these conditionals could be satisfied, it would be a safe bet that the impulse to censor approaches unanimity. For a list of expressions officially censored in the United States, see Cline (1974, pp. 7–8).

Objections

Critics have advanced two major objections to commission con-clusions: (1) that the data are too weak to support policy pre-scriptions, and (2) that the conception of "harm" implicit in the com-missions' work is narrow.

The data are weak because they are based on limited samples, some of them self-selected. They are weak, too, because they are based on limited observations, on laboratory research rather than lon-gitudinal study, and because they confuse short-term effects with possible long-term effects. Data are deficient also because they em-ploy correlations to substantiate causation, divorced from theory and a corpus of other research. The last weakness leads to inconsistency. Thus elimination of laws against pornography in Denmark was asso-ciated during the 1960s with reduced *reporting* of some sex crimes (Kutschinsky 1970). The Pornography Commission cites this study as demonstrating obscenity's lack of harm. However, in the United States, where forcible rape is more frequent than in Denmark, a con-trasting correlation reveals an increase in *reports* of forcible rape, and of *arrests* for it, with increased distribution of obscene materials (Cline 1974, p. 192, Kupperstein & Wilson 1970). The Pornography Commission drew no causal conclusion from the American statistics as it did from the Danish data.

Conceptions of harm implicit in these studies have also been chal-lenged as too narrow and vague. Although attention was directed to "damage of a personal or social nature," the scope of such damage was limited, in the Pornography Commission reports, to (1) changes in "sex crimes" with the freeing of obscene expression; (2) com-parisons between sex offenders—a heterogeneous lot—and non-offenders in their self-confessed consumption of erotica; and (3) changes in opinions and behavior induced by manipulations in labo-ratories. Such research tests a limited notion of "harm." It omits from its purview long-range, cumulative effects and the possibility of dam-age to taste and to a fabric of social relations.

The narrow conception of harm flows, in turn, from a fuzzy con-ception of the social system. None of us has the definitive picture of the "social system,"[3] but some background image is implicit in all prescriptions for policy. To think of programs of action as if they op-erated in a sparse system is politically convenient, but inappropriate

[3] Wildavsky (1979, p. 31) calls the "sociologist's view of the social system, non-existent." Other policy analysts agree (Sheldon & Freeman 1970).

for social *scientists.* To think this way is to guarantee unforeseen consequences. By contrast, imagining programs operating in a dense web broadens one's time-horizon, refers judgment to historical experience as well as to fresh data, and promotes prudence.

Combining common sense, history, and research data confirms some truisms about moral atmospheres.

TRUISMS

Research on the effects of massively distributed messages is voluminous and need not be summarized in detail here (Comstock 1975b, Comstock & Fisher 1975, Eysenck & Nias 1978, Liebert & Schwartzberg 1977, Weiss 1969, Withey & Abeles 1980). When research findings are coupled with case histories and some verified socio-psychological hypotheses, they yield conclusions that conform to common sense. Some of these truisms are outlined below.

1. In the "Short Run," Most People are Stimulated by Erotic and Violent Scenes

Age makes a difference, of course, but, with some personality differences allowed for, watching violent or sexual acts stimulates appetite for them. We have no exact measure of how long the stimulation lasts or how far it spreads from the witnessed acts to substitute acts, but a short-term effect is apparent.

Stimulation is accentuated as observers "identify" with actors. The stimulation is also accentuated if the scenes are played so as to *justify* the expression of sexual and aggressive passions. Of violence in particular, we note that it is more frequently employed as it is approved by others. And "approval" includes *tacit* approval—being *permitted* to do violence—as well as *explicit* approval—being *encouraged* to do it (Berkowitz 1968, Liebert & Baron 1972, Sears 1961, Siegel 1974).

2. Violent People Like Violence

We commented earlier (p. 16) that people who act violently in one arena tend to adopt the violent style in other places. Thus physically aggressive boys like to *watch* violence as well as practice it (Bandura 1973, Lefkowitz et al. 1972, McCarthy et al. 1975).

The fact that we self-select the stimuli to which we are exposed makes it difficult to disentangle the effect of any particular exposure from the personality that seeks it. For example, Eron and his colleagues (1971, 1972) attempted to test the long-range consequences of a taste for televised violence by following a group of youngsters for 10 years. They studied 875 children in the third grade and found that, at that age, "children who preferred violent television programs were more aggressive in school as rated by peers than children who preferred less violent programs" (1972, p. 262).

Of these youngsters, 427 were studied again ten years after the original observations. This group was almost equally divided between boys and girls. *For the boys only,* a continuing correlation was discovered between early television habits and aggressive behavior as teenagers. Since the correlation between teenagers' viewing habits and measures of their "violence" (+.31) is slightly higher than the correlation that was obtained when these boys were eight and nine years old (+.21), the investigators conclude that television viewing had an *enduring, independent causal impact* upon adolescent aggressive behavior. This effect appears both when adolescents are rated for aggression by their peers and when they are scored for "aggression" on a standard psychometric, the MMPI. The researchers conclude that the television effect "explains a larger portion of the variance than does any single factor which we studied, including IQ, social status, mobility aspirations, religious practice, ethnicity, and parental disharmony" (1971, p. 623).

A comparable conclusion is reached by Belson (1978) who, with his associates, interviewed 1,565 London boys 13 to 16 years of age about their television-viewing habits during the period 1959 to 1971. On the basis of boy's avowed preference for violent or non-violent programs, comparisons were made of the self-reported violent behaviors of those with different viewing tastes. Belson believes that "the evidence is strongly supportive of the hypothesis that long-term exposure to television violence increases the degree to which boys engage in serious violence." He also found taste for violent programs associated with boys' use of foul language and their violence in sports.

Some "violent" programs induce more violent effects than others, according to Belson. Seeing violence in sports, cartoons, science fiction, or slapstick comedy does not increase youthful aggression. But long-time exposure to Western movies and to realistic fictional violence increases the violent propensities of boys. So, too, do violent stories in which the actors have close personal relationships and abuse one another physically and verbally or in which the violence is justified by the "good cause" for which the actors are fighting.

Belson also found what common sense assumes: that individuals vary in their susceptibility to suggestion. A small minority of boys disproportionately respond to the violent images on television.

3. Stimulating Males Erotically Stimulates Them Aggressively

Sexual expression in the male is prone to coupling with the pleasures of injury as well as the pleasures of affection. "Physiologically and psychologically there is a close connection between violence and sex" (Eysenck & Nias 1978, p. 33). Freedom "to fuck in the streets," as demanded by an English schoolgirl writing in the children's issue of *Oz,* cannot be assumed to be a pacifiier.

The causal train runs both ways. Stimulating men sexually stimulates them aggressively and, conversely, "tough guys" like to exhibit their sexual powers; it is part of their being tough.

We noted earlier (pp. 121–124) the persistent association of aggression with male sexuality. Laboratory research confirms that sexually stimulated males tend to behave more aggressively, depending on the context[4] (Donnerstein 1980, Donnerstein et al. 1975, Meyer 1972, Tannenbaum & Zillman 1975, Zillman 1971, Zillman et al. 1974). Donnerstein adds that his subjects—"normal, healthy, college males"—*enjoy* the violence they see in erotic, aggressive films, like the rape movies that one can buy via advertisements in *Penthouse* and *Hustler.*

Studies "in the field" confirm laboratory findings. For example, one type of aggressive sex offender is called, from the French, a *frotteur.* The crime is known as frottage (Thoinot 1930). A frotteur is a male "rubber-upper" who gets satisfaction from rubbing his penis against women, and sometimes against young men, in crowded places. Victims are usually strangers and, for the frotteur, this is part of the exploitative excitement. (Incidentally, neither my reading nor my clinical experience has found a female "rubber-upper," a *frotteuse,* although I have met women who manipulate themselves with clothing, hands, and other objects in public places as a sexual thrill).

Beller and her associates (1980) studied the characteristics of frotteurs apprehended in New York subways. These investigators report incidents such as these:

> Defendant was observed on platform wearing a raincoat (sunny day; temperature 90 degrees) and manipulating his penis. Male boarded train and immediately crowded female complainant and bumped and rubbed his naked penis on her buttocks. Complainant tried to move away and Defendant did grab her by the waist and breast and held her until he ejaculated.

---

[4] Context is important. Sexual arousal may *distract* the male from aggression, *if* the aggression has been produced by a non-sexual stimulus.

> [Another offender was] observed to rub his penis in a lewd manner
> and to make sounds to passing females, causing alarm and fear. Defend-
> ant was also observed to crowd various unidentified females boarding
> trains and bump his erect enclosed penis on their buttocks and with his
> hand to squeeze their buttocks (p. 37).

What interests us in the study of violent crimes is that "contrary to
psychiatric stereotypes," Beller et al. say (p. 35), "50% of recidivists
in these crime categories prove to have arrest records for violent
crimes, including nonsexual ones." In addition to previous arrests for
rape and sodomy, the 150 recidivists in this sample had been convicted of a total of 221 *violent non-sexual* crimes (Beller et al. 1980, p.
44).

4. Familiarity Breeds Preference

Repeated exposure to stimuli produces preference for the stimuli.
Such an "exposure effect" is well documented, and it occurs
whether or not the person exposed is aware of the influence (Harrison 1977, Harrison & Hines 1970, Kunst-Wilson & Zajonc 1980, Wilson 1975, Zajonc 1968).

Watching erotic scenes reduces inhibition and encourages experi-
mentation (Byrne & Lamberth 1971, Cairnes et al. 1971, Kobasigawa
1966, Mann et al. 1971, Mosher 1971). Watching violence increases
tolerance of it (Averill et al. 1972, Berger 1962, Cline et al. 1973,
Dominick & Greenberg 1972, Drabman & Thomas 1974).

As one wit put it, "Familiarity breeds attempt." Alexander Pope's
poem tells a truth about vice, that:

> Seen too oft, familiar with her face;
> we first endure, then pity, then embrace.

5. Human Beings Imitate

Children, in particular, are "adhesive." Images of action "stick" to
them.

Reminding ourselves of the obvious does not tell us,. of course,
who imitates what, how much, and how long. Susceptibility to suggestion varies among individuals just as does susceptibility to disease.
Evidence points to the possibility that persons in "poor psychological
and social health" are more vulnerable to lethal suggestions (Comstock 1975b, Flanders 1968, Liebert & Schwartzberg 1977). Poor psychological and social health, in this context, refers to a history of failure, to low self-esteem, and to estrangement from cultural bonds.

There are no exact tallies of the proportions of populations that may be in such "poor health." However, some unknown number of miserable people, living drab lives, find zest in copying crimes. Anecdotes, and some research, illustrate the contagion:

a. Woodrick et al. (1977) report that 71 percent of parents have observed their children imitate TV characters. The imitation includes adoption of accents, slang phrases, and costumes.

b. "In Manila, the popular Viet Nam war movie, *The Deer Hunter,* inspired Russian-roulette killings. The youths dress up like Americans . . . put a single round in a revolver, and dare each other. . . ." (Pilger 1979).

c. A movie of gang fighting, *The Warriors,* inspired imitative fights in major American cities (Christopher 1979).

d. A "Juvenile Awareness Program" that tried to frighten potential delinquents into "going straight" with visits to prison and threatening lectures by tough "cons" increased the delinquency of some of those who were exposed (Finckenauer 1979).

e. A cinema projectionist is charged with a forcible rape during which he imitated the guttural sounds he heard in *The Exorcist* (Eysenck & Nias 1978, p. 57).

f. "In 1973 a young woman was assaulted by a gang of youths in Boston who poured petrol on her and then set her afire. The Boston police were sure that the hoodlums had copied a very similar scene shown just the day before on a very popular TV crime program" (Berkowitz et al. 1978, pp. 59–60).

g. "Inspired by the television program *Starsky and Hutch,* a 17-year-old retarded boy tried to extort $50,000 from the city's mayor. . . ." (Canadian Press 1978).

h. Grant Hendrick (1977), himself a "lifer," interviewed 208 of his fellow inmates in Marquette State prison, Michigan. Ninety percent of his informants claimed to have learned new tricks or improvements of their old techniques from watching TV. Forty percent said that they had attempted specific crimes copied from television. One fellow reported that he had wanted for some three weeks to rape a woman and that he succeeded after following a tactic depicted in *The Streets of San Francisco.*

i. "The television play *Doomsday Flight,* broadcast in the U.S. and elsewhere, told the story of an attempt to extort money from an airline. A telephone caller in the movie warns the airline officials that one of their planes then in flight carried a bomb which was set to explode if the plane descended below a certain altitude. If they paid him the money he wanted, he would tell them where the bomb could be found. The telecast triggered a number of very similar extortion attempts both in America and abroad" (Berkowitz et al. 1978, p. 60).

"While this film was still on the air, a bomb threat (which turned out to be a hoax) was telephoned to one U.S. airline. Within twenty-four hours of the show, four more had been phoned in. Within the week following the show, eight such hoax calls . . . were received by various U.S. airlines, including American, TWA, Eastern, Pan-American, and Northwest" (Siegel 1974, p. 131).

j. A nine-year-old San Francisco girl and her parents sued the National Broadcasting Corporation and station KRON-TV for $11 million after the girl had been sexually attacked by four teenagers who copied a technique—using a broom handle—from a scene in the TV program, "Born Innocent." The judge dismissed the case on the ground that the plaintiff could not demonstrate the network's *intention* to stimulate such a crime.

k. "In the fall of 1977, the television violence issue was made a central feature of the defense brought in the case of a 15-year-old Florida boy, Ronald Zamora, accused (and ultimately convicted) of killing a neighbor. His attorney sought to prove that his client's ability to make moral judgments had been destroyed by his long exposure to a diet of televised violence" (Bogart 1980, p. 123).

Research confirms these anecdotes about imitation. In a series of studies Phillips (1974, 1977, 1978, 1979, 1980) has shown that contagion spreads across dimensions of aggression—murder, suicide, and fatal "accidents." Phillips reports that:

1. After publicized murder-suicide stories, both non-commercial and commercial airplane crashes increase.

2. Such increase persists for approximately nine days before airplane "accidents" return to normal.

3. The greater the publicity given by the mass media to a murder-suicide story, the greater the increases in both commercial and non-commercial airplane crashes.

4. The less publicity given stories about murder-suicide, the smaller the consequent increase in "accidental" deaths. Mortal stories reported on newspapers' inside pages have no effect and geographical areas in which these stories go unnoticed also experience no increase in subsequent mortality.

5. Highly publicized stories about suicide are followed by an increase in single-person, single-car "accidents." This correlation confirms the suspicion that some proportion of such single-driver car crash is "autocide."

LIMITATIONS OF SOCIAL SCIENCE AS POLICY SCIENCE

These comments on social research and common sense, and on efforts of governments to improve judgment through social science, illuminate limitations in the application of facts to decisions. The limitations derive from (1) asking *vague causal questions;* for which (2) the *content* of causes and effects is narrowed by availability of data; for which (3) the *nature of the causal system* is unknown; and for which (4) the *values* to be assigned probabilities are unspecified. These limitations work together to assure that (5) *consequences of policies ramify.* This means that acting upon such poorly informed policies produces unforeseen consequences.

A first limitation results from asking vague questions—questions, for example, about the production of "personal and social harm," where the content of "harm" is not defined. Thus, government asked the Pornography Commission "to study the causal relationship of such [obscene] materials to antisocial behavior." Although the Commission listed a number of such possible antisocial effects (Johnson 1971, p. 197), it could study only a few.

A second limitation is imposed by the availability of data. When governments ask social scientists to test for social effects, the quality of the work depends on the relevance of available data. To do empirical social research one must be able to isolate the events termed causes and effects so as to be able to measure them. This tempts one to study what is available rather than what is conceivable.

In the debates that follow such limited research and its interpretation, one side accuses the other of short-sightedness—of leaving things out—and the other side responds by arguing, in effect, that "if you can't 'operationalize' a concept, its referent does not exist." In this vein Johnson (1971, p. 199) defends the narrow conception of harm employed by the Pornography Commission by saying that critics' concern with harm "to mind and character is not so much wrong as simply impossible to deal with at the level of research. What indeed are we talking about?"

The danger of this kind of empirical attitude is that it pays verbal respect to complexity but accords actual worth to simplicity. The danger is that of assuming that, if we can't count an effect, it does not exist.

A third limitation results when one asks about the *causes* of social behaviors without being able to specify the nature of the system in which the proposed causes operate. One does not know, therefore, whether the causes to be looked for are to be conceived as few and powerful, or, what is more likely, multiple and independently weak, but forceful in league with other causes and with repetition.

A fourth limitation derives from the inability of a social science to tell legislators and other decision-makers what *values* to assign risks of different sorts. Every recommendation of experts to governments *implicitly* trades the true positives and true negatives assumed in the prescription against its false positives and false negatives. To advise that a law be changed because "it won't hurt" and "might do some good" is to make a judgment that the negation will be a true negative and that the affirmation will be a true positive. But every such forecast carries a risk that both the negation and the affirmation will be somewhat false.

We are returned to judging the price to be paid for rare, bad events against the price to be paid for some unknown quantity of good events. Evaluation of the possible harms induced by widespread messages of a certain sort is, with necessary changes made, comparable to estimating the dangerousness of individuals. Messages that do not move most people toward damaging action will move a few.

Balancing the values to be assigned our hits on target against the values to be assigned our misses is *not* a job social scientists can perform. Scientists can estimate the *relative frequency* of events, but they cannot *price* those events. They cannot do such work *practically* because they have no authority to assign numbers to the worth of their hits and misses. They cannot do such work *ethically* because they are not held accountable for results.[5] And they also cannot do such work *ethically* because, in one kind of "just society," those who pay the prices of decisions get to make them.

Legal decisions and legislative changes involve risks. Risks can be individual or collective; they can be "immediate or delayed, cumulative or ephemeral, and can affect future generations or our own or both" (Starr & Whipple 1980, p. 1118). Whenever "experts" decide for others what risks they should take, conflict is inevitable.

These limitations of the social scientist as policy advisor work in concert to assure that recommendations made in a dense web of causes will have ramifications. Ramifications include unforeseen consequences. According to Wildavsky's *Law of Large Solutions* (1979, Chapter 3), the larger the "social problem," the bigger "the solution," and the more "the solution" creates unanticipated consequences with which future public policy must contend.

---

[5] Charles Frankel (1955, p. 203) defines "being responsible" this way: "A decision is responsible when the man or group that makes it has to answer for it to those who are directly or indirectly affected by it."

A difficulty with this definition is that of determining "indirect" effects.

SUMMARY

A moral atmosphere is a web of many influences. The many influences reverberate. They bounce off one another and they rub off, selectively, on persons exposed to them.

It is incorrect to assume, as some research has, that our moral environment is segmented, or that it can be segmented. It is incorrect to assume, for example, that morality in the sexual sphere is an independent province of behavior.

It is more correct to assume that attitudes and practices toward self and others ramify. They branch out; they run across dimensions of action artificially categorized as sexual, aggressive, recreational, vocational, and on. Common sense assumes more of a holistic, than an atomistic, image of the social system. So, too, do historians. Scholars who study cultures and changes in their vitality assume that the quality of social relations is patterned. This means that lessons on "how to be" are *not* compartmentalized.

In heterogeneous societies, and in changing societies, there are competing lessons, but there are, at the same time, reinforcing ones. The street invades the school. Themes in the theater both reflect and encourage practices in the home. The games we play, and how we play them, are projections of our values. Aesthetic taste *bespeaks* moral judgment, *influences* it, and *is influenced* by it. Philosophers and artists have powers, even if we cannot assign quantities to them.

Sampling

The point can be made by examining a small sample of how art affects, and sometimes infects, the moral atmosphere, at the same time that it reflects it. For example, in recent years the art of window display in retail stores changed. Displays often became scenes, rather than just poses. The scenes became sexual *and* violent—not one or the other, note, but both.[6]

[6] The movement of eroticism toward degradation and violence has been noted repeatedly. A recent survey of the distribution of pornography in Canada finds the usual amalgam of books, films, and video-cassettes depicting sadistic and masochistic acts and adult exploitation of children. Two items from Scandinavia particularly offended police trying to control the profitable flow of obscenity: a movie depicting a middle-aged man having intercourse with a 12-year-old *feeble-minded* girl and a "how-to-murder" manual (Melnyk 1980b).

According to a popular researcher of eroticism (Talese 1980), the atomic bomb dropped on Hiroshima had attached to it a rear-end photograph of Betty Grable, one of the American soldiers' favorite "pin-ups."

We may think it a mystery that demoralized (that is, "open") sexuality should so frequently be associated with brutality. Explanation of this association may be a mystery, but its probability remains a fact.

Some passersby object, but others are attracted. Business increases. Melnyk (1980a) describes one such window in an Edmonton clothing store. It depicts a rape scene under flashing disco lights:

> One man holds a knife blade against the woman's throat while his other hand clutches her breast. The other man crouches at her side, his hand reaching up under her dress near her buttocks.
>
> One of the men [has] the fly to his trousers undone... In another corner a male, dressed in black with "Madness" printed on his T-shirt and a beer bottle in hand, looms over a semi-prone female. An open pair of scissors lies inexplicably by the pair's side. Black graffiti scrawled against a white backdrop announces ominously: "It happens in the Alley."

Practitioners of such art excuse it as "commentary," rather than moral influence. Thus Robert Currie, director of "visual planning" in one of New York's major retail stores, confides to his interviewer, Selzer (1979, p. 31):

> My windows *are* making a social comment. Depravity may not be overt, but certainly from where I go and from what my friends tell me, I can see depravity in styles of life. *My* life style is depraved. I go to the sleaziest bars in town. My sexual conduct is depraved. And since we're in an age of depravity, I thought there should be a comment on it, and I'm commenting on it in my windows (emphasis his).

Dense Webs Again

Display art is, of course, but one small facet of the moral climate. Other fashions in art and ideas permeate the atmosphere. If one asks, then, what has caused the rise in domestic violence within wealthy countries, the intelligent answer cannot nominate a few causes with singular effects. One looks, instead, at a tightly packed network of influences that affect one another as they move us.

Any nomination of causes is, therefore, partial. It is never complete. And, given rapidly changing moral climates, such nomination says nothing about causal *powers,* but only something about causal *possibilities.*

Furthermore, nomination of the causes of disapproved events produced in a dense system accepts the possibility that "good" causes can have "bad" consequences and, conversely, that "private vices," in Mandeville's (1714) phrase, may produce "public benefits."

We do not assume that bad acts have only bad causes, and good acts, good ones. On the contrary, a closely woven web of influences can result in approved actions generating costly effects. Good intentions do not lead only to happy endings. Values have prices.

There *are* preferences, including moral ones, that have suicidal consequnces.[7]

THREADS IN THE WEB

With these qualifications, we can list some of the causes of violence in modern civil societies. These nominated causes are tied together by strands of assumption.

It is assumed that harmonious relations between human beings are constantly threatened by our appetites. It is assumed that pacific relations are achieved at the cost of constraining lessons.

Those populations that have produced arrangements called "civilized" are those that have attempted to reduce physical force from the court of first resort to that of last resort. The fact that this effort has had only limited success, and temporary success, indicates the magnitude of the struggle of civil life against the appeals of barbarism. This fact confirms Sigmund Freud's (1958, p. 62) conclusion that we would not have to preach neighborly love so vehemently if the practice came more readily.

The list to be outlined assumes, with Santayana (1953, p. 142), that "every generation is born as ignorant and wilful as the first man" and needs, therefore, to be cultured. It assumes that whatever breaks the bonds of pacific influence between parents and their children reduces altruism. It claims that whatever diminishes apprenticeship of the young in a *specific, civil way* of being an adult produces violent people.

Our list admits that some tribes recommend internecine combat and teach their young violent lessons—the Yanomamö (Chagnon 1977), for example, and the Ik (Turnbull 1972), and the Albanovesi

---

[7] Study of suicidal ethics is reserved for other volumes. However, some intellectuals find it difficult to believe that their "good thoughts, good intentions, and good policies" can have unhappy consequences.

The tenor of suicidal ethics can be briefly described. For example, Booth (1979, p. 172) tells us that "when well-meaning liberal societies have valued peace at almost any price and have abjured the use of the military instrument, international politics have fallen under the sway of those countries willing to manipulate and use force."

Suicidal ethics are also apparent in response to "the tragedy of the commons." The tragedy of "an unmanaged commons [is that] greedy herdsmen drive out considerate ones, grasping hunters drive out moderate ones, polluting industries drive out clean, and rapidly reproducing parents displace those who accept the limits to growth" (Hardin 1977b, p. 131).

There are occasions when philanthropy kills the philanthropist. These are occasions on which good intentions ignore causal webs.

(Wolfgang & Ferracuti 1967). "Community," then, is not enough to assure pacific life. Reduction of deadly assault requires the discipline of manners against the pleasures of self-expression. Freud was more accurate than Rousseau. Civilization *is* bought at the cost of repression, where "repression" refers to inhibition of impulse.

An outline of contemporary violence-generators is, therefore, an inventory of *dis*inhibiting forces. Such an inventory lists causes one at a time, but they are better thought of as occurring all at one time and as interacting. Several sources of disinhibition are discussed below.

1. Frustration

A popular thesis says that human beings act violently when they are frustrated. It is then claimed that one kind of social system, rather than another, is frustrating.

As with other common hypotheses, there is truth in this one, but the truth is obscure. It is obscure because people who use the "frustration-aggression hypothesis" slip back and forth between two meanings of "frustration."

A first meaning is *objective*. In this sense (*F-1*), to be frustrated is to be blocked, thwarted, prevented from getting what one wants. Frustration here is measured by failure—more or less objectively. Observers can watch animals strive for goals and can agree about their success or failure: whether the ape gets the banana or the runner wins the race.

A second meaning of frustration is *subjective* (*F-2*). It refers to a psychological state—to feelings of despair, or anger, or to a free-floating discontent.

According to the frustration-aggression thesis, it is the psychological state, *produced* by the objective condition, that ignites violent action. No one denies that violent people are often angry first and violent later. But, as we have seen, this is not always so, and some deadly actors are coolly cruel. However, what is crucial, and unanswered by this popular causal story, is what converts objective failure into subjective anger.

If being prevented from getting what we want were sufficient to produce anger, and anger, violence, then we would be in a constant state of domestic war because *frustration (F-1) is a condition of social life.*

Living with others means that we cannot have everything we want, when we want it, in the manner we would like it. To apply the frustration-aggression hypothesis, then, we need to know the conditions under which particular kinds of people are angered by particular kinds of failure. We need a map coordinating dimensions of objective frustration with degrees of subjective frustration. At present we have no such chart, and no one knows which persons under which circumstances *feel* more or less frustrated by which failure. In fact, the very ideas of success and failure have not been adequately diagrammed for people of diverse ways of life.

In addition to our lack of a map locating the longitude of failure and the latitude of anger, we have another difficulty in using the frustration-aggression hypothesis. The difficulty, again, is that of locating causes. When a person loses at a game and becomes angry, we often say he is a "poor sport." This saying locates the causes of the anger in the actor, not the situation. But when we move from the regulated arenas of sports into the disorderly forums of moral contests, our sympathies may move causes from the hostile dispositions of actors to the "unjust" obstacles to satisfaction of their desires.

This differential location of causation with the frustration-aggression hypothesis is morally determined, not scientifically fixed. It rests on beliefs about how life ought to be, about what we have "the right" to expect, and about which of our aspirations should be fulfilled. When we locate causes by moral criteria, we quarrel about whether the anger felt by actors upon disappointment is to be attributed to their aspirations or to their situations. This dispute raises the issue of whether "frustration" should be appeased by lowering expectations or by demanding changes in the quality of our lives.

Given this moral debate, and given our lack of a guide reliably translating objective conditions into psychological states, the assumption that frustration produces aggression is more useful *after the fact* of violence, as an ad hoc explanation of it, than it is before the fact as a predictive tool.

Deficiency of this thesis as an explanatory story is also apparent when anger and despair increase as objective conditions improve—a correlation of events observed over the past few decades in Western countries and often associated with revolution (Brinton 1938, Davies 1962, Moss 1972b). For example, the political observer Alexis de Tocqueville (1805–1859) noted in his *The Old Regime and the French Revolution* (1856) that:

> It was precisely in those parts of France where there had been most improvement that popular discontent ran highest. . . . Patiently endured so long as it seemed beyond redress, a grievance comes to appear intolerable once the possibility of removing it crosses men's minds. . . . At the height of its power feudalism did not inspire so much hatred as it did on the eve of its eclipse (1955 trans., pp. 176–177).

Attention turns, then, from objective circumstances as adequate causes of deadly dispute to psychological aspects of the moral atmosphere. With this shift, the psychology of relative deprivation becomes more important than objective frustration, and one attends to conditions that encourage people to *feel* deprived.

2. Relative Deprivation

A psychological fact of life is that happiness is a by-product rather than an achievement[8] and that it varies with comparisons. Happiness, when it is not simply a matter of one's "glandular juices," is a "contrast effect." The comparisons that affect how we feel about ourselves are made against the lives of others we know. These comparisons depend, too, upon where we are relative to where we have been and hope to be. This explains why some people who have gone through hell seem happier than others in similar present circumstances. It explains why refugees from oppressive states are so often greater patriots in their new-found-land than natives of the host country.

The *comparative* basis of contentment produces a predicament. It is the possibility that *opening opportunities increases discontent.*

This possibility says nothing about justice; it refers only to consequence. The consequence of elevated aspiration may be disaffection. The contingencies under which this effect is likely are these:

1. The achievement that becomes possible requires abilities that the aspirant does not have.

2. Actors operate in an ideological climate that denies the rules of the game under which differences in outcome occur.

3. Past achievements have been divorced from merit, that is, have been *given* rather than *earned.* This condition describes the career of a "spoiled child" who, we note, can't stand frustration.

4. A neighbor's "luck" is better.

5. Objective inequalities in wealth, health, prestige, and happiness are apparent in a culturally heterogeneous population. This condition may be expected to aggravate a sense of relative deprivation as such

---

[8] Some intelligent people believe that happiness can be planned and they find it surprising when their plans go awry. So the novelist Virginia Woolf (1921) exclaims, "And the other way about it was equally surprising—that is, when everything was arranged—music, weather, holidays, every reason for happiness was there—then nothing happened at all. One wasn't happy. It was flat, just flat, that was all."

unequal peoples meet. Opportunity to meet people whose fortune has been better increases with residential and occupational mobility. Such mobility also increases opportunity to meet people whose "luck" has been worse than ours, but feelings of relative deprivation come from comparing ourselves with those who are a bit better off, not with those who are worse off.

Research on the production of the sentiment of relative deprivation demonstrates the unpleasant paradox that people may do more poorly because "too much" is expected of them and they may feel more disgruntled because their "consciousness has been raised." In brief, *given the contingencies listed above,* we may have it better and feel worse.

For example, Joan McCord (1980) has followed the careers of men who were part of a juvenile delinquency prevention program started in 1939—the Cambridge-Somerville Youth Study. In this research boys between the ages of 5 and 11 who were living in factory-dominated neighborhoods in eastern Massachusetts were paired on such relevant variables as age, family background, home environment, IQ, and histories of delinquency. One member of each pair was randomly assigned to a "treatment" group and one remained in a control group. Treatment consisted of counselling which included developing rapport, help with school work, athletics, some vocational training, walks and talks, driving lessons, medical and psychiatric help, and job assistance for parents.

A follow-up of 343 of these men begun in 1975 revealed that the treated group did *worse* on almost every measure of outcome. Compared with their controls, the treated men were more likely to have been criminal repeaters, to have been diagnosed as schizophrenic or manic-depressive, to have trouble with alcohol, to be dissatisfied with their jobs, to have experienced marital difficulties, and to be more pessimistic about their futures. Moreover, the more intense the treatment and the longer it persisted, the more damaging its effects.[9]

---

[9] One should not generalize from this study to every attempt to rehabilitate offenders. Some programs may work, as the text by Ross and Gendreau (1980) claims. However, research to date may be summarized as showing that the better controlled the study, and the more objective the measures of results, the less frequently do reform programs achieve their objectives. But, since institutions for the "correction" of offenders are themselves so damaging (and, in my opinion, immoral), almost any experiment with less punitive modes of responding to inmates is justified. They are justified not just as hopeful experiments, but also because they are less costly than present prisons and more humane.

McCord tries to explain these findings. In a provisional test of four competing hypotheses, she concludes that the only hypothesis that makes sense, if any explanation does, is that the treated group suffered the bitterness that comes from frustrated hope. In McCord's words, "Of the four explanations for damaging effects ... the one which seems to have the greatest support suggests that the program created unrealistically high expectations among clients, thus setting the stage for disillusion" (p. 87).

McCord's conclusion was more dramatically demonstrated by some of the findings of the largest social science research ever conducted, that on the American soldier in World War II. Stouffer and his colleagues (1949) studied factors affecting military morale among American armed services. These investigators discovered that dissatisfaction with promotions was *greatest* where the probability of promotion was *highest* (in the Air Force) and that discontent was *least* where the chance of promotion was *lowest* (in the Military Police).

Such patterns of relative discontent have been produced experimentally as well as observed historically. Thus "game theorists" have shown that the schedule of outcomes—how rewards are distributed—makes a difference in players' satisfactions. In these laboratory games, *people who win the same amount of money experience different degrees of satisfaction* depending upon how their winnings have been apportioned. Within a range of possible gain, those who win in smaller units are less happy than those players who win *the same amount,* but with some bigger portions.

Disappointment and its accompanying anger are dispositions that vary with personality. Allowing for that, these emotions are stimulated by a comparative process, one that compares where we are, and have been, with what others are getting and what we believe is "our due." Envy remains a constant stimulus to violence.

3. Entitlement

The feeling of being relatively deprived rests on a conception of being entitled. This is a matter of interpretation, obviously. Interpretation varies with a climate of opinion. Domains of entitlement expand and contract with ideologies and conceived possibilities.

Democratic ideology, as opposed to autocratic ideology, expands demands. Democratic politics enlarges the domain of entitlement. The way to office is through promise, and the justification of promise is that one "has a right to. . . ." When we compete for votes by enlarging the zone of entitlement, there is no end until disaster humbles us. Votes *are* "bought," in a variety of ways (Kiplinger 1980, Shilling 1979, Tufte 1978). State treasuries can then be bankrupted by attempts to pay off (Auletta 1975a, 1975b, 1979, Shefter 1977, Whalen 1980) and this "pressure" provides one of the many sources of fraud (Volume Three, Chapter 3).

Competition to attain and maintain power by appeasing conflicting interests makes effective, democratic government difficult, as The Brookings Institution reports (Pechman 1980). The difficulty is a consequence of expanded conceptions of governments' obligation to take care of citizens. The expansion is novel and dangerous in that contemporary demand for more "rights" acknowledges no necessity to balance rights with obligations.

These comments on the age of entitlement again say nothing about justice, which is itself a shifting concept. One can agree or disagree with the justice of any particular claim to an expanded right. The present point is that expansion carries risk—the risk of failed promise, disappointment, anger, and violence.

Ortega's thesis

In one of the few prophetic books of this century, the Spanish philosopher José Ortega y Gasset (1883–1955) wrote of *The Revolt of the Masses* (1932). He assumed the revolt would be violent.

Ortega's thesis is simple and devastating. It is that people who enjoy the benefits of Western civilization do not understand the bases of that civilization. They do not know what makes it possible. They assume its benefits are there, perhaps always were there, only for the demanding. Ortega's "massmen" know no history and therefore have no comprehension of how it came to be that thousands of people can do such commonplace things as flush a toilet, turn an electric switch, fly through the air, or see a tele-transcribed image bounced off a man-made moon.

Ortega describes "massmen" as persons who make no special demands of themselves, who assume themselves "to be just like everyone else," and for whom "simply being," in contrast with any doing, constitutes an entitlement. In the philosophy of "the mass," one is entitled to all the privileges of civil life "just as a right." For Ortega's "massmen":

> The material and social organisation, placed at their disposition like the air, is of the same origin, since apparently it never fails them. . . . The very perfection with which the XIXth Century gave an organisation to certain orders of existence has caused the masses benefited thereby to consider it, not as an organised, but as a natural system. Thus is ex-

plained and defined the absurd state of mind revealed by these masses; they are only concerned with their own well-being, and at the same time they remain alien to the cause of that well-being. As they do not see, behind the benefits of civilisation, marvels of invention and construction which can only be maintained by great effort and foresight, they imagine that their role is limited to demanding these benefits peremptorily, as if they were natural rights. In the disturbances caused by scarcity of food, the mob goes in search of bread, and the means it employs is generally to wreck the bakeries. This may serve as a symbol of the attitude adopted, on a greater and more complicated scale, by the masses of today towards the civilisation by which they are supported (pp. 64–65).

The violent pressures of expanding zones of entitlement have supporting sources in other challenges to pacifying standards.

4. Relativism and Nihilism

The American Supreme Court Justice, Oliver Wendell Holmes, Jr. (1841–1935), wrote Harold Laski (5 August 1926):

Pleasures are ultimates and in cases of difference between ourself and another there is nothing to do except in unimportant matters to think ill of him and in important ones to kill him" (cited by Wilson 1962, p. 762).

If we are not to kill one another whenever we disagree about important matters, there must be some standard to which we can jointly appeal in resolving our differences. Reasoned resolution of conflict is only possible when disputants have already accepted a common principle by which to adjudicate contests. Lacking such a principle, reason becomes footless; it has no ground on which to stand.[10] Negotiation breaks down, and compromise is replaced with dominance and submission or warfare. This is the meaning of the battle cry of the 1960s and 70s: "non-negotiable demands."

Within populations that attempt to be societies, the attitude of non-negotiable demand is stimulated by the erosion of moral and epistemological foundations. Whatever assists dissolution of these bases is part of the web of influences generating conflict. On this assumption, a wide range of influences is seen to be at work. However, one must point out again that naming some of these influences says

[10] The philosopher Blanshard (1962, p. 25) reminds us that the word "reason" draws much of its meaning from the Latin *ratio* denoting "relation" or "order." Reason, then, relates this to that, but without a standard of truth, beauty, and goodness, the relational work becomes futile.

nothing about the validity, or the intellectual appeal, of any one of them. It only says that these are strands in the causal matrix of violence.

One strand consists of philosophical movements that have attacked supernatural and other absolute justifications of morality. If God is dead, all is permitted. Such a Nietzschean statement is but a metaphor expressing the principle that, without firm footing in conceptions of truth, beauty, and goodness, reason drifts and negotiation becomes impotent to assuage conflict.

Twentieth century philosophers have challenged foundations of knowledge, morality, and taste. Their challenges have not remained within academic walls, but have spread outside them and have been disseminated by journalists and artists.

The extent of the attack on absolutes and universals, and discussion of its impact, can be read elsewhere (Blanshard 1962, Ladd 1973, Schoeck & Wiggins 1961). The tone of the attack, and its probable relation to violence, is what concerns us here.

Some important modern philosophers have subverted the belief that acts can be designated absolutely good or evil. "Naturalistic ethics" denies that statements of right and wrong are empirical propositions. Talk about "moral knowledge" and "moral truth" is deemed to be meaningless. Logical positivism teaches that a sentence such as, "Murder is wrong," proposes nothing empirical, but only voices the speaker's emotion. The distinguished Oxonian philosopher A.J. Ayer (1946, p. 107) puts it this way:

> We begin by admitting that the fundamental ethical concepts are unanalysable, inasmuch as there is no criterion by which one can test the validity of the judgments in which they occur. . . . The presence of an ethical symbol in a proposition adds nothing to its factual content. Thus if I say to someone, "You acted wrongly in stealing that money," I am not stating anything more than if I had simply said, "You stole that money." In adding that this action is wrong I am not making any further statement about it. I am simply evincing my moral disapproval of it. It is as if I had said, "You stole that money," in a peculiar tone of horror, or written it with the addition of some special exclamation marks.

It bears repeating here that neither the logical coherence of an argument, such as Ayer's, nor the empirical validity of any of its propositions says anything about the moral consequences of believing the argument. The "emotive theory of morality" may be logical and it may even be true, and yet it may be harmful for a group to accept it.

Awareness that moral judgments may be relative, rather than absolute, was stimulated by cultural anthropologists and sociologists who demonstrated the variety of preferences people enjoy. Wester-marck's massive study, *The Origin and Development of the Moral Ideas* (1906) and Sumner's *Folkways* (1906) were followed by Frazer's *Golden Bough* (1915) and then by a torrent of ethnological descriptions of the varied morals of remote human beings. "The mores (customs) can make anything right," Sumner assured us, and generations of students were so taught—with varying degrees of their acceptance, of course. But, if one believes Sumner, then there is no firm ground for moral judgment other than the customs of one's tribe. Every moral commandment can be doubted. One might as well do what one wants, and this, precisely, was one lesson extracted from observation of the varied ways in which human beings lived.

Challenge to moral standards never stands still. The challenge extends to other spheres of activity. Skepticism spreads to aesthetics, knowledge, workmanship, and all institutional arrangements. Cultural relativism teaches that beauty is only in the eye of the beholder. "Each to her own taste," said the woman as she kissed the pig.

Knowledge, too, becomes relative. Following some ideas of Marx and Engels, Karl Mannheim (1893–1947) developed what he called a "sociology of knowledge" (1936). This study starts with the cogent argument that what one can know depends on one's social context. It holds that the categories through which we define events are "social constructions," and this, of course, is correct. But the sociology of knowledge does not rest on these premises. It goes on to transform all theories into ideologies and to deny meaning to the concept of "objectivity." Its challenge ends with doubts about the independent existence of anything. Carried to its logical outcome, a sociology of knowledge dissolves reality. Reality becomes not that which can be perceived with some degree of objectivity, but only that which is construed in a process of social interaction. On this assumption, all facts can be made different—"transcended"—by acts of "social construction" and we become free of the limitations of a real world.

Epistemological relativism, like ethical relativism, may be true, but it cannot be believed. No group of people that lives together in some degree of harmony can *act* on such assumption, however much they may attest it. All people act as if there were some aspects of nature that were "real" and that did not move about willy-nilly with thought. Moreover, no group can live together peacefully and productively without assuming some common ground of right and wrong conduct. And the assumption of this common ground is always justified (Ladd 1957), whether or not you and I find *their* justification justifiable.

On this score, it is amusing to observe ethical relativists fudge on their doctrine[11] as they simultaneously demand "respect" for other people's ways—some of them, at least—while they reserve the right to condemn the mores of abhorrent groups. Blanshard (1962, pp. 40–41) comments that:

> There was something large and tolerant about the relativist view that won it many youthful converts between the two wars. In practice the most effective argument against it was provided by Hitler. Sociologists who were committed to the view that the Nazis' approval of their own action made it right found themselves vehemently denouncing that action, not merely as jarring to their feelings, but as irrational, inhuman, and intolerable. It was plain that they could not stay where they were. They must either return to some kind of objectivity or adopt a more wholehearted irrationalism.

Irrationalism has been the response of some individuals who, bereft of a tribe and a culture, and confused by their schooling, become enraged. It may not seem to follow that one should become angry because standards of beauty, truth, and right action have been eroded. Yet it is a consequence—although only one of the consequences—of deracination. Human beings do not thrive as culture-free, unbounded individuals. Cut loose from emotional and intellectual anchors, alienated individuals drift toward destruction of themselves and their worlds. A privileged Harvard undergraduate shows us the connection between being morally uprooted and enraged. Richard Hyland (1969) writes:

> The only reason I wouldn't blow up the Center for International Affairs is that I might get caught. But the desire is there. As it is for the 7094 Computer, the Instrumentation Labs, and the Center for International Studies at M.I.T., draft boards, army bases, the Pentagon, the White

---

[11] The logical positivist Ayer cannot himself *believe*—that is, say *and* act according to—his analysis of ethics. In a later essay Ayer (1966) urges that he and other "humanists"—meaning in this context, atheists—have a "moral obligation" to relieve "mankind in general ... of the ignorance, helplessness, and material want" that has been the lot of most human beings throughout history.

In response to Ayer, another philosopher (Hush 1966) points out that it seems inconsistent for an ethical relativist and "emotivist" to preach moral obligation to others. Apropos this argument, Mitchell (1980) shows that many secular philosophers "possess a traditional conscience which they find it hard to defend in terms of an entirely secular world-view." In sum, myths may be necessary for social solidarity and personal integrity.

House, the Capitol, New York City, Los Angeles, Las Vegas, and Harvard University. . . .

What has happened to our generation is that we never got what we wanted. We've only been led to believe that we have. Many of us know now what we want. Or at least we know what we don't want. We don't want the war or any part of the whole civilization. It might be necessary to go back two hundred years and start again.

We have an irreconcilable tension in our existence, all the way from breakfast to bedtime. Blowing up a bad thing will relieve much of that tension. So that the preceding sentence doesn't become evidence for any of the rampant psychological reductionist theories about radicals, it should be pointed out that the psychological problems most of us have are very directly capitalism's fault.

I may have learned only two things in my four years at Harvard. The first is that an equally intelligent, rational, and valid argument can be made on all sides of any question from any and all premises. The second is that those arguments have no relationship to anything but themselves. To make this more clear, I will affirm that I do not think there exists any argument that can justify American foreign policy. The point is that arguments are based on reason and the valid laws of discourse can prove anything within their system. It is the feeling I have in my stomach against the war that matters. Any argument in favour of it does not.
. . .

Terrorism could help restore the understanding of transcendence. Blowing up buildings destroys the product. It destroys what was once thought to be permanent. If buildings begin to blow up all around, people may well ask for a new inquest into the permanent. People might abandon the idea of suffering through life to build a permanent monument. They might adopt the idea of enjoying and participating in the humility towards something else but oneself. This might be possible only after a socialist revolution where self could be rejected for community. Exploding buildings may help the transition.

We are told continually that knowledge will make us free. We are taught to ignore irrational consequences and to put our faith in reason. Anyone who has tried to organize against the war knows that it is not the mind alone that defends the war, but the whole personality. We are fed reason in order to give an inferiority complex to the rest of our emotions and senses. What capitalism requires is a decision-maker who thinks his choices are rational.

We are trapped in a philosophical system of cause and effect. Rationality binds the mind and restricts the soul. It might even destroy the brain cells. We need to be liberated. We should be constrained no longer by possible rational consequences. We should begin to allow other emotions to dictate our actions.

. . .

The very virtue of terrorism, in fact, is that it allows a spontaneous release of the frustrations caused by capitalism. Capitalism should receive the blows from the pent-up hostility that it causes.

With all of the words and images we have around us, it may be that action is the only way to open fresh areas of consciousness. In any case, it will take a very concrete destruction of the material foundations of the wrongs we are fighting before we are rid of them. Only then will we be able to plant trees and flowers all over our woes, and begin again (Reproduced by permission of *The Harvard Crimson*).

One can empathize with a young American, like Hyland, faced with the possibility of being conscripted to fight a war he regards as unjust. However, his defense of indiscriminate violence does not make him a man of peace.

What is relevant to our concern is the rage associated with having learned that anything can be proved true or false, and that neither epistemology nor morality have any "relationship to anything but themselves." What is also relevant is the lack of education Hyland received from four years of expensive schooling, a lack demonstrated by his talking causally while rejecting cause-and-effect, appealing to reason while rejecting rationality, proposing a millennium, and assuming that whatever one wants is what one should have received.

The poet W.B. Yeats (1865–1939) believed that "civilization is a great struggle to achieve self-control." Relativism puts one on a slippery slope toward nihilism, and nihilism denies the value and the necessity of self-control. Reason and reasonableness are derided as bridles upon self-expression as, of course, they are. The function of reason *is* to constrain the spontaneity of thought, as Aaron (1971) contends. Nihilism frees one from such constriction. Why cogitate if results are so uncertain? And, asking this question, the expressive artist and colleagues in barbarism recommend "thinking with one's blood." Thus the novelist D.H. Lawrence (1937):

My great religion is a belief in the blood, the flesh, as being wiser than the intellect. We can go wrong in our minds. But what our blood feels and believes and says, is always true. The intellect is only a bit and a bridle. What do I care about knowledge? All I want is to answer to my blood, direct, without fribbling intervention of mind or moral, or what not.

Thinking with one's blood is exhilarating. It is one meaning of being free. However, such "liberation" seems to make people miserable, rather than happy, and it gives license to destruction. The great French sociologist Emile Durkheim (1858–1917) tried to test this thesis with epidemiological data on suicide (1951). Of course, floating definitions of "suicide" reduce the value of such data, as Douglas (1967) shows. Nevertheless, the probable causal connection between becoming "deregulated"—that is, free of social constraint—and becoming violent—against self or others—is a repeated lesson from the clinic and from history. It is a lesson that may therefore be debated, but it is one that should be given a hearing.

Habituation to standards of taste, truth, and right action channels conduct. It *is* a limitation, and a limitation of the kind required by civil life.

5. Useless Youth

For most human beings in all times and places, careers have been guided by institutions. Institutions are regular practices justified by their practitioners as legitimate. Grounds of legitimacy vary, of course, from appeals to the gods to requirements of survival and other functions.

Tribes and more widely dispersed populations have always reared offspring in a shifting complex of habitual practices governing reproduction, production, play, obligations to the living and dead, and other matters. However, institutions are not fixed. When cultures meet, regular practices are challenged. When the material bases of life change, institutions that were accommodated to old bases may decay.

The decay that is of contemporary interest as a generator of violence is the decline of institutions that apprentice youth to adult roles. With such decline, embarrassing proportions of both youth and adults find themselves useless.

To be useless is to have no talent that one wishes to exercise or that one's lawful economy is prepared to purchase. There are two sides to this coin: the individual side, describing what one can do and wants to do, and the social side, describing the economic needs of a particular society.

The two sides deserve emphasis because, with dissemination of the entitlement theme, what a person *can do* economically and lawfully may come to be defined as unworthy—not a "decent" job—and, given other options, some individuals *will not do* what they can do.

One option is to "free ride" on parents and governments. Another option is to do what one likes to do, and what is more rewarding than time-bound, lawful work. Given the appropriate tastes, this can be stealing and dealing. And some kinds of stealing and dealing, particularly in the lucrative distribution of illegal comforting chemicals, gets one into fights.

Estimates of the numbers of people who are "useless," as we have defined it, are difficult to extract. Measures of "unemployment" provide one such measure, but, as we have seen in Volume One, Chapter 4, these measures are subject to some unknown amount of error:

1. *How* we count "being unemployed" is one issue: Shall we ask people questions, count compensation claims, relate either or both of these indicators to "job vacancy" rates?

2. *What* we count is another matter: Shall we count seekers of part-time jobs, full-time jobs, auxiliary income, all of these or some of these, and how shall we identify the happily idle who reside outside the labor market?

3. How we *interpret* any of these measures is yet another issue: Do these numbers reflect hardship or preference or some mixture? For example, one commentator notes that 24 percent of persons classed as "unemployed" in a populous Canadian province list their principal vocation as "artist" (Wagemakers 1980). Shall we give credence to this preference?

We can acknowledge these many uncertainties in using "unemployment" as an indicator of being "useless" and still remain impressed that some uncomfortable proportion of young people in some Western countries are unemployed and unapprenticed. In the United States Ginzberg (1980) reports that surveys show one-fourth of white male teenagers, and one-third of nonwhite male teenagers, to be unemployed. Since these numbers include people in school, the concept, "unemployment," must refer to those without part-time jobs as well as those without full-time work. But, among males between the ages of 20 and 25, about eight percent of white men are unemployed compared with about 20 percent of nonwhite men.

Ginzberg recognizes "the many different (and often contradictory) explanations . . . offered to account for the trends" that he reviews. He believes that "there may be something" to the view that these statistics reflect a decline in "the work ethic," but he does not think this is a significant factor. Ginzberg proposes two other explanations, one of which is but a variation on the "work ethic" theme. Ginzberg mentions:

> the lack of orientation to work and the limited competence that characterize many young people, particularly among minority populations in the inner city. [The other hypothesis is] that many inner-city youngsters prefer to work at a somewhat questionable occupation rather than at a dirty, low-paying job; they can earn more on less time and do not have

to submit to the discipline of the work place. . . . The American economy is increasingly a service economy. Only about one job in three is in the production of goods, that is, in agriculture, manufacturing, mining or construction. Many, if not most, jobs in the service sector require some literacy, facility with numbers and communications skills: competence most young people acquire in school. Approximately one black youngster in four currently fails to graduate from high school. For many of them effective schooling really stops long before they leave or are pushed out, since a significant proportion become truants by the time they are 12 or 13 and many who remain in school pay little or no attention to their studies (pp. 46-47).

Ginzberg's explanations refer to some causes that lie within the economic marketplace and to some that are external to it. External factors that affect economic careers, and that therefore make violent vocations more or less probable, are the conditions under which children are produced and nurtured. Any conditions that allow people to reproduce outside institutional forms for the training of children may be expected to increase crime rates in general and violent crimes in particular.

6. Fragmented Families

All the many influences that make family life problematic are criminogenic influences. Substitutes for the present form of family are possible, as in Israeli kibbutzim, but until such substitutes evolve, children who are spawned and abandoned are candidates for crime. And there are, of course, many styles and intensities of "being abandoned." Polansky and his colleagues (1981) describe some of these.

Families in industrialized Western states are no longer strong links transmitting a culture from one generation to another. Outside religious enclaves—Amish, Hutterite, Mormon, for example—the most prevalent union is one of individuals bound by little else than personal gratification. The economy does not make marriage necessary, or even rational. Social expectations, including religious prescriptions, have become vague, and the goodness of life with families is questioned and caricatured by the mass media.

Many modern unions depend upon romantic love and mutual personal satisfaction to make marriage palatable. These are fragile sentiments upon which to base an enduring friendship. Marriages so contracted place a heavy burden upon the bare meeting of two individuals romantically attached but culturally denuded. Such unions are not well equipped to cultivate offspring.

ADDITIONS

The above inventory of disinhibiting influences is suggestive, but not exhaustive. Other sources of culture-breaking and disaffection can be named, but a full list would take us beyond present purposes. However, it should be noted briefly that the movement of large numbers of people is disruptive of cultural continuity and so are frequent changes of occupation and the separation of workplace from residence. Residential transience and job transience are both reflections of, and contributors to, dissolution of patterned modes of existence.

Furthermore, a market economy that stimulates the production of wealth competitively and that aggressively promotes the consumption of its products provides opportunities for thefts of various sorts (Volume Three, Chapter 4) and opportunities for that multi-faceted form of brigandage called "gangsterism." As we know (Chapter 10), gangsterism differs from legitimate business and from those frauds that range from the "shady" to the outright larcenous in its use of violence to settle business disputes.

Rich, free societies invite racketeering by virtue of their affluence and openness. In addition, whenever a relatively inelastic demand for products or services meets a short supply—as when gambling, sex, and some habituating "drugs" are made illegal—then there are opportunities for "organized crime" to meet the demand. These opportunities exist in all societies, whatever the titles given their economies—"capitalist," "socialist," or whatever. However, the freer the economy and the larger the market, the more opportunity for illegal as well as legal enterprise. And, to return to our concern with violence, among the "business instruments" employed by those illegal enterprises called "rackets" are assault, homicide, and their threat.

Demand for "comforting chemicals" is one of these business chances and it is a demand that contributes both directly and indirectly to homicide. These so-called "drugs" also have more subtle influences upon the moral atmosphere and crime rates.

COMFORTING CHEMICALS

Human beings ingest a fantastic pharmacy of mood-altering substances—organic and inorganic, natural and synthetic. Many of these agents have been used for as long as we have history—and this is particularly true of alcoholic beverages and *Cannabis sativa* in its various forms such as marijuana, hashish, ganja, and charas.

We incorporate these many mood-changers in wonderful ways. We eat these substances in food, on food as condiments, and by themselves. We drink them, swallow them as tablets, smoke them, sniff and suck them. We rub them on our flesh and inject them under our skin and into our veins.

These chemicals are popularly called "drugs," but that term is inexact since it connotes several things. For example, "drug" suggests a medicinal substance used to prevent or cure disease. However, the verb, "to drug," suggests something that stupefies or poisons. The phrase, "comforting chemicals," is more exact because these agents are taken principally for the comfort they provide rather than for their nutritional or medicinal value. Moreover, these chemicals range in effects from varieties of *depressant,* to varieties of *stimulant,* to those agents whose major effect is *psychotropic* ("mind-turning").

Some of the more popular comforting chemicals have no disinhibitory effect. This can be said, for example, of the stimulants coffee and tobacco (what tobacco does to physical health is another matter). The powerful opiates also do not disinhibit so much as they incapacitate; that is, in sufficient concentration, they take people "out of the action." The depressant, ethyl alcohol, remains the principal source of "release" followed, increasingly, by some of the narcotic and psychotropic agents. Neither alcoholic beverages nor psychotropic chemicals can be ingested for long, in high dosage, without physical damage. But what is of concern here are the criminogenic effects of these comforts. These effects are direct and indirect.

A direct effect appears in crimes generated by markets for illegal "drugs." The mark-up from the cost of producing these chemicals to the price commanded by them "on the street" is tremendous. For example, the legal American price (1980) for a 40 milliliters (about 1.5 oz.) bottle of Demerol—a synthetic analgesic similar in effect to morphine—is $10. The street value runs about $5,000., or about seven times the price for the same quantity of gold (Pound 1980). With such profit to be made, robberies and burglaries of pharmacies have increased. For example, a survey of selected American cities places the risk of victimization among Pennsylvania drugstores at 60 percent every five years. The average druggist in that state experienced two thefts in the past five years (Pound 1980).

Some of the robberies result in homicide. Robbers killed four American pharmacists in 1979 and one during the first three months of 1980. In turn, a pharmacist killed one robber during the first quarter of 1980 (Pound 1980). Pharmacists' associations are urging members to secure their stores and to lobby for harsher penalties for theft of "controlled substances."

Legal mood-changers also contribute to crime. Chapter 3 commented on the relationship between alcohol and violence. The causal connection is both direct and indirect. It is indirect in that it is a function of the kinds of people who do the drinking. It is direct in that it is a function of what alcohol does. Ethyl alcohol induces a progressive, descending anesthesia of the central nervous system (cns). "Progressive" means that the more one drinks, the more of the nervous system that is put out of operation. The effect is cumulative. "Descending" refers to the fact that the anesthesia starts with the "highest," most distinctively human, portions of the cns—those that evolved last in the development of the species—and "progressively descends" to anesthetize those portions that are more rudimentary. The "highest" portion of the cns is the cortex of the frontal lobes, the cerebral zone in which conscience resides. In brief, booze relieves us of conscience. It also relieves us of self-consciousness, one of the pleasures that stimulates its use. Alcohol is a social lubricant, but it exacts a price.

Ethyl alcohol is strongly involved in violent crime. Wolfgang's (1958) study of killings in Philadelphia from 1948 to 1953 found alcohol in either the victim or his murderer or both in almost two-thirds of the cases. Similarly, Fisher (1951) reports for Baltimore that close to 70 percent of homicide victims had been drinking. Bowden et al. (1958) publish a figure of nearly 50 percent for murder victims in Australia, and Cleveland (1955) finds a similar rate in his study of homicides in Cincinnati, Ohio. Bullock (1955) tells us that almost 30 percent of homicides in Texas occur in bars. Shupe (1954) measured alcohol concentrations by urinalysis among 882 persons arrested during or immediately after the commission of a felony (indictable offense) in Columbus, Ohio, during the 1950s. He concludes that:

> Crimes of physical violence are associated with intoxicated persons. Cuttings (11 to 1 under the influence of alcohol), the carrying of concealed weapons (8 to 1 under the influence of alcohol), and other assaults (10 to 1 under the influence of alcohol). . . . (p. 663).

The record of violence released by psychotropic agents is thus far anecdotal rather than statistical. However, attention to the moral atmosphere, as opposed to the direct effects of specific agents, suggests that we cannot become countries of "pill-poppers" without some elevation of crime rates. This, of course, may change if, as in Huxley's *Brave New World* (1960), something like *Soma* is invented that puts people to sleep without first intoxicating them. Meanwhile, "bending the mind" is a risky pastime.

"Mind" is the behavioral control center. Anesthetizing the brain can be more safely experienced in rituals where culture prescribes the appropriate behavior under intoxication. But uncultured intoxication is associated with frenzy, and some of the frenzy turns violent.

Multiple Use

The moral atmosphere changes as more people experiment with a greater variety of comforting chemicals of varied potency. It is not that any one agent is an inevitable "stepping stone" to heavier use or more dangerous chemicals. The concern is that widespread advocacy, and use, of the comforting chemicals challenges the boundaries of moderate use. The hazards of this challenge are both physical and social.

There *are* "stepping stones" toward multiple drug use, and abuse, but these stones are not "in" the chemicals; they are "in" people. Research finds the following correlations (Reprinted, with permission, from Nettler 1976, pp. 162–164):

1. If any chemical is *the* stepping-stone to multiple drug use, it is tobacco. Almost all tobacco addicts drink alcoholic beverages, but some drinkers—probably a minority—do not smoke.

2. Almost all North Americans who try marijuana have first tried tobacco and alcohol (Petersen et al. 1972, p. 47). This finding is probably true also of European marijuana users.

3. Young people who use tobacco and alcohol are more likely to try marijuana than those who abstain from the more popular chemicals. For example, a survey of drug use among high school seniors in Michigan (Bogg et al. 1969) reports that among students who drink alcoholic beverages, 20 percent had smoked marijuana at least once. Among abstainers from alcohol, the proportion that had tried marijuana was only 1.6 percent. Similarly, while 24 percent of tobacco users had tried marijuana, only 5 percent of tobacco abstainers had done so. The correlations between using alcohol, tobacco, and marijuana were the most significant associations discovered by this study.

4. Almost all North American users of the opiates, barbiturates, cocaine, "speed," and the stronger psychotropic drugs like LSD have also tried marijuana, but most people who have tried marijuana do not use the more dangerous drugs (Petersen et al. 1972, p. 47).

5. People who use marijuana frequently, and in particular those who become habituated to its use, are more likely to use heavier drugs than those who use marijuana experimentally or casually. For example, a survey among American teenagers (Josephson et al. 1972) finds that the more regularly youngsters have used marijuana, the more likely they were to have tried heroin, glue, "ups," and

"downs." Probabilities increase dramatically from non-users of marijuana, to occasional users, to regular users.

6. There is more than one road to H (heroin). There is more than one mode of introduction to opiates and more than one pattern of opiate use (Ball et al. 1968).

Learning to use the comforting chemicals is, for the most part, a social event. There are exceptions, such as the physician or nurse who becomes a narcotics addict through the availability of opiates, through familiarity with them, and through some pain relieved by them. But, allowing for such exceptions, most people are introduced to the chemical pleasures by others. The probability of escalating use of "drugs" is, then, partly a function of the people one knows. One's choice of preferred people is, in turn, a function of the kind of person one is. However, as use of the comforting chemicals becomes more widespread and more frequent, people "at the margin" become more vulnerable. They are more likely to meet devotees and be subject to their advocacy. In this manner the cultural climate is changed.

Change in the moral climate is evidenced by increases in the proportions of young "drug" users since the surveys of the 1960s reported on preceding pages. A recent American study (Johnston et al. 1979) finds that, between 1962 and 1979, the proportion of adults 18 to 25 years of age that has tried marijuana increased from four percent to 68 percent and the proportion that has used cocaine, angel dust, or heroin increased from three percent to 33 percent. Among younger Americans, those 12 to 17 years of age, the proportion that has used marijuana or cocaine doubled during the 1970s.

A Defense

One line of defense against the spread of a "drug culture" is the spread of physical culture. There is preliminary evidence that individuals who resist chemical comforts are "biologically self-protective" (Berkson 1955). This applies, in particular, to people who are outside the defense perimeter of a religious community.

Individuals who respect their physical selves—including such lovers of their bodies as muscle-builders—resist the chemical addictions. This does not mean that they have never tried depressants or stimulants. It means that the pleasures of health override the pleasures of chemical changes of mood.

This kind of protective "narcissism" has been measured by the extent to which one takes care of one's health, uses preventive hygiene, and keeps "in shape." Macmillan (1964) tested this hypothesis with a survey of self-care habits. She found a significant correlation between "love of self," in this sense, and freedom from tobacco addiction. The range of this defense deserves further testing.

RESUMÉ

The intent of the foregoing discussion is to divert attention from singular causes and simple explanations of changes in homicide rates. In place of this popular style of thought, it is suggested that human action is channeled by a multiplicity of changing influences. Whatever these many causes of action are, they do not have constant weights—the same today that they were yesterday.

This theme accommodates the many roads to homicide and explains our poor powers of prediction. It allows, again, that we can know what the causes of particular events can be without knowing what they will be.

This theme has run through our description of homicidal occasions. It also pertains to the many occasions on which people lie, cheat, and steal. Some of these injuries are described in Volume Three.

REFERENCES

Aaron, R.I. 1971. *Knowing and the Function of Reason.* Oxford: Clarendon.

Adler, F. 1975. *Sisters in Crime: The Rise of the New Female Criminal.* New York: McGraw-Hill.

Alexander, H.H. 1881. *The Life of Guiteau and the Trial of Guiteau for Assassinating Pres. Garfield.* Philadelphia: National.

Alexander, Y. (ed). 1976. *International Terrorism: National, Regional, and Global Perspectives.* New York: Praeger.

Allen, C. 1969. *A Textbook of Psychosexual Disorders.* London: Oxford U.P.

Allen, J. 1977. *Assault with a Deadly Weapon: The Autobiography of a Street Criminal.* Ed. by D. Kelly and P. Heymann. New York: Pantheon.

Allison, P.D. 1978. "Measures of inequality." *Amer.Sociol.Rev.,* 43:865–880.

Almond, G.A. & S. Verba. 1963. *Civic Culture: Political Attitude and Democracy in Five Nations.* Boston: Little, Brown.

Alper, S. et al. 1976. "The implications of sociobiology." *Science,* 192:424, 426–427. (April 30).

Alpert, J. 1972. Introduction to S. Melville, *Letters from Attica.* New York: Morrow.

American Anthropological Association. 1947. "Statement on human rights." *Amer.Anthro.,* 49:539–543.

Amiot, M. et al. 1968. *La violence dans le monde actuel.* Paris: Desclée, De Brouwer.

Anonymous. 1942. "An analysis of Jewish culture." In I. Graeber & S.H. Britt (eds.), *Jews in a Gentile World: The Problem of Anti-Semitism.* New York: Macmillan.

Archer, D. & D. Gartner. 1976. "Violent acts and violent times: A comparative approach to postwar homicide rates." *Amer.Sociol.Rev.,* 41:937–963.

Arenberg, G.S. 1980. Personal communication from the Chief of Staff Services, American Federation of Police. (March 5).

Arendt, H. 1964. *Eichmann in Jerusalem: A Report on the Banality of Evil.* New York: Viking.

Armor, D.J. 1972. "The evidence on busing." *Pub.Int.,* #28:90–126.

Arnold, D.O. (ed.). 1970. *The Sociology of Subcultures.* Berkeley: Glendessary.

Aron, R. 1973. *Histoire et dialectique de la violence.* Paris: Gallimard.

Arthur, A.E. 1969. "Diagnostic testing and the new alternatives." *Psych.Bull.,* 72:183–192.

Ash, P. 1949. "The reliability of psychiatric diagnoses." *Jour.Ab.Soc.Psych.,* 44:272–277.

Associated Press. 1979. "Vexed him with lawsuits, she's guilty of barratry." (June 19).

Atkinson, A.B. 1975. *The Economics of Inequality.* Oxford: Clarendon.

Auletta, K. 1975a. "Who's to blame for the fix we're in?" *New York,* 8:29–41 (Oct.27).

——. 1975b. "Should these men go to jail?" *New York,* 8:36–41 (Dec.1).

——. 1979. *The Streets Were Paved With Gold.* New York: Random House.

Averill, J.R. et al. 1972. "Habituation to complex emotional stimuli." *Jour.Ab.Psych.,* 80:20–28.

Ayer, A.J. 1946. *Language, Truth, and Logic.* New York: Dover.

——. 1966. "Humanism and reform." *Encounter,* 27:13–15.

Baker, J.R. 1974. *Race.* New York: Oxford U.P.

Baker, R.K. & S.J. Ball. 1969. *Violence and the Media: A Staff Report to the National Commission on the Causes and Prevention of Violence.* Washington, D.C.: U.S. GPO.

Baldwin, J. 1972. *No Name in the Street.* New York: Dial.

Ball, J.C. et al. 1968. "The association of marihuana smoking with opiate addiction in the United States." *Jour.Crim.Law, Crim., & Police Sci.,* 48:259–274.

Bandura, A. 1962. "Social learning through imitation." In M.R. Jones (ed.), *Nebraska Symposium on Motivation.* Vol. 10. Lincoln: Univ. Nebraska Press.

——. 1973. *Aggression: A Social Learning Analysis.* Englewood Cliffs, N.J.: Prentice-Hall.

Banfield, E.C. 1974. *The Unheavenly City Revisited.* Boston: Little, Brown.

Baraka, I.A. 1972. "Black people!" In R. Barksdale & K. Kinnamon (eds.), *Black Writers of America.* New York: Macmillan.

Barnett, A. et al. 1975. "On urban homicide: A statistical analysis." *Jour.Crim.Justice,* 3:85–110.

Barzini, L. 1972. "Feltrinelli." *Encounter,* 39:35–40.

Barzun, J. 1962. "In favor of capital punishment." *Amer.Scholar,* 31:181–191.

Bauer, P.T. & J. O'Sullivan. 1977. "Ordering the world about: The new international economic order." *Policy Rev.,* 1:55–69.

Becker, J. 1977. *Hitler's Children: The Story of the Baader-Meinhoff Gang.* Philadelphia: Lippincott.

Begin, M. 1977. In C. Moritz (ed.), *Current Biography.* New York: Wilson.

Beichman, A. 1978. "Terrorism: War without end." *Amer.Spectator,* 11:20–23.

Bell, D. 1960. *The End of Ideology: On the Exhaustion of Political Ideas in the Fifties.* Glencoe, Ill.: Free Press.

Beller, A. et al. 1980. "Sex crimes in the subway." *Crim.,* 18:35–52.

Belson, W.A. 1978. *Television Violence and the Adolescent Boy.* Farnborough, Eng.: Saxon House.

Bensing, R.C. & O.J. Schroeder. 1960. *Homicide in an Urban Community.* Springfield, Ill.: Thomas.

Bentham, J.R. 1980. Personal communication from the Superintendent of the Public Relations Branch, Royal Canadian Mounted Police. (June 3).

Bereiter, C. 1973. "Education, socioeconomic status, IQ, and their effects." *Contemp.Psych.,* 18:401–403.

Berelson, B. & G.A. Steiner. 1964. *Human Behavior: An Inventory of Scientific Findings.* New York: Harcourt, Brace, World.

Berger, S.M. 1962. "Conditioning through vicarious instigation." *Psych.Rev.,* 69:450–466.

Berkowitz, L. 1968. "Impulse, aggression, and the gun." *Psych.Today,* 2:18–22.

Berkowitz, L. et al. 1978. "Experiments on the reaction of juvenile delinquents to filmed violence." In L.A. Hersov et al. (eds.), *Aggression and Anti-Social Behaviour in Childhood and Adolescence.* Toronto: Pergamon.

Berkowitz, L. & R.E. Goranson. 1964. "Motivational and judgmental determinants of social perception." *Jour.Ab.Soc.Psych.,* 69:296–302.

Berkowitz, L. & J. Macaulay. 1971. "The contagion of criminal violence." *Sociometry,* 34:238–260.

Berkson, J. 1955. "Smoking and lung cancer, some observations on two recent reports." *Jour.Amer.Stat.Assoc.,* 53:28.

Berns, W. 1979. *For Capital Punishment: Crime and the Morality of the Death Penalty.* New York: Basic Books.

Bethell, T. 1980a. "Treating poverty." *Harper's Magazine,* 260:16–24.

Bickel, A.M. 1974. "Watergate and the legal order." *Commentary,* 57:19–25.

Bierce, A. 1958. *The Devil's Dictionary.* New York: Dover.

Biggs, J., Jr., 1955. *The Guilty Mind: Psychiatry and the Law of Homicide.* Baltimore: Johns Hopkins U.P.

Biskind, P. & M.N. Weiss. 1975. "The Weather Underground, take one: On location with Bernardine Dohrn, Kathy Boudin, Jeff Jones, Bill Ayers, and Cathy Wilkerson." *Rolling Stone,* #199:36–88.

Blakeslee, A.F. 1932. "Genetics of sensory thresholds: Taste for phenyl thio carbamide." *Proc.Nat.Aca. Sci.,* 18:120–130.

Blanshard, B. 1962. *Reason and Analysis.* La Salle, Ill.: Open Court.

Block, A. 1980. *East Side—West Side.* Cardiff, Wales: University College, Cardiff Press.

Block, R. 1975. "Homicide in Chicago: A nine-year study (1965–1973)." *Jour.Crim.Law & Crim.,* 66:496–510.

———. 1977. *Violent Crime: Environment, Interaction, and Death.* Lexington, Mass.: Lexington Books.

Bloom, L. & R. Riemer. 1949. *Removal and Return: The Socio-Economic Effects of the War on Japanese Americans.* Los Angeles: Univ. Calif. Press.

Blue, J.T., Jr. 1948. "The relationship of juvenile delinquency, race, and economic status." *Jour. Negro Educ.,* 17:469–477.

Blum, A. & G. Fisher. 1978. "Women who kill." In I.L. Kutash et al. (eds.), *Violence: Perspectives on Murder and Aggression.* San Francisco: Jossey-Bass.

Blumenthal, M.D. 1972. "Predicting attitudes toward violence." *Science,* 176:1296–1303 (June 23).

Blumenthal, M.D. et al. 1972. *Justifying Violence: Attitudes of American Men.* Ann Arbor: Institute for Social Research.

———. 1975. *More About Justifying Violence: Methodological Studies of Attitudes and Behavior.* Ann Arbor: Institute for Social Research.

Blumstein, A. et al. (eds.), 1978. *Deterrence and Incapacitation: Estimating the Effects of Criminal Sanctions on Crime Rates.* Washington, D.C.: National Academy of Sciences.

Bogart, L. 1980. "After the Surgeon General's report: Another look backward." In S.B. Withey & R.P. Abeles (eds.)., *Television and Social Behavior: Beyond Violence and Children.* Hillsdale, N.J.: Erlbaum.

Bogg, R.A. et al. 1969. "Some sociological and social psychological correlates of marihuana and alcohol use by Michigan high schools studentw." Paper presented at the Midwest Sociological Societ? meeting. Indianapolis (May 2).

Bogue, D.J. 1969. *Principles of Demography.* New York: Wiley.

Bohannon, P. (ed.). 1960. *African Homicide and Suicide.* Princeton: Princeton U.P.

Bohannon, P. 1963. *Social Anthropology*. New York: Holt, Rinehart, Winston.

Bohman, M. 1978. "Some genetic aspects of alcoholism and criminality." *Arch.Gen.Psychiatry*, 35:269–276.

Bonger, W. 1969. *Criminality and Economic Conditions*. Abridged, with Intro. by A.T. Turk. Bloomington, Ind.: Indiana U.P.

Booth, K. 1979. *Strategy and Ethnocentrism*. London: Croom Helm.

Bottoms, A.E. 1967. "Delinquency among immigrants." *Race*, 8:357–383.

Bowden, K.M. et al. 1958. "A survey of blood alcohol testing in Victoria (1951–1956)." *Med.Jour.Australia*, 2:13–15. (July 5).

Braucht, G.N. et al. 1980. "Victims of violent death: A critical review." *Psych.Bull*, 87:309–333.

Brearley, H.C. 1932. *Homicide in the United States*. Chapel Hill: Univ. North Carolina Press.

Brien, A. 1965. "The monster within." *The London Spectator* #7168:614 (Nov. 12).

Brill, A.A. 1941a. "Necrophilia. Part I." *Jour.Crim.Psychopathology*, 2:433–443.

———. 1941b. "Necrophilia. Part II." *Jour.Crim.Psychopathology*, 3:51–73.

Brinton, C. 1938. *The Anatomy of Revolution*. New York: Norton.

Brittain, R. 1968. "The sexual asphyxias." In F.E. Camps (ed.), *Gradwohl's Legal Medicine*. 2nd ed. Baltimore: Williams & Wilkins.

Brittan, S. 1975. "Full employment policy: A reappraisal." In D. Worswick & D. Thomas (eds.), *The Concept and Measurement of Involuntary Unemployment*. London: Allen & Unwin.

Bryan, A.L. 1963. "The essential morphological basis for human culture." *Current Anthro.*, 4:297–306.

Buckley, W.F., Jr. 1969. "On experiencing Gore Vidal." *Esquire*, 72:108–113, 122–132.

Bugliosi, V. & C. Gentry. 1974. *Helter Skelter: The True Story of the Manson Murders*. New York: Norton.

Bullock, A. 1962. *Hitler: A Study in Tyranny*. New York: Harper & Row.

Bullock, H.A. 1955. "Urban homicide in theory and fact." *Jour.Crim.Law & Crim.*, 45:565–575.

Bumpass, L.L. & R.R. Rindfuss. 1978. *Children's Experience of Marital Disruption*. Paper read at the Institute for Research on Poverty. Madison, Wis.

———. 1979. "Children's experience of marital disruption." *Amer.Jour.Sociol.*, 85:49–65.

Bumpass, L.L. & C.F. Westoff. 1970. "The 'perfect contraceptive' population." *Science,* 169:1177–1182 (Sept. 18).

Burchinal, L.G. 1964. "Characteristics of adolescents from unbroken, broken, and reconstituted families." *Jour.Marr.Fam.Living,* 26:44–51.

Burlingame, R. 1954. *Henry Ford.* New York: New American Library.

Burnham, D. 1973. "Murder rate for blacks in city 8 times that for white victims." *New York Times,* 1, 46 (Aug. 5).

Bustamente, M.E. & M.A. Bravo. 1957. "Epidemiología del homicidio en México." *Higiene,* 9:21–33.

Byrne, D. & W. Griffitt. 1966. "A developmental investigation of the law of attraction." *Jour.Person.Soc.Psych.,* 4:699–702.

Byrne, D. & J. Lamberth. 1971. "The effects of erotic stimuli on sex arousal, evaluative responses, and subsequent behavior." In Technical Report of the Commission on Obscenity and Pornography. Vol. 8. Washington, D.C.: U.S. GPO.

Cahn, S. 1970. *The Treatment of Alcoholics: An Evaluative Study.* New York: Oxford U.P.

Cairns, R.B. et al. 1971. "Psychological assumptions in sex censorship: An evaluative review of recent research (1961–1968). Technical Report of the Commission on Obscenity and Pornography. Vol. 1. Washington, D.C.: U.S. GPO.

Callahan, D. 1972. "Ethics and population limitation." *Science,* 175:487–494 (Feb. 4).

Camus, A. 1955. *The Myth of Sisyphus.* Trans. by J. O'Brien. London: Hamilton.

Canadian Corrections Association. 1967. *Indians and the Law.* Ottawa: The Canadian Welfare Council.

Canadian Press. 1978. "Idea for extortion plot inspired by TV program." (Jan. 19).

——. 1979. "Liquor a way of life and death on reserve." (Nov. 2).

Card, J.J. 1977. *Consequences of Adolescent Childbearing for the Young Parent's Future Personal and Professional Life.* Palo Alto: American Institutes for Research in the Behavioral Sciences.

——. 1978. *Long-Term Consequences for Children Born to Adolescent Parents.* Palo Alto: American Institutes for Research in the Behavioral Sciences.

Carroll, L. 1974. "Race and sexual assault in a prison." Unpublished ms. Kingston, R.I.: Department of Sociology, University of Rhode Island.

——. 1977. "Humanitarian reform and biracial sexual assault in a maximum security prison." *Urban Life,* 5:417–437.

Castan, N. 1971. "La criminalité familiale dans le ressort du parlement de Toulouse, 1690–1730." *Cahiers des Annales,* #33:91–107.

Castro, F. 1959. *Discursos para la Historia.* Habana: Oficina del Historiador de la Ciudad de la Habana.

Cattell, R.B. 1949. "The dimensions of culture patterns of factorization of national characters." *Jour.Ab.Soc.Psych.,* 44:443–469.

——. 1950. "The principal culture patterns discoverable in the syntal dimensions of existing nations." *Jour.Soc.Psych.,* 32:215–253.

Cattell, R.B. et al. 1951. "An attempt at a more refined definition of the cultural dimensions of syntality in modern nations." *Amer.Sociol.Rev.,* 17:408–421.

Cattell, R.B. & R.L. Gorsuch. 1965. "The definition and measurement of national morale and morality." *Jour.Soc.Psych.,* 67:77–96.

Chadwick, R. 1963. "An analysis of the relationship of domestic to foreign conflict behavior over the period 1955–1957." First-year paper, mimeog. Evanston, Ill.: Northwestern University.

Chagnon, N.A. 1977. *Yanomamö: The Fierce People.* New York: Holt, Rinehart, Winston.

Chai, C.K. 1967. *Taiwan Aborigines: A Genetic Study of Tribal Variations.* Cambridge, Mass.: Harvard U.P.

Chalidze. V. 1977. *Criminal Russia: Essays on Crime in the Soviet Union.* Trans. by P.S. Falla. New York: Random House.

Chandler, D.B. 1976. *Capital Punishment in Canada.* Toronto: McClelland & Stewart.

Chappell. D. et al. (eds.). 1977. *Forcible Rape: The Crime, the Victim, and the Offender.* New York: Columbia U.P.

Charlé, S. 1979. "The Tokyo police academy: Training the body, mind, and spirit." *Police Magazine,* 2:49–53.

Christie, N. 1960. *Unge Norske Lovovertredere (Young Norwegian Lawbreakers).* Oslo: Universitetsforlaget.

Christopher, R. 1979. "Putting the hex on *The Warriors.*" *MacLean's,* 92:23 (Apr. 2).

Clark, L. & D. Lewis. 1977. *Rape: The Price of Coercive Sexuality.* Toronto: The Canadian Women's Educational Press.

Clark, M.E. 1977. "Sociobiology and scientific debate." *Science,* 197:822 (Aug. 26).

Clarke, G. 1980. "A lethal delusion." *Time,* 116:27 (Dec. 22).

Clarkson, K.W. & R.E. Meiners. 1977. "Government statistics as a guide to economic policy: Food stamps and the spurious increase in the unemployment rates." *Policy Rev.,* 1:27–51.

——. 1978. "Deflating Unemployment statistics." *Amer.Spectator,* 11:26–28.

Cleaver, E. 1968. *Soul on Ice.* New York: McGraw-Hill.

Cleckley, H. 1964. *The Mask of Sanity.* 4th ed. St. Louis: Mosby.

Cleveland, F.P. 1955. "Problems in homicide investigation: IV: The relationship of alcohol to homicide." *Cincinnati Jour.Med.,* 36:28–30.

Clinard, M. & D.J. Abbott. 1973. *Crime in Developing Countries: A Comparative Perspective.* New York: Wiley.

Cline, V.B. (ed.). 1974. *Where Do You Draw the Line?: An Exploration into Media Violence, Pornography, and Censorship.* Provo; Utah: Brigham Young U.P.

Cline, V.B. et al. 1973. "Desensitization of children to television violence." *Jour.Person.Soc.Psych.,* 27:360–365.

Clutterbuck, R.L. 1978. Cited by E.H. Kahn, Jr., "Profiles: How do we explain them?" *The New Yorker,* 54:37–62. (June 12).

Coggin, D. & D. Moser. 1968. "Indonesia runs amok, 1965–1966." In C. & S. Mydans (eds.), *The Violent Peace.* New York: Atheneum.

Cohen, M.L. et al. 1975. "The psychology of rapists." In S.A. Pasternack (ed,), *Violence and Victims.* New York: Spectrum.

Cohen, M.R. & E. Nagel. 1934. *An Introduction to Logic and Scientific Method.* New York: Harcourt, Brace.

Coleman, J.S. 1974. "Review essay: Inequality, sociology, and moral philosophy." *Amer.Jour.Sociol.,* 80:739–764.

Comstock, G.A. 1975a. "The effects of television on children and adolescents: The evidence so far." *Jour.Communic.,* 25:25–34.

——. 1975b. *Television and Human Behavior: The Key Studies.* Santa Monica: Rand Corp.

Comstock, G.A. et al. (eds.). 1972. *Television and Social Behavior. Vol. V: Television's Effects—Further Explorations.* Washington, D.C.: U.S. GPO.

Comstock, G.A. & M. Fisher. 1975. *Television and Human Behavior: A Guide to the Pertinent Scientific Literature.* Santa Monica: Rand Corp.

Comstock, G.A. & E.A. Rubinstein (eds.). 1972a. *Television and Social Behavior. Vol. 1: Media Content and Control.* Washington, D.C.: U.S. GPO.

——. 1972b. *Television and Social Behavior. Vol. 3: Television and Adolescent Aggressiveness.* Washington, D.C.: U.S. GPO.

Connor, W.D. 1973. "Criminal homicide, USA/USSR: Reflections on Soviet data in a comparative framework." *Jour.Crim.Law & Crim.,* 64:111–117.

Conquest, R. 1968. *The Great Terror.* New York: Macmillan.

Coon, C.S. 1962. *The Origin of Races.* New York: Knopf.

Coon, C.S. & E.E. Hunt. 1966. *The Living Races of Man.* London: Cape.

Cornuelle, R.C. 1968. *Reclaiming the American Dream.* New York: Vintage Books.

Coser, L.A. 1956. *The Functions of Social Conflict.* Glencoe, Ill.: Free Press.

Costantini, E. & K.H. Craik. 1980. "Personality and politicians: California party leaders, 1960–1976." *Jour.Person.Soc.Psych.,* 38:641–661.

Cousineau, F.D. 1976. *General Deterrence of Crime:* An Analysis. Ph.D. dissertation. Edmonton: Department of Sociology, The University of Alberta.

Cousineau, F.D. & J.E. Veevers. 1972. "Juvenile justice: An analysis of the Canadian Young Offenders' Act." In C. Boydell et al. (eds.), *Deviant Behavior and Societal Reaction.* Toronto: Holt.

Cramer, J.C. 1980. "Fertility and female employment: Problems of causal direction." *Amer.Sociol.Rev.,* 45:167–190.

Cuddihy, J.M. 1974. *The Ordeal of Civility: Freud, Marx, Levi-Strauss, and the Jewish Struggle with Modernity.* New York: Basic Books.

Curtis, L.A. 1974. *Criminal Violence: National Patterns and Behavior.* Lexington, Mass.: Lexington Books.

——. 1975. *Violence, Race, and Culture.* Lexington, Mass.: Lexington Books.

Davidson, W.S., II. 1974. "Studies of aversive conditioning for alcoholics: A critical review of theory and research methodology." *Psych.Bull.,* 81:571–581.

Davies, J.C. 1962. "Toward a theory of revolution." *Amer.Sociol.Rev.,* 27:5–19.

Davis, A.J. n.d. (ca. 1969). *Report on Sexual Assaults in the Philadelphia Prison System and Sheriff's Vans.* Unpublished ms. Philadelphia: Police Department and District Attorney's Office.

Davis, J.C. 1959. "A formal interpretation of the theory of relative deprivation." *Sociometry,* 22:280–296.

Davis, M. & J.F. Krauter. 1971. *The Other Canadians: Profiles of Six Minorities.* Agincourt, Ont.: Methuen.

de Boer, C. 1979. "The polls: Terrorism and hijacking." *Pub.Opin.Quart.,* 43:410–418.

deCarufel, A. & J. Schopler. 1979. "Evaluation of outcome improvement resulting from threats and appeals." *Jour.Person.Soc.Psych.,* 37:662–673.

Della Fave, L.R. 1974. "On the structure of egalitarianism." *Soc.Probs.,* 22:199–213.

Delury, G.E. (ed.). 1978. *World Almanac and Book of Facts for 1979.* New York: Newspaper Enterprise.

Demaris, O. 1977. *Brothers in Blood: The International Terrorist Network.* New York: Scribner's.

Deutsch, M. 1979. "Education and distributive justice: Some reflections on grading systems." *Amer.Psych.,* 34:391–401.

Devine, P.E. 1979. "The conscious acceptance of guilt in the necessary murder." *Ethics,* 89:221–239.

DiCara, L.V. 1970. "Learning in the autonomic nervous system." *Sci.Amer.,* 222:31–39.

Dickinson, R.L. & L. Beam. 1931. *A Thousand Marriages: A Medical Study of Sex Adjustment.* Baltimore: Williams & Wilkins.

Dienstbier, P.A. 1977. "Sex and violence: Can research have it both ways?" *Jour.Communic.,* 27:176–188.

Dietz, P.E. 1978. *Kotzwarraism: Sexual Induction of Cerebral Hypoxia.* Unpublished ms. Belmont, Mass.: McLean Hospital.

Dinitz, S. et al. 1973. "Psychopathy and autonomic responsivity: A note on the importance of diagnosis." *Jour.Ab.Psych.,* 82:533–534.

DiRenzo, G.J. (ed.). 1974. *Personality and Politics.* Garden City, N.Y.: Doubleday.

Dominick, J.R. & B.S. Greenberg. 1972. "Attitudes toward violence: The interaction of television exposure, family attitudes, and social class." In Technical Reports to the Commission on Obscenity and Pornography. Vol. 3. Washington, D.C.: U.S. GPO.

Donnerstein, E. 1980. "Aggressive erotica and violence against women." *Jour.Person.Soc.Psych.,* 39:269–277.

Donnerstein, E. et al. 1975. "Erotic stimuli and aggression: Facilitation or inhibition?" *Jour.Person.Soc.Psych.* 32:237–244.

Donovan, R.J. 1955. *The Assassins.* New York: Harper.

Dostoyevsky, F. 1871. *The Possessed.* Trans. 1936 by C. Garnett. New York: The Modern Library.

Douglas, J.D. 1967. *The Social Meanings of Suicide.* Princeton: Princeton U.P.

Douglas-Hamilton, I. & O. Douglas-Hamilton. 1975. *Among the Elephants.* London: Collins & Harvill.

Douglass, J.D., Jr. & A.M. Hoeber. 1979. *Soviet Strategy for Nuclear War.* Stanford: Hoover Institution.

Downes, D.M. 1966. *The Delinquent Solution.* New York: Free Press.

Drabman, R.S. & M.H. Thomas. 1974. "Does media violence increase children's toleration of real-life aggression?" *Develop.Psych.,* 10:418–421.

Driver, E. 1961. "Interaction and criminal homicide in India." *Soc.Forces,* 40:153–158.

Drucker, P.F. 1978. "Meaningful unemployment figures." *Wall St.Jour.,* 99:16 (Nov. 3).

Dryden, J. 1700. "On the characters in the Canterbury Tales." Preface to his *Fables, Ancient and Modern; Translated into Verse, from Homer, Ovid, Boccace, and Chaucer: with Original Poems.* Reprinted 1973. London: Scholar Press.

Dudley, R.C. 1977. Personal correspondence. (Jan. 7).

Duhamel, R. (ed.), 1962. *Office Consolidation of the Criminal Code and Selected Statutes.* Ottawa: Queen's Printer and Controller of Stationery.

Durkheim, E. 1924. *Sociologie et philosophie.* Paris: Alcan.

——. 1950. *The Rules of Scientific Method.* New York: Free Press.

——. 1951. *Suicide: A Study in Sociology.* Ed. by G. Simpson. Glencoe, Ill.: Free Press.

Durrell, L.G. 1957. *Bitter Lemons.* New York: Dutton.

Easterlin, R.A. 1973. "Does money buy happiness?" *Pub.Int.,* #30:2–10.

Eble, C.C. 1972. *How the Speech of Some is More Equal Than Others.* Paper read at the meeting of the Southeastern Conference on Linguistics. Chapel Hill: Univ. of North Carolina.

Eckstein, H. 1962. "The incidence of internal wars, 1946–1959." Appendix I in H. Eckstein (ed.), *Internal War: The Problem of Anticipation.* Washington, D.C.: Smithsonian Institution.

Economist. 1980. "Smoke in whose eyes?" 275:8–9 (Apr. 12).

Edmonton Journal. 1971. "Quebec will be independent within 10 years—separatist." p. 3 (Feb. 24).

Edwards, J.H. 1981. "Genetic disorders among the Jewish people." *The Lancet,* #8221:642–643 (Mar. 21).

Efron, D. 1941. *Gesture and Environment.* New York: King's Crown.

Ehrenreich, G.A. 1960. "Headache, necrophilia, and murder: A brief hypnotherapeutic investigation of a single case." *Bull.Menninger Clinic,* 23:273–287.

Ehrlich, I. 1974. "Participation in illegitimate activities: An economic analysis." In G.S. Becker & W.M. Landes (eds.), *Essays in the Economics of Crime and Punishment.* New York: National Bureau of Economic Research.

Eliot, T.S. 1948. *Notes Towards a Definition of Culture.* London: Faber.

Elliott, F. 1978. "Neurological aspects of psychopathic behaviors." In W. Reid (ed.), *The Psychopath: A Comprehensive Study of Antisocial Disorders and Behaviors.* New York: Brunner/Mazel.

Ellul, J. 1965. *Propaganda: The Formation of Men's Attitudes.* New York: Random House.

——. 1979. "Politicization and political solutions." In K.S. Templeton, Jr. (ed.), *The Politicization of Society.* Indianapolis: Liberty Press.

Elms, A.C. 1976. *Personality in Politics.* New York: Harcourt, Brace, Jovanovich.

Elster, J. 1979. *Ulysses and the Sirens: Studies in Rationality and Irrationality.* Cambridge: Cambridge U.P.

Elwin, V. 1950. *Maria Murder and Suicide.* 2nd ed. London: Oxford U.P.

Emshwiller, J.R. 1980. "In atom-bomb scare, Federal NEST team flies to the rescue." *Wall St.Jour.,* 103:1, 17 (Oct. 21).

Encounter. 1973. "Sartre's arthritis." 40:96.

——. 1980. "Love & hate . . . Good & evil." 54:25.

Ennis. H.P. 1967. *Criminal Victimization in the United States: A Report of a National Survey.* Washington, D.C.: U.S. GPO.

Eron, L.D. et al. 1971. *Learning of Aggression in Children.* Boston: Little, Brown.

——. 1972. "Does television violence cause aggression?" *Amer.Psych.,* 27:253–263.

Evans, K.M. 1962. *Sociometry and Education.* London: Routledge & Kegan Paul.

Evans, R. & R. Novak. 1965. "Inside report: Civil rights disaster." Syndicated column, Nov. 24.

Eysenck, H.J. & D.K.B. Nias. 1978. *Sex, Violence, and the Media.* London: Maurice Temple Smith.

Fanon, F. 1963. *The Wretched of the Earth.* New York: Grove Press.

Farnsworth, P.R. 1937. "Changes in attitudes toward men during college years." *Jour.Soc.Psych.,* 8:274–279.

Farrington, D.P. 1978. "The family backgrounds of aggressive youths." In L. Hersov et al. (eds.), *Aggression and Antisocial Behaviour in Childhood and Adolescence.* Oxford: Pergamon.

Farrington, D.P. et al. 1978. "The persistence of labelling effects." *Br.Jour.Crim.,* 18:277–284.

Farris, J. & B.M. Jones. 1977. "Alcohol metabolism among American Indians and Caucasians." *Alcoholism, Clin.Exper.Res.,* 2:77082.

Federal Bureau of Investigation. 1977. *Crime in the United States: Uniform Crime Reports—1976.* Washington, D.C.: U.S. GPO.

Federal Bureau of Investigation. 1978. *Crime in the United States—1977: Uniform Crime Reports.* Washington, D.C.: U.S. GPO.

Fenna, D. et al. 1971. "Ethanol metabolism in various racial groups." *Can.Med.Assoc.Jour.*, 105:472–475 (Sept. 4).

Ferracuti, F. 1968. "European migration and crime." In M.E. Wolfgang (ed.), *Crime and Culture: Essays in Honor of Thorsten Sellin.* New York: Wiley.

Ferri, E. 1895. *L'omicidio nell'Antropologia Criminale.* Torino: Bocca.

Fiedler, F.E. et al. 1952. "Unconscious attitudes as correlates of socio-metric choice in social groups." *Jour.Ab.Soc.Psych.*, 47:790–796.

Finckenauer, J.O. 1979. "Scared crooked." *Psych.Today,* 13:6.

Fiora-Gormally, N. 1978. "Battered wives who kill: Double standard out of court, single standard in?" *Law & Hum.Beh.*, 2:133–165.

Fisher, R.S. 1951. "Symposium on the compulsory use of chemical tests for alcohol intoxication." *Maryland Med.Jour.*, 3:291–292.

Fisher, S. 1973. *The Female Orgasm: Psychology, Physiology, Fantasy.* New York: Basic Books.

Flanders, J.P. 1968. "A review of research on imitative behavior." *Psych.Bull.*, 69:316–337.

Fletcher, J. 1966. *Situation Ethics.* Philadelphia: Westminster Press.

Foa, U.G. et al. 1976. "Some evidence against the possibility of uto-pian societies." *Jour.Person.Soc.Psych.*, 34:1043–1048.

Forslund, M.A. 1970. "A comparison of Negro and white crime rates." *Jour.Crim.Law,Crim., & Police Sci.*, 61:214–217.

Fox, A.L. 1932. "The relationship between chemical constitution and taste." *Proc.Nat.Aca.Sci.*, 18:115–120.

Fox, J. & T.F. Hartnagel. 1979. "Changing social roles and female crime in Canada: A time series analysis." *Can.Rev.Sociol.Anthro.*, 16:96–104.

Francescato, G. et al. n.d., ca. 1979. *Resident's Satisfaction in HUD-Assisted Housing: Design and Management Factors.* Washington, D.C.: U.S. GPO.

Franchini, A. & F. Introna. 1961. *Delinquenze Minorile.* Padova: Cedam.

Frankel, C. 1955. *The Case for Modern Man.* New York: Harper & Row.

Frazer, J.G. 1915. *The Golden Bough.* 12 vols. London: Macmillan.

Fredlund, M.C. 1975. "The economics of animal systems." In G. Tullock (ed.), *Frontiers of Economics.* Blacksburg, Va.: University Publications.

Freedman, D.G. 1974. *Cradleboarding and Temperament: Cause and Effect.* Paper read at the annual meeting of the American Associ-ation for the Advancement of Science. San Francisco (Feb. 28).

Frégier, H.A. 1840. *Des classes dangereuses de la population dans les grandes villes, et des moyens de les rendre meilleures.* Paris: Baillière.

Freud, S. 1938. "Totem and taboo." Reprinted in his *The Basic Writings of Sigmund Freud.* New York: Modern Library.

——. 1958. *Civilization and Its Discontents.* Trans. by J. Riviere. Garden City, N.Y.: Doubleday.

Friedan, B. 1973. Cited by *Newsweek,* 81:63 (May 14).

Friedman, M. 1968. *Dollars and Deficits.* Englewood Cliffs, N.J.: Prentice-Hall.

Friedrich, C.J. 1969. "The evolving theory and practice of totalitarian regimes." In C.J. Friedrich et al. (eds.), *Totalitarianism in Perspective: Three Views.* London: Pall Mall.

Friedrich, P. 1962. "Assumptions underlying Tarascan political homicide." *Psychiat.,* 25:315–327.

Fromm, E. 1973. *The Anatomy of Human Destructiveness.* New York: Holt, Rinehart, Winston.

Gager, N. & C. Schurr. 1976. *Sexual Assault: Confronting Rape in America.* New York: Grosset & Dunlap.

Gaito, J. & A. Zavala. 1964. "Neurochemistry and learning." *Psych.Bull.,* 61:45–62.

Gall, N. 1971. "How Castro failed." *Commentary,* 52:45–57.

Gardiner, M. 1976. *The Deadly Innocents: Portraits of Children Who Kill.* New York: Basic Books.

Gardiner, P. 1967. "Irrationalism." In P. Edwards (ed.), *The Encyclopedia of Philosophy.* New York: Macmillan.

Gastil, R.D. 1971. "Homicide and a regional culture of violence." *Amer.Sociol.Rev.,* 36:412–427.

Gebhard, P.H. et al. 1965. *Sex Offenders.* New York: Harper & Row.

Geen, R.G. & D. Stonner, 1974. "The meaning of observed violence: Effects on arousal and aggressive behavior." *Jour.Res.Person.,* 8:55–63.

Getschow, G. & B.R. Schlender. 1981. "Family portrait: Friends view parents of Hinckley as loving, devoted to children." *Wall St.Jour.,* 104: 1, 17 (Apr. 6).

Gibbens, T.C.N. & R.H. Ahrenfeldt (eds.). 1966. *Cultural Factors in Delinquency.* London: Tavistock.

Gibbon, E. 1776–1788. *The Decline and Fall of the Roman Empire.* 6 vols. Abridged by M. Hadas, 1962, as *Gibbon's The Decline and Fall of the Roman Empire.* New York: Putnam's Sons.

Gibson, E. & S. Klein. 1969. "Murder, 1957–1968." *Home Office Studies in the Causes of Delinquency and the Treatment of Offenders, #4.* London: HMSO.

Giddings, F.H. 1911. *The Elements of Sociology.* New York: Macmillan.

Giere, R.N. 1979. *Understanding Scientific Reasoning.* New York: Holt, Rinehart, Winston.

Gilbert, J.A.L. 1976. "Royal Alexandra Hospital survey." *Edmonton Journal,* p. 17 (Sept. 17).

Gilder, G. 1973. *Sexual Suicide.* New York: Quadrangle Books.

———. 1974. *Naked Nomads: Unmarried Men in America.* New York: Quadrangle Books.

———. 1978. *Visible Man.* New York: Basic Books.

———. 1979a. "The aftermath of slavery's last days." *Wall St.Jour.* 101:12 (July 13).

———. 1979b. Personal correspondence. (Feb. 4).

———. 1981. *Wealth and Poverty.* New York: Basic Books.

Gillioz, E. 1967. La criminalité des étrangers en Suisse." *Revue pénale suisse.* 2:178–191.

Ginzberg, E. 1980. "Youth unemployment." *Sci.Amer.,* 242:43–49.

Given, J.B. 1977. *Society and Homicide in Thirteenth-Century England.* Stanford: Stanford U.P.

Glad, B. 1973. "Contributions to psychobiography." In J.N. Knutson (ed.), *Handbook of Political Psychology.* San Francisco: Jossey-Bass.

Glazer, N. & D.P. Moynihan. 1963. *Beyond the Melting Pot.* Cambridge, Mass.: M.I.T. Press and Harvard U.P.

——— (eds.). 1975. *Ethnicity: Theory and Experience.* Cambridge, Mass.: Harvard U.P.

Glenn, N.D. 1974–1975. "Recent trends in white-nonwhite attitudinal differences." *Pub.Op.Quart.,* 38:596–604.

Gleser, G.C. et al. 1959. "The relationship of sex and intelligence in choice of words: A normative study of verbal behavior." *Jour.Clin.Psych.,* 15:182–191.

Gold, M. 1981. "The cells that would not die." *Science 81,* 2:28–35.

Goldberg, L.R. & C.E. Werts. 1966. "The reliability of clinicians' judgments: A multi-trait-multimethod approach." *Jour.Consult.Psych.,* 30:199–206.

Goldberg, S. 1973. *The Inevitability of Patriarchy.* New York: Morrow.

Goldman, P. 1981. "American nightmare." *Newsweek,* 97:29 (Apr. 13).

Goldman, P. et al. 1976. "Death wish." *Newsweek,* 88:26–33 (Nov. 29).

Goldsby, R.A. 1971. *Race and Races.* New York: Macmillan.

Goldstein, A.S. 1967. *The Insanity Defense.* New Haven: Yale U.P.

Goldstein, J.H. & R.L. Arms. 1971. "Effects of observing athletic contests on hostility." *Sociometry,* 34:83–90.

Goode, W.J. 1956. *After Divorce.* Glencoe, Ill.: Free Press.

———. 1964. *The Family.* Englewood Cliffs, N.J.: Prentice-Hall.

Goodman, R.M. 1979. *Genetic Disorders Among the Jewish People.* Baltimore: Johns Hopkins U.P.

Goodman, R.M. et al. 1980. *Population Structure and Genetic Disorders.* New York: Pergamon.

Goodman, R.M. & A.G. Motulsky (eds.). 1979. *Genetic Disorders Among Ashkenazi Jews.* Grand Rapids, Mich.: Raven.

Goodrich, H. 1977. "Uses and abuses of the terms 'racism' and 'racist'." *ASA Footnotes,* 5:4, 8.

Goodwin, D.W. 1976. *Is Alcoholism Hereditary?* New York: Oxford U.P.

———. 1978. "The genetics of alcoholism: A state of the art review." *Alcohol Health Res. World,* 2:2–12.

———. 1979. "Alcoholism and heredity." *Archs. Gen. Psychiat.,* 36:57–61.

Gorer, G. 1962. "The Marquis de Sade." *Encounter,* 18:72–78.

Graham, H.D. & T.R. Gurr. 1969. *Violence in America: Historical and Comparative Perspectives: A Report to the National Commission on the Causes and Prevention of Violence.* Washington, D.C.: U.S. GPO.

Graven, J. 1965. "Le problème des travailleurs étrangers délinquants en Suisse." *Revue internationale de criminologie et de police technique,* 19:265–290.

Gray, J.G. 1959. *The Warriors: Reflections of Men in Battle.* New York: Harper & Row.

Green, E. & R.P. Wakefield. 1979. "Patterns of middle and upper class homicide." *Jour. Crim. Law & Crim.,* 70:172–181.

Greenstein, F.I. 1969. *Personality and Politics.* Chicago: Markham.

Greenwald, A.G. 1975. "Consequences of prejudice against the null hypothesis." *Psych. Bull.,* 82:1–20.

Groth, A.N. 1979. *Men Who Rape: The Psychology of the Offender.* New York: Plenum.

Gurr, T.R. 1970. *Why Men Rebel.* Princeton: Princeton U.P.

Guttmacher, M. & H. Weihofen. 1952. *Psychiatry and the Law.* New York: Norton.

Haas, A. 1979. "Male and female spoken language differences: Stereotypes and evidence." *Psych.Bull.*, 86:616–626.

Hagan, J.L. 1977a. "Criminal justice in rural and urban communities: A study of the bureaucratization of justice." *Soc.Forces*, 55:597–612.

———. 1977b. "Finding 'discrimination': A question of meaning." *Ethnicity*, 4:167–176.

Hakeem, M. 1958. "A critique of the psychiatric approach to crime and corrections." *Law & Contemp.Probs.*, 23:650–682.

Hall, E.T. 1959. *The Silent Language.* Garden City, N.Y.: Doubleday.

Halperin, M. 1974. *The Rise and Fall of Fidel Castro: An Essay in Contemporary History.* Berkeley: Univ. Calif. Press.

Hamburg, D.A. & J. Van Lawick-Goodall. 1973. *Factors Facilitating Development of Aggressive Behavior in Chimpanzees and Humans.* Unpublished paper. Stanford: Stanford University.

Hamparian, D.M. et al. 1978. *The Violent Few: A Study of Dangerous Juvenile Offenders.* Lexington, Mass.: Lexington Books.

Hardin, G. 1977a. "Ethical implications of carrying capacity." In G. Hardin & J. Baden (eds.), *Managing the Commons.* San Francisco: Freeman.

———. 1977b. "Rewards of pejoristic thinking." In G. Hardin & J. Baden (eds.), *Managing the Commons.* San Francisco: Freeman.

Hare, R.D. 1966. "Psychopathy and choice of immediate vs. delayed punishment." *Jour.Ab.Psych.*, 71:23–29.

———. 1968. "Psychopathy, autonomic functioning, and the orienting response." *Jour.Ab.Psych.*, 73: entire supplement.

———. 1981. "Psychopathy and violence." In J.R. Hays et al. (eds.), *Violence and the Violent Individual.* Jamaica. N.Y.: Spectrum.

Hare, R.D. & D.N. Cox. 1978. "Clinical and empirical conceptions of psychopathy, and the selection of subjects for research." In R.D. Hare & D. Schalling (eds.), *Psychopathic Behavior: Approaches to Research.* New York: Wiley.

Harlow, H.F. & M. Harlow. 1967. "The young monkeys." *Psych.Today*, 1:40–47.

Harmon, N.B. (ed.). 1952. *The Interpreter's Bible.* Vol.1. New York: Abingdon-Cokesbury.

———. 1953. *The Interpreter's Bible.* Vol.2. New York: Abingdon-Cokesbury.

Harries, K.D. 1974. *The Geography of Crime and Justice.* New York: McGraw-Hill.

Harrison, A.A. 1977. "Mere exposure." In L. Berkowitz (ed.), *Advances in Experimental Social Psychology.* Vol.10. New York: Academic Press.

Harrison, A.A. & P. Hines. 1970. "Effects of frequency of exposure at three short exposure times on affective ratings and exploratory behavior. *Proceedings,* 78th Annual Convention of the American Psychological Association. 5:391–392.

Hart, B. 1974. "Gonadal androgen and sociosexual behavior of male mammals." *Psych.Bull.,* 81:383–400.

Hartley, S.F. 1970. "The decline of illegitimacy in Japan." *Soc.Probs.,* 18:78–91.

———. 1975. *Illegitimacy.* Berkeley and Los Angeles: Univ. Calif.Press.

Hartmann, D.P. 1969. "Influence of symbolically modeled instrumental aggression and pain cues on aggressive behavior." *Jour.Person.Soc.Psych.,* 11:280–288.

Harvey, P. 1970. "Problems in Chinatown." *Hum.Events,* 30:21 (May 16).

Hastings, D.W. 1965. "The psychiatry of presidential assassination." *Jour.Lancet,* 84 (Mar., Apr., May, July).

Hause, J.C. 1975. "Ability and schooling as determinants of life-time earnings, or if you're so smart, why aren't you rich?" In F.T. Juster (ed.), *Education, Income and Human Behavior.* New York: McGraw-Hill.

Havender, W.R. 1978. "Defining racism." *Science,* 199:934 (Mar. 3).

Hawryluk, B. 1979. *Uniform Crime Reporting.* Mimeog. Edmonton: Department of Sociology, University of Alberta.

Haynes, R. 1980. Interview with Dick Cavett. PBS-TV (Feb. 1).

Helson, R. 1980. "Challenger and upholder syndromes in critics." *Jour.Person.Soc.Psych.,* 38:825–838.

Hendrick, G.H. 1977. "When television is a school for criminals." *TV Guide,* 1:4–10 (Jan. 29).

Henissart, P. 1970. *Wolves in the City: The Death of French Algeria.* New York: Simon & Schuster.

Henry, A.F. & J.F. Short, Jr. 1954. *Suicide and Homicide: Some Economic, Sociological, and Psychological Aspects of Aggression.* New York: Free Press.

Heppenstall, R. 1972. "A verdict and its consequences: The murder of Jean Jaures." *Encounter,* 39:51–55.

Hermann, M.G. (ed.). 1977. *A Psychological Examination of Political Leaders.* New York: Free Press.

Herrnstein, R.J. 1973. "Education, socioeconomic status, IQ, and their effects." *Contemp.Psych.,* 18:403–405.

Herskovits, M.J. 1941. *The Myth of the Negro Past.* New York: Harper.

Hetherington, E.M. & E. Klinger. 1964. "Psychopathy and punishment." *Jour.Ab.Soc.Psych.,* 69:113–115.

Higgins, J.W. & M.B. Katzman. 1969. "Determinants in the judgment of obscenity." *Amer.Jour.Psychiat.*, 125:147.

Hinsie, L.E. & R.J. Campbell. 1960. *Psychiatric Dictionary.* 3rd ed. New York: Oxford U.P.

Hirsch, C.A. 1953. "La criminalité nord-africaine." *Revue internationale de criminologie et de police technique*, 7:298–302.

Hobsbawm, E.J. 1969. *Bandits.* London: Weidenfeld & Nicolson.

Hockett, C.F. 1973. *Man's Place in Nature.* New York: McGraw-Hill.

Hoffman-Bustamente, D. 1973. "The nature of female criminality." *Issues in Crim.*, 8:117–136.

Hogan, R. 1973. "Moral conduct and moral character: A psychological perspective." *Psych.Bull.*, 79:217–232.

Hogan, R. & E. Dickstein. 1972. "Moral judgment and perceptions of injustice." *Jour.Person.Soc.Psych.*, 23:409–413.

Hollander, P. 1973. *Soviet and American Society: A Comparison.* New York: Oxford U.P.

Holyst, B. 1967. *Detection of Criminal Homicides.* Warsaw: Juridical Edition.

——. 1969. "Factors connected with homicides and their importance in investigations." *Internat.Crim.Police Rev.*, 226:78–80.

Home Office. 1978. *Criminal Statistics: England and Wales 1977.* Command paper #7289. London: HMSO.

Hopkins, A. 1980. "Controlling corporate deviance." *Criminol.*, 18:198–214.

Horner, C. 1980. "The facts about terrorism." *Commentary*, 69:40–45.

House, T.H. & W.L. Milligan. 1976. "Autonomic responses to modeled distress in prison psychopaths." *Jour.Person.Soc.Psych.*, 34:556–560.

Howe, I. 1976. *World of Our Fathers: The Journey of the East European Jews to America, and the Life They Found and Made.* New York: Harcourt, Brace, Jovanovich.

Hsu, F.L.K. 1953. *Americans and Chinese: Two Ways of Life.* New York: Abelard-Schuman.

Hush, N. 1966. "Are humanists reformers?" *Encounter*, 27:92–95.

Hutt, C. 1972. *Males and Females.* Middlesex, Eng.,: Penguin Books.

Huxley, A. 1960. *Brave New World.* New York: Harper & Row.

Hyland, R.E. 1969. "In defense of terrorism." *The Harvard Crimson*, special supplement. (Oct. 22).

Ingram, J.H. (ed.). 1978. *Annual Abstract of Statistics—1979 edition.* London: HMSO.

Introna, F. 1963. "Aspetti degenerativa e criminologici delle migrazioni interne." *La Scuola Positiva,* 5:668–692.

Isaacs, H.R. 1975a. *Idols of the Tribe: Group Identity and Political Change.* New York: Harper & Row.

——. 1975b. "Basic group identity: The idols of the tribe." In N. Glazer & D.P. Moynihan (eds.), *Ethnicity: Theory and Experience.* Cambridge, Mass.: Harvard U.P.

Jackson, D. 1964. "The evolution of an assassin." *Life,* 56:68A-80 (Feb. 21).

Jackson, R.H. 1947. *The Nürnberg Case.* New York: Knopf.

Jacoby, S. 1977. "Hers." *New York Times,* Sec.III:2 (Dec. 1).

James, E.W. 1979. "A reasoned ethical incoherence?" *Ethics,* 89:240–253.

Janus, S. et al. 1977. *A Sexual Profile of Men in Power.* New York: Warner Books.

Jarvie, I.C. 1967. *The Revolution in Anthropology.* London: Routledge & Kegan Paul.

——. 1975. "Cultural relativism again." *Phil.Soc.Sci.,* 5:343–353.

Jayewardene, C.H.S. 1964. "Criminal homicide in Ceylon." *Probs.Child Care Jour.,* 3:15–30.

Jayewardene, C.H.S. & H. Ranasinghe. 1963. *Criminal Homicide in the Southern Province.* Colombo: The Colombo Apothecaries.

Jencks, C. et al. 1972. *Inequality: A Reassessment of the Effect of Family and Schooling in America.* New York: Basic Books.

Jenkins, B.M. 1981. *Embassies Under Siege: A Review of 48 Embassy Take-Overs, 1971–1980.* Santa Monica: Rand Corp.

Jennings, D. 1979. "Slain student's boyfriend held: Campus murder aftermath." *San Francisco Chronicle,* #201:1, 18 (Sept. 7).

Johnson, P.H. 1967. *On Iniquity: Some Personal Reflections Arising out of the Moors Murder Trial.* London: Macmillan.

Johnson, R.N. 1972. *Aggression in Man and Animals.* Philadelphia: Saunders.

Johnson, W.T. 1971. "The pornography report: Epistemology, methodology, and ideology." *Duquesne Law Rev.,* 10:190–219.

Johnston, L.D. et al. 1979. *Drugs and the Class of '78: Behaviors, Attitudes, and Recent National Trends.* Washington, D.C.: U.S. GPO.

Jonassen, C.T. 1949. "A re-evaluation and critique of the logic and some methods of Shaw and McKay." *Amer.Sociol.Rev.,* 14:608–617.

Jones, J. 1972. *Prejudice and Racism.* Reading, Mass.: Addison-Wesley.

Jones, M.R. 1976. "Time our lost dimension: Toward a new theory of perception, attention, and memory." *Psych.Rev.*, 83:323–355.

Josephson, E. et al. 1972. "Adolescent marijuana use: Report on a national survey." In S. Einstein & S. Allen (eds.), *Proceedings of the First International Conference on Student Drug Surveys*. Farmingdale, N.Y.: Baywood.

Kamin, L.J. 1974. *The Science and Politics of IQ*. Potomac, Md.: Erlbaum.

Kantner, J.F. & M. Zelnik. 1973. "Contraception and pregnancy: Experience of young unmarried women in the United States." *Fam.Planning Perspecs.*, 5:21–35.

Kapsis, R.E. 1979. "Black streetcorner districts." *Soc.Forces*, 57:1212–1228.

Karpman, B. 1954. *The Sexual Offender and His Offenses: Etiology, Pathology, Psychopathology, and Treatment*. New York: Julian Press.

Katz, A.J. et al. 1976. *Progress Report: The Pilot Alberta Restitution Centre*. Calgary: The Centre.

Katzman, M.B. 1970. "Photograph characteristics influencing the judgement of obscenity." In *Technical Report to the Commission on Obscenity and Pornography*. Vol. 9. Washington, D.C.: U.S. GPO.

Kempner, R.M.W. 1978. "A prosecutor on 'Nuremberg reconsidered'." *Encounter*, 51:92–93.

Kesey, K. 1964. *One Flew Over the Cuckoo's Nest*. New York: Compass Books.

Keyfitz, N. 1973. "Can inequality be cured?" *Pub.Int.*, #31:91–101.

Kimmel, S. 1940. *The Mad Booths of Maryland*. Indianapolis: Bobbs-Merrill.

Kiplinger, A. 1980. *The Kiplinger Washington Letter*. 57:1 (July 3).

Kitchin, L. 1966. *Drama in the Sixties*. London: Faber & Faber.

Klebba, A.J. 1975. "Homicide trends in the United States, 1900–1974." *Pub.Health Reports*, 90–195–205.

Klein, T.W. & J.C. DeFries. 1973. "Racial and cultural differences in sensitivity to flickering light." *Soc.Biol.*, 20:212–217.

Klemming, L.G. 1967. *Grekers och Jugoslavers Kriminalitet*. Stockholm: Institute for Criminal Science.

Kobasigawa, A. 1966. "Observationally induced disinhibition of inappropriately sex-typed responses in young children." *Jap.Jour.Educ.Psych.*, 14:9–14.

Koch, J.L.A. 1891–1893. *Die psychopathischen minder wertigkeiten*. Ravensburg: Maier.

Koch, S. 1974. "Psychology as science." In S.C. Brown (ed.), *Philosophy of Psychology*. London: Macmillan.

Koch, S. 1981. "The nature and limits of psychological knowledge: Lessons of a century qua 'Science'." *Amer.Psych.*, 36:257–269.

Koestler, A. 1956. *Reflections on Hanging*. London: Gollancz.

Kopun, M. & P. Propping. 1977. "The kinetics of ethanol absorption and elimination in twins supplemented by repetitive experiments in single subjects." *European Jour.Clin.Pharmacology*, 11:337–344.

Krafft-Ebing, R. von. 1935. *Psychopathia Sexualis: With Especial Reference to the Antipathic Sexual Instinct: A Medico-Forensic Study*. New York: Physicians & Surgeons Book Co.

Krige, E.J. 1936. "Changing conditions in marital relations and parental duties among urbanized natives." *Africa*, 9:1–23.

Kunstler, W. 1976. "Unradical chic." *Wall St.Jour.*, 94:6 (Mar. 5).

Kunst-Wilson, W.R. & R.B. Zajonc. 1980. "Affective discrimination of stimuli that cannot be recognized." *Science*, 207:557–558 (Feb. 1).

Kupperstein, L. & W.C. Wilson. 1970. "Erotica and anti-social behavior: An analysis of selected social indicator statistics." In *Technical Report to the Commission on Obscenity and Pornography*. Vol. 7. Washington, D.C.: U.S. GPO.

Kutschinsky, B. 1970. *Studies on Pornography and Sex Crimes in Denmark*. Copenhagen: New Social Science Monogs.

Ladd, J. 1957. *The Structure of a Moral Code*. Cambridge, Mass.: Harvard U.P.

—— (ed.). 1973. *Ethical Relativism*. Belmont, Calif.: Wadsworth.

Lalli, M. & S.H. Turner. 1968. "Suicide and homicide: A comparative analysis by race and occupational levels." *Jour.Crim.Law, Crim., & Police Sci.*, 59:191–200.

Lambert, J.R. 1970. *Crime, Police, and Race Relations: A Study in Birmingham*. London: Oxford U.P.

Lamm, M.R. et al. 1976. "Sex and social class as determinants of future orientation (time perspective) in adolescents." *Jour.Person.Soc.Psych.*, 34:317–326.

Lamont, A.M. 1961. "Forensic psychiatric practice in a South African mental hospital." *South African Med.Jour.*, 35:833–837.

Lancet, 1979. "Born to drink?" #8106:24–25 (Jan. 6).

Landau, S. 1961. "Cuba: The present reality." *New Left Rev.*, #9:14–15, 17–18, 20, 22.

Landau, S.F. & I. Drapkin. 1968. *Ethnic Patterns of Criminal Homicide in Israel*. Jerusalem: Institute of Criminology, Hebrew University.

Lane, H.L. 1977. *The Wild Boy of Aveyron*. London: Allen & Unwin.

Langer, S.K. 1967. *Mind: An Essay on Human Feeling.* Baltimore: Johns Hopkins U.P.

Lansky, D. et al. 1978. "Blood alcohol level discrimination by alcoholics: The role of internal and external cues." *Jour.Consult.Clin. Psych.,* 46:953–960.

Laqueur, W. 1976. "The futility of terrorism." *Harper's Magazine,* 252:99–105.

———. 1977. *Terrorism.* Boston: Little, Brown.

——— (ed.). 1978. *The Terrorism Reader.* New York: New American Library.

Lasky, M.J. 1972. "Lady on the barricades." *Encounter,* 39:17–31.

Lasswell, H.D. 1977. *Psychopathology and Politics.* Chicago: Univ.Chicago Press.

Laue, J.H. 1978. "Advocacy and sociology." In G.H. Weber & G.J. McCall (eds.), *Social Scientists as Advocates: Views from the Applied Disciplines.* Beverly Hills: Sage.

Lawrence, D.H. 1937. Letter to Herbert Asquith, reprinted in Asquith's *Moments of Memory,* p. 187. London: Hutchinson.

Lefever, E.W. 1979. *Amsterdam to Nairobi: The World Council of Churches and the Third World.* Washington, D.C.: Ethics & Public Policy Center.

Leighton, A.H. 1955. "Psychiatric disorder and social environment." *Psychiat.,* 18:367–383.

Levin, D. 1977. "A dirge for the harp." *Sports Illus.,* 46:80–82 (Apr. 18).

LeVine, R.A. 1966. "Outsiders' judgements: An ethnographic approach to group differences in personality." *S.W.Jour.Anthro.,* 22:101–116.

Levine, S. 1966. "Sex differences in the brain." *Sci.Amer.* 214:84–90.

———. 1971. "Sexual differentiation: The development of maleness and femaleness." *Calif.Med.,* 114:12–17.

Levy, J.E. & S.J. Kunitz. 1974. *Indian Drinking: Navajo Practices and Anglo-American Theories.* New York: Wiley.

Lewis, O. 1959. *Five Families: Mexican Case Studies in the Culture of Poverty.* New York: Basic Books.

———. 1961. *The Children of Sanchez: Autobiography of a Mexican Family.* New York: Basic Books.

———. 1966a. "The culture of poverty." *Sci.Amer.,* 215:19–25.

———. 1966b. *La Vida: A Puerto Rican Family in the Culture of Poverty—San Juan and New York.* New York: Random House.

Liben, G. 1963. "Un reflet de la criminalité itallienne dans la région de Liège." *Revue de Droit Pénal et de Criminologie,* 44:205–245.

Litchtheim, G. 1968. "Devaluation." *Commentary,* 45:65–71.

Liebert, R.M. & R.A. Baron. 1972. "Some immediate effects of televised violence on children's behavior." *Develop.Psych.,* 6:469–475.

Liebert, R.M. & N.S. Schwartzberg. 1977. "Effects of mass media." In M.R. Rosenzweig & L.W. Porter (eds.), *Annual Review of Psychology.* Vol. 28. Palo Alto: Annual Reviews.

Life. 1966. "The Pied-Piper of Tucson." 60:18–24b, 80c–90 (Mar. 4).

Lindesmith, A.R. 1965. *The Addict and the Law.* Bloomington, Ind.: Indiana U.P.

Lippmann, W. 1956. *Essays in the Public Philosophy.* New York: Mentor.

Liston, R.A. 1977. *Terrorism.* New York: Thomas Nelson.

Lloyd, R.W., Jr. & H.C. Salzberg. 1975. "Controlled social drinking: An alternative to abstinence as a treatment goal for some alcohol abusers." *Psych.Bull.,* 82:815–842.

Loftin, C. 1980. "The deterrent effects of punishment." In S.E. Fienberg & A.J. Reiss, Jr. (eds.), *Indicators of Crime and Criminal Justice: Quantitative Studies.* Washington, D.C.: U.S. GPO.

Lovaas, O.I. 1961. "Effect of exposure to symbolic aggression on aggressive behavior." *Child Develop.,* 32:37–44.

Lowie, R.H. 1940. *An Introduction to Cultural Anthropology.* New York: Farrar, Rinehart.

Lundberg, G.A. & L. Dickson. 1952. "Inter-ethnic relations in a high-school population." *Amer.Jour.Sociol.,* 58:1–10.

Lunde, D.T. 1973. *Sex Hormones, Mood, and Behavior.* Paper presented at the Sixth Annual Symposium, Society of Medical Psychoanalysis. New York.

———. 1975. *Murder and Madness.* Stanford: Stanford Alumni Assoc.

Lundsgaarde, H.P. 1977. *Murder in Space City: A Cultural Analysis of Houston Homicide Patterns.* New York: Oxford U.P.

Lundy, R.M. 1956. "Self-perceptions and descriptions of opposite sex sociometric choices." *Sociometry,* 19:272–277.

Lynn, R. 1961. "Introversion-extraversion differences in judgements of time." *Jour.Ab.Soc.Psych.,* 63:457–458.

Lyster, W.R. 1974. "Homicide and fertility rates in the United States." *Soc.Biol.,* 21:389–392.

Maas, P. 1975. *King of the Gypsies.* New York: Viking.

Maccoby, E.E. & C.N. Jacklin. 1974. *The Psychology of Sex Differences.* Stanford: Stanford U.P.

Mack, J.A. & H-J Kerner. 1974. *The Crime Industry.* Lexington, Mass.: Lexington Books.

Mackie, M.M. 1973. "Arriving at 'truth' by definition: The case of stereotype accuracy." *Soc.Probs.,* 20:431–447.

Macmillan, B. 1964. *Personality and Tobacco Addiction.* Mimeog. Edmonton, Department of Sociology, University of Alberta.

Maeder, T. 1981. *The Unspeakable Crimes of Dr. Petiot.* London: Hutchinson.

Mailer, N. 1960. "The white Negro: Superficial reflections on the hipster." Reprinted in his *Advertisements for Myself.* New York: New American Library.

Malabre, A.L., Jr. 1979. "The outlook: Review of current trends in business and finance." *Wall St.Jour.,* 101:1 (July 9).

Malamuth, N.M. et al. 1980. "Sexual responsiveness of college students to rape depictions: Inhibitory and disinhibitory effects." *Jour.Person.Soc.Psych.,* 38:399–408.

Malamuth, N. & B. Spinner. 1979. *A Longitudinal Content Analysis of the Best-Selling Erotica Magazines.* Paper read at the annual meeting of the Western Psychological Association. San Diego (April).

Malaparte, C. 1964. *The Skin.* Trans. by D. Moore. New York: Avon Books.

Mandeville, B. 1714. *The Fable of the Bees.* Reprinted 1962. New York: Capricorn Books.

Mann, G. 1978. "Thoughts on our anti-terrorist illusions." *Encounter,* 51:86–87.

Mann, J. et al. 1971. "Effects of erotic films on sexual behavior of married couples." In *Technical Report of the Commission on Obscenity and Pornography.* Vol.8. Washington, D.C.: U.S. GPO.

Mannheim, K. 1936. *Ideology and Utopia: An Introduction to the Sociology of Knowledge.* New York: Harcourt, Brace.

Manor, F.S. 1980. "The new world disorder." *Amer.Spectator,* 13:19–21.

Mao, Tse-tung. 1967. *Quotations from Chairman Mao Tse-tung.* New York: Bantam Books.

Marighella, C. 1971. *Minimanual of the Urban Guerrilla.* Reprinted as an appendix in R. Moss, *Urban Guerrilla Warfare.* London: International Institute for Strategic Studies.

Mark, V. & F.R. Ervin. 1970. *Violence and the Brain.* New York: Harper & Row.

Martin, J.C. & I. Cartwright (eds.) 1974. *Martin's Annual Criminal Code.* Agincourt, Ont.: Canada Law Book.

——. 1978. *Martin's Annual Criminal Code.* Agincourt, Ont.: Canada Law Book.

Martin, M.B. 1977. "On human love." *Nat.Rev.,* 29:998 (Sept. 2).

Master, W.H. & V.E. Johnson. 1979. *Homosexuality in Perspective.* Boston: Little, Brown.

Mazur, A. 1968. "The littlest science." *Amer.Sociol.,* 3:195–200.

McCarthy, E.D. et al. 1972. "The effects of television on children and adolescents: Violence and behavior disorders." *Jour.Communic.,* 25:71–85.

McClelland, D. 1961. *The Achieving Society.* Princeton: Van Nostrand.

McClintock, F.H. et al. 1963. *Crimes of Violence: An Enquiry by the Cambridge Institute of Criminology into Crimes of Violence Against the Person in London.* London: Macmillan.

McClintock, F.H. & E. Gibson. 1961. *Robbery in London.* London: Macmillan.

McCord, J. 1978. "A thirty-year follow-up of treatment effects." *Amer.Psych.,* 33:284–289.

——. 1980. "The treatment that did not help." *Soc.Action & Law,* 5:85–87.

McCord, W. & J. McCord. 1964. *The Psychopath: An Essay on the Criminal Mind.* Princeton: Van Nostrand.

McCormick, D. 1962. *Blood on the Sea: The Terrible Story of the Yawl "Mignonette."* London: Muller.

McDowell, E. 1973. "Tending the spirit." *Wall St.Jour.,* 88:1, 11 (Mar. 26).

McGuigan, F.J. 1978. *Cognitive Psychophysiology: Principles of Covert Behavior.* Englewood Cliffs, N.J.: Prentice-Hall.

McNamara, H.P. 1975. *Newsletter.* Hackensack, N.J.: National Council on Crime and Delinquency.

McNish, B. 1979. *A Study of Homicide in Alberta.* Unpublished report. Edmonton: Department of Sociology, University of Alberta.

McPheters, L.R. 1976. "Criminal behavior and the gains from crime." *Crim.,* 14:137–152.

Meadows, E. 1978. "Why the unemployment rate is out of touch with the real world." *Fortune,* 97:136–146 (May 8).

Meehl, P.E. 1962. "Schizotaxia, schizotypy, and schizophrenia." *Amer.Psych.,* 17:827–838.

——. 1973. *Psychodiagnosis: Selected Papers.* Minneapolis: Univ.Minnesota Press.

Megargee, E.I. 1966. "Undercontrolled and overcontrolled personality types in extreme social aggression." *Psych.Monogs.,* 80: entire #611.

Melnyk, H. 1980a. "Rape scene in store window." *Edmonton Journal,* pp. A-1, A–3 (May 15).

——. 1980b. "Wrapper stripped off Alberta's porn trade." *Edmonton Journal,* p. B–3 (June 28).

Melville, S. 1972. *Letters from Attica*. With a profile by J. Alpert. New York: Morrow.

Menken, J. et al. 1978. *Experience with Contraceptive Methods in Developed Countries*. Paper read at the Symposium on Contraceptive Technology. Washington, D.C.: National Academy of Sciences (May 16–17).

Messner, S.F. 1980. "Income inequality and murder rates: Some cross-national findings." *Comp.Soc.Res.,* 3:185–198.

Metzger, L.P. 1971. "American sociology and black assimilation: Conflicting perspectives." *Amer.Jour.Sociol.,* 76:627–647.

Meyer, A. 1905. "Suggestions concerning a grouping of facts according to cases." Pages 140–163 of *The Seventeenth Annual Report of the New York State Commission on Lunacy*. Reprinted in E.E. Winters (ed.), *The Collected Papers of Adolf Meyer*. Vol.2, 1951. Baltimore: Johns Hopkins U.P.

Meyer, T.P. 1972. "The effects of sexually arousing and violent films on aggressive behavior." *Jour. Sex Res.,* 8:324.

Miller, N.E. 1969. "Learning of visceral and glandular responses." *Science,* 163:434–445 (Jan. 31).

Miller, W.B. 1958. "Lower class culture as a generating milieu of gang delinquency." *Jour.Soc.Issues,* 14:5–19.

Mills, C.W. 1959. *The Sociological Imagination*. New York: Oxford U.P.

Mitchell, B. 1980. *Morality: Religious and Secular*. New York: Oxford U.P.

Money, J. & A.A. Ehrhardt. 1972. *Man & Woman, Boy & Girl: The Differentiation and Dimorphism of Gender Identity from Conception to Maturity*. Baltimore: Johns Hopkins U.P.

Montgomery, P. L. 1974a. "Jurors hear officers describe finding 27 bodies near Houston." *New York Times,* p. 16 (July 9).

——. 1974b. "Henley trial a San Antonio attraction." *New York Times,* p.10 (July 15).

Morgenstern, O. 1965. Personal communication (Nov. 15).

Morris, C. 1956. *Varieties of Human Value*. Chicago: Univ.Chicago Press.

Morris, N. 1966. "Impediments to penal reform." *Univ.Chicago Law Rev.,* 33:627–656.

Morris, T.P. 1957. *The Criminal Area: A Study in Social Ecology*. London: Routledge & Kegan Paul.

Morris, T.P. & L. Blom-Cooper. 1964. *A Calendar of Murder: Criminal Homicide in England Since 1957*. London: Michael Joseph.

Morselli, E. 1879. *Il Suicidio*. Milano: Dumolard.

Morton, N.E. 1980. "Diseases determined by major genes." *Soc.Biol.*, 26:94–103.

Moser, D. 1966. "He cruised in a golden car, looking for the action." *Life*, 60:23–24b, 80c–90 (Mar. 4).

Moses, E.R. 1970. "Negro and white crime rates." In M.E. Wolfgang et al. (eds.), *The Sociology of Crime and Delinquency*. 2nd ed. New York: Wiley.

Mosher, D.L. 1971. "Psychological reactions to pornographic films." In *Technical Report of the Commission on Obscenity and Pornography*. Vol.8. Washington, D.C.: U.S. GPO.

Moss, H.A. & E.J. Susman. 1980. "Constancy and change in personality development." In O.G. Brim, Jr. & J. Kagan (eds.), *Constancy and Change in Human Development*. Cambridge, Mass.: Harvard U.P.

Moss, R. 1972a. "Marighella: Letter from South America." *Encounter*, 39:40–43.

——. 1972b. *The War for the Cities*. New York: Coward McCann.

Moynihan, D.P. et al. 1965. *The Negro Family: The Case for National Action*. Washington, D.C.: U.S. GPO.

Mullin, H.C. 1980. "Cuba then and now." *The Economist*, 275:10 (Apr. 26).

Munford, R.S. et al. 1976. "Homicide trends in Atlanta." *Crim.*, 14:213–232.

Munger, M.D. 1977. *Growing Utility of Political Terrorism*. Springfield, Va.: National Technical Information Service.

Murray, W. 1980. "Letter from Rome." *The New Yorker*, 56:64–93 (Sept. 15).

Mushanga, M.T. 1970. *Criminal Homicide in Western Uganda: A Sociological Study of Violent Deaths in Ankole, Kigezi, and Toro Districts of Western Uganda*. M.A. thesis. Kampala: Makarere University.

Mussen, P.H. & E. Rutherford. 1961. "Effects of aggressive cartoons on children's aggressive play." *Jour.Ab.Soc.Psych.*, 62:461–464.

Mydans, C. & S. Mydans. 1968. *The Violent Peace: A Report on Wars in the Postwar World*. New York: Atheneum.

Nader, L. 1975. Address at the First International Symposium on Restitution. Minneapolis (Nov. 10–11).

Nader, R. 1974. Public address. Edmonton: University of Alberta (Nov. 28).

Nann, E. 1967. *Die Kriminalität der italienischen Gastarbeiter im Spiegel der Ausländer Kriminalität*. Hamburg: Kriminalistik Verlag.

Nash, J. 1967. "Death as a way of life: The increasing resort to homicide in a Maya Indian community." *Amer.Anthro.,* 69:455–470.

Nechaev, S.G. 1895. "Catechism of a Revolutionary." In M. Bakunin, *Sozial-politischer Briefwechsel mit Alexander Herzen und Ogarev.* Trans. by B. Minzes. Stuttgart: Cotta.

Nettler, G. 1970. *Explanations.* New York: McGraw-Hill.

——. 1972. "Knowing and doing." *Amer.Sociol.,* 7:3, 5–7.

——. 1975. "Social science and social policy." In D. Macfarlane (ed.), *Report of the Proceedings: A Crime Prevention Workshop.* Toronto: Centre of Criminology, University of Toronto.

——. 1976. *Social Concerns.* New York: McGraw-Hill.

——. 1977. "Description without explanation; treatment without cure." Review of D.T. Lunde, "Murder and Madness." *Contemp.Psych.,* 22:397–398.

——. 1978. *Explaining Crime.* 2nd ed. New York: McGraw-Hill.

——. 1979. "Criminal justice." In A. Inkeles et al. (eds.), *Annual Review of Sociology.* Vol. 5. Palo Alto: Annual Reviews.

——. 1980. "Sociologist as advocate." *Can.Jour.Sociol.,* 5:31–53.

Neumann, K. 1963. *Die Kriminalität der italienischen Arbeitskräfte in Kanton Zürich.* Zürich: Juris Verlag.

Newsweek. 1973. "Friedan vs. Schlafly." 81:63 (May 14).

New York Times. 1921. "Charges filed against paper in Chicago." p.3 (Sept. 9).

——. 1922. "Ford says libelous attacks on Jews will cease." p.9 (Jan. 6).

——. 1977a. "Woman denied acquittal for killing of ex-husband." p.16 (Nov. 1).

——. 1977b. "Michigan woman acquitted for ex-husband's slaying." p.14 (Nov. 4).

Nietzsche, F. 1907. *Beyond Good and Evil: Prelude to a Philosophy of the Future.* Trans. by H. Zimmern. New York: Macmillan.

Nisbet, R.A. 1974a. "The pursuit of equality: Review essay." *Pub.Int.,* #35:103–120.

——. 1974b. "Rousseau and equality." *Encounter,* 63:40–51.

——. 1975. *The Twilight of Authority.* New York: Oxford U.P.

Niswander, J.D. et al. 1975. "Congenital malformations in the American Indian." *Soc.Biol.,* 22:203–215.

Nordhaus, W. 1975. "The political business cycle." *Rev.Econ.Studies,* 42:169–190.

Norman, E.R. 1979. *Christianity and the World Order.* New York: Oxford U.P.

Novak, M. 1972. *The Rise of the Unmeltable Ethnics.* New York: Macmillan.

Nye, F.I. 1957. "Child adjustment in broken and unhappy unbroken homes." *Jour.Marr.Family Living,* 19:356–261.

Olson, R.G. 1967. "Nihilism." In P. Edwards (ed.), *The Encyclopedia of Philosophy.* New York: Macmillan.

Orford, J. & G. Edwards. 1977. *Alcoholism: A Comparison of Treatment and Advice, with a Study of the Influence of Marriage.* Oxford: Oxford U.P.

Ormrod, R. 1977. "The McNaughton case and its predecessors." In D.J. West & A. Walk (eds.), *Daniel McNaughton: His Trial and the Aftermath.* Ashford, Eng.: Gaskell Books.

Ortega y Gasset, J. 1932. *The Revolt of the Masses.* New York: Norton.

Osgood, C.E. et al. 1957. *The Measurement of Meaning.* Urbana: Univ.Illinois Press.

Oswald, I. 1980. "Domestic violence by women." *The Lancet,* #8206:1253–1254 (Dec. 6).

Outerbridge, W.R. 1968. "The tyranny of treatment . . . ?" *Can.Jour.Corrections,* 10:378–387.

Paglin, M. 1979a. "Poverty in the United States: A reevaluation." *Policy Rev.,* 8:7–24.

Parloff, M.B. 1979. "Can psychotherapy research guide the policymaker?: A little knowledge may be a dangerous thing." *Amer.Psych.,* 34:296–306.

Parrington, V.L. 1930. *Main Currents in American Thought: On Interpretation of American Literature from the Beginnings to 1920.* Vol.3. New York: Harcourt, Brace.

Pascal, B. 1955. *Thoughts: An Apology for Christianity.* Trans. by T.S. Kepler from *Pensees de M. Pascal sur la religion et sur quelques autres sujets* (1670). Cleveland: World.

Pattison, E.M. et al. (eds.). 1977. *Emerging Concepts of Alcohol Dependence.* New York: Springer.

Pearson, B.E. (ed.). 1978. *Canada Year Book.* Ottawa: Statistics Canada.

Pechman, J.A. (ed.). 1980. *Setting National Priorities: Agenda for the 1980s.* Washington, D.C.: The Brookings Institution.

Peter, L.J. 1977. *Peter's Quotations: Ideas for Our Time.* New York: Morrow.

Petersen, R.C. et al. 1972. *Marihuana and Health: Second Annual Report to Congress from the Secretary of Health, Education, and Welfare.* Washington, D.C.: U.S. GPO.

Petersen, W. 1969a. *Population.* 2nd ed. New York: Macmillan.

———. 1969b. "The classification of subnations in Hawaii: An essay in the sociology of knowledge." *Amer.Sociol.Rev.*, 34:863–877.

———. 1979. *Malthus.* Cambridge, Mass.: Harvard U.P.

Petersilia, J.R. & P.W. Greenwood. 1977. *Mandatory Prison Sentences: Their Projected Effects on Crime and Prison Populations.* Report P-6014. Santa Monica: Rand Corp.

Peterson, J. 1972. "Thunder out of Chinatown." *Nat.Observer,* 11:1, 18 (Mar. 8).

Peterson, R.A. et al. 1962. "Stabilities in deviance: A study of assaultive and non-assaultive offenders." *Jour.Crim.Law, Crim., & Police Sci.,* 53:44–48.

Pettigrew, T.F. & R.B. Spier. 1962. "The ecological structure of Negro homicide." *Amer.Jour.Sociol.,* 67:621–629.

Phillips, D.P. 1974. "The influence of suggestion on suicide: Substantive and theoretical implications of the Werther effect." *Amer.Sociol.Rev.,* 39:340–354.

———. 1977. "Motor vehicle fatalities increase just after publicized suicide stories." *Science,* 196:1464–1465 (June 24).

———. 1978. "Airplane accident fatalities increase just after newspaper stories about murder and suicide." *Science,* 201:748–750 (Aug. 25).

———. 1979. "Suicide, motor vehicle fatalities, and the mass media: Evidence toward a theory of suggestion." *Amer.Jour.Sociol.,* 84:1150–1174.

———. 1980a. "Airplane accidents, murder, and the mass media; Towards a theory of imitation and suggestion.: *Soc.Forces,* 58:1001–1024.

———. 1980b. "The deterrent effect of capital punishment: New evidence on an old controversy." *Amer.Jour.Sociol.,* 86:139–148.

Pilger, J. 1979. "Outrage in the name of the boat people." *Edmonton Journal,* p. A-6 (July 27).

Pipes, R. 1980. "Soviet global strategy." *Commentary,* 69:31–39.

Pittman, D.J. & W. Handy. 1964. "Patterns in aggravated assault." *Jour.Crim.Law, Crim., & Police Sci.,* 55:462–470.

Pohlman, E. 1967. "Unwanted conceptions." *Eugenics Quart.,* 14:143–154.

Pokorny, A.D. 1965. "A comparison of homicides in two cities." *Jour.Crim.Law, Crim., & Police Sci.,* 56:479–487.

Polansky, N.A. et al. 1981. *Damaged Parents: An Anatomy of Child Neglect.* Chicago: Univ. Chicago Press.

Pope, A. 1734. *An Essay on Man.* Edited 1965 with an introduction by F. Brady. Indianapolis: Bobbs-Merrill.

Post, R.H. 1962a. "Population differences in red and green color vision deficiency: A review, and a query on selection relaxation." *Eugenics Quart.,* 9:131–146.

———. 1962b. "Population differences in vision acuity: A review, with speculative notes on selection relaxation." *Eugenics Quart.,* 9:189–212.

———. 1965. "Selection against 'colorblindness' among 'primitive' populations." *Eugenics Quart.,* 12:28–29.

Pound, K. 1980. "Drug crimes shooting up at pharmacies." *Wall St. Jour.,* 102:15 (June 30).

Powers, T. 1971. *Diana: The Making of a Terrorist.* Boston: Houghton, Mifflin.

President's Commission on Mental Health. 1978. *Report to the President.* Vol. 4. Washington, D.C.: U.S. GPO.

Prichard, J.C. 1835. *A Treatise on Insanity and Other Disorders Affecting the Mind.* London: Sherwood, Gilbert, Piper.

Quadagno, D. et al. 1977. "Effects of perinatal gonadal hormones on selected non-sexual behavior patterns: A critical assessment of the nonhuman and human literature." *Psych. Bull.,* 84:62–80.

Quinney, R. 1974. "The ideology of law: Notes for a radical alternative to legal oppression." In J. Susman (ed.), *Crime and Justice: 1971–1972.* New York: AMS Press.

R. v. Ward. 1978. Toronto: Ontario Supreme Court.

Rada, R.T. (ed.). 1978. *Clinical Aspects of the Rapist.* New York: Grune & Stratton.

Rado, S. 1956. *Psychoanalysis of Behavior.* New York: Grune & Stratton.

Rado, S. & G. Daniels. 1956. *Changing Concepts of Psychoanalytic Medicine.* New York: Grune & Stratton.

Radzinowicz, L. 1946. "Crime by size of communities." Mimeog. London: University of London.

Rainwater, L. 1960. *And the Poor Get Children: Sex, Contraception, and Family Planning in the Working Class.* Chicago: Quadrangle.

———. 1970. "Neutralizing the disinherited: Some psychological aspects of understanding the poor." In V.L. Allen (ed.), *Psychological Factors in Poverty.* Chicago: Markham.

Raphael, D.D. (ed.). 1967. *Political Theory and the Rights of Man.* London: Macmillan.

———. 1980. "Claims and obligations." *Times Lit. Suppl.,* #4021:449 (Apr. 18).

Rapoport, A. 1974. "War and peace." *Annals Amer.Aca.Pol.Soc.Sci.,* 421:152–162.

Rapoport, D.C. 1971. *Assassination and Terrorism.* Toronto: CBC Learning Systems.

——. 1977. "The politics of atrocity." In Y. Alexander & S.M. Finger (eds.), *Terrorism: Interdisciplinary Perspectives.* New York: John Jay Press.

Reckless, W.C. 1967. *The Crime Problem.* 4th ed. New York: Appleton-Century-Crofts.

Redfield, R. 1957. "The universally human and the culturally variable." *Jour.Gen.Educ.,* 10:150–160.

Reed, J.S. 1975. *The Enduring South: Subcultural Persistence in Mass Society.* Chapel Hill: Univ.North Carolina Press.

Reed, P. et al. 1976. *Homicide in Canada: A Statistical Synopsis.* Ottawa: Statistics Canada.

——. 1978. "Homicide in Canada: A statistical synopsis." In M.A.B. Gammon (ed.), *Violence in Canada.* Toronto: Methuen.

Reed, T.E. 1977. "Racial comparisons of alcohol metabolism: Background problems and results." *Alcoholism: Clin.Exper.Res.,* 2:83–87.

Reich, C.A. 1970. *The Greening of America.* New York: Random House.

Reichard, G.A. 1938. "Social life." In F. Boas (ed.), *General Anthropology.* Boston: Heath.

Reinisch, J. & W. Karow. 1977. "Prenatal exposure to synthetic progestins and estrogens: Effect on human development." *Archs.Sex.Beh.,* 6:257–288.

Reiser, L.I. & L.C. Warden (eds.). 1972. *American Jurisprudence.* 2nd ed. San Francisco: Bancroft-Whitney.

Rhoads, S.E. 1978. "What is life worth? I: How much should we spend to save a life?" *Pub.Int.,* #51:74–92.

Richardson, L.F. 1960a. *Arms and Insecurity.* Chicago: Quadrangle.

——. 1960b. *Statistics of Deadly Quarrels.* Chicago: Quadrangle.

Rife, D.C. 1948. "Genetic variability within a student population." *Amer.Jour.Phys.Anthro.,* 6:47–62.

Rindfuss, R.R. & L.L. Bumpass. 1977. "Fertility during marital disruption." *Jour.Marr.Fam.,* 39:517–528.

Roberts, R. et al. 1972. *Fischer/Spassky: The New York Times Report on the Chess Match of the Century.* New York: Bantam Books.

Robertson, F. 1978. *Triangle of Death: The Inside Story of the Triads—the Chinese Mafia.* London: Routledge & Kegan Paul.

Robinson, D.N. 1980. *Psychology and Law: Can Justice Survive the Social Sciences?* New York: Oxford U.P.

Rohner, R.P. 1975. *They Love Me, They Love Me Not: A Worldwide Study of the Effects of Parental Acceptance and Rejection.* New Haven: Human Relations Area Files Press.

Rose, R. & G. Peters. 1978. *Can Government Go Bankrupt?* New York: Basic Books.

Rosenfeld, A. 1981. "Tippling enzymes." *Science 81,* 2:24–25.

Rosenthal, A.M. 1964. *Thirty-Eight Witnesses.* New York: McGraw-Hill.

Rosenthal, R. 1978. "How often are our numbers wrong?" *Amer.Psych.,* 33:1005–1008.

——. 1979. "The 'file drawer problem' and tolerance for null results." *Psych.Bull.,* 86:638–641.

Ross, H.L. & I.V. Sawhill. 1975. *Time of Transition: The Growth of Families Headed by Women.* Washington, D.C.: The Urban Institute.

Ross, R.R. & P. Gendreau (eds.). 1980. *Effective Correctional Treatment.* Toronto: Butterworths.

Rossi, P.H. 1971. "The city as purgatory." *Soc.Sci.Quart.,* 51:817–820.

Roth, J.A. 1978. "Prosecutor perceptions of crime seriousness." *Jour.Crim.Law & Crim.,* 69:232–242.

Rousseau, J.J. 1762. *Émile, or On Education.* Trans. 1979 by A. Bloom. New York: Basic Books.

Royal Commission. 1955. *Report of the Royal Commission on Law of Insanity as a Defence in Criminal Cases.* Ottawa: Queen's Printer & Controller of Stationery.

Rubin, J. 1970. *Kill Parents, Burn Suburbs—Rubin.* Speech at Kent State University, as reported by the *Akron Beacon Journal* (Apr. 11).

Rummel, R.J. 1963. "Dimensions of conflict behavior within and between nations." *Gen. Systems,* 8:1–50.

——. 1966. "Dimensions of conflict behavior within nations. 1946–1959." *Jour. Conflict Resol.,* 10:65–73.

——. 1969. "Dimensions of foreign and domestic conflict behavior: A review of empirical findings." In D.G. Pruitt & R.C. Snyder (eds.), *Theory and Research on the Causes of War.* Englewood Cliffs, N.J.: Prentice-Hall.

Runciman, W.G. 1966. *Relative Deprivation and Social Justice: A Study of Attitudes to Social Inequality in Twentieth-Century England.* London: Routledge & Kegan Paul.

Rutstein, D.D. & R.L. Veech. 1978. "Genetics and addiction to alcohol." *New Eng.Jour.Med.,* 298:1140–1141 (May 18).

Rutter, M. et al. 1964. "Temperamental characteristics in infancy and the later development of behavioural disorders." *Br.Jour.Psychiat.,* 110–651–661.

Ryle, G. 1949. *Concept of Mind.* London: Hutchinson's.

Sade, D.A.F. de 1904. *The 120 Days of Sodom.* Reprinted in *The Complete Marquis de Sade.* Ed. and trans. by P.J. Gillette, 1966. Los Angeles: Holloway House.

Salili, F. et al. 1976. "Achievement and morality: A cross-cultural analysis of causal attribution and evaluation." *Jour.Person.Soc. Psych.,* 33:327–337.

Sandler, M. et al. 1978. "Phenylethylamine overproduction in aggressive psychopaths." *The Lancet,* #8103:1269–1270.

Santayana, G. 1951. *Dominations and Powers: Reflections on Liberty, Society, and Government.* London: Constable.

———. 1953. *Persons and Places. Vol.3: My Host the World.* New York: Scribner's Sons.

Sarat, A. 1977. "Studying American legal culture: An assessment of survey evidence." *Law & Soc. Rev.,* 11:427–488.

Sarte, J-P. 1973. Interview cited in *Encounter,* 40:96.

Schachter, S. & B. Latané. 1964. "Crime, cognition, and the autonomic nervous system." In D. Levine (ed.), *Nebraska Symposium on Motivation.* Lincoln: Univ.Nebraska Press.

Schaefer, J.M. 1979. "Ethnic differences in response to alcohol." In R.W. Pickens & L.L. Heston (eds.), *Psychiatric Factors in Drug Abuse.* New York: Grune & Stratton.

Schalling, D. & A.S. Rosen. 1968. "Porteus Maze differences between psychopathic and non-psychopathic criminals." *Br.Jour.Soc.Clin. Psych.,* 7:224–228.

Schickel, R. 1972. "Letting go." *Commentary,* 54:104–108.

Schloss, B. & N.A. Giesbrecht. 1972. *Murder in Canada: A Report on Capital and Non-Capital Murder Statistics 1961–1970.* Toronto: Centre of Criminology, University of Toronto.

Schmauk, F.J. 1970. "Punishment, arousal, and avoidance learning in sociopaths." *Jour.Ab.Psych.,* 76:325–335.

Schmeiser, D.A. et al. 1974. *The Native Offender and the Law.* Ottawa: Information Canada.

Schmidt, H.O. & C.P. Fonda. 1956. "The reliability of psychiatric diagnosis: A new look." *Jour.Ab.Psych.,* 52:262–267.

Schmitt, R.C. 1956. "Illegitimate birth rates in an atypical community." *Amer.Jour.Sociol.,* 61:476–477

Schoeck, H. 1966. *Envy: A Theory of Social Behavior.* New York: Harcourt, Brace.

Schoeck, H. & J.W. Wiggins (eds.). 1961. *Relativism and the Study of Man.* Princeton: Van Nostrand.

Schoenberger, R.A. 1968. "Conservatism, personality, and political extremism." *Amer.Pol.Sci.Rev.,* 62:868–877.

Schuckit, M.A. & V. Rayses. 1979. "Ethanol ingestion: Differences in blood acetaldehyde concentrations in relatives of alcoholics and controls." *Science,* 203:54–55 (Jan. 5).

Schuessler, K.F. 1962. "Components of variations in city crime rates." *Soc.Probs.,* 9:314–323.

Schwartz, L.R. 1972. "Conflict without violence and violence without conflict in a Mexican mestizo village." In J.F. Short, Jr., & M.E. Wolfgang (eds.), *Collective Violence.* Chicago: Aldine.

Seagle, W. 1932. "Homicide." In E.R.A. Seligman & A. Johnson (eds.), *Encyclopedia of the Social Sciences.* New York: Macmillan.

Sears, R.R. 1961. "Relation of early socialization experiences to aggression in middle childhood." *Jour.Ab.Soc.Psych.* 63:466–492.

Seitz, S.T. 1972. "Firearms, homicides, and gun control effectiveness." *Law & Soc.Rev.,* 6:595–613.

Seligman, D. 1978a. "A macrodefinitional approach to full employment." *Fortune,* 97:63 (Feb. 13).

——. 1978b. "Intimations of full employment." *Fortune,* 98:36 (Sept. 25).

——. 1978c. "Numbers game." Fortune, 98:36 (Dec. 4).

Selzer, M. 1979. *Terrorist Chic: An Exploration of Violence in the Seventies.* New York: Hawthorn.

Shapiro, N.H. 1974. "Who merits merit?" *So.Calif.LawRev.,* 48:318–370.

Shaplen, R. 1980. "Profiles: Eye of the storm." *The New Yorker,* 56:43–89 (June 2).

Shaw, C.R. & H.D. McKay. 1942. *Juvenile Delinquency and Urban Areas.* Chicago: Univ.Chicago Press.

Shaw, G.B. 1934. *The Complete Plays of Bernard Shaw.* London: Oldham's Press.

Sheehan, S. 1976. *A Welfare Mother.* Boston: Houghton, Mifflin.

Shefter, M. 1977. "New York City's fiscal crisis: The politics of inflation and retrenchment." *Pub.Int.,* #48:98–127.

Sheldon, E.B. & H.E. Freeman. 1970. "Notes on social indicators: Promises and potential." *Policy Scis.,* 1:97–111.

Shepard, R.N. & P. Arabie. 1979. "Additive clustering: Representation of similarities as combinations of discrete overlapping properties." *Psych.Rev.,* 86:87–123.

Shields, J.V.M. & J.A. Duncan. 1964. *The State of Crime in Scotland.* London: Tavistock.

Shilling, A.G. 1979. "Too many feet in the trough?" *Wall St.Jour.,* 101:18 (Dec. 10).

Shoham, S. 1966. *Crime and Social Deviation.* Chicago: Regnery.

Short, J.F., Jr. et al. 1969. *Staff Reports to the National Commission on the Causes and Prevention of Violence.* 13 volumes. Washington, D.C.: U.S. GPO.

Shupe, L.M. 1954. "Alcohol and crime: A study of the urine alcohol concentration found in 882 persons arrested during or immediately after the commission of a felony." *Jour.Crim.Law & Crim.,* 44:661–664.

Siegel, A. 1974. "The effects of media violence on social learning." In V.B. Cline (ed.), *Where Do You Draw the Line?: An Exploration into Media Violence, Pornography, and Censorship.* Provo, Utah: Brigham Young U.P.

Siegel, R.A. 1978. "Probability of punishment and suppression of behavior in psychopathic and nonpsychopathic offenders." *Jour.Ab.Psych.,* 87:514–522.

Silberman, C.E. 1978. *Criminal Violence, Criminal Justice.* New York: Random House.

Simon, H.A. 1977. *Models of Discovery.* Boston: Reidel.

Simon, W.E. 1978. *A Time for Truth.* New York: McGraw-Hill.

Simondi, M. 1970. *Dati Su Attanta Casi Di Omicidio.* Firenze: Department of Mathematics and Statistics, University of Florence.

Singer, M. 1978. "What is life worth? II: How to reduce risks rationally." *Pub.Int.,* #51:93–112.

Singer, R. 1953. "The sickle cell trait in Africa." *Amer.Anthro.,* 55:634–648.

Small, D. & J.D. Singer. 1970. "Patterns in international warfare, 1816–1965." *Annals Amer.Aca.Pol.Soc.Sci.,* 391:145–155.

Smart, R.G. 1964. "The importance of negative results in psychological research." *Can.Psych.Rev.,* 5:225–232.

Smith, B.F. 1977. *Reaching Judgment at Nuremberg.* New York: Basic Books.

Smith, C. 1976. *Carlos: Portrait of a Terrorist.* New York: Holt, Rinehart, Winston.

Smith, J.C. & B. Hogan. 1973. *Criminal Law.* 3rd ed. London: Butterworths.

Smith, K.J. 1965. *A Cure for Crime: The Case for the Self-determinate Sentence.* London: Duckworth.

Smith, R.J. 1978. *The Psychopath in Society.* New York: Academic Press.

Smith, S.M. & C. Braun. 1978. "Necrophilia and lust murder: Report of a rare occurrence." *Bull. Amer.Aca.Psychiat. & Law,* 6:259–268.

Snyder, C.R. 1958. *Alcohol and the Jew: A Cultural Study of Drinking and Society.* Glencoe, Ill.: Free Press.

Soares, L.M. & A.T. Soares. 1969. "Social Learning and social violence." *Proceedings of the 77th annual meeting of the American Psychological Association.* Washington, D.C.: The Association.

Sokal, R.R. 1966. "Numerical taxonomy." *Sci.Amer.,* 215:106–116.

Sommer, R. 1969. *Personal Space: The Behavioral Basis of Design.* Englewood Cliffs, N.J.: Prentice-Hall.

Sonnenfeld, J. & P.L. Lawrence. 1978. "Why do companies succumb to price fixing?" *Harvard Bus.Rev.,* 56:145–157.

Sorokin, P.A. 1937–1941. *Social and Cultural Dynamics.* 4 vols. New York: American.

———. 1944. "The conditions and prospects for a world without war." *Amer.Jour.Sociol.,* 49:441–449.

Sorrells, J.M. 1977. "Kids who kill." *Crime & Delinq.,* 23:312–320.

Spielman, R.S. et al. 1974. "Regional linguistic and genetic differences among Yanomamö Indians." *Science,* 184:637–644. (May 10).

Spilerman, S. & D. Elesh. 1971. "Alternative conceptions of poverty and their implications for income maintenance." *Soc.Probs.,* 18:358–373.

Spinley, B.M. 1964. *The Deprived and the Privileged.* London: Routledge & Kegan Paul.

Spivak, J. 1979. "Hungary's Gypsies, poor and unpopular, embarrass regime." *Wall St.Jour,* 100:1, 25 (June 11).

Starr, C. & C. Whipple 1980. "Risks of risk decisions." *Science,* 208:1114–1119 (June 6).

State of Indiana vs. Ford Motor Company. 1980. Cause #11–431.

Statistical Abstracts of the United States. 1974. Washington, D.C.: Department of Commerce.

Statistics Canada. 1976. *Homicide in Canada: A Statistical Synopsis.* Ottawa: Statistics Canada.

———. 1978. *1976 Census of Canada: Population: Demographic Characteristics—Mother Tongue.* Ottawa: Statistics Canada.

———. 1979. *Crime by Offence—1977.* Ottawa: Statistics Canada.

Stein, B. 1979. *The View from Sunset Boulevard: America as Brought to You by the People Who Make Television.* New York: Basic Books.

Stekel, W. 1929. *Sadism and Masochism: The Psychology of Hatred and Cruelty.* New York: Grove.

Stephenson, R.M. & F.R. Scarpitti. 1968. "Negro-white differentials and delinquency." *Jour.Res.Crime & Delinq.,* 5:122–133.

Sterling, C. 1978. "The terrorist network." *Atlantic Monthly,* 242:37–47.

———. 1981. *The Terror Network.* New York: Holt, Rinehart, Winston.

Sterling, T.D. 1959. "Publication decisions and their possible effects on inferences drawn from tests of significance—or vice versa." *Jour.Amer.Stat.Assoc.,* 54:30–34.

Stouffer, S.A. et al. 1949. *The American Soldier.* Princeton: Princeton U.P.

Straus, M. 1980. "Victims and aggressors in marital violence." *Amer.Beh.Sci.,* 23:681–704.

Strauss, J.H. & M.A. Strauss. 1953. "Suicide, homicide, and social structure in Ceylon." *Amer.Jour.Sociol.,* 58:461–469.

Strong, E.K., Jr. 1962. "Nineteen year follow-up of engineer interests." *Jour.Appl.Psych.,* 36:65–74.

Sumner, W.G. 1906. *Folkways: A Study of the Sociological Importance of Usages, Manners, Customs, Mores, and Morals.* Boston: Ginn.

Surgeon General's Scientific Advisory Committee on Television and Social Behavior. 1972. *Television and Growing Up: The Impact of Televised Violence.* Washington, D.C.: U.S. GPO.

Sutherland, A. 1975. *Gypsies: The Hidden American.* New York: Free Press.

Svalastoga, K. 1956. "Homicide and social contact in Denmark." *Amer.Jour.Sociol.,* 62:37–41.

Sveri, K. 1966. "Culture conflict and crime." In D. Schwarz (ed.), *Svenska Minoriteter.* Stockholm: Aldus.

Talese, G. 1980. *Thy Neighbor's Wife.* London: Collins.

Tannenbaum, P.H. & D. Zillman. 1975. "Emotional arousal in the facilitation of aggression through communication." *Adv.Exper.Soc.Psych.,* 8:149–192.

Tanter, R. 1965. "Dimensions of conflict behavior within and between nations, 1958–1960." *Jour.Conflict Resol.,* 10:41–64.

Tarde, G. 1890. *Le criminalité compareé.* 2nd ed. Paris: Alcan.

Tardiff, G. 1966. *La Criminalité de violence.* M.A. thesis. Montreal: University of Montreal.

Taylor, R. 1967. "Causation." In P. Edwards (ed.), *The Encyclopedia of Philosophy.* New York: Macmillan.

tenBroek, J. et al. 1968. *Prejudice, War, and the Constitution.* Berkeley & Los Angeles: Univ. California Press.

Terman, L.M. 1938. *Psychological Factors in Marital Happiness.* New York: McGraw-Hill.

——. & L.E. Tyler. 1954. "Psychological sex differences." In L. Carmichael (ed.), *Manual of Child Psychology,* 2nd ed. New York: Wiley.

Ternowetsky, G.W. 1977a. "Income maintenance and the culture of poverty in Australia." *Internat.Soc.Work,* 20:2–13.

——. 1977b. "Work orientations of the poor and income maintenance." *Austral.Jour.Soc.Issues,* 12:266–280.

——. 1977c. *Intergenerational Poverty, Life Styles, and Income Maintenance: An Analysis of the Cultural and Situational Views of Poverty.* Canberra: Report to the Australian Government Department of Social Security.

——. 1979. "Income security and attitudes of the poor: A restricted cross-lagged test of causality and change." *La Trobe Sociology Papers #5.* Melbourne: Department of Sociology, La Trobe University.

Thoinot, L. 1930. *Medicolegal Aspects of Moral Offenses.* Philadelphia: Davis.

Thomas, A. et al. 1970. "The origin of personality." *Sci.Amer.,* 223:102–109.

Thomas, D.S. 1952. *The Salvage: Japanese American Evacuation and Resettlement.* Berkeley & Los Angeles: Univ.California Press.

Thomas, D.S. et al. 1946. *The Spoilage: Japanese American Evacuation and Resettlement.* Berkeley & Los Angeles: Univ.California Press.

Thomas, H. 1971. *Cuba: The Pursuit of Freedom.* New York: Harper & Row.

——. 1979. *A History of the World.* New York: Harper & Row.

Thomas, W.I. 1937. *Primitive Behavior: An Introduction to the Social Sciences.* New York: McGraw-Hill.

Thompson, H.S. 1966. *Hell's Angels: A Strange and Terrible Saga.* New York: Random House.

Thurow, L.C. 1973. "Proving the absence of positive associations." *Harvard Educ.Rev.,* 43:106–112.

Tietze, C. 1979. "Unintended pregnancies in the United States, 1970–1972." *Fam.Planning Perspecs.,* 11:186–188.

Time. 1964. "Crime: A savage stalks at midnight." 83:17–18 (June 26).

Ting, S.K. & K.K. Tan. 1969. "Post-mortem survey of homicides in Singapore, 1955–1964." *Singapore Med.Jour.,* 10:248–258.

Toby, J. 1950. "Comment on the Jonassen-Shaw and McKay controversy." *Amer.Sociol.Rev.,* 15:107–108.

——. 1957. "The differential impact of family disorganization." *Amer.Sociol.Rev.,* 22:505–512.

Tocqueville, A. de. 1856. *The Old Regime and the French Revolution.* Reprinted, 1955. Garden City, N.Y.: Doubleday.

Townsend, P. 1874. "Poverty as relative deprivation: Resources and style of living." In D. Wedderburn (ed.), *Poverty, Inequality, and Class Structure*. Cambridge, Eng.: Cambridge U.P.

Trillin, C. & E. Koren. 1978. "Our far-flung correspondents: Low and slow, mean and clean." *The New Yorker,* 54:70–74 (July 10).

Tuchman, B.W. 1978. *A Distant Mirror: The Calamitious 14th Century.* New York: Knopf.

Tufte, E.R. 1974. *Data Analysis for Politics and Policy.* Englewood Cliffs, N.J.: Prentice-Hall.

——. 1978. *Political Control of the Economy.* Princeton: Princeton U.P.

Turnbull, C. 1972. *The Mountain People.* New York: Simon & Schuster.

Turner, C.F. 1978. *Longitudinal and Experimental Perspectives on the Social Psychology of Socioeconomic Attainment.* Ph.D. dissertation. New York: Columbia University.

Tversky, A. 1977. "Features of similarity." *Psych.Rev.,* 84:327–352.

Tversky, A. & D.H. Krantz. 1969. "Similarity of schematic faces: A test of inter-dimensional additivity." *Perception & Psychophysics,* 5:124–128.

United Nations. 1965a. *Comparative Survey on Juvenile Delinquency. Part V: Middle East.* New York: United Nations.

——. 1965b. *Third United Nations Congress on the Prevention of Crime and the Treatment of Offenders.* New York: United Nations.

——. 1973. *Report of the Ad Hoc Committee on International Terrorism.* New York: United Nations Document A/9028.

United Press International. 1980a. "Gacy: 'Clowns can get away with murder'." (Feb. 14).

—— 1980b. "Illinois needs executioners." (Mar. 27).

——. 1980c. " 'Pitiful' people still want to join Manson's 'family'." (Mar. 3).

Valentine, C.A. 1968. *Culture and Poverty: Critique and Counter-Proposals.* Chicago: Univ.Chicago Press.

Vandenberg, B. 1978. "Play and development from an ethological perspective." *Amer.Psych.,* 33:724–738.

van den Haag, E. 1968. "On deterrence and the death penalty." *Ethics,* 78:280–288.

van Lawick, H. & J. van Lawick-Goodall. 1971. *Innocent Killers.* Boston: Houghton, Mifflin.

Verden, P. & D. Shatterly. 1971. "Alcoholism research and resistance to understanding the compulsive drinker." *Mental Hygiene,* 55:331–336.

Verkko, V. 1951. *Homicides and Suicides in Finland and Their Dependence on National Character.* Copenhagen: G.E.C. Gads Forlag.

Vesell, E.S. 1972. "Ethanol metabolism: Regulation by genetic factors in normal volunteers under a controlled environment and the effect of chronic ethanol administration." *Annals New York Aca.Scis.,* 197:79–88.

Vicker, R. 1979a. "Bone of contention: North Yemen, a relic of 15th century, stirs 20th century rivalries." *Wall St.Jour.* 100:1, 23 (May 25).

Vogel, E.F. 1979. *Japan as Number One: Lessons for America.* Cambridge, Mass.: Harvard U.P.

Voltaire, F.M.A. 1767. *L'Ingenu: Histoire Véritable.* Reprinted 1957. Paris: Librairie Minard.

von Clausewitz, C. 1977. *On War.* Princeton: Princeton U.P.

Voss, H.L. & J.R. Hepburn. 1968. "Patterns in criminal homicide in Chicago." *Jour.Crim.Law, Crim., & Police Sci.,* 59:499–508.

Wade, N. 1976. "Sociobiology: Troubled birth for new discipline." *Science,* 191:1151–1155.

Wagemakers, S. 1980. Interview, CBC-FM, "Arts national." (Jan. 14).

Waid, W.M. 1976. "Skin conductance response to both signaled and insignaled noxious stimulation predicts level of socialization." *Jour.Person.Soc.Psych.,* 34:923–929.

Wainwright, L. 1964. "A very special murderer." *Life,* 57:21 (July 3).

Walker, R.L. 1955. *China Under Communism: The First Five Years.* New Haven: Yale U.P.

Wall Street Journal. 1979. "Tax report: A special summary and forecast of federal and state tax developments." 101:1 (July 11).

Wallis, C.P. & R. Maliphant. 1967. "Delinquent areas in the county of London: Ecological factors." *Br.Jour.Crim.,* 7:250–284.

Walters, R.H. et al. 1962. "Enhancement of punitive behavior by audio-visual displays." *Science,* 136:872–873.

Waltz, K. 1959. *Man, the State, and War.* New York: Columbia U.P.

Warren, D.I. & R.B. Warren. 1975. "Six kinds of neighborhoods." *Psych.Today,* 8:74–80.

Warriner, C.K. 1958. "The nature and functions of official morality." *Amer.Jour.Sociol.,* 64:165–168.

Wason, P.C. & P.N. Johnson-Laird. 1972. *Psychology of Reasoning: Structure and Content.* London: Batsford.

Watt, R.M. 1963. *Dare Call It Treason.* New York: Simon & Schuster.

Waxman, C.I. 1977. *The Stigma of Poverty: A Critique of Poverty Theories and Policies.* Toronto: Pergamon.

Weil, S. 1946. "Words and war." *Politics,* 3:69–73.

Weinberg, T.S. 1978. "Sadism and masochism: Sociological perspectives." *Bull.Amer.Aca. Psychiat. & Law,* 6:284–295.

Weisman, A. 1965. "Self-destruction and sexual perversion." In E.S. Shneidman (ed.), *Essays in Self-Destruction.* New York: Science House.

Weiss, W. 1969. "Effects of the mass media of communication." In G. Lindzey & E. Aronson (eds.), *The Handbook of Social Psychology.* 2nd ed. Reading, Mass.: Addison-Wesley.

Weller, R.H. 1978. "Wanted and unwanted child-bearing in the United States: 1968, 1969, and 1972 National Health Surveys." *Vital and Health Statistics,* Series 21, #32. Washington, D.C.: National Center for Health Statistics.

Wellford, C.F. 1974. "Crime and the dimensions of nations." *Internat.Jour.Crim.Penol.,* 2:1–10.

Wenzky, O. 1965. "Analyse zur Ausländer Kriminalität." *Kriminalistik,* 1:1–5.

West, D.J. 1965. *Murder Followed by Suicide.* London: Heinemann.

West, D.J. et al. 1978. *Understanding Sexual Attacks.* Lond: Heinemann.

Westermarck, E. 1906. *The Origin and Development of the Moral Ideas.* 2 volumes. London: Macmillan.

Whalen, R.J. 1980. "Negotiable instruments: Redeeming America's promises." *Harper's Magazine,* 260:24–27.

Wheeler, L. & A.R. Caggiula. 1966. "The contagion of aggression.: *Jour.Exper.Soc.Psych.,* 2:1–10.

Whiting, B. & C. Pope. 1973. "A cross-cultural analysis of sex differences in the behavior of children aged three to eleven." *Jour.Soc.Psych.,* 91:171–188.

Widom, C.S. 1976. "Interpersonal and personal construct systems, in psychopaths." *Jour.Consult.Clin.Psych.,* 44:614–623.

———. 1977. "A methodology for studying noninstitutionalized psychopaths." *Jour.Consult.Clin.Psych.,* 45:674–683.

Wiers, P. 1939. "Juvenile delinquency in rural Michigan." *Jour.Crim.Law & Crim.,* 30:148–157.

Wildavsky, A. 1979. *Speaking Truth to Power: The Art and Craft of Policy Analysis.* Toronto: Little. Brown.

Wilkenfeld, J. 1968. "Domestic and foreign conflict behavior of nations." *Jour.Peace Res.,* 5:56–69.

Wilkins, J.L. et al. 1974. "Personality type, reports of violence, and aggressive behavior." *Jour.Person.Soc.Psych.,* 30:243–247.

Wilkinson, P. 1977. *Terrorism and the Liberal State.* New York: Wiley.

Williams, W.T. et al. 1971. "Controversy concerning the criteria for taxonometric strategies." *Computer Jour.,* 14:162–165.

Willmott, P. 1966. *Adolescent Boys in East London.* London: Routledge & Kegan Paul.

Wilson, E. 1962. *Patriotic Gore: Studies in the Literature of the American Civil War.* New York: Oxford U.P.

Wilson, J.Q. 1974. "Violence, pornography, and social science." In V.B. Cline (ed.), *Where Do You Draw the Line?: An Exploration into Media Violence, Pornography and Censorship.* Provo, Utah: Brigham Young U.P.

Wilson, W.R. 1975. *Unobtrusive Induction of Positive Attitudes.* Ph.D. dissertation. Ann Arbor: Department of Psychology, University of Michigan.

Wilson, R.S. 1974. "Twins: Mental development in the pre-school years." *Develop.Psych.,* 10:580–588.

——. 1978. "Synchronies in mental development: An epigenetic perspective." *Science,* 202:939–948 (Dec. 1).

Wilt, G. & J. Bannon. 1974. *A Comprehensive Analysis of Conflict Motivated Homicides and Assaults: Detroit 1972–1973.* Washington, D.C.: The Police Foundation.

Winegarten, R. 1974. "Literary terrorism." *Commentary,* 57:58–65.

Wirth, L. 1936. "Preface." In K. Mannheim, *Ideology and Utopia: An Introduction to the Sociology of Knowledge.* New York: Harcourt, Brace.

Wistrich, R. 1980. "Kreisky, Arafat, and friends: Young in spirit." *Encounter,* 54:40–43.

Wolfgang, M.E. 1957. "Victim-precipitated criminal homicide." *Jour.Crim.Law, Crim., & Police Sci.,* 48:1–11.

——. 1958. *Patterns in Criminal Homicide.* Philadelphia: Univ.Pennsylvania Press.

——. 1978. "Rethinking crime and punishment." *Across the Board,* 15:55–61.

Wolfgang, M.E. & F. Ferracuti. 1967. *The Subculture of Violence: Toward an Integrated Theory in Criminology.* London: Tavistock.

Wong, W. 1977. "Behind the facade: San Francisco killings jolt nationwide myth of carefree Chinatown." *Wall St.Jour.,* 97:1, 16 (Nov. 16).

Wood, A. 1961. "A socio-structural analysis of murder, suicide, and economic crime in Ceylon." *Amer.Sociol.Rev.,* 26:744–753.

Woodrick, C. et al. 1977. "Television-viewing habits and parent-observed behaviors of third-grade children." *Psych.Reports,* 40: Part I.

Woolf, V. 1921. "The new dress." In *A Haunted House and Other Short Stories.* New York: Harcourt, Brace.

Wootton, B. 1978. *Crime and Penal Policy: Reflections of Fifty Years' Experience.* London: Allen & Unwin.

Wright, Q. 1942. *A Study of War.* 2 volumes. Chicago: Univ.Chicago Press.

Yochelson, S. & S.E. Samenow. 1976. *The Criminal Personality. Vol.I: A Profile for Change.* New York: Aronson.

Yolton, J. 1973. "Action: Metaphysic and modality." *Amer.Phil.Quart.,* 10:71–85.

Zaehner, R.C. 1974. "The wickedness of evil: On Manson, murder, and mysticism." *Encounter,* 42:50–58.

Zajonc, R.B. 1968. "Attitudinal effects of mere exposure." *Jour.Person.Soc.Psych.,* 9:1–28.

——. 1980. "Feeling and thinking: Preferences need no inferences." *Amer.Psych.,* 35:151–175.

Zeiner, A.R. et al. 1976. "Physiological responses to ethanol among the Tarahumara Indians." *Annals New York Aca.Scis.,* 273:151–158.

Zeldin, T. 1977. *France 1848–1945. Vol.II: Intellect, Taste, and Anxiety.* Oxford: Clarendon.

Zelnik, M. & J.F. Kantner. 1972. "Sexuality, contraception, and pregnancy among young unwed females in the United States." In C.F. Westoff & R. Parke, Jr. (eds.), *Demographic and Social Aspects of Population Growth.* Vol.I. Washington, D.C.: U.S. GPO.

——. 1973. "Sex and contraception among unmarried teenagers." In C.F. Westoff (ed.), *Toward the End of Growth: Population in America.* Englewood Cliffs, N.J.: Prentice-Hall.

Zelnik, M. et al. 1979. "Probabilities of intercourse and conception among U.S. teenage women, 1971 and 1976." *Fam.Planning Perspecs.,* 11:177–183.

Zigler, E. & L. Phillips. 1965. "Psychiatric diagnosis and symptomatology." In O. Milton (ed.), *Behavior Disorders.* Philadelphia: Lippincott.

Zillman, D. 1971. "Excitation transfer in communication-mediated aggressive behavior." *Jour.Exper.Soc.Psych.,* 7:419–434.

Zillman, D. et al. 1974. "Strength and duration of the effect of aggressive violent and erotic communications on subsequent aggressive behavior." *Communic.Res.,* 1:286–306.

Zimmerman, H.G. 1966. "Die Kriminalität der ausläandischern Arbeiter." *Kriminalistik,* 2:623–625.

Zimring, F.E. 1979. "Determinants of the death rate from robbery: A Detroit time study." In H.M. Rose (ed.), *Lethal Aspects of Urban Violence.* Lexington, Mass.: Lexington Books.

Zimring, F.E. et al. 1976. "Punishing homicide in Philadelphia: Perspectives on the death penalty." *Univ.Chicago Law Rev.,* 43:227–252.

——. & G.J. Hawkins. 1973. *Deterrence: The Legal Threat in Crime Control.* Chicago: Univ. Chicago Press.

Zinn, H. 1967. "History as private enterprise." In K.H. Wolff & B. Moore (eds.), *The Critical Spirit.* Boston: Beacon Press.

NAME INDEX

SUBJECT INDEX

A